MATCHED
for Eternity

Carmen Lin

WESTBOW
PRESS®
A DIVISION OF THOMAS NELSON
& ZONDERVAN

WestBow Press books may be ordered through booksellers or by contacting:

WestBow Press
A Division of Thomas Nelson & Zondervan
1663 Liberty Drive
Bloomington, IN 47403
www.westbowpress.com
1 (866) 928-1240

ISBN: 978-1-5127-8230-1 (sc)
ISBN: 978-1-5127-8231-8 (hc)
ISBN: 978-1-5127-8232-5 (e)

Library of Congress Control Number: 2017905136

Print information available on the last page.

WestBow Press rev. date: 06/01/2017

To Rev. and Mrs. Harral A. Hall and to my husband of thirty-six years, Rev. Dr. Yishan Lin. And to my three daughters, Angela Lin Yee, Leslie Liu, and Corrie Haffly, without whom this book would be much inferior.

Contents

Introduction

*W*hen Carmen asked me to write an introduction to a book she had written, I agreed out of a sense of obligation. I was the new pastor, and she was a member of the church, a sweet little Asian lady, and very enthusiastic about her writing project. Then she sent me the manuscript. It was long. It was filled with detail, and I would have to read it all before writing my piece. I felt trapped!

At first, I thought I could get away with only reading a bit of it. My introduction would be adequate if I expanded on my first impressions. My duty would be done.

But then I began to read. I was caught up in a world both familiar and strange and drawn to both. She is from a different generation, a different culture, a different background and language and traditions. But in spite of these big differences (and sometimes because of them), I recognized common and compelling themes. Our shared humanity was in evidence as she described her experience with a remarkable degree of candor and insight. This was not only a journal of events or a sweet sentimental journey ... and certainly not just another inspirational memoir.

Carmen dares to tell the truth in this book. Her story unfolds like real life, only she is paying attention in ways most people don't. She confronts reality, even dives into it, not knowing the outcome, unflinching in her faith and in her willingness to acknowledge pain and peril. When I call her faith "unflinching," I don't mean that she has no doubts or struggles. She struggles mightily, at times on the brink of despair, and even goes over the edge. And yet her faith never dies. It is never defeated, even though she runs out of answers and the strength to keep going. She never gives up even when she is in a free-fall. Somehow, she always knows there is more, that God will always show up.

The trials she encounters are ordinary at times, and she provides a wonderful perspective on how to go through them. Other times the suffering is great, a threat to anyone's sense of well-being. The lessons here are costly, not easy, and they force the reader to identify with her in her deep vulnerability. That could be me. That is me! And Carmen becomes a humble yet experienced guide, whose grit is admirable, whose wisdom is hard-fought.

She not only shares her own challenging circumstances but the ordeals of others—whose journey she joins. Carmen has an unshakable sense of calling. And so she engages with others as they face troubles, as they wrestle with major life issues, as they search for the God who seems elusive, as their situations seem so hopeless. Better to avoid such entanglements, we would think, but this is her calling!

Even when she feels helpless, Christ compels her! And she wagers everything on His presence, power, and utter reliability. She has no backup plan. This book is an advanced course on perseverance. Which is another word for courage. Which is the best translation of *faith*—a word often used glibly by Christians who live on the surface, not really knowing the meaning of the word as it operates in the battlefields of life.

Carmen herself is often overlooked and underestimated by others. She feels demeaned and struggles with self-confidence and against self-pity. She is astonishingly open about all of this. Sometimes the put-downs come from those who are closest to her—her friends, others in the church, her extended family, her own husband. Yishan, her husband, is the most prominent character in the book, but the ambivalence in their relationship over the years cannot be missed because Carmen will not cover it up. She can be furious with him, even to the point of imagining their marriage ending. But she continues to believe that they are called to live together and serve together and that severing this sacred partnership for any reason would be a sin. She notes his shortcomings but also honestly specifies her own. She finally finds a compassion that transforms her whole view of him.

Ministry marriages can be tough. I've been half of one for forty-four years—I know! Seldom has this particular pressure been so transparently expressed. Even here. (Especially here!) God is at work, providing resources for personal healing (that goes all the way back to childhood), for relational restoration, and for renewal of a ministry that can bless many others. Carmen's recounting does not hesitate to take us into the most difficult and demoralizing places, but it never leaves her there (or leaves us there).

So often in her story, the word *miracle* is mentioned. She is not exaggerating. She has trained herself to trace the fingerprints of God in the scenes of life. She knows the knack of prayer to produce the impossible. Every answer to another plea from Carmen only adds fuel to the fire of her faith. In this, she both elevates others and offends them. The personality of Carmen almost demands a response toward one extreme (full obedience) or another (total rejection). It's hard to be indifferent to her version of what God is doing.

Lest anyone think Carmen is some sort of mystic, let me assure you that this is one hardworking woman who values education and has a practical mind. She is one who is never too certain or dogmatic in the face of life's perplexities. She is sure of God but not of her own feelings or opinions or judgments. She ultimately defers to Him and is willing to wait ... and to look foolish.

The high view and value of Scripture is evident in this book ... and must align all of our wonderings and wanderings. Carmen becomes increasingly sensitive to signs of God's intervention in the here and now but seeks to place every assumption within the context of Scripture, seeking confirmation in God's Word.

This book has much to teach us about following Christ faithfully on a daily basis and in the stormy seasons. Her writing constantly models the spiritual maturity of a severe self-examination. Instead of resorting to excuses and defensiveness, fixing the blame on others, resorting to religious clichés, or simply changing the subject to something more pleasant, Carmen forces herself to look in the mirror and stay with that reflection for a while. "God, show me the truth about myself and what changes You want to make inside me." She is fearless in doing this, and she becomes incredibly helpful to others in her ever-widening circle— and to us, the readers, as a result.

This is true humility. I see a lot of it in her ... and not much in myself. But recognize how invaluable it is for growth and breakthrough beyond our current self-imposed limitations. We must be willing to die to our own impatient, insecure egos in order to produce fruit for the kingdom. This is obvious as the book pushes us into a fierce, uncompromising trust in God's goodness. And a relinquishment of our own self-focused agendas.

If I step back for a moment, having read the entire book, I am more convinced than ever of this: To come alive, to experience real freedom, to make a real difference in this world, we must be completely assured that Jesus Christ is alive, that the Holy Spirit is active in our world today, that God is always at work behind the scenes to produce the result that will be best, and that we are called to live constantly overwhelmed by the glory of God manifest all around us—no matter the denials blasting back at us from the darkness.

I am grateful for this elaborate tribute to the grace of God operating on real life as articulated by my sister in Christ—an immigrant who has lived in many worlds and accumulated strong convictions from her beautiful, heartbreaking, soul-mending journey.

Whoever you are, I recommend that you read this book because you will relate to the discouragement caused by disappointments and damage done by the sins of others and by sins that are self-inflicted. But you will also resonate with the longings of one who is on her own quest for the God who promises to meet us in the low places. And you will discover the answer to one of life's greatest questions. Does God really answer our prayers? The answer may surprise you, but it'll ring true.

Thank you, Carmen, for the invitation to read this surprisingly provocative book!

Doug Stevens
Transitional Lead Pastor
University Covenant Church, Davis, CA
June 2013–October 2014

Prologue

*W*henever I had a chance to share my stories with people, I almost always was told, "You should write a book."

Me? Writing a book? Who would want to buy it? Outside of my circles of friends, I'm practically a nobody. Who will read my book?

Yet when I looked back at my own life and that of Yishan, who went home to be with the Lord on June 15, 2002, I felt I owed our Lord and Savior, Jesus Christ, a great debt. Jesus has saved me out of a life of despair and delivered Yishan from a life without God, and then in turn, He put us together to serve in His vineyard so that through our messages and testimonies many people were saved. Toward the end the Lord even kept our marriage intact, which otherwise would have been disintegrated.

Once at a woman's retreat where I was the sole speaker, I shared a story about Yishan and me. Upon hearing this story, these women exclaimed, "Just like in the movies!"

So what should I do but write down all these stories to glorify the name of our Lord Jesus Christ? After all, these are *His* stories, not really ours. Without Him, there would be no stories to tell.

Okay then, I'll first ask two questions. Fact or fiction: a scientist and atheist turned to Christ and eventually became a pastor? Yes, that was true. This person was my husband.

A dying marriage was saved and thus glorified the Lord? There were at least two such cases in this book.

God did wonderful things in Yishan's life, although this world's media never paid attention to him. His name appeared in the newspaper only twice—the first time in 1966 when we were married and the second and final time in 2002 in the obituary column.

Yet there was something special about Yishan, something that attracted people to him when he preached or witnessed. Six hundred people attended his memorial service, which was far beyond my estimation. (Even in Taiwan, where both Yishan and I were born, a funeral with six hundred in attendance is considered large.) And more than ten years after his death, I was still being told by people he had ministered to how they missed him. Of course, the reason for all this was what the Lord did to this man. I believe those stories are worthy of being told.

Both Yishan and I came from Buddhist families, and both of us were the first ones in our respective families to become Christians. I was baptized in my junior year at college in 1963, and he was not converted until eight years after our marriage in 1974. What made his conversion even more remarkable was the fact he had been trained to believe in the theory of evolution, which denied God.

Throughout my adolescent years, I dreamed of a number of roles in which I wanted to be, but never did I imagine in all my wildest dreams that I would be a pastor's wife someday.

Perhaps being a pastor's wife is no big deal. Yet from my own perspective, having seen how my husband struggled through his atheism as a scientist and then turned into a believer of Jesus Christ and eventually was "apprehended" (Philippians 3:12) by the Lord to be His chosen minister, it was with great awe and excitement that I saw how the Lord led me and my husband into His service. It was as if I were seeing the Lord performing miracle after miracle, although at times I also felt some sense of pain when my husband was so totally engrossed in doing the Lord's work that he seemed to forget about my existence.

Now that the Lord has called Yishan to be home with Him, I'm feeling a sense of obligation to tell the story how the Lord has used a seemingly ordinary man. In this story I have been privileged to see the glory of the Lord interspersed throughout many parts of our lives.

I want to tell this story so that His work may not be forgotten and that He may receive all the honor due His name.

In writing about Yishan, it is inevitable to include my own story as well since the Lord has called me first and at times used me to help my husband. So this is a book written from my own perspective.

When I began writing this book, I had another purpose in mind. Incredible as it may sound, our marriage probably would have been dissolved sometime during the last few years of Yishan's life. Bear in mind we're talking about two sinners, not saints. It was totally by the grace of God and His wonderful intervention that our marriage was kept intact to the end. Among many reasons, our problems arose primarily from the fact that Yishan was a pastor. In 1996 or 1997, I happened to read in one of the three major US news magazines an article about half of pastors' marriages in the United States ending up in divorce, which was not any different from ordinary couples! (That was a shocking and unacceptable figure to me at that time.) Although some of those divorces were caused by infidelity or financial troubles just as in the other marriages, a lot of those were caused because that those pastors' wives felt that their husbands had neglected them, which was just how I had felt a lot of times! So I've learned my marriage problem was not unique only because Yishan and I were from Taiwan. This is really an issue that needs to be dealt with! I want this book to serve as a mirror and warning to many pastors so that their wives may not have to go through the many headaches and heartaches that I went through.

May Christ's kingdom be strengthened and His name be praised!

—December 2012

Chapter 1

A Providential Match

*I*magine yourself standing in a large hall filled with five or six hundred people packed like sardines. You think you are surrounded by people you do not know, but all of a sudden, you spot a familiar face. What would you do?

To me, this was not an imagined scenario. It was how I met my future husband, Yishan, again in September of 1964 after having not seen each other for four years.

Here, before going on to tell you what happened next, perhaps it's better for me to start with a common Chinese idiom that Yishan quoted many times when talking about our marriage.

Yishan used to comment on our marriage as a match of "door to door and window to window." Usually, this idiom means a good match of social status on both sides. What Yishan referred to, however, actually concerned not only our social statuses but our fathers as well. Both of us had well-to-do grandfathers, but both of our fathers squandered away their inheritances, and thus, we both came from poor families.

So in the summer of 1958 when Yishan and I met for the first time, we felt a common bond besides our mutual interest in music. That summer I had just finished tenth grade and was attending a government-sponsored summer camp learning to drive a military jeep. Very few people owned cars in those days, so learning to drive was great excitement to young people. Every summer a driving camp

1

attracted a lot of high school and college students. That summer the driving camp was based in Provincial Hsinchu High School, Yishan's alma mater. Yishan was a college sophomore then, but he was not a camp participant. It was rather providential that we met there that summer.

While Yishan was in junior high at that school, he started to learn piano. His piano was mostly self-taught. By the time he was in senior high, he became the official pianist for the school's famous choir. (His alma mater's choral team often won championships in national contests.) Since his family did not own a piano, he used to practice on the piano in the school auditorium, and while in college he still went back there to practice piano during the summer.

The driving camp program was set up in a way that half of the participants attended classes in the school auditorium for half of the day while the other half of the participants learned to drive on the road. In this way all the participants were able to attend both activities. During the lunch hour while no class was in session, Yishan came to use the piano, and there he got to meet some of the camp participants.

In the second week of our camp, there was a singing contest. I was urged to join the contest, and Yishan was introduced to me as my accompanist. I never had formal voice training, but after I practiced a few times with Yishan and received some suggestions from him on how to improve my singing, I won that contest, and thus began our friendship.

That first segment of our friendship lasted about a year and a half. Since both of us were students and neither one had a telephone, it was rather inconvenient for us to see each other. To keep in touch, we had to write letters, or I had to go visit him at his dorm. A few times when I went there, I was disappointed to learn that he had gone home for the holidays. It was not until we were married in 1966 when he told me why he had to go home without telling me ahead of time. Since his family was poor, he had to go home for the holidays. Otherwise, he would have to pay extra for meals. At that time he was too bashful to tell me the truth.

Well, back in 1958 and 1959 when I repeatedly found out that he had gone home without informing me, I began to think that I was not as important to him as his family. Gradually, I stopped seeing him, and by the summer of 1960 when I received a letter from him saying that he was going into the army for the required two-year military service, I decided I had had enough of him. That summer of 1960 was graduation time for both of us—me from high school and him from college. I sent him a "Dear John" letter to end our friendship, and four years later when we met again, he told me he had been heartbroken to receive that letter.

The next four years saw me very busy in college. I went to Taiwan Normal University (TNU), the provincial (later changed to national) university for training future high school teachers. I picked this university for the reason that it was completely cost-free and that I could receive a small monthly allowance since I commuted instead of living in the dorm. Besides commuting, I was also busy working my way through college because the small monthly allowance was not enough for me. I tutored students and also worked for my former English teacher, grading student exams and assignments for her. On top of that, I wanted to keep my good academic records since I had received top scores in the college entrance exam among TNU students, and I had to study hard.

Those four years were also hard for me in other ways. The first summer (1961) I lost my mother to a sudden illness. Since I was very close to my mother, her death was a hard blow to me. She was a Buddhist all her life, and I was still not a Christian then. So there was no hope of eternal life for her or for me, and when she died, I cried my heart out until my voice became hoarse.

Actually, I had been going to a church for a year by then, but during that year I went to church every Sunday only to join the choir. Every time the pastor began to preach, I would begin to doze off, and almost without exception, I would wake up suddenly to find the sermon near the end. I was ashamed of my own behavior and tried to pinch myself in order to stay awake. However, it was of no use, and I wondered at the lullaby effect of those sermons. As I look back now, I understand it to be the work of Satan—the birds came snatching away the seeds (Matthew 13:4, 19). It was pathetic that I did not know how to pray when my mother became ill, even though I knew I should.

The second summer I received a severe burn on my face and legs. In those days we were using a freestanding round coal stove, and I had a large stockpot on the stove, which was full of hot water to be used for bathing. I removed the pot so that I could cook dinner, and when I finished cooking, I put the large pot of hot water back to the stove. However, one of the handles on the pot was already damaged and had become loose. When I tried to put the pot back on the stove, I lost grip of that handle and the pot tipped over. Most of the hot water immediately spilled on my legs. Part of it ran down on the hot coals and produced a hot mixture of ash and steam that came up to the right side of my face. I let out a loud yell, and everybody in the house heard it and instantly ran to me. My elder brother rushed me to a nearby private hospital, and when the doctor saw me, he lamented, "Oh, a girl, and it's on the face." He immediately gave me an injection of antibiotics to prevent complications.

The Lord really had mercy on me, for no permanent scars were left on my face except a tiny dot that was barely visible. There were some scars left on my legs, even to this day, but people hardly noticed them.

In the third summer (1963) there was a big flood in the area where I lived. At that time we were living in a rented old house constructed of mud bricks. After soaking in water for several hours, those bricks became soft and gave in, and the house collapsed. From the fifth floor of a neighbor's concrete building, my younger brother and I watched our house caving in. We had fled to our neighbor's building only less than thirty minutes before the house collapsed. It was a traumatic experience. I cried when the house fell, and my brother tried to comfort me. Instantly, we became homeless, but luckily, our eldest sister, who had been married for many years, took us to her home the next day.

A few months later, my maternal grandmother died. She had lived with us most of my life until the flood made us homeless and forced her to live with an aunt. Needless to say, it was another loss for me, but it was not such a hard blow as my mother's death, possibly because I had become a Christian by then. Earlier that year I had accepted Jesus Christ as my Lord and Savior and was baptized on Easter Sunday. I was beginning to learn to pray and to turn to Jesus in my times of need.

With the coming of the year 1964, I was brought to the last semester of my senior year. With my regular tutoring, the exam-grading work, and my own studies—plus church activities three times a week—my life was pretty full, and I had no time to worry about graduation or the future. Then one day about a month or two before graduation, I suddenly found that all of my classmates (twenty-nine students in our English center class) had found a school for the required one-year postgraduation practical teaching, me and another female student being the only exceptions. I had assumed that the government would assign me a school, but on that day I learned for the first time that if I did not find a school of my own choice, the government probably would send me to a far-out area where few students would want to go.

Therefore, I panicked, but a classmate informed me of a city school where he knew there were two openings. I went to the academic dean of that school the next day, but he said, "We have no openings." I was disappointed, to say the least, and that afternoon I went back to the classmate, telling him that he had given me some wrong information. Yet he said, "Oh, you are so dumb. You have no connections and no VIP recommendations. Of course they will not easily give you a job."

What was I to do? Well, I prayed. I was not ambitious, and I did not ask for an elite school. So long as I could get a school in the city of Taipei, any school, I would be content.

About a week or two after I prayed, I was called to our director's office. She said, "The principal of your alma mater just called. She asked for an alumna, and I immediately thought of you."

It was interesting that she thought of me first. In our class of twenty-nine students, there were a total of thirteen and half alumnae of my alma mater. (The one counted as half went to my alma mater for junior high but went to another school for senior high.) Why did our director think of me first instead of my classmates? Some said it was because I was a good student, but if she had thought of any one of my classmates instead of me, I would not have had a chance. Obviously, this was an answer to my prayer.

That afternoon I went to my alma mater for an interview with the principal. She did not give me the job on the spot, and after I went home, I continued to pray. About a week later, I was called to our director's office again. She informed me that principal of my alma mater had called to offer me a teaching position. That very afternoon the principal of the city school where I had inquired before also called to offer me a job. Of course I accepted my alma mater's position and turned down the other offer.

My alma mater, Taipei First Girls' High School, has always been considered the most prestigious high school in Taiwan. In the end I found out that I got the most elite job offer among our class of twenty-nine students. Some of my classmates had parents who had very good connections, and I was probably the one with the least amount of social and political connections. However, I learned that *I* had the best connection after all, for I was connected to the heavenly hot line (Jer. 33:3). I'm very thankful that the Lord of the universe should choose to bestow His grace upon a poor young Christian such as me so that I could learn to depend on Him for my needs. I truly learned how the Lord could lavish His rich grace on the one least deserving.

Throughout my four years of college, I got to meet several young men. As time went on, however, I realized that none of them was as good as Yishan, and I began to long for the opportunity to see him again. In the summer of 1963, I got that opportunity when I attended the Second Summer Institute in American studies (again, another grace of the Lord to enable me to attend that institute that summer since we had to pass some tests to be selected), which was held in National Taiwan University, from which Yishan had graduated back in 1960. One day during recess time I was walking down the corridor outside the classrooms when I saw Yishan holding a camera and taking pictures of a friend. He was so focused on taking pictures that he did not see me. I did not greet him right away. I had a bag full of heavy books in my hand, and I wanted to put the bag in the classroom first. I was going to greet him later, but by the time I came out again, both he and his friend were nowhere to be found. *Well*, I thought, *Perhaps he and I were not meant to meet again.*

Then on the first Sunday of September 1964, the first Sunday right after I began my job as a teacher, I went to Taipei Sung-San International Airport to see three friends off. They were leaving for the United States to study, and I was in a huge area where hundreds of people had crowded together, trying to get a view through the glass of partition of those walking toward the airplane. All of a sudden, I saw Yishan standing with a friend, just five or six people away from me. Our eyes met simultaneously, and seeing me alone, he introduced his friend to me.

It was really providential that Yishan and I met again. That day that area must have been packed (like sardines) with five or six hundred people, yet Yishan and I happened to be standing so close to each other. Our chance meeting was really not by chance at all when I learned later from Yishan how he should have been on that airplane that day instead of being the one to see someone off. As he said, he did not pass the US Embassy's English proficiency test as required for students coming to the United States. So he had to apply to an ESL school in DC, and he was waiting for an I-20 from that school. If he had passed that proficiency test, he would have been among those boarding the plane that day, and I probably would not have been able to see him standing there. It also happened that one of his former college classmates had a brother-in-law boarding the plane that day, but that classmate was in southern Taiwan receiving some kind of training and was not able to go to the airport himself. Instead he had asked Yishan and another former classmate to go in his place. However, Yishan and his friend arrived in the airport too late. By the time they arrived the man they were supposed to see off had gone into the airplane, but they met me instead.

Indeed, I believe it was the Lord who had brought us together in the airport that day. *He was our matchmaker.* Very shortly after that

7

we began seeing each other again, and eventually, we were married less than two years later on June 8, 1966, in Macomb, Illinois. As I learned later, I also believe that God had brought us together for a special purpose, namely so that we might serve Him for the glory of His kingdom.

Chapter 2

The Ignorant Days

*I*n September 1965, I came to the United States with a graduate teaching assistantship. I had then the lofty goal of pursuing graduate studies and getting my master's and PhD degrees. Within less than a year, however, I lost my ambition, specifically for two reasons. First, during my last summer in Taiwan, I began to experience pain in my right back, and after becoming a graduate student in Brookings, South Dakota, the pain seemed to become more frequent. My adviser, Miss Brown, took me to the local medical clinic for tests, and they examined my stomach but did not find anything wrong. The unremitting pain served to frustrate and distract me from concentrated studies. (I continued to suffer that pain for twenty-two years; however, in 1987, I was finally able to find out that I had gallstones, but that is another story in itself.)

Second, Yishan and I were separated from each other by two vast Midwestern states and a whole day of travel by train or buses. We could not see each other except during semester/quarter breaks or long weekends. Our time together was far and sparse and seemed very short. Long-distance calls were expensive then, and we could afford one only infrequently. We began to look for time to be together, and I thought of giving up my graduate studies.

I prayed about my situations, and God seemed to be silent. It wasn't that He did not care, but rather I felt He was leaving the matter in my own hands. Yishan reasoned that I should try to finish my

9

master's degree, but I told him that I did not want to be separated from him anymore. I said that if we got married, I still could continue with my graduate studies later. We then began to plan for a June wedding.

The day I arrived at Macomb, Illinois, happened to be my birthday, so I will always remember that. I traveled from Brookings, South Dakota, by Greyhound, and I had to transfer to the Crownline from Davenport, Iowa, to get to my destination. The Greyhound bus I boarded was pretty much full, but when I boarded the Crownline bus, I found only one other passenger, a woman slightly older than me. Possibly because it was a weekday and not a weekend, there were not many passengers. That other passenger traveled some distance and then got off the bus, and then I was the only passenger left.

In those days I never heard of the term sex predator, and it was, of course, not for the reason of safety precaution at all that I chose a midsection seat. A little while after that other passenger left, the bus driver asked me to sit in the front so that he could talk to me. At first I hesitated since he was a total stranger. After he asked it the second time, however, I moved to the front as he seemed to be so sincere. Bus drivers were mostly friendly in those days, and this driver was especially so. We did have quite a good conversation, but I can no longer recall very much of it.

I do remember that he asked me why I had come to the United States, and I told him I had come as a graduate student. Then after we had talked for a while, he asked, "You're not going there [meaning Macomb] to get married, are you?" And I said yes. Well, at the next bus stop, which was a general store, he got off, and when he came back to the bus, he handed me a wedding gift. It was a special gadget for name lists and phone numbers with a convenient index for quick access. It cost a dollar. It wasn't exactly expensive, but I felt overwhelmed. (In those days you could buy many useful things with a dollar. A gallon of gasoline cost only nineteen cents if you lived in the big city. It cost thirty-nine cents in the small town where I lived, and chickens usually cost nineteen cents a pound. Just remember that in those days chickens were pretty much all organic. You'll appreciate how much nineteen cents was actually worth compared to our price system now. Oranges on sale were five cents a pound, and cabbages on sale were ten cents for three pounds. Again, all produce items were natural with no GMOs in those days. So you can understand that one dollar at that time was really no small money.) I never expected a total stranger to give me a wedding gift, but it seemed that God was really showing me He would be with me and bless me no matter where I went.

When Yishan and I were married in June 1966, I was, of course, already a Christian, but I was very ignorant as far as the biblical teaching was concerned. I was faintly aware of the biblical injunction "Do not be unequally yoked," but I understood neither why nor what it meant. I only knew the Constitution permitting the freedom of religion, and I thought I had the freedom to marry a non-Christian so long as he did not interfere with my faith. As far as I was concerned, I thought Yishan and I loved each other, and that was enough. I also wanted a church wedding, and he agreed to it. That was sufficient to make me happy. I did not see the necessity of having the same faith between husband and wife.

Well, I soon found out.

Yishan went to church with me the first Sunday after our wedding since the pastor of that Baptist church was the minister who officiated our wedding. Yishan felt obligated to go, but I noticed he dozed off during the sermon. I attributed it to his lesser English ability, but it was really due to his lack of interest. He refused to go to church after that, and I had to go alone the next Sunday. It was surely inconvenient when I realized I had to go to church by myself, but I was so blissfully ignorant that I still had to learn more about *why* not to be unequally yoked.

Being a newlywed then, I was naturally more interested in spending time with Yishan than leaving him alone at home, so I skipped churches a few times. Moreover, during the second month after the wedding, I began feeling nauseous and soon found out I was pregnant. Sometimes nausea also prevented me from attending church.

After the wedding Yishan and I did not take a honeymoon trip because we could not afford one. Yishan said that there was no need for both of us to get PhDs. So long as one person got it, it was enough, he said. I bought his argument, gave up my graduate teaching assistantship as well as my student status, and became a poor student wife. So we spent our honeymoon together in our apartment while Yishan finished up his lab experiments, and I helped him with his master's thesis. I was really happy just to be together with Yishan, and I did not ask more of anything else.

I tried to find a job, yet during that summer in Macomb, Illinois, all that I could find was a dishwashing job in a small café. The meager salary of one dollar per hour was not glamorous, but I took it gladly anyway. Love had a way of motivating one for self-sacrifice. Yishan also found a job in a manufacturing factory, working on the graveyard shift, 11:00 p.m. to 7:00 a.m. This job, Yishan told me, required tremendous amounts of strength, and every morning at 7:40, when Yishan came home from work, he seemed totally exhausted. As a newlywed, I had to spend the night by myself. Naturally, every night I begrudgingly saw him off, and every morning I woke up early to wait for him to come home.

My own dishwashing job did not last long, however. In the summer of 1966, having been in the United States for less than a year, I was also ignorant in many other areas. I did not know I should get a pair of latex gloves when I used commercial detergent to wash dishes in a café. By the end of three days' work, my hand could not tolerate the detergent, and the skin began to peel off one layer after another. It was also the first time I learned the hard way that I had many layers of skin on my hand.

(Now I recall something unusual. That cafe where I worked was very small, so small that the dishwashing area was not in the kitchen but just a small area where I had to stand washing the dishes while the customers could see me. I remember one of those evenings when I was washing dishes when I heard one of the customers saying to someone while walking toward me, "That dishwasher is working so hard. I think I'm going to tip her." And presently, he came up to me and gave me a quarter. Amazing! I never heard of this before, but I'm very thankful. Especially now almost fifty years later, when I think of it, I'm really thankful that the Lord showed me one of His blessings in my ignorance days.)

Hastily, I quit working, and after several days of resting and allowing my hands to heal, I got a job again. It was another dishwashing job at the only Chinese restaurant in town. The restaurant business was tremendous, and every afternoon when I checked in for work, the dishes were already high in piles waiting for me. They had a hot water dishwashing machine, but I had to hand-wash the dishes in detergent first and load them in the racks for the machine to rinse. Unfortunately, I had the same peeling problem with my hands and, again, so after working on the job for three days, I had to quit.

I then found another job, working as a waitress in a restaurant that had a separate lounge that served food and alcohol. The pay was only a little better than the dishwashing job—a dollar per hour *plus* tips. The part of the restaurant where I worked did not serve alcohol, and hence, I did not get fat tips. The tips I got were usually dimes or quarters. Sometimes when customers were dissatisfied with the food and sometimes for no reason at all, I was simply left no tip.

Life might be hard for another couple, but Yishan and I were so much in love in Macomb that summer that I wonder if you could find another happier or more content couple than the two of us. Our attention was so focused on each other that everything else seemed insignificant.

A month and a half after the wedding, we found ourselves to be prospective parents. In 1966, instead of dreading the news as some young couples do nowadays, Yishan and I welcomed it with joy and great expectations. Back then, medical science was not advanced enough to allow us to find out the sex of the baby, and I asked Yishan, "Would you prefer a boy or a girl?"

"If it's a boy, I think I'll be strict with him," he said. "But if it's a girl, I'll love her very much." I did not think he was prejudiced, but I was glad to know that he preferred a girl just as I did. My own preference was at least partially influenced by the way my two

13

sisters-in-law treated my mother, and I did not want to have sons who would later bring wives to trouble me.

Well, God gave me a girl, and not just one but two for two years in a row. Angela was only seven months old when Leslie was conceived, but I did not know of her existence until she began to kick inside of me.

When I learned I was to be a first-time mother, Yishan and I went to an ob-gyn in Macomb, and he informed us the total medical cost would be $280, including the doctor's and the county hospital bills. Toward the end of the summer when Yishan finished his master's requirements and we moved to Carbondale for his PhD study at Southern Illinois University (SIU), I had to find another ob-gyn. Since we thought the doctor's bill was only $280, we took $99 out of our $350 savings and bought a hi-fi set. Soon after that, I went to Dr. Bennett, who informed us the total cost would be $500 because I would be having my baby in Holden Hospital, a private hospital, instead of a county hospital. Considering the amount of savings we had, Yishan exclaimed, "We can afford only a head, not a whole baby!"

Well, God was gracious, and we had our whole baby. Seven months later when Angela was born, we did have enough savings to pay for the medical bills. We had student health insurance that did not cover maternity expenses, and henceforth, we ourselves had to shoulder every penny of the medical bills, but we did not have to go into debt. And fifteen months later when Leslie was born, it cost us another $500. We were able to pay for that as well.

Soon after Leslie was born, Yishan came home one day from the university and said to me, "Recently, another graduate student in my lab has repeatedly said to me that he is poor. I wonder why he said that."

At that time we were living solely on the income of Yishan's teaching assistantship, which was $240 minus tax (a little more than $220 per month). The other graduate student Yishan mentioned had a research assistantship, which was $240 tax-free. His wife had a master's degree and was working full-time for the university. We did not know how much she earned; however, obviously, they were much better off than we were, and they still had no children then.

I reasoned that Yishan's lab mate was afraid Yishan might want to borrow money from him. When I told him of my thought, he said, "*Well*, two of my high school friends have finished their master's and are working full-time, and both have offered to help me financially. If I had to borrow money, I could borrow from them. I would *not* have to borrow from him!"

Those two friends of Yishan's had come from St. Louis to visit us a month or two before Angela was born. They stayed with us overnight. We had extra beds in the living room to accommodate them. I also cooked a full meal of Chinese food to treat them. I cooked so much food that there was leftover for them to take back to St. Louis the next day. Needless to say, when my daughters were born, both times they sent us gifts.

God was really gracious on us. Just as His eyes are on the sparrows, His eyes were also on us in those days. When we first moved to Carbondale, someone found an apartment for us that would cost $100 a month. However, we were able to find a furnished full-basement apartment that only cost $60. Despite the fact that Yishan had to send home to his parents back in Taiwan thirty or forty dollars each month, we were still able to save enough for everything we had to pay.

Another friend of Yishan's was working on his master's paper about the same time Yishan's two friends came from St. Louis to visit. This friend was so confident in his paper when he finished it that he challenged me, "If you can find a single mistake, typing or grammatical, for each mistake I'll treat you to a movie." He sent his paper for me to proofread, and I found a total of twenty-one mistakes. Of course, I did not get to see twenty-one movies, but he sent us a huge package of baby gifts, including clothing and a baby blanket for Angela.

Another couple, Yvonne and Edward, whom we came to know after we moved to Carbondale, became our close friends. Their daughter was born seven months prior to Angela, and they gave us everything their daughter had outgrown, including anything from clothing to baby bottles. They also gave us a brand-new high chair. In fact, so many friends gave us gifts that we did not need to buy much.

At that time we had no car. One day we were told of an ad in the newspaper. Cousin Fred had baby bathtubs on sale for only fifty cents each. Cousin Fred was a store located on Highway 13, but the only way Yishan and I could get there was by foot. So on one afternoon the two of us set out from our basement apartment and walked to and back from the store. It was good exercise for us, and we did not mind the distance. However, as we were walking on the side of the highway, we found ourselves to be the only pedestrians. With cars speeding by us in both directions at forty to forty-five miles per hour, those cars seemed more like airplanes to me than automobiles, and both Yishan and I felt it was not a very pleasant experience. Nevertheless, we were happy to be able to bring home a baby bathtub at such a good price. I guess it showed how wonderfully God provided for our needs.

Nowadays people go to garage sales or Goodwill stores to get used items, but in 1967, I was not aware of those places. Besides, it was our first baby, and I was kind of expecting to have brand-new items for a brand-new baby. Again, the good Lord did not leave me disappointed.

We needed a stroller, a must. My two-time (junior high and college) classmate Heather and her roommate gave us one. Heather was also a student in Carbondale at that time. On some occasions I invited her (and sometimes her roommate also) over for dinner. On one occasion I stayed up overnight typing a term paper for her. If I had not done that for her, she would have to hand in her paper late. I guessed she was so grateful that she and her roommate gave us that big gift.

Before Angela's birth Dr. Bennett asked me which anesthesia I preferred, and I chose a spinal injection over gas mask because I wanted to stay awake when my baby was born. I did not expect the side effect from the anesthetic though—a headache when I lay down and a greater headache when I sat or got up. Hence, I was very weak after the delivery and greatly needed someone to care for me and the baby once I went home from the hospital.

The Lord fulfilled most of my other needs through a kind couple,

Rev. and Mrs. Harold A. Hall. I'm going to talk about them in a later chapter. Suffice it for me to say here that both of them are with the Lord now, but I owed them a great deal. They were also instrumental in helping Yishan become a Christian.

So during those ignorant days, it was really the Lord who took care of me like a newborn babe. I can only thank Him and praise Him for His loving kindness.

Perhaps I should add this here. It was definitely not because I was not doing well as a graduate student that I lost my ambition. I recall a special event from that period. That day all the foreign students from SDSU were invited to visit a small town called Marshall in Minnesota, near the border of Minnesota and South Dakota. We arrived in a bus and were welcomed by the Rotary Club members there to attend their meeting. During the meeting we were introduced, and following that, there were two special arrangements on the agenda after their meeting ended. The first one was a short talk given by one of the faculty members of SDSU, a man from India who talked about India and then answered questions. I have no memory of what he said or what those questions and answers were. I only remember that he was not very well received. After his talk I gave a slide presentation about Taiwan. I had asked for those slides from Miss Lillian Lu, who was the adviser to our Evergreen Fellowship when I attended Grace Baptist Church in Taipei. She had been a graduate student in the United States before she returned to Taiwan, and she certainly knew what slides to send me. Some of them were pictures of women from the church attending a fellowship meeting. The most impressive slide to me to this day was the picture of a young boy sitting on a water buffalo while playing a bamboo flute. When I showed that slide, I said, "This is an Oriental cowboy." All the listeners laughed. It was obvious they were very delighted with my presentation. After the meeting was over, I went with a senior couple to their home. They were my host family. At their home they took a couple pictures of me and sent them to me later. That evening at their home, they told me they felt honored to have me as their guest. (Miss Lillian Lu, sadly for me, later developed breast cancer and went to be with the Lord within a few years after I came to the United States.)

That visit was from so long ago that I have forgotten a lot of the details, but I still remember part of the agenda was for us to visit an ice cream factory. When we were in the factory, it was *very* cold. We were told they had to keep the temperature at -40 degrees Fahrenheit, and when we went outside, we all felt much warmer, even though it was -27 degrees, the coldest day I ever encountered when I was living in South Dakota. Yet when we returned to Brookings, my heart felt very warm because of the welcoming reception from the people in that small town.

I also remember another meeting I attended. It was the state convention of AAUW (Association of American University Women) held at Mitchel that year. I was told I could not be a member since I had not earned a US degree, but I was taken along by a professor to attend the meeting. (As a graduate teaching assistant, I was considered a faculty member of the university.) During the meeting the group was split into smaller sessions. Now I realized they must have arranged for me to speak in a small session. The memory of this event has somehow faded until now. I gave a talk about Taiwan, and I probably also presented those slides. After that, there was a Q and A session. I only remember one of those questions asked, "How about your prince?" I was puzzled and said, "Prince? We have no prince." Then it dawned on me that the person was asking about the son of Chiang Kai Shek, the president of the Republic of China who had lost the whole country to Chairman Mao of the Communist Party and fled to Taiwan. His eldest son later did succeed him to be the president of a supposedly democratic country. So I understood the intention of the questioner, and I answered, "To me, it is no problem that he is the son of Chiang Kai Shek. The question is if he has the ability to be the president." Only in recent years have I learned that this son turned out to be a better ruler than his father. So my answer turned out to be correct.

My answer was actually longer, but I cannot recall much of what I said. My only memory is that I did enjoy that meeting, and I also got along very well with the two other female graduate teaching assistants who shared the same office with me. They also attended that convention, but I was the only foreign student there to be presented as a speaker. Now I can see it was also another privilege the Lord had given me. One of those two TAs gave me a can containing some seaweeds, my very favorite food!

Although I eventually lost my ambition for advanced degrees, I have always had a fond memory of my Brookings days.

Chapter 3

The Predawn Darkness

In 1967, shortly after Angela was born, partly because of the influence of Mrs. Hall and partly because of my own inner need, I resumed my custom of attending church on Sundays. Yishan, of course, did not come along, and I had to take Angela with me. Though a newborn, she was quite opinionated; she didn't like the nursery. When she saw the Caucasian lady who took her from my arms, she began to yell, and no amount of cooing or comforting could calm her down.

This reminded me of an incident that happened not too long before that. One day I put her in the stroller and took her to the doughnut shop one block away from our apartment. At the entrance to the shop, a Caucasian lady happened to come by. She held the door open for me and said hello to Angela, but Angela took a look at the lady and let out a loud wail. The lady said to Angela, "Oh, I'm sorry," and I felt embarrassed. She did not stop crying until I came out of the store.

The first Sunday I took Angela to church, I stayed with her in the nursery for about forty minutes. By the time I went into the sanctuary, the worship was almost over. The next Sunday I went to the nursery, the lady in charge said to me, "Leave her with me, and you go to the worship." I did just that. When I returned to the nursery, Angela was asleep. The lady told me she cried for twenty minutes and eventually was tired and fell asleep. In my memory she never for once failed to cry when I left her at the nursery with the Caucasian lady during her first year.

One evening Yishan and I attended some social function and had to leave Angela home. We asked a Chinese student to babysit her. That student was young and still single, and I did not know if she had babysitting experience or not. When we got home, we were told Angela did not cry at all. Our friend played peekaboo with her, and she even giggled. I suspected that Angela *was* "racially biased" as a baby, and I did not know where she got that idea. I'm glad that she eventually overcame the fear of white ladies. By the time Leslie was born, Angela was happy when I left both her and Leslie at the nursery.

Well, Angela's fear of white ladies (except for Mrs. Hall) was not the only difficulty I faced when going to church. One Sunday the pastor must have preached too long a sermon or somebody had dragged the worship a bit too far. I don't remember which was the case. Anyway, that day I went home later than usual, and Yishan's stomach must have been growling. When he saw me, he complained, "You're going to starve me to death!"

Despite his humorous nature, he was not joking when he said those words. I could tell he was definitely quite upset. That day I learned for sure the inconvenience of being unequally yoked.

Around that time I learned of a weekly Bible study for Chinese students led by Mr. Hall. Even though I was no longer a student, I went anyway since all were welcome. Of course, I had to take Angela along. Quite a few times, she would not sleep or stay still by herself, and I had to pick her up. Otherwise, she would cry or make noise. It was naturally not easy for me to concentrate on listening to Rev. Hall. However, I tried to hang on and did manage to pick up a few things. As I look back now, I think it was the grace of God that kept me there under those inconvenient circumstances.

The Chinese Student Bible Study was held at the Baptist Foundation when I first joined the group. Later it was moved to the home of a Chinese student couple who became the leaders of the group. By then the group had gotten larger. The hostess was very hospitable and had invited many students to come for dinner, and of course, they stayed for the Bible study after the meal was served. Occasionally, I pitched in and helped prepare the food.

At first, Yishan tried to resist the invitation for Bible study. Very quickly, he gave in. Once I received the invitation to join the group for meals, he had to come along. Otherwise, he had to stay home and cook for himself. After the meal, however, I noticed that he almost always dozed off during the discussion of the Bible. I sighed whenever I saw him going into his own dreamland. Most of the time during the Bible study, I had to take Angela and Leslie into another room to keep them from distracting the group since Leslie was only a year old at that time. Needless to say, I was there for Yishan's sake. I sacrificed myself in the hope that Yishan would somehow learn some Bible truth.

I did not know how much Yishan learned during that period, but it was surely a period of spiritual awakening for me. By and by, I got more involved with the group, and before long I began to attend their prayer meetings on Saturday mornings as well. I don't remember how I struck the deal with Yishan to babysit the two girls, but I was able to leave them home when I went to the prayer meetings. There I was free to share with fellow believers, and almost every time I basked in the working of the Holy Spirit among us.

Such a wonderful period did not last long, however. In June 1971, we had to move away. A friend of Yishan's asked us to join him to open up a Chinese restaurant in Chicago. By then Yishan had graduated with a PhD and was still unable to find a job in his field. Our friend asked us to help at least temporarily, and he promised that we could leave any time Yishan found a job in his field.

We moved to Chicago to work in the Chinese restaurant, but I ended up being the chef, an arrangement I did not expect in the beginning. Originally, I was told that three men, Yishan with his friend and another man, would be working in the kitchen and that I only had to serve as the cashier. However, I turned out to be the only one there who knew about menus and was also the only one who could actually cook Chinese food for a restaurant.

So Yishan and I worked there together as a team. It was a

bittersweet experience. We were so busy that we had no time to buy furniture and had to sleep on the hardwood floor of our apartment for two months. We were happy to be working together, but it was another period of hard life for us.

Fortunately, that phase of our life lasted only two months for me and three months for Yishan. I quit to find an office job in downtown Chicago. When Yishan quit the restaurant, he also found a typing job a number of blocks away from my workplace. (Since Yishan was a pianist, he was able to type quite fast, much faster than I could.) Thus, we commuted together in the morning. I got off the train one station ahead of him. He came to join me during the lunch hour and went back after the lunch, and then we commuted home together at the end of the workday.

Once we arrived home, I would plunge myself into preparing supper while Yishan went downstairs to wait for the school bus to bring the girls home. The nursery school that the girls attended served them lunch, but they were always very hungry when they got home. Yishan would take care of the girls to make sure they got fed. By the time I finished cooking, the girls still had room in their stomachs for more food, and we always enjoyed a family meal. After dinner Yishan washed the dishes while I took the girls to the bathroom for their bath. We kept this routine during the workdays, but it was a period of happy family life for us.

At the turn of the new year for 1972, Yishan found a job in his field. His place of work was in another part of Chicago, and he drove every day. That ended our commuting together. Then seven months later, his parents came from Taiwan to live with us, and our family life took a wrong turn.

Before Yishan's parents joined us, he said, "When Mother comes, I want you to cook since her cooking is not as good as yours." It was arranged that Yishan's mom would cook the rice (using a rice cooker) and also wash/cut the meat and vegetables according to my specifications so that they would be ready for me to cook when I got home. It was all well-arranged, although sometimes I still had to do some preparations myself.

The big surprise came after the first meal. Yishan went to the sink to wash dishes as usual, but his mom chased him away. She chided, "How come a man is washing dishes? Men do not belong in the kitchen. Go away. Let me wash the dishes."

Obediently, Yishan went to join his father and the girls in their bedroom. (We lived in a two-bedroom apartment without a family room. Yishan's parents slept in the girls' bedroom, and the girls slept in the living room.) I'm sure Yishan was happy to be relieved of the dishwashing job. When my mother-in-law finished the dishes, however, I was dismayed and greatly distressed when I found the dishes dirtier than unwashed. Because of the cataract condition she had at that time, she had poor eyesight and did not do the dishes properly. Before she washed the dishes, they were dirty only on the inside, but after she washed them, they became dirty both inside and out. From then on, I refused to let her wash the dishes. This also meant that from then on, I had to perform all the housework by myself without Yishan's lending a helping hand.

Nineteen years later in August 1991, Yishan's mother and two sisters came to California for Angela's wedding, and two of my sisters also came. All of them stayed with us. At that time Yishan's mother told my sisters of her first experience with us in Chicago in 1972. According to her own confession, when she saw Yishan washing dishes for me, she felt so sad for Yishan that she shed tears after she went to her room. Of course, by 1991, she knew it was *no* big deal for a husband to wash dishes. By then it had become common experience when she saw her granddaughter's husband washing dishes. She realized *then*, when both the husband and wife were working, the husband should help the wife wash dishes. However, back in 1972, it was a shock for her when she saw Yishan washing dishes. At that time she only cared for her own son and definitely had no concern for me.

My in-laws also brought another problem for me when they came to live with us in Chicago. Yishan's father was a chain-smoker. According to his own calculation, he smoked "twenty-two cigarettes a day." It might not sound so awful for another person, but it was disastrous for me.

Ever since my childhood, I had learned that I was extremely sensitive and allergic to cigarette smoke. Between my fifth and eighth grades when my family was living with an uncle and his family, I would always begin to cough and feel choked whenever my uncle lit a cigarette in the next room.

In 1972, when my in-laws came, I was working in the national headquarters of a company where almost two-thirds of the employees smoked. Every afternoon around three o'clock, the large office became foggy with smoke, and I began to have a headache. By 5:00 p.m., when I left for home, I desperately needed a clean space for breathing. Unfortunately, when Yishan's parents came to live with us, I had to go home every evening to an apartment already filled with cigarette smoke. Nowadays we all know the hazards of secondhand cigarette smoke, but in 1972, nobody had sympathy for me for what I had to go through day in and day out.

Needless to say, every evening when I came home from work, I was already tired. Then I had to continue working in the kitchen all alone and also continue suffering with the cigarette smoke while Yishan and the two girls were laughing in the bedroom with his parents. With a fatigued body working under those circumstances, I felt more like a housemaid than a housewife. The only time when the rest of the family came to the kitchen was when the dinner was ready. And of course, after dinner they all went back together to the bedroom. I was left all alone in the kitchen again, washing dishes. Then after that, I had to give the girls their bath, and Yishan *never* lent a helping hand.

I was lonely and miserable. And it made it even worse when Yishan stopped going to church with me.

The first Sunday after my in-laws arrived, we took them to church with us. My in-laws were Buddhists. Yishan was not a believer yet, but he had been dutifully attending church after he got the job in his field. After attending church with us once, my in-laws refused to go on the second Sunday, and Yishan stayed home with them. He said, "On weekdays both of us are working and have to leave my parents home alone. On weekends I shouldn't leave them home alone. I'll stay home with them."

I actually tried very hard to please my in-laws. I cooked the best food for them. I also asked a colleague living in Indiana to buy cartons of cigarettes for Yishan's father since the price was cheaper there despite my own adverse reaction to cigarettes. I even purchased three new coats for Yishan's mother and his two sisters; I did not buy any for my own sisters. I thought I did the best any woman could have done to please her in-laws, yet I found my in-laws to be quite distant. No matter what their needs were or how I pleaded with them, they never spoke directly to me. They always relayed their requests or messages *through* Yishan.

Indeed, it's an understatement to say that I felt frustrated. I suffered, and Yishan never saw the need to help me out or to try to improve my in-laws' relationship with me. But the saddest fact was that my relationship with Yishan began to deteriorate. One day I exploded, and Yishan raised his hand to slap me. His hand landed on my face when his mother rushed out and got hold of it, but then she coldly commented, "*You yourselves* fell in love and got married. How come you are quarreling!"

I was angry but also in great anguish. Life became meaningless to me, and I began to contemplate suicide. We were then living about four blocks from Lake Michigan. Quite a few times I thought of jumping into the lake. Whenever I had the suicidal thought, however, I would also think, *Who is going to take care of my two girls when I die?* The Lord really had mercy on me. He used my love for the two girls to keep me from taking my own life.

It was perhaps the darkest period of my life up to that time. I've heard it said, "The hour before dawn is the darkest." What a long night! I thought I would never see the light of day, but the Lord in His mercy moved the hearts of my in-laws and eventually they returned to Taiwan. They stayed with us nearly eight months. Those eight months were pretty much like eight years to me.

A week before they left, I overheard Yishan's mother commanding him, "After I leave, don't follow her to become a Christian." I then heard him answer with great assurance, "Mother, don't worry. I've been married almost seven years, and I'm still not a Christian. I don't think I'll ever become a Christian in my life."

Well, God works in mysterious ways. Within less than a year after his parents left, Yishan joined a baptismal class and decided to get baptized. The predawn darkness was finally over.

Chapter 4

Love Manifested

In September 1966, shortly after we moved to Carbondale, Illinois, where Yishan embarked on his PhD studies, we attended Sunday worship service at a church a block away from our apartment. When the service was over, the two of us, being first-time visitors, were asked to stand in the front and a lot of people lined up to shake hands with us. Of those who came up, there was a couple who introduced themselves as Rev. and Mrs. Harral A. Hall. There was something special about them that quite impressed me during that brief encounter. Whether it was their smiles or their warm welcome (or maybe both), I could not tell.

After that Sunday, we did not go back to church because of Yishan's lack of interest. However, a few weeks later, Rev. and Mrs. Hall came to knock on our door. They saw me in a maternity dress that Sunday, so they knew I was expecting and had come to inquire if we needed help. Did we need help!

To me, they were really a godsend. We were still new in town and did not have many friends. My first baby was due in a few months, and I was almost unprepared.

First, I needed a sewing machine to make some baby clothes. Mrs. Hall lent me her electric sewing machine. We also needed a crib. A few weeks later, Rev. and Mrs. Hall came to visit and brought us one. It was smaller than a regular crib but sufficient for us. A neighbor left the crib out in the dump, Mrs. Hall told us, but they took it home. Mr.

Hall added two legs that had been sawed off to fit a trailer home. They still had no grandchildren, they said. So we could keep it for a while.

Rev. and Mrs. Hall were then in their midsixties. Rev. Hall was a retired minister and was working at the administration office of SIU at that time. Quite frequently, he also filled in the pulpit needs of some area churches.

When Angela was born, Mrs. Hall came to visit me in the hospital. She came every day and stayed with me during the whole visiting hours. Yishan, being a graduate student at that time, could not come to the hospital during the daytime visiting hours. Mrs. Hall's visits provided me not just with much-needed company, but they also kept me from feeling homesick. Since my siblings were in Taiwan and none of them could come to visit, the Lord really sent her to provide me with important emotional support.

In those days we still owned no car. On the day I was discharged, we needed a car to bring me and the baby home. Rev. and Mrs. Hall came to the hospital to help Yishan do the job of a new father. Except for the color of their skin, their smiles and willingness to help really made them look like they were brand-new grandparents.

Once they got me and Angela comfortably settled at home, Mrs. Hall then went on to instruct Yishan on how to wash diapers. Pampers were then the first disposable diapers available on the market, but we could not afford them all the time and we usually used cloth diapers. As time went on, I also discovered that Angela could not wear paper diapers too long. Every time I put disposable diapers on her, she always got rashes.

Before 8:00 a.m. the next morning when Rev. Hall went to work, he dropped off Mrs. Hall at my apartment first. Yishan had to go to classes, and because of my physical condition, I needed someone to take care of me and the baby. Mrs. Hall came to fill in the need.

I was recuperating and slept a lot during the first two weeks after I went home. When Mrs. Hall came, she let me sleep most of the time. When the baby woke up, Mrs. Hall would first change her diapers before bringing the baby to me to nurse.

When I was growing up in Taiwan, I had many opportunities to babysit nephews and nieces. Being a new mother, however, I was not familiar with the American way of mothering. So the first morning Mrs. Hall was with me, she showed me how to bathe the baby step by step.

As far as lunch was concerned, she was unprepared the first day. According to Taiwanese customs, Yishan had prepared some pork with special broth, which was usually served to a postpartum nursing mother. I showed Mrs. Hall the lunch I would have, but I had to get up and cook some fried rice to serve her for lunch.

Well, when Mrs. Hall came the following morning, she brought two sacks of lunch, one for herself and the other for Yishan. Besides showing her hospitality, she also took all the soiled diapers and clothes home when Rev. Hall came to pick her up at the end of each day. Again, in the morning when she came, she brought all the clothes and diapers back, clean and fresh. Not until many years later did I learn that each time she took the soiled diapers and clothes home, she washed them in her own washing machine, but she also had to dig into her own pocket to get them dried at the Laundromat since she did not own a dryer at that time.

The first day when I cooked lunch for Mrs. Hall, as I was adding salt to the fried rice, she saw that my salt was running out. The very next morning, she brought me a fresh box of Morton salt and refused to let me pay her for it. On top of that, when she saw that I did not have enough cloth diapers, she also bought me a dozen new diapers and some baby clothes as gifts. A month or two later, she also had the ladies at her church pool some money and give me and Angela a baby shower, presenting me a brand-new playpen.

As one who was relatively new in the New World at that time, I used to think that elderly American ladies had plenty of leisure time so that Mrs. Hall could afford helping me. How wrong and ignorant I was! As I got to know her better later, I learned that she was actually a busy lady. Besides being an active member of her church, attending Sunday services both mornings and evenings, she also taught a Sunday school class to foreign students and was actively involved with the ladies of the church. During those two weeks when she came to help me, sometimes I woke up seeing her writing something. When she saw me, she would put her writing aside. As I got to know her better, I realized that she was actually writing letters. She really made a lot of sacrifices for me during those two weeks!

After those two weeks of rest and nourishment, I was fully recuperated and could be on my own. Mrs. Hall was released to go back to tend to her own needs at her home.

When Angela was a month old, we invited all our Chinese friends to our apartment for a traditional Taiwanese celebration. Mr. and Mrs. Hall, of course, were invited, and after the dinner I presented to Mrs. Hall two special gifts as a token of my appreciation for her sacrificial help to me. Obviously, if I had not been fully recovered after those two weeks, I would not have been able to make those gifts. One was a small bag with a very special flap in triangular shape for cover and also a crocheted ball added on top of the bag for fastening, and I crocheted it using a special nylon yarn from Taiwan. The other was a still smaller bag. I used the same material that I had crocheted, and I sewed on the top a metal clasp to be used as a coin purse. (It was a fad among Taiwanese girls/women to crochet all sorts of bags using that kind of nylon yarn during those years. However, I believe it was an inspiration from the Lord to give me the idea to make that special bag for Mrs. Hall since I had never seen one like that before. She was very pleased to receive it and later used it as a cosmetic bag.)

Mrs. Hall presented with the gift

Sometime after that, Mrs. Hall organized the ladies at her church and started a weekly meeting called "Friendship Center," which met at the basement of her church. I attended the meetings regularly. Friendship Center was actually geared at the many foreign student wives, me included, who had small children and had to stay home.

I considered myself lucky, since our apartment was near the center of the town and close to stores. Once I put Angela into the stroller, I could easily do all the shopping even without a car. Some of those student wives were not so lucky. A lot of them lived in the university housing, which was farther away from the center of the town. As a result, they were mostly housebound. They had to wait for weekends when their husbands could provide them the transportation for shopping.

Mr. and Mrs. Hall devoted practically all of their spare time to helping foreign students. On weekdays they usually would visit either the sick or some housebound ladies with special needs. On Saturdays they often gave rides to foreign students and took them to supermarkets or do other weekend shopping. Years later I realized the

Halls had left such indelible marks on me that I was myself following their footsteps, helping people whenever I could.

The Halls got to know many foreign students and knew the loneliness of the student wives with small children. Friendship Center provided an outlet for those women, not just as a social activity but also as a chance to learn (or to share) crafts and recipes and different cultures. It actually also provided an environment for women of different religions to meet Christians.

Almost two decades later in the 1980s, friends of Mr. and Mrs. Hall in Carbondale held a special eightieth birthday celebration for Mr. Hall and presented to him and Mrs. Hall a thick collection of letters and articles of appreciation by people from all over the world, people who had been recipients of Mr. and Mrs. Hall's benevolence and generosity. Yishan and I were living in Schaumburg at that time, hundreds of miles away from Carbondale. To this day it is still one of my life regrets that I could not go back to Carbondale to physically participate in that celebration. Besides giving a check as a gift, I can only take comfort in the fact that I did contribute a letter of appreciation to that collection.

In the first year after I joined the Chinese Students Bible Study, all of us lived in small apartments. None of us had a place large enough to accommodate all the participants. We met at the Baptist Student Foundation at that time. When we wanted to hold a potluck dinner, we would go to Mr. and Mrs. Hall's home. It seemed to me that everyone felt quite at home at their place. While most of us sat in the living room discussing the Bible, a few students would be boiling noodles in the kitchen. After the dinner most of us pitched in to help with cleaning up. Yet I'm sure that after all of us had left, Mrs. Hall would still have had to spend time putting her house back in order.

During the years I attended Chinese Students Bible Study, Mr. and Mrs. Hall were usually present. They actually did not understand a single Chinese word, and yet they patiently sat there listening while the participants discussed topics in Mandarin. Occasionally, someone would translate part of the discussion into English for them, but most of the time, they just sat there until a question that none of us knew how to answer came up. Then someone would translate the question for Mr. Hall so that he could help answer it. Watching the soft-spoken Mr. and Mrs. Hall sitting there and answering questions, I felt that I was seeing the embodiment of love and patience.

Since I lost my mother while I was still in college, it was really Mrs. Hall who played the motherly role to me after I got to know her. She taught me many valuable tips on how to save money and how to salvage items people would normally throw away and how to reuse them long before the word *recycle* was ever heard. She was a role model for me not just in mothering but more importantly, as a Christian woman and wife. Whenever I needed someone for good advice, I would call on her, even after we moved to Chicago and later to Schaumburg. I really looked up to her as my own mother, more than a close friend.

When I applied to Moody Summer School in 1982, I was required to have three letters of recommendation. One of those three people I asked to write the recommendation was Mr. Hall. When I saw him some time later in Carbondale, I asked him what he had written in that letter. I knew it was supposed to be confidential, and I really did not expect him to tell me its content. I was just curious. Without revealing the secret to me, Mr. Hall said, "Let's put it in this way. When those people read that letter, they're going to think that you are my daughter." Since I was never fond of my own father and often felt the lack of a father's love, I think God really had provided me the fatherly love through Mr. Hall.

The greatest gratitude I owed to the Halls was their influence on Yishan. As I have already mentioned, Yishan was not a Christian when we got married. For years he used two delay tactics against my evangelistic approach. Whenever I said to him, "I think you should believe in Jesus Christ," he would immediately shoot back a dart and say, "Tell me how to believe." Woe to me, I had not myself been trained in evangelism. Nor had I completed reading the whole Bible. I did not know how to tell him. I could only hand him the Bible and tell him to read it for himself. I did not even know I should tell him to start in the New Testament. When he took the Bible, naturally, he turned to the first page where it says, "In the beginning God created the heavens and the earth." Then he would give the Bible back to me and commented, "It's full of myths. I'd rather read the kung fu stories." I felt defenseless.

For the second tactic Yishan employed, at my mention of believing in Jesus, he would bring up the names of two former classmates whom Yishan had identified as Christians; however, these two had performed many unchristian acts. Then Yishan would remark, "Like those guys, why should I become a Christian? I'm actually better than either one!" Again, I was speechless.

However, as time went on and Yishan had more opportunities to observe the Halls, he gradually came to see the difference between so-called Christians and the real followers of Jesus Christ. He confessed years later that from the beginning he did see the difference between me, a Christian who wanted to attend church every Sunday, and his former classmate who did not care about attending church at all. Nevertheless, possibly because I was too close to him for him to see my real value, the Halls' self-sacrifice really touched Yishan's stony heart and removed all his animosity against Christians.

When Rev. Hall was young, he originally wanted to follow his father's footsteps in his medical practice. However, while he was in his premed studies, the Lord called him into Christian service, and he became a preacher instead. To me—and to Yishan as well—Mr. and Mrs. Hall's action actually spoke even louder than the words they preached. By their very acts of love, patience, and sacrifice, they had testified to the words in the Bible. "For God is love. By this the love of God was manifested in us, that God has sent His only begotten Son into the world so that we might live through Him ... No one has beheld God at any time; if we love one another, God abides in us, and His love is perfected in us" (1 John 4:8–9, 12 NASB).

During the summer of 1988, we drove down to Carbondale to visit the Halls. It was the last time we saw them. Shortly before Thanksgiving of 1989, a few months after we moved to the West Coast, we received word that Mr. Hall had gone home to be with the Lord. Mrs. Hall survived her husband and lived on six or seven more years. I am very thankful that Yishan, my daughters Corrie and Angela, and I (Leslie was in Boston) made that trip in 1988 to Carbondale and were able to see them one more time. Of course, now *even* Yishan is with the Lord, and I'm sure they are all having sweet fellowship with one another in heaven. But I really miss them all.

I feel so privileged not just to have known Mr. and Mrs. Hall but also to have been intimately involved with them and to have personally benefited so much because of them. Indeed, God is love, and even though I have never seen God with my own eyes, the Lord has allowed me to see His love manifested through His loving servants, Mr. and Mrs. Hall. To God be all glory and gratitude!

Chapter 5

A Strange Encounter

$\mathscr{I}$n 1971, a few months after we moved to Chicago, we were told of a Chinese church not too far from where we lived. We went where we were told, but we could not find that church. After searching for some time, we were finally able to locate their meeting place. Thus, on January 2, 1972, we attended the Sunday worship service of FC Church for the first time. We met our friend Bob, whom we had not seen for six months. That day he learned that Yishan was still without a job in his field.

The next evening Bob came to our apartment to inform Yishan of a job opening in his field. A dorm mate of Bob's was quitting work to return to school. His boss told him to find his own replacement, and Bob just found out that this dorm mate was in the same field as Yishan. Yishan went for interview the next morning, and two days later he started working.

To Yishan, this seemed rather out of the ordinary. For *two years* he had been looking for a job, and they always seemed to have eluded him. Now that he went to a Chinese church for the first time, the job came in his way without his own active seeking. Even though he could not see the existence of God, he did see the connection of attending church and getting this job. From then on, he went to church every Sunday without my nagging or reminding him.

As for me, of course, I was very thankful, to say the least. For two years my prayers for Yishan's job seemed to have been lost in the air.

Yet deep down in my heart, I knew unless Yishan capitulated himself to the Lord, the Lord would be in no hurry to help him. So after he started working on the new job and continued going to church with me, life itself seemed to be complete.

However, as the saying goes, good times never last long. Within months, when Yishan's parents came to live with us, our family life took a down turn and tragedy almost resulted when life seemed unbearable to me. What I did not know was that it was really a period in the Lord's plan for me to learn His new grace.

As I have already mentioned, at that time Yishan stopped going to church in order to stay home with his parents. It was one of those Sundays when I went to church alone that the Holy Spirit opened my eyes to see the need of praying for Yishan's salvation. That day as the preacher was talking about a Christian in Tokyo who knelt nightly on the concrete bathroom floor to pray for her husband's salvation, he said, "Even a stony, steely heart will be softened, and ten years later her husband was saved." As I listened to those words, tears streamed down my face, and I thought, *If I start praying for Yishan today, how will I be able to go on for ten years with life like this?*

Nevertheless, I did start to pray for Yishan's salvation, and that was just the beginning of the road the Lord was leading me on to learn of His ways in my life.

A few months later, a pastor's wife from LA came to preach. She talked about how she was once the speaker for a YWCA retreat during the Sino-Japanese War. As she arrived at the conference, she was told that her scheduled interpreter was sick and could not come. That meant she would have to speak without an interpreter.

That night, she said, she knelt in her hotel room and prayed, "Lord, I need the ability to speak the local dialect." "Local dialect" in Chinese is the same as the word "tongue" (Acts 2) in the Chinese New Testament. She said that she could understand the local dialect, but she had never been able to speak it. However, as she prayed, she was filled with the Holy Spirit and began to speak in a tongue that *was* the local dialect. "I testify to the power of the Holy Spirit and the ability to speak in tongues," she said.

As I listened to her message, I felt the power of the Holy Spirit on myself as tears flowed down my cheeks. There was nothing sad about the message at all. When the service was over, I stood in line with others to shake hands with the speaker. When it was my turn, I had meant to say to her, "Thank you, Mrs. Chao, for your message. I was greatly touched by it." However, I was so overpowered by the Holy Spirit that I began to cry and said, "Mrs. Chao, my husband is still not saved!" She took my name and address and promised to send me a book when she went back to LA.

A few weeks later, I received a book from her—*From Prison to Praise* by Chaplain Carother. When I finished reading the book, I was convinced of its message on how to praise God even in the midst of the most difficult situations. Thus, I began to offer praises to the Lord in my prayers, "Lord, even though Yishan is still not saved, I want to praise You. You must have a good purpose in this."

It was around that time (1973) that I invited the church's weekly Friday night Bible study group to meet at our apartment. When they came, I happened to open my Bible to the front leaf where I saw the date of my baptism. This Bible had been given to me by Grace Baptist Church of Taipei when I was baptized. I felt ashamed when I realized that it had been nearly ten years since I had received this Bible, and yet the Bible was almost a total stranger to me. That evening I vowed in front of the group to get myself familiar with the Bible, and I did start to read it diligently.

About two months later (May), Yishan's parents went back to Taiwan. My relationship with Yishan began to improve, but he still refused to go to church. Then in July, we took a two-week vacation and drove to Yellowstone and Glacier National Parks and all the way to Banff National Park in Canada. On the way back, we visited some friends in Minneapolis. There Yishan witnessed a strange encounter with the supernatural, and his attitude toward God was turned around.

Up to that time, my Bible knowledge was limited, and I was very ignorant as far as the teachings on angels and demons were concerned. I had come from a Buddhist-animist background where I used to hear my mother talk about her many encounters with spirits. When I became a Christian, I decided that my mother's stories were due to her superstition, and I refused to believe in any spirit beings other than God and angels (good angels). I did not know anything about demons at that time.

When my Minneapolis friends told us how they had been encountering spirits through something similar to the Ouija board, I discounted them as impossible. (In Chinese, they call it "the Dish Fairy.") Yishan was, of course, an atheist, and no one could convince him of the existence of God or any other form of spirits.

That morning as we were ready to leave, a couple unexpectedly came to visit my friends. As we lingered around a little longer, the weather suddenly changed, and it became very dark and windy and began to rain heavily. My friend's husband said, "Now it's a good time to play the Dish Fairy." He was serious about convincing us and began to cut pieces of paper and then write letters and numbers on them. He then placed those pieces of paper in a circle and put a goblet upside down in the center.

My friend's husband had three of us place our hands on the goblet. "Only lightly touch the edge," he instructed us.

I was one of those three touching the goblet. I was also the only Christian of all the three couples present. My Bible knowledge was limited, and naturally, I was not aware of the prohibition in the Bible against occult involvement. However, I warned my friends, "I'm a Christian. I do not believe in ghosts (the term used by our friends for spirits). Even if they do exist, they'll be afraid of Jesus, and I don't think they'll come near."

My friend's husband had all of us close our eyes and ask repeatedly, "Is anybody there? Is anybody there?"

After the chanting went on for a while and nothing moved, I opened my eyes and said, "See? I told you. There is nothing *there!*"

"Right, perhaps it's because you're a Christian," my friend's husband said. "Why don't you remove your hand and let me take over?"

I withdrew my hand, and he placed his on the edge of the goblet. We all closed our eyes and began to ask again, "Is anybody there?"

Within a minute or two, the goblet began to shake and move around. All of us opened our eyes, and indeed the goblet was shaking and moving. We began to ask questions.

"Do you know him?" somebody asked, pointing toward Yishan.

"Yes," the goblet answered by moving to the side of the word.

"Where did he come from?" Again, the question was about Yishan.

"C-H-I-C-A-G-O." The goblet spelled out the answer.

"How many people came with him?"

"Three." Again the goblet moved to answer the question. The answer was correct.

"What's his name?"

"Yishan." Again the name was correctly spelled out. In fact, I did not think my friends (or theirs) knew how Yishan's name should be spelled. A lot of our Chinese friends often misspelled Yishan's name.

"What's his wife's name?"

This time the goblet just moved within the circle without giving an answer.

"Do you know my name?" I persisted in asking. However, the goblet continued to move around, totally ignoring any question concerning me or asked by me.

"What's his eldest daughter's name?" somebody asked another question about Yishan.

"Angela." The answer was correct.

"What's his second daughter's name?"

"Leslie." Again, that was a correctly spelled answer.

Up to this point both Yishan, and I had doubts whether the goblet was moving on its own or not. My friend's husband was quick to point out that the hands were not pushing the goblet but rather just following along instead.

"If you don't believe it, why don't you put your hand here?" he said, and then he gave his place to Yishan.

Another person also let me take over his place. With my own

hand on the edge of the goblet, I knew for sure that I could not push it. But it had a power of its own, and I had to follow wherever it wanted to go.

As it turned out, with only two exceptions, all the questions we asked that day were correctly answered. The first exception was regarding *me*. Whenever I asked a question or whenever a question was asked concerning me, the goblet did not answer but only moved around within the circle.

The second exception was Yishan's birthday. Both the year and the month of his birth were answered correctly, but the wrong date was given. Except this, all the other people's birthdays were given correctly, including Angela's and Leslie's.

Later as I learned more of the Bible, I realized that there *was* really some demonic power moving the goblet. Demons are fallen angels. They are more knowledgeable than human beings. They know a lot about us, but they are not omniscient as God is. That's why Yishan's date of birth was given incorrectly.

That experience also helped me to understand the meaning of Colossians 1:13 (NASB), which says, "For He delivered us from the domain of darkness, and transferred us to the kingdom of His beloved Son." Since I no longer belonged in the spirit realm controlled by Satan, there was no way for a demonic spirit to know or tell anything about me. Ignorant as I was, I knew I was genuinely saved and therefore belonged to the Lord, Jesus Christ. I'm very thankful for God's love and faithfulness, which were demonstrated to me that day clearly, marking me out from the rest who were not believers of Jesus Christ.

True, as some Christians were quick to accuse me of and pointed out, I should not have been involved in any occult practice. Yet because of my own ignorance of biblical knowledge, it was really inevitable. And for all that happened, I was all the more thankful to the Lord for His protection on me and especially for the way He allowed things to develop, and in the end He was the one to receive all the honor and glory. Romans 8:28 was thus proven true not only on me but on Yishan as well.

That day when Yishan saw with his own eyes the different ways the goblet responded to me and to the questions asked by others, he really saw the *difference* between a Christian and non-Christian. This led him to the conclusion that if there were spirit beings, then God might exist too. It also led him to ponder further the question, "Is Jesus Christ truly God?"

This really piqued Yishan's interest in the spiritual search, and when we came back from the vacation, he started attending church without lapses. The only exception was the Sunday after we moved to Schaumberg, a western suburb of Chicago. That Sunday, we were both exhausted after moving into the new house we had purchased. Otherwise, every Sunday, he would voluntarily go to church without my prodding or nagging. The Holy Spirit was working in answer to my prayer for Yishan. By the next Easter, he joined a baptismal class and was baptized in July 1974.

Here I need to mention what Yishan's mother said to him about a week before she and her husband went back to Taiwan. He was talking with them in their room (actually Angela and Leslie's bedroom), and I overheard her saying to Yishan, "After I leave, don't you ever follow her in becoming a Christian." He answered her with great self-confidence, "Mother, you can be assured. I've been married almost seven years and I'm still not a Christian. I don't think I'll ever become a Christian in this life!" (Hence, I often caution people against boasting in front of an all-knowing God.)

His mother said that in early May of 1973, but he joined the baptismal class in April of 1974, less than a year from his saying those words. And later he decided to be baptized.

Glory be to God! He deserves all praises. All things really work together for good to those who love Him (Romans 8:28). How true His word is!

Chapter 6

The Choir Director

$\mathcal{A}$ few weeks after I went to FC Church, I joined the choir just as I used to in other churches. When I joined the FCC choir, we had a capable choir director whose name was Roseanna. A little more than a year later, however, she resigned. The reason? She and her husband were planning to leave as foreign missionaries.

We had a new choir director. Or I should say that someone volunteered to take the job. It happened while Yishan and I were away on vacation. When I came back, I was a little dismayed to see how the new choir director directed the choir, and hence, I did not go back to choir practices. I found out I was not alone. Three or four other members stopped going as well.

One day, these former choir members happened to get together and talk about the choir. I casually said, "Too bad Yishan is not a Christian. Otherwise, I think he'd make a fine choir director." I recalled how he had coached me before that singing contest.

"We should pray for the Lord to convert Mr. Lin so that he can be our choir director," said one of those present. Later this sister told me that she put Yishan's name on her prayer list and prayed for his salvation daily.

For some reason, Roseanna stayed on in church and did not leave. That day when we were talking about the choir, she was also present. I urged her to take back the directorship. She consented under one condition. "If I direct the choir again, you have to promise me to take it over when I leave," she said.

I did not promise her anything. I confessed my love for music, but I said, "I don't think my musical ability is sufficient for me to be a choir director." It was then I brought up the prospect of Yishan's potential as a choir director that prompted the other sister's response to pray for Yishan to be a choir director.

Not too long after that, Roseanna came back to direct the choir, and I rejoined her. Approximately a year later, she resigned again. This time it was for real. She and her husband *were* leaving for foreign mission field.

About a month after Yishan was baptized, our pastor together with an elder came to talk to me.

"Roseanna has resigned," said the pastor. "And she has recommended you to be the choir director."

"Oh, no," I said. "I love music, and I only know how to sing. I don't know how to direct the choir."

"But," I continued, "if the church doesn't mind, I'd like to recommend my husband, Yishan. I think he's more suitable to be the choir director, even though he is a new Christian. I do not think that *any* person can be a choir director. One has to have some musical talent, and I think he has it. If he needs help spiritually, I'd be glad to help on the side."

I said all this genuinely from my heart. Quite unexpectedly, though, the pastor responded to my words in a different light and said to the elder, "This sister is very spiritual. She's upholding her husband."

As a result, Yishan became our new choir director.

It was quite interesting to watch how he handled the new job. Since he was a new Christian, he still had to learn the biblical teaching concerning how to serve God in the church. I was by that time a little more knowledgeable in spiritual principles, and somehow, the Lord was able to use me to help Yishan.

At the beginning Yishan was very enthusiastic and went all out to recruit new choir members. The response, however, was far from enthusiastic, and he felt a little dejected. When he told me this on the way home from church (a forty-five-minute drive) that Sunday afternoon, I said, "Don't be discouraged. We can pray together and ask the Lord to move the hearts of those people to join the choir."

Not only did we pray together that evening, but I prayed about it every day too. I knew Yishan did it every day in his own devotional time as well. He usually had his devotion at work during the lunch hour.

The next Sunday we went to church as usual. When the worship service was over, quite a number of people came to Yishan, wanting to join the choir. One mother in particular came to inquire for her son and daughter, both of whom were interested in singing.

This, of course, impressed Yishan very much since he was able to see the difference prayers made, and therefore, he learned the importance of prayers.

As a result of prayers and with the Lord using Yishan, the choir significantly grew, not only in the number of people but also in the quality of presentations. Whereas the choir used to seem out of proportion with more women than men, now it became well-proportioned with more male voices in the choir. One Sunday, there were enough brothers in the choir to sing an all-male piece, thus giving the sisters a break.

It was September of 1974 when Yishan took over the choir. Pretty soon it was time to start practicing for the annual Christmas program. I suggested two selections from Handel's *Messiah*, the two very well-known choral pieces "For Unto Us a Child Is Born" and the hallelujah chorus. Yishan liked both pieces too, and we decided to do them.

However, a few Sundays later, it seemed that no progress was made. The reason was that the fluctuation in the attendance of some choir members was affecting their learning, and therefore, it seemed that the choir was not progressing.

That Sunday at choir practice, Yishan seemed frustrated. He asked the members whether we should continue practicing *Messiah* or choose something easier instead. Handel's two choral pieces were by no means easy unless one was willing to devote the time to learn and practice.

We took a vote. It was a unanimous decision. We'd stick to *Messiah*. Amazingly, by the next Sunday, all the choir members attended the practice, and from then on, we progressed nicely.

The original plan of the Christmas program was also to include four solos, all of them selections from Handel's *Messiah*—an alto singing "He Is Like a Shepherd" followed by a soprano singing "Come Unto Me All Ye That Labor," a tenor solo of "Comfort Ye," and then a bass solo of "The Trumpet Shall Sound".

To me, with the two choral pieces plus the four solos from Messiah and with Yishan directing his first Christmas program, it would be a perfect Christmas. Naturally, I could sing the soprano solo. Another woman in the choir could sing the alto solo. We also had a brother who was a good tenor for the solo piece. Best of all, there was Andrew, whose voice was excellent for "The Trumpet Shall Sound". We were told that before coming to the United States, he had studied voice and won a contest in Hong Kong.

However, early on in our practice, Andrew told Yishan that he was planning to go to Canada during Christmas so that he would not be able to sing in the choir. When I heard that, I thought about how imperfect our Christmas program would be without Andrew. I earnestly prayed and asked the Lord to change Andrew's mind so that he would stay to join us for the Christmas program.

A few weeks later, Andrew told Yishan he would be around for Christmas, but the best he could do was only sing in the choir. He definitely would not sing the bass solo. From then on, Yishan gave up praying for Andrew's singing the solo, even though he still continued to pray for the choir and the Christmas program as a whole.

However, I continued to feel that our Christmas program would be imperfect without Andrew's solo because no one else could replace him. Therefore, I did not give up and continued to pray, "Lord, please give us a perfect Christmas program. Please move Andrew's heart so that he will consent to sing the solo."

In order to give the choir more time for practice, knowing that everybody would be off on the afternoon of December 24, I suggested that we gather at 4:00 that afternoon for rehearsal. I also announced that I would cook enough food for all choir members so that they did not have to worry about cooking.

Some choir members did not own cars and were in need of transportation. Yishan arranged rides for them, and the day before Christmas Eve, he called up Andrew to inform him the name of the person who would pick him up for the choir rehearsal. When Yishan was about to hang up the phone, Andrew said, "Could I sing a solo tomorrow night?"

"What song?" asked Yishan.

"The Trumpet Shall Sound," answered Andrew.

Praise the Lord! He did give us a perfect Christmas after all. Besides Andrew's solo, we had fourteen women and fourteen men singing in the choir that Christmas. Perfect numbers. The Lord is really to be praised!

A few months after Yishan became the choir director, he was elected to be one of the church deacons. This got him involved with more services beyond the scope of the choir and eventually got him into church politics. Of course, neither one of us had heard of the term *church politics* at that time. Yet as I look back now, that was evidently what happened. I can also see that it was really one of Satan's schemes to wreck the church, but very few of us were able to clearly see it then. In the beginning some discontentment with the pastor brewed, and eventually, it split the church into two sides, pitting one against the other. Of course, this inevitably created some *enemies* for Yishan, and some people began to *boycott* the choir director by staying out of the choir.

Romans 8:28 continued to stand true for us even during that difficult period. The situation just drove us to be more diligently on our knees, pleading with the Lord to raise up more choir members. He did. In fact, the Lord so blessed the choir to the extent that the choir thrived despite the fact that every church fellowship suffered during that period.

I don't consider this as something to brag about. I only thank the

Lord for His continued faithfulness on all of us. Those of us in the choir were somehow not so much affected by the turmoil around us and continued to experience joy. Thus, we were less discouraged and were able to continue in serving the Lord.

The Holy Spirit was very actively working in our life during that period, even when I was weak. During that time I was so affected by the disharmony that I stopped my daily Bible reading for a while without being consciously aware of it. One Monday morning I realized what was happening, and immediately, I picked up the Bible. However, since I had stopped reading the Bible for a while, I felt lost, not knowing where to begin, so I just randomly opened up the book.

As soon as I opened up the Bible, my eyes saw a portion of the Scripture on the right-hand page in bold print as if a magnifier were placed over it. It was the Chinese Bible given to me at the time of my baptism, but up to that time, I had not read that part of the Scripture. There were no highlights or notes written on that page. If the Lord had not magnified that part of Scripture for me, I would not have been able to notice the words He wanted me to read at that time.

It was a passage in Deuteronomy 12.

> You shall not do at all what we are doing here today, every man doing whatever is right in his own eyes; for you have not as yet come to the resting place and the inheritance which the Lord your God is giving you. When you cross the Jordan and live in the Land which the Lord your God is giving you to inherit, and He gives you rest from all your enemies around you so that you live in security, then it shall come about that the place in which the Lord your God shall choose for His name to dwell, there you shall bring all that I command you: your burnt offerings and your sacrifices, your tithes." (Deuteronomy 12:8–11 NASB)

That passage stayed magnified for a few seconds, and then it went back to normal. But it remained long enough for me to pay attention to it and read those words and get the message the Lord intended for me.

At that time we were so unhappy with the pastor that we stopped giving our tithes to the church. We sent it someplace else. I felt the Lord was saying, "You are doing what is right in your own eyes, but I want you to stop it in the future when this is over. I'm going to give you peace, and then you have to bring the tithes to the church again."

At that moment I remembered the song our choir was rehearsing for the coming Sunday just the day before. It was one Yishan had picked from the *Volunteer Choir,* "On the Stormy Banks of the Jordan River." (I do not think Yishan had deliberately picked that song for its message, for he seldom paid attention to the lyrics but mostly selected songs for the melody. As I think back now, I cannot help praising the Lord for the way He guided us.)

Since that Scripture passage had these words, "When you cross the Jordan," I also felt the Lord was giving not just me but the whole church a message of comfort and promise. When I shared this with the whole church that following Sunday before the choir sang that song, a lot of brothers and sisters were encouraged, but some were unhappy. Later I heard some criticism against me, but I did not care since I knew I had shared a message from the Lord.

Eventually, the storm was over, but the church was devastated. Attendance dropped from an average between 150 and two hundred to fewer than seventy. The choir was somewhat used by the Lord as a sort of anchor for the church during that time.

I do not attribute any merit to the choir director at all. On the contrary, I'd rather say it was all due to the Lord's mercy just as promised in Jeremiah 2:20–23.

To be honest, however, I'd admit that God uses different people at different times, and He certainly used Yishan in a special way during that time. I'll just cite a few more examples here.

One day Yishan realized a certain choir member had missed two Sunday rehearsals. He called the brother after church. "I have been sick at home for two weeks, and you're the first person to call," he told

Yishan. Immediately, we went to visit him that very afternoon. We had a very good time of sharing then.

If we had not visited that brother in time, he might have been discouraged. Who knows what might have happened?

Another time choir attendance was down. One day in a prayer meeting at church Yishan asked the Lord to bring more people to join the choir. As he prayed, the Holy Spirit took control of him, and he uncontrollably broke down and wept. Later he told me he was not feeling sad at all when he wept. However, words got out and spread, and people said, "Brother Lin cried at the prayer meeting because not enough people showed up for choir practice." This rumor was only a half-truth, but the Lord used it anyway. It generated a lot of sympathy for Yishan, and the choir became vibrant with members again.

One summer, according to that year's church calendar, the choir was to sponsor a musical evangelistic meeting. Yishan, being the choir director, was assigned to coordinate the whole event. He started to plan and pray for the whole thing, asking the Lord to help him pick the music pieces for enough people to sing in the choir, for nonbelievers to come, and especially for a suitable speaker.

However, he forgot to ask the Lord to pick the right date. As he started to plan, he just decided on August 22, thinking it was a good date. However, when he first made known the date to the choir, two members immediately objected, saying they would not be able to join the choir that Sunday since by then they would be back to their college campus. If it was moved a week earlier to August 15, there were still others who would not be able to come.

Seeing this dilemma, Yishan realized his own neglect of prayers concerning the date. During the next several days, he expressly prayed for the Lord's guidance concerning this matter. It was a hard-pressed problem. After many days' prayers, he was still at a loss. Finally, he said to the Lord, "Well, Lord, I'm still not sure of Your will. I'm going to pick a date between the two. If it's not Your will, please stop me immediately. If it is correct, please give Your blessing." He then decided on August 15.

Toward the end of July, there was still no available speaker. Yishan had called up a preacher, and that preacher said he was already booked for August 15. He said more prayers. A few days later, Yishan received a phone call informing him that a certain evangelist who also had great musical gifts was in Chicago and was available for speaking engagement on August 15. Yishan was overjoyed. When he contacted this evangelist, the latter immediately consented to speak and also offered to play three musical instruments that day. An added plus was that his daughter could also sing a solo.

August 15 came, and the meeting turned out to be a success. That evangelist indeed was musically gifted. He also delivered a moving evangelistic message. The Holy Spirit worked on that day, and someone raised his hand (or hers, I don't remember) to receive Jesus as Lord and Savior.

The following Sunday, August 22, very few people joined the choir. At first, Yishan thought the choir members were having an emotional down after a big event. However, when the worship service was over, he saw some members sitting in the back rows were either blowing their noses or had watery eyes. *Hay fever season had started!* If he had picked August 22 as he had originally decided, it would have been disastrous. Very few choir members would have been able to sing for the big event. We did see the Lord answering prayers in a marvelous way again!

As I look back now, I can see the Lord used the choir as His training ground for the choir director to learn how to depend on Him so that when the time came, he could be called into full-time Christian service.

(Perhaps it is better for me to add a note here about this pastor who was the center of controversy while Yishan was the choir director. Although we were dissatisfied with him at that time, the Holy Spirit worked in such a beautiful way in Yishan's life and mine that a few years later we invited that pastor to preach at the Cedar Church, which Yishan and I started sometime after we moved to Schaumburg. God gave us a chance to reconcile. Still many more years later in the late 1990s, when we were living in F City, California, we heard that this pastor and his wife had also moved to F City. Again the Lord gave us an opportunity to visit them at their home and we had a very good sharing time. Still later, when Yishan went home to be with the Lord, I invited this pastor, who had baptized Yishan, to give the benediction at the end of Yishan's memorial service. I'm very thankful that the Lord has led me in learning His high and holy way rather than the worldly way. He certainly wants us to be perfect like Him. Praise Him, and give Him all the glory!)

Chapter 7

The Microbiologist

When Yishan started his job as a microbiologist, he was not required to conduct researches. However, his daily routine work took relatively little time, and he had plenty of time on hand. So he developed some research projects on his own. Within several months he formulated a new medium for detecting wild yeasts. After repeatedly testing the media successfully, he decided to attend a trade convention and publish this formula.

After his company submitted his name for enrollment in the convention, his new medium suddenly lost its potency, and no wild yeast could be detected. He immediately started experiments to find out the cause.

His new medium was formulated by mixing some chemicals with a basic ingredient that was considered neutral and nonfunctional for the past century or so. Shortly before the new medium lost its function, his lab supplies were running out, and he ordered a batch of new supplies. The fluctuation in the function of the new medium occurred after he received the shipment and began using the new supplies.

Trying to find out where the problem was, Yishan tested on every chemical in the ingredients. After trying out every single chemical and still finding no answer, he was desperate.

By that time he had already sent out the abstract to the convention committee, and it was not good to back out. He definitely had to find out a solution, or his formula would become a laughing stock when people found out that it did not work.

At that time he was not yet a Christian. Still, he had heard enough Christian testimonies on how God answered prayers and solved problems for believers. So when he saw that he was at the end of the rope, he bowed his head and prayed, "I don't know if there is really a God or if the salvation of Jesus Christ is true or not. God, if You are really there, please help me now. I have not been able to find out why the new medium does not work. I'm at my wit's end. Please help me solve the problem."

Although Yishan did tests on every single chemical ingredient of the new medium, he had left out the basic ingredient that was traditionally held as neutral and nonfunctional. He did not consider it necessary to test on that item. However, after he finished his sincerely uttered prayer, he thought he should give that basic ingredient a try. After he tested it, he got the surprise of his life. *Eureka!* Not only did he find the culprit, but he also had a new discovery. The traditional idea concerning this basic ingredient, he realized, was actually faulty. Not only did he find this basic ingredient played a pivotal role in his new formula, thus shattering the traditional wisdom, but he also found that the same product from the same chemical supplier actually fluctuated in its purity and thus needed to be monitored. Its purity affected the function of the other chemicals and so the concentration of the other chemicals had to be adjusted accordingly.

When the Lord helped Yishan solve the problem of the new medium, the greatest discovery Yishan made was not about the basic ingredient but the existence of God. Surely, the Lord used that to bring Yishan one step closer to Himself. Within months of that convention, Yishan was baptized. A little more than a month after his baptism, he became the choir director.

Once Yishan started his research project, he brought home research journals from work and read them after dinner. He felt he needed to read other people's research to keep informed. His reading the journal while listening to classical music practically became a nightly ritual.

The first two weeks after he took over the choir, his nightly ritual changed. Instead of reading research journals, he sat on the carpeted floor of his study, surrounded by choir music scattered around him. Being a new choir director, he was rather serious and also very nervous. He spent every night of those two weeks choosing music for the choir to sing. Only when he thought he had picked up enough songs for the choir did he then go back to the research journals.

One night after he picked up a research article to read, an idea flashed like a light in his head, and his heart beat wildly. It was an idea for further research on his new medium. The next day when he went to work, he quickly jotted down a research outline from the idea that came the night before. He then went ahead and carried out the experiments in his lab. Quite surprisingly, three weeks later he completed all the lab work. All that was left to be done was writing it down into a paper.

Usually in his field, it would take at least six months to a year to finish the required lab work for a research project. To Yishan, this was another miracle that he was able to complete that research in only three weeks. Then he realized it was *not* due to his own intelligence or good luck. He knew the Lord did it again. He had spent two weeks on choosing music for the choir, but the Lord had saved more time for him in his research work, far more than what he had given to the Lord's work!

A year later he embarked on still further research on the new medium. After several months of lab work, the research was near its end. However, he needed to come up with a new method to bring the research to completion. He proposed several methods and carried each out one by one, but one by one, they failed. Finally, he thought he would have to give it up.

Yet he felt great reluctance in giving it up. If he had to leave this research unfinished, it would mean he had wasted several months' time and effort. So he prayed, "O Lord, You see that I only have one step left of this research project, but I don't know how to go on. If You think this research is worth publishing, please give me a method to bring it to completion. If it is not worthy of any value in Your sight, please help me feel at peace with the loss of the past several months' time and effort. Let it be done in Your will."

After Yishan finished praying, when he opened his eyes, he thought of two methods. One was simple and direct, the other very complicated, requiring a lot of twists and turns.

Immediately, he set out to carry out those two methods. When he examined the results, he got a surprise again, but it was a pleasant surprise. Both methods worked. The Lord really doubled His recompense.

I see the Lord's humor in thus guiding Yishan. As Yishan himself had confessed, both methods manifested the wisdom of the Lord. "How come I'm so dumb not to be able to come up with such a simple and direct method!" Yishan mused. "As to the other method, it is so complicated that it's definitely beyond my simple mind to conjure it up!"

As much as Yishan enjoyed his work, for a number of years, he tried to find a higher-paying job. There were many opportunities, but he was not successful in achieving his goal. Finally, a good opportunity came. That job opening seemed to have been tailor-made for him, requiring a PhD with the kind of training and experience that fit him perfectly. To him it was also an opportunity to move out of the bitter cold winters of Chicago. Both of us prayed that the Lord would give him this job.

A few days after Yishan sent out his resumes/applications, he happened to be reading 1 Corinthians 16:8–9 (NASB), "But I shall remain in Ephesus until Pentecost, for a wide door for effective service has opened to me, and there are many adversaries."

As Yishan read those words, he said in his mind the word *Ephesus* was clearly substituted with *Chicago*, and he understood the Lord was telling him he would not get that job. Indeed, several weeks later he received a letter saying, "Our budget has been cut," and they hired a fresh PhD graduate with no experience.

Of course in that Scripture passage, the Lord also promised Yishan to open a wide door for effective service, but how was that to be fulfilled?

Every other year (later changed to yearly), Yishan's company sponsored an eleven-week training class for the industry his company serviced worldwide. Part of Yishan's job was to teach this class microbiological techniques and labs. Three years after Yishan became a Christian, a young man (I'll call him Ching) was sent from Taiwan to attend this class.

Three months before Ching came, when we learned that he was coming, Yishan and I began to pray for him. When Ching came, Yishan immediately welcomed him to his lab office and began witnessing to him. Ching was the only Taiwanese in that class, and his wife, son, and parents were in Taiwan. Even though he only spent eleven weeks away from home, he was lonely and homesick. When Yishan invited him to attend church on Sunday, Ching quickly consented.

The very first Sunday Ching went to church, he felt the effect of the Holy Spirit on him, but he did not know it. When the congregation rose to sing a hymn, he just followed along even though he had never been in a church before and did not know the hymn. As soon as he began to sing, he felt choked as if he was going to cry. Not knowing it was the Holy Spirit working on him, he felt ashamed and tried to stop it. However, later when the choir was singing, he could not control his tears, and still, he felt more ashamed.

Yishan tried to explain to him that this was the work of the Holy Spirit. Indeed, the Spirit was working mightily on Ching, for that Sunday he even felt the speaker was talking to him. Moreover, Ching voluntarily asked Yishan to take him to church the following Sunday.

I asked Yishan to bring Ching home to dine with us several times, and almost from the start, he was quite at home with us. Each time we shared the gospel message and testimonies with him. We also lent him a Bible, and I encouraged him to write down any questions he might have in his reading.

One Saturday I asked Yishan to drive to Chicago to pick up Ching and bring him home. He was staying in a motel that was a forty-five-minute drive one way. Naturally, on the way home, Yishan used that time to witness to Ching.

After I finished cooking, I went to the living room where Yishan was still talking to Ching. I asked Ching if he would like to receive Jesus as his Lord and Savior. He said he had two questions that needed to be answered first. One was, "How can I know the Bible is the Word of God?" The other was, "How can I be sure Jesus is the Son of God and not merely a man?"

After I answered both questions, Ching said he still had more questions from his reading of the Bible. I asked him, "Are they concerning accepting Jesus as Lord and Savior?"

Ching answered no. I then encouraged him to pray to accept Jesus first, and I told him later I would answer his questions about the Bible.

Before Ching prayed, he explained that he had not personally experienced God, but he believed in all that we had told him about God and the Bible. I assured him by saying, "Of course we have told you everything that we know to be true. Why should we try to deceive you? As to your own experience, don't worry. Once you accept Jesus into your heart and the Holy Spirit comes in, you'll begin to experience Him."

After Ching prayed the prayer of acceptance, I said to him, "Now you can ask your questions from the Bible."

He took out a piece of paper from the Bible and looked at it, and he was puzzled.

"Strange," he said. "When I read the Bible at the motel, I did not understand this verse. Even though I understood the meaning of every word, but the whole sentence just did not make sense to me. Yet I understand it now. How come?"

"Well," I said, "there you have it. At the motel you had not accepted Jesus. It was natural you could not understand the Bible. Now that you have accepted Jesus, you have the Holy Spirit in your heart to be your teacher. In John 14:26, Jesus promised, 'But the Helper, the Holy Spirit, Whom the Father will send in My name, He will teach you all things.' You said you did not have any experience about God, but here is your experience already."

Indeed, the Holy Spirit made His manifestation to Ching that evening. Of all the questions he wrote on that piece of paper, I did have to answer and explain some, but others he understood by himself without necessitating my explanation.

Five days later on the following Thursday, I asked Yishan again to bring Ching home after work. I knew he missed home-cooked meals, and he really enjoyed my cooking. That evening when Yishan and I were about to pray together as we usually did, we invited Ching to pray with us.

He replied, "I would like to, but I don't know how to pray."

"Don't worry," I said. "We understand you are a new Christian, and we won't laugh at you. Prayer is actually talking to God. Just talk to God the way you're talking to us. The important thing is to say things genuinely out of your heart. Only a short prayer will do."

Ching then said, "Okay."

The three of us knelt by the sofa, and I began to pray. After I finished, it was Yishan's turn. When he finished, there was silence. As we waited, I wondered if Ching was ever going to pray. Then a short moment later, Ching started. Once he began, words just kept pouring out of his mouth like a river, praising God and praying for the salvation of his colleague and family back in Taiwan. Immediately, I thought of Romans 8:26, and I knew the Holy Spirit was praying for him.

While listening to Ching's prayer, I kept praising the Lord in my heart. No mature Christians could have prayed like that. No, not even Billy Graham could have done it. For being a Christian for less than a week, he really could not have prayed such a powerful prayer by himself. Even today I still remember these words he uttered that night. "Lord, within a few weeks, I'm returning to Taiwan. Please help me to bring the gospel to my family members." Many people who have been Christians for many years never feel the burden to spread the gospel, let alone one who had trusted Christ for less than a week.

When Ching's prayer ended, he stood up, stunned but very excited.

"I experienced it! I experienced it!" He could not contain his excitement. "Wonderful! It was so wonderful! When the two of you prayed, I was not listening but constructing a speech in my mind. When it was my turn, my brain just went blank, and I could not remember a single word of the speech I just prepared. I was at a loss and did not know what to say. Then I just opened my mouth and sentences kept coming out. I knew it was not myself praying but God helping me. Now I know He is real, a living God. He is with me. I will tell my family the good news when I go back to Taiwan."

God did open "a wide door for effective service," and Ching was only the first fruit. I'll cite one more example here.

Another year two men, one older and one younger, came from Taiwan to attend the eleven-week training class. The older one of the two was named Hsiao. He was married, and he was forty years of age. When Yishan first met him, he had been in Chicago a week. What specifically drew Yishan's attention about Hsiao was that he looked pale and haggard. Hsiao confided in Yishan about his anxiety and homesickness. He told Yishan he was worried that in his absence his wife might be harassed by his parents who lived with them. He said his parents were very harsh, especially his father. He was so worried and homesick that he had been tempted to pack up and fly back to Taiwan. As a result, he had suffered from insomnia for that whole week after arriving in Chicago.

Back then it was a rare opportunity for people to be sent by the Taiwanese government to the United States for advanced studies. Hsiao actually had an opportunity of a lifetime, the envy of many colleagues. Yet he was so worried that he was ready to give it up. Yishan saw this as an opportunity to witness to the power of prayer, and he immediately taught Hsiao how to pray and ask Jesus for help.

The next morning Hsiao came to Yishan's lab/office all beaming and told Yishan, "The prayer you taught me was very effective. Last night I was homesick again. I knelt down and prayed to Jesus for help. As I prayed, I felt warmth in my head, and it went down my whole body. When I finished praying, I felt great peace, and I was able to fall asleep very quickly. I didn't wake up until this morning. For the first time in more than a week, I was fully rested when I woke up."

From that day on, Hsiao was interested in the name of Jesus and started attending the Chinese church near his motel. A few weeks later, we invited him to spend the weekend with us. There in our living room, Yishan and I shared with him the gospel truth, and he accepted Jesus as his Lord and Savior.

After Hsiao prayed to accept Jesus, it was easy to see the joy on his face.

"Now I realize it's so good to be a Christian!" He said, "If I had not come to the United States, I would not have had the opportunity to hear the good news. In Taiwan, I have two close friends who are both Christians. We have been friends for over two decades, but they never told me the salvation of Jesus. I don't consider them good friends anymore. They have been so selfish and never shared the good news with me. When I go back to Taiwan, I'm going to rebuke them!"

Truly, Hsiao was so happy with the newfound joy in the Lord Jesus that one could see it spilling over. The very next day when he went to church, he told a number of people that he had accepted Jesus as his Lord and Savior. Words spread around, and many people came to shake hands with him and congratulate him on becoming a Christian. He was as happy as a little child. He truly had tasted the goodness of the Lord.

Now I can see clearly why the Lord gave Yishan that job as a microbiologist. I'm sure He used it as another training ground for Yishan to spread the gospel. As the Lord opened the door wider and wider for Yishan to effectively serve Him, he became less and less interested in research work. Eventually, when the Lord's time came, the microbiologist was ready to quit his job.

Visiting St. Louis Botanical Gardens

Chapter 8

An Uphill Battle

The Lord began calling me not too long after I was saved. The first time it occurred while I was in Taiwan. Several months after I was baptized, I went to a winter conference for college students. I went with some church friends, but the day we went was the last day of the conference. At the end of the meeting, the speaker gave an altar call for full-time Christian service. I was a relatively new Christian, not quite knowing the Bible or the full significance of Christian calling. Yet when the speaker was giving the call, I felt my heart pounding and an urge to walk to the front. However, I suppressed myself and reasoned, "God could not be calling me. I'm only a new believer. He must be calling those long-time Christians."

The Lord called me the second time a few years later. I was attending the Chinese Student Bible Study at SIU at that time. That evening we had a meeting with a special speaker, a well-known Chinese speaker named Rev. Wang. At the end of that meeting, Rev. Wang gave two calls, one for nonbelievers to put their trust in Jesus and the other for Christians to go into full-time service.

When Rev. Wang gave the second call, I felt my heart pounding again and also an urge to raise my hand. But I suppressed myself again. This time I told myself, "God could not be calling me. I'm married now and a mother of two. Only those who are single and younger than I could respond to God's call." My own ignorance had kept me from responding properly to God's calling.

My third calling came in late 1972. It was at a special celebration banquet at church. We had a featured speaker that evening named Rev. Frank Harris, a former missionary to China. Of course, 1972 was the year President Nixon made the historic visit to China. In his speech Rev. Harris said, "In the future when God lifts the *Bamboo Curtain* and the door of gospel is open again for China, I believe the way to bring gospel to China cannot be the same again. I don't think the door will be open for Western missionaries. At that time it will be open only for Chinese professionals who go to China to work in their fields and secretly bear witness for the gospel."

I don't remember if Rev. Harris gave any altar call that evening. However, as I listened to him, my heart was stirred, and I felt the Lord was calling me to bring the gospel to the Chinese people. From that day on, I started praying for the Lord to open the door of China for the gospel.

Of course, that evening Yishan did not attend the banquet. He was staying home with his parents. Naturally, he did not hear Rev. Harris's message. Nor did he know about my calling. I did not tell him about any of my callings.

The Lord's calling came a fourth time in 1974, a month after Yishan's baptism. We were attending NACOCE (North American Congress on Chinese Evangelism), held at Wheaton College, which was about a thirty-minute drive from our home in Schaumburg. Yishan and I attended only the evening sessions of that conference. At the end of the second evening's meeting, Rev. Wang came to the podium, the same Rev. Wang that I heard at SIU. He was not the speaker for that evening, but I believe he was one of the main organizers of that conference. As he stood at the podium, I heard him calling young people who had decided to go into full-time Christian service to walk to the front. As Rev. Wang talked to those young people, I remained in the back and talked to a sister from our church. Both of us felt the urge to serve the Lord, but we both felt unworthy. She thought that she did not have good academic credentials, and I thought being a wife and mother disqualified me.

On the third evening of NACOCE, I heard a powerful message.

In fact, I think it was the Holy Spirit working His power on me. The speaker of that evening was a former mechanical engineer. His text was Acts 1:8, "But you shall receive power, when the Holy Spirit has come upon you; and you shall be My witnesses both in Jerusalem, and in all Judea and Samaria, and even to the uttermost part of the earth."

I still remember the speaker's words that evening. "I'm a former mechanical engineer. I know the power involved in getting man to outer space. At NASA, it took thousands of hours of manpower and millions of dollars in sending a rocket to the space. Yet Jesus Christ was able to ascend to heaven without the aid of any single human being. It was a demonstration of the power of the Holy Spirit."

As I listened to those words, I felt the power of the Holy Spirit, and tears streamed down my face while I was taking notes. I had the habit of taking notes while listening to sermons. There was definitely nothing sad about that message, but I could not control my tears. In fact, the impact of the Holy Spirit was such that I felt listening to that sermon only once was not enough. When we got home, I took out my notes and read them one more time. The notes I took were at best sketchy of what I heard that evening. Yet the power of the Holy Spirit was so strong on me that tears streamed down my face again when I read those notes. Then I prayed for quite a while before I reluctantly went to bed.

In the middle of that night, I woke up. While I was still half awake, I heard some words in my head. The words were in Mandarin, and they said, "Compose music. Compose music." Then I was fully awake.

Earlier that evening before the sermon began, a Chinese music professor from a university in Mississippi sang. Before she sang, she said, "Chinese church choirs, if possible, should endeavor to sing songs composed by Chinese Christians."

Since I was not a music major, those words did not carry any weight for me. By the time I went to bed that night, I had completely forgotten what that professor had said. So when I was awakened by the command to write music, I was puzzled by what I just heard. Like the little boy Samuel who ran to Eli when the Lord called him,

"Samuel, Samuel," I also went to the living room and prayed, "Lord, was it You who just talked to me? You know I have not learned how to write music. If You want me to compose music, I'm willing to obey You, but You'll have to give me the music."

When I finished praying, I immediately went back to bed. As I lay down, I felt a toothache. The toothache had actually been with me two or three days. When I was praying in the living room, I was so concentrated on talking to the Lord that I was not aware of the toothache. Once I was in bed, however, I was fully aware of the pain and felt uncomfortable. I thought, *Perhaps I should get up again and pray about my toothache.*

However, I felt tired and sleepy and did not get up. I just lay in bed and said in my heart, "O Lord, have mercy on me." (What I prayed in Chinese were actually five words.)

Immediately, the response came, faster than the blink of the eye and much faster than a telephone call or telegraph. I felt two hands tapping my shoulders and simultaneously heard a truly small, still, and audible voice in my right ear, saying five Chinese words, "I want to heal you." The voice was so small that I'm sure not a second person could have heard it. It was unlike a regular human voice since it carried no vibration. It was literally still, but it was the most wonderful voice I had ever heard. As soon as I heard those five Chinese words, my toothache was instantly gone.

I was full of joy and thanksgiving. I kept saying in my heart, "Thank You, Lord. Thank You, Lord." I kept repeating that until I fell asleep.

The next morning when I woke up, I was reminded of what had transpired in the night, and immediately, I was full of excitement. I quickly got out of bed. Yishan was also awake, and I told him what had happened.

After Yishan had left for work and the two girls left for school, I was all by myself. I went to the living room and knelt down where I prayed the night before. Immediately, I was overwhelmed with such a strong sense of Christ's love that I felt unworthy that He should have died for me, and once again I could not control the tears that freely flowed out.

When I opened my mouth to pray, I felt a strong force coming out of my bosom, and I could not help but pray out very loud. It was good that I was all by myself. Otherwise, if someone else was present, he or she might think that I was out of my mind shouting so loud. Thus, I kept praying, or should I say shouting! When I finally felt I had prayed long enough and ended the prayer, twenty or thirty minutes had elapsed. I was amazed! It was the first time my own prayer had lasted that long. They were usually only five minutes long.

From that day forward, every time I prayed, I felt the same power on me, and my prayers never went back to the old lame way of short prayers. Even when I prayed at church, I would pray out very loud as well. I couldn't help it. Yet Yishan did not understand, and once he complained to me, "When you prayed, why did you have to shout?"

From then on, not only did my prayers become longer, but I began to spend more time reading the Bible as well. Actually, I began to feel a great yearning to receive seminary training. At first, I told Yishan I wanted to take courses at Moody Bible Institute. He objected, saying it was not safe for me to go by myself. Years later he confessed that he was using it only as a pretext. Even back then, however, I knew it was a lame excuse, but unless he gave his consent, I did not want to fight his will.

After I heard the command to compose music, I told Yishan about going to a nearby Christian college to study music. Again, he objected. The only thing I could do then was pray. I asked the Lord to give me the music. Three weeks later while I was taking a shower, I felt music floating in my head, and I started to sing. After I got out of the shower, I quickly took a piece of paper and wrote down the melody. Once I finished the melody, I knelt down and prayed. I thanked the Lord for giving me the music and asked Him to give the lyric as well. As I prayed, words came in both English and Chinese. Once I got up from my knees, I wrote down the lyric and titled the song "My Shepherd Died for Me". It was the only song that came to me in both Chinese and English. Of all the other songs I have written so far, the lyrics are predominantly in Chinese. One is in English ("The Lord's Prayer"), and a few are bilingual; however, most of them I had to work on the translation myself.

Here I might as well mention how the Lord gave me that song "The Lord's Prayer". It was during a time when I was reading Matthew 6:9–13.

> Our Father who art in Heaven,
> Hallowed be thy name,
> Thy kingdom come,
> Thy will be done,
> On earth as it is in heaven.
> Give us this day our daily bread.

I was reading the Revised Standard Version at that time. (It was the first Bible I bought after I arrived in Brookings, South Dakota, as a graduate student. It was the only version I knew besides the KJV in those days.) As I was reading these words, I began to *feel the intonation* of each sentence as if I were reading them out loud, and the up and down movement of the intonation became music like the melody of a song. I stopped and read those words very slowly again, and the music continued to float in my head. I quickly jotted down the melody. Then I began to match the words of this passage to the melody. I did have to rework a little part of the melody later. But as a whole it was a song given to me from the Lord, and sometime later I was able to sing it at two weddings as a soloist.

Of course this song, "The Lord's Prayer," like most of other songs I wrote, has only the melody and no accompaniment since I did not know enough about music to do that. However, the pianist who accompanied me for those weddings was very talented, and she was able to do a very good job. And when the wedding was over, she commented that *that* song sounded very nice.

Since I could not go to Bible school to receive formal training, I decided to get myself equipped anyway. I began to spend two or three hours a day studying the Bible. I got a commentary and compared the

Chinese verses with the two English versions I had. Whenever I had difficulty understanding a passage, I prayed, asking the Lord for help. I have since found out the Holy Spirit *is* the best teacher. He usually answered prayers and opened my eyes to understand the Scriptures. I was full of joy.

Sometimes I was so engrossed in discovering the riches of the Scripture that I neglected my duties as a housewife. When Yishan came home, he was not happy to see the mess in the house, and he would chide me and ask, "What have you spent the whole day doing?" I did not tell him what I did. I reasoned that he would not understand. So I just kept silent.

I also began to spend more time praying, especially praying for my unbelieving friends and relatives. As I prayed, the Lord impressed upon me the importance of teaching my children the Scripture and praying for them. I asked myself, "What would it matter to me if I saved the whole world and my own children were lost?"

Thus, I began the habit of reading the Bible with Angela and Leslie. Usually, I did this on weekdays. Each morning after they finished breakfast, I would use the spare time they had before going to school to read the Bible with them. I had them take turns reading the verses, and then I explained the verses or asked them questions to make sure they understood them. Even if they had only five or ten minutes left, we would read the Bible together. Sometimes they were in a rush to go to school. Then I would wait until they came home in the afternoon. After giving them snacks, I would have them read the Bible, and naturally, we would be able to spend a little more time on it. Later when they were older (I think they were in sixth grade by that time), I told them to begin memorizing Scripture passages, teaching them to write down the verses on index cards. I wanted them to have a disciplined life and love God's Word. (As I remember now, I do not think I did this with my third child. She was very independent by the time I should be doing this with her, and thus, I was not able to assert any influence on her.)

Of course, I was also spending time writing songs whenever I sensed a melody coming. Sometimes it took me one whole hour sitting at the piano, hammering out the melody. Sometimes it took even longer to get the right lyric. A few times I had difficulty setting the music right. I guess it was due to the fact that I never had formal training in music composition. Once in a while, Yishan criticized my music when I asked for his opinion or when I asked him for help. I felt frustrated. I knew my music was not perfect, but what could I do? I really do not know why the Lord wants me to compose songs when He knows that I have not been trained in this respect. I've learned enough not to ask why. Was He just trying to see my obedience? Up to this day, I still do not have the answer, but I will always try to do my best whenever He gives me the song to write, no matter how long it takes. Perhaps I'll perfect it when I go to heaven.

One day a woman asked me, "Your girls are older now. Why do you still stay home? Why don't you go out and find a job?"

This woman was a nonbeliever. I did not blame her for not understanding me. I did not tell her the Lord had called me. What frustrated me most was Yishan. By then he was a believer and the choir director. He was serving the Lord with his full heart, and yet he seemed not able to accept the fact that I should be serving the Lord with my full heart as well. A few times I felt he was pressuring me to find a secular job so that I could bring some income to help the family.

It was an uphill battle for me to serve the Lord and give Him my best while being a housewife at the same time. No wonder I felt frustrated easily. I had no one to turn to but the Lord. He is always faithful. Many times while praying I was filled with the Holy Spirit and I would be full of joy and receive the strength to carry on, while at the same time, tears kept rolling down my cheeks. I praise and thank the Lord for keeping me on course in this uphill battle.

Chapter 9

Home Bible Study

*I*n November 1973, we moved into a new home in a northwestern suburb of Chicago called Schaumburg, where we found out later they had built Woodfield Mall, an indoor mall that was then the world's largest.

The way that led us to purchase that new home was quite a twisted one, and it led me to think God must have had a purpose in moving me to Schaumburg. Shortly after we moved, I got to know three Chinese families (all from Taiwan), two in the same subdivision as ours and one in a nearby town. Since none of them were Christians and I was the only believer then, I reasoned that the Lord had given me a mission to bring the gospel to them.

I started witnessing to them and tried to invite them for Bible study. They were not very responsive. I reasoned with myself, "If they don't want to come, I can go to their home. They surely will not refuse me."

Sure enough, they did not refuse me. So I went to one of their homes and had all the three women together. But these young mothers were so distracted by the crying and needs of their children that their ears were obviously not with me.

I stopped mentioning Bible studies to those women, but I began praying for them. Six months later one of them called me up, "When are you going to have a Bible study at your home? We would like to come."

By that time our church was in such disarray I did not want to take these women to the church's Bible study. Instead I organized one at my home and invited them and their families for dinner and Bible study. By that time I had also met other Chinese families in the neighboring towns, more than the three I knew initially. So that evening there were six or seven couples that came. A woman I had invited even brought another couple.

Yishan was by that time baptized, but his Bible knowledge being limited, he was not of much help during the Bible study. I was the one leading the study, but I felt very inadequate. At our second meeting, I invited a Christian couple from church and a retired pastor. All of them lived quite far away from us. The elderly pastor had actually come out of his retirement and had started a new church about twenty minutes away from where we lived.

I had originally wanted a weekly Bible study, but one of the women told me, "Weekly meetings are too much for us. Once a month is just right." So we met only once a month. However, I could see the Holy Spirit working in our midst. Every time we met, the discussion was always animated. Once it went on so late that I saw the kids falling asleep one by one on the carpet, and then I realized it was past midnight. I had to stop the meeting right then.

When the time came for our second or third monthly meeting, one of them said, "It's not good that we let you cook all the food alone. Next time we'll each bring a dish." So our monthly dinner became a potluck. Then each of the families also wanted to host a meeting. So our Bible study rotated to different locations each month.

At our first meeting I noticed one of the men was reading a comic book during our Bible study time. Obviously, he had come with his wife only for the dinner. If he had stayed home, he probably would have difficulty cooking for himself. He, of course, reminded me of how Yishan used to react to Bible studies before his conversion. I could only pray for the Holy Spirit to work in that man's heart.

From the beginning I tried to invite these people to go to church with us. They did once, but they did not go again. The problem was the distance. These nonbelievers were not willing to drive a long distance to go to a church in the city of Chicago.

Later on, however, when the elderly pastor invited these nonbelievers to attend *his* church, they happily went quite regularly. For the sake of the Lord's kingdom, I was grateful that elderly pastor was willing to drive almost an hour to help with our Bible study. I also rejoiced that my nonbelieving friends were willing to go to his church. Others at my own church did not share my vision, however. One specifically rebuked me to my face. "You're spreading the gospel for other people's church."

I felt hurt to be wrongfully rebuked, but I kept on with the monthly meetings. I knew I had done nothing wrong. As long as Christ's kingdom was being advanced, I was willing to suffer misunderstandings by others.

Perhaps I should have been satisfied with these monthly meetings, but I was not. I wondered how long it would take before these nonbelievers could turn into Christians. I began to ask the Lord to motivate these nonbelievers for weekly meetings or to bring more Christians so that we could begin meeting on a weekly basis.

I was fully aware that without the working of the Holy Spirit, these monthly meetings would not have started at all. And to keep the meetings going, not only was He working in our midst, but He also gave us a wonderful miracle as a sign of His presence with us. It happened not too long after our monthly meeting started, about a little more than a year after I received the healing miracle on my toothache.

One day I called up a woman that I had not talked to for one or two months. At the end of the conversation, I asked her, "By the way, how's your sister-in-law doing?"

This woman had given birth to a baby boy a few months earlier. Prior to that, she had told me she and her husband were in the process of helping her sister-in-law through immigration in order that the latter might come to the United States in time to help this woman when she gave birth. As it turned out, the immigration process was slow, and by the time the younger sister-in-law arrived, the baby was already more than a month old, which was far past the time when the woman needed care. I actually had made some food for the woman during that first month.

After the younger sister-in-law came, Yishan and I went to visit that family. We witnessed to them and shared the gospel. At the end we asked if any of them would like to receive Jesus as Lord and Savior.

"I'm a biology major. I do not believe in any God in the universe," said that young sister-in-law. She had a master's degree in biology.

Her brother followed, "I'm a civil engineer. I do not believe in any God either."

I thought in my heart, *My husband has a PhD in biology. He believes in God.* Of course, I said nothing.

The engineer's wife responded, "I believe there is a God in the universe, but I cannot yet believe that Jesus is God."

Then a month or two later when I called to inquire about that young woman, the woman told me, "My sister-in-law is not doing well. She has been bleeding for about a month."

She went on to inform me of her plight. "Last month my sister-in-law continued to bleed after her menstrual period was over. I took her to a gynecologist who prescribed some medication for her. When she took the medication, she started to react as if she were pregnant. She's so nauseous that she is weak and can no longer come downstairs for meals. Instead of her helping me, now *I* have to wait on her and bring food upstairs to her three times a day."

I asked if the gynecologist was giving her the correct medication and if she had asked for a second opinion.

"Yes," she said. She took her sister-in-law to another gynecologist who said the prescription was correct, but it was obviously not suitable for the sister-in-law. The doctor told her to discontinue using it. The medication was discontinued, but the bleeding also returned. So altogether the sister-in-law had been hemorrhaging for the total of a whole month. The second doctor was going to schedule an appointment for the patient to go into the hospital for a D and C.

As soon as I heard the story, I thought of another woman's hemorrhaging story, the one recorded in Matthew 9, Mark 5, and

Luke 8. Into my mind also came the scene of our last visit with this family. However, I was bolstered with faith and courage by my own healing miracle, and I thought perhaps the Lord could use me to help bring this family to Him if He should choose to heal her just as He did with that hemorrhaging woman nineteen hundred years ago.

I proposed to pray for the hemorrhaging sister-in-law. I said over the phone, "I've never prayed over another person for healing. I don't know if I've got a healing gift or whether God is going to heal your sister-in-law or not. All that I know is that if God is willing to heal her, when I pray for her, she'll be well."

The woman at the other end of the phone line said, "I have to ask my sister-in-law whether she will let you pray or not."

A minute later she said, "My sister-in-law would like you to pray for her."

Immediately, I drove over to their house and was led upstairs to the young woman's bedside. Her loss of blood was obvious. Her face and limbs completely ashen in color. Up to that time, I had never seen a person so depleted of blood. She seemed to me not much different from a corpse lying in a casket except that she could still talk. When she saw me, she struggled to get up, but she was too weak.

"Never mind getting up," I said to her. "Just stay there in bed. You're too weak to get up."

I then told her how the Lord had healed me of my toothache and also the story of the hemorrhage woman recorded in the Bible. Before I continued, she interrupted me, "But I don't know how to pray."

"I know that," I said. "You're still not a believer in Jesus. It's *me* who's going to pray for you, but you'll have to pray with me in your heart when I ask Jesus to heal you."

She consented, and I began to pray. It was a simple and direct prayer, praising God and asking for His mercy. When I ended, I simply left and went home.

Shortly before nine the next morning, the phone rang.

"My sister-in-law was able to come downstairs for breakfast this morning. She would like you to come pray for her again."

Praise the Lord! I was very happy to hear that, and I quickly drove over to their house. I was led upstairs again to the sister-in-law's bedside.

Before I was able to open my mouth, she said first, "Very strange. Yesterday as soon as you prayed for me, I felt much better."

I then asked her, "Do you believe in Jesus now?"

"Very hard," she said.

I knew it was hard for her. She would have to overcome several hurdles. First, she had to believe in a God in the universe. Then she'd have to believe that Jesus is God. However, I could see her atheistic belief was shaken up when she said, "Very strange."

Although she was still not willing to commit herself to the Lord Jesus, I went ahead and prayed for her continued healing anyway.

Earlier that morning I had made breakfast for Yishan and the girls and did not feel anything wrong. However, as I opened my mouth to pray for the continued healing of that young woman's hemorrhage condition, I felt terribly weak myself *as if* I had been sick for months and was completely depleted of strength.

It was then and there that I learned of the difference between physical strength and spiritual power. Earlier that morning I had used my physical strength to cook breakfast, and there was nothing wrong with my physical condition. When I prayed for the healing of that young woman, what I needed was spiritual power, not physical, and alas, I had none left in me.

It was a valuable lesson the Lord allowed me to experience and learn. As a believer in Jesus Christ, I have a spiritual battery in me that needs to be recharged daily. I had used up its power the day before when I prayed for that young woman and made her feel much better. I should have asked the Lord to recharge me with His power before I went ahead to pray for her the second time. However, being ignorant of my own spiritual need, I had recklessly run out of the house as soon as I got that phone call without being in contact with the Lord first. It was not until several months later when I read Mark 1:35 that I saw the *imperative need of prayers in receiving spiritual power.* If Jesus Christ, being the Son of God, needed to go to the wilderness to pray after He performed some healing miracles on people, how much more necessary for me as His believer to be in tune with Him in my spiritual upkeep!

When I prayed for that patient and felt so weak myself, I was scared. In my ignorance I was afraid of confessing my own spiritual depletion, and I just quickly ended my prayer and ran home.

The third morning my phone rang again. They still wanted me to go over to pray for the patient. I was told her condition remained the same. My second prayer for her was ineffective, but the result of the first prayer was so obvious that they still desired more of it.

I had a different thought. I told my caller, "Prayer is more effective when more people pray. I'd rather wait for tonight when my husband can come and pray with me."

So Yishan and I went to their home that evening. When I prayed, I detected a little more strength, but I still felt rather weak. At that time I had not yet learned I needed to replenish my strength with more prayers for myself.

When Yishan prayed, I did not feel a lot of difference. However, a year later the woman told me of the difference. She gingerly mentioned it over a phone call, "I would like to tell you something. I hope you don't mind. A year ago when you and your husband prayed for my sister-in-law, I felt your prayer to be rather weak. And even though your husband was a relatively new Christian, his prayer was a lot more powerful than yours. When he prayed, I felt as if the earth shook."

Praise the Lord. Though I did not feel the difference, she did. And although her sister-in-law was not completely healed right away, she never had to go to the hospital for that surgery (D and C). About two weeks later her bleeding completely stopped, and after some more time of recuperation, she completely regained her strength and went to Columbia, Missouri, to attend graduate school.

When this young woman's brother saw how she had gotten better through prayers, he said to his wife, "We should start attending church." They did. Eventually, the wife professed her faith in Jesus and attended a baptismal class, getting ready to receive water baptism. Unfortunately, before she was baptized, her husband got a new job in the Silicon Valley, and they moved away. After they moved, she wrote me once, and eventually, the correspondence stopped. I was never able to find out if she was ever baptized.

However, the Lord did answer my prayers for weekly meetings. A year after our monthly meetings started, two Christian couples joined us. One was brought along by a nonbeliever who had regularly attended the monthly meetings. Another was introduced to me by a friend of mine.

With the addition of these two Christian couples, we began to meet every Friday night. Then the Lord also added more people to us. One night I counted a total of thirty-two, including adults and children. Our living room was bursting at the seams, and we began to feel the need to start Sunday worship services.

We began to pray for a suitable location for Sunday meetings. It was not quite easy. I called several churches. Some asked, "Are you going to pay rent?" Others did not even call back when I left an inquiry message.

Eventually, I located a Baptist church. When I told her our purpose for using their facility was to bring the gospel to the Chinese people in the area, the receptionist gleefully responded, "That's great." Later when I talked to her pastor, Rev. Michael Green, he echoed similar sentiments and said, "For years we had wanted to bring gospel to the Chinese, but we could not do it. It's wonderful that you can do that for us. Our building belongs to the Lord. If He wants to use it, we have to let Him."

Rev. Green even called up the local newspaper, which sent a reporter and a photographer to my home and ran a story with my picture in the newspaper. (When that story appeared in the newspaper and I read it, to my consternation, I found some mistakes in the story. It was then I learned that news reporters could twist up your stories when they wrote them up.)

So the home Bible study grew into a church. It went from one meeting each month to three meetings a week—midweek prayer meeting, Friday night Bible study, and Sunday worship service.

Indeed, the Lord did give us far above what we had asked. "Eye hath not seen, nor ear heard, neither have entered into the heart of man, the things which God hath prepared for them that love him" (1 Corinthians 2:9).

A few years later, all of the couples that came to the first Bible study dinner moved away to other states. Two of those families, both husbands and wives, became believers and were baptized in other states. Another woman, the last of the original participants in my first dinner, told me something wonderful shortly before she moved to Virginia.

Her husband had actually found a new job in the state of Virginia and had begun working there in the previous fall. She and her daughter stayed behind in Illinois, waiting for their house to be sold. That winter happened to be quite mild. I still remember that time, and there was no snowfall, which was rather unusual for the Chicago area up to that time. Their house was set back quite far from the street, and so their driveway leading to the garage was quite long. She told me, "I think the Lord was watching over me. With my husband absent from home, I would have had a hard time shoveling the driveway if there had been a snowfall."

Of course, I was very delighted to hear that because I recalled how she used to ask questions during the Bible study. "If there is a God, then He is neither fair nor kind. Why would He let those serving Him suffer?" Or whenever she heard some testimony about God's wonderful work in a believer's life, she would say, "If I can also see God or hear Him, then I'll believe."

I used to try to convince her not to wait for the opportunity to see a miracle in order to put her trust in Jesus, but my persuasion was to no avail. However, the Lord had His own timetable of working on this woman. Eventually, she told me the following story that occurred that spring before she moved to the East Coast.

One day she took her car to a car wash. When she got there, the attendant told her to leave her car but not to turn it off. She left the shift in the drive position, not knowing she should have left it in neutral. After she got out of her car, she walked from the entrance of the wash to the exit, thinking the attendant would drive her car. As a result, the car continued to go forward after it came out of the exit and crossed the street until it was stopped by the curb on the other side of the street. When she saw her car continue going forward, she said she almost tried to stand in front of it in order to stop it. I commented to her, "If you had tried, you would have been run over by your car."

Then when she saw her car cross the street and finally stop at the curb, she felt dismayed and was sure some accident would occur. "The car wash was located on a busy street near an intersection," she told me. "Some coming traffic on either direction of that street was bound to hit my car. Or another car from the nearby cross street would come and collide with it."

Yet at that critical moment, no car came from the left side because of the red light at the intersection. Nor did anyone come from the right side. Neither was there traffic from the nearby cross street. "It was impossible that there was no traffic on that busy street," she said. Therefore, she had ample time to walk over to her car and drive it away before causing any accident. She believed it was God's invisible hand blocking traffic from all directions for her.

Around May or June of 1981, this woman moved to the East Coast to join her husband. On the evening of the following year's Easter Sunday, I received a long-distance call from her. "I was baptized today," she joyfully told me. "I felt very honored to have known you. It's through your influence that I received Jesus and was baptized. You're the first person I called to inform of my baptism."

Still a few years later, her whole family moved across the country from the East Coast all the way to the West Coast, specifically Southern California. After she moved there, she called me again to tell me about their move. Once when they were in Kentucky, her husband was tired and sleeping in the back of the car while she was driving. That part of Kentucky was hilly with the highway built on different sections, the eastbound lanes on the lower part and the westbound lanes on the upper hills. Sometime after she took over driving, it began to rain, and worse, it was raining sleet! She was inexperienced, and her car slipped and completely turned around

180 degrees so she was on the lower eastbound lanes! Her husband was jerked awake, and so was her mother, who was sitting on the passenger side next to her. Her mother was a Buddhist, and when she saw what happened, she said to her daughter, "You have a big life!" (Buddhists believe a person who is able to escape certain death has a big life.) However, she told me that she believed the Lord had protected her so that neither her family nor her car was harmed, and she said to me over the phone that day, "Now I know if a person does not know Jesus Christ, then he has lived his life in vain!"

I felt honored to have been used by the Lord in bringing her not only to receive Jesus Christ as her Savior and get baptized but also to know Him on a deeper level. Yet all the glory and honor should belong to Jesus Christ. Without the work of the Holy Spirit in those people's lives, I would not have been able to see those years of home Bible study bearing any fruit. Praise the Lord, and all glory be given to Him!

Chapter 10

A New Baby

In 1978, my third child, Corrie, was born, exactly ten years and two weeks after Leslie's birth and more than eleven years from Angela's. Friends used to think Corrie was conceived by accident. Actually, it was God's answer to my prayer, but boy, what a surprise God had in store for me.

After Leslie was born, my doctor advised me to use a contraceptive. Yishan also urged me to use it. Being a poor graduate student, he was scared after becoming a father of two, although he had joked when we first got married that he wanted a dozen children to form a choir. I felt forced to accept the use of contraceptives—first pills and then an IUD. I did not like either one. My body told me none of them were suitable for me. I felt trapped because of our financial strain.

My heart yearned for more children. Having come from a family of seven children, I was used to large families, and I always enjoyed being with children. Being the only one of my family in the United States often made me feel lonely. April of 1972 was the only time I got a surprise visit from my eldest sister when she was on her way home from Brazil to Taiwan. Without a US visa, she could stay in Chicago for only seven days. During that week I talked with my sister day and night until my voice became hoarse. Then after she left, I began to miss my siblings even more.

After Yishan was baptized in 1974, our financial situation somewhat improved. At least because of the health insurance his company was paying for us, I felt we could afford another child. In 1975, the Vietnam War ended, and when I read and heard stories about the Vietnamese orphans and refugees, I even thought about adopting an orphan. As I began to pray and ponder it, I also thought, *Why can't I have a child of my own instead?*

Thus, I began to talk Yishan into letting me have at least one more child. At first, he persistently withstood me, but I was not discouraged. About a year later, Yishan relented. In September of 1977, I went to the doctor to have my IUD removed, and Corrie was born the next July. I named the new baby after Corrie ten Boom.

As I look back now, I realize I was then still quite naive and sentimental and was not able to take many things into consideration. My longing for my family members in Taiwan had blinded me in knowing my true need. After only two months into the third pregnancy, I felt very awkward as if I were carrying a full-term baby. Because of my physical condition, I began to regret that I had wanted this pregnancy.

Mentally and emotionally, however, I was thankful that the Lord was giving me another child. Yishan even showed extra care and kindness for me. When I wanted to wash the kitchen floor and the living room carpet, he told me to rest while he did it for me, the only time he did it in all our thirty-six years of marriage. As the baby started to kick inside, I often had Angela and Leslie rest their hands on my tummy. They were delighted when they detected the baby's movement.

Nevertheless, as the pregnancy progressed, I felt worse, physically at least. During the last three months, I could not lie down in bed. If I did, I would feel the weight of the baby pressing against my chest, and I would feel suffocated. So during those three final months, at night I could only sit on a sofa with a pillow on top of the sofa back for my head and stretch my legs on chair. It was a wonder I could sleep in that position for three months.

Of course, it was no surprise that I would wake up very early each morning during that period. Then I would feel an urge to read the book of Job. Every morning soon after waking up, I would go out to the patio to pray and read the book of Job. I felt I could identify myself with Job in his suffering. However, it was not until Corrie's birth then I realized that the Lord was using the book of Job to prepare me for more suffering.

Earlier that year Yishan and I had started praying for the Lord to give us enough funds so that we could go back to Taiwan to visit our relatives. Ever since Yishan's baptism, we had prayed for the salvation of his parents and my own siblings. We wanted to use our trip to Taiwan to witness to our relatives.

The Lord answered our prayers for the funds, and by the time my pregnancy was in full term, we were planning on a family trip to Taiwan in December.

Two nights before I went to the hospital to have Corrie delivered, Yishan and I knelt together by our bed to pray. As usual, we prayed for the ministry of our church and the needs of friends as well as our upcoming trip. We especially prayed for the conversion of our family members in Taiwan.

When it was Yishan's turn, something very unusual happened.

Perhaps here I should first refer to an earlier time and also talk about my theological standing. In our church we rarely heard teachings on how to receive the gifts of the Spirit. We considered ourselves evangelicals. Then one day I found a book in the public library authored by John Sherrill titled *They Speak with Other Tongues*. It was a thick book, but I checked it out, finished the reading, and gave it to Yishan. He also finished the reading. Both of us were impressed and convinced by the stories given in the book, and we began to pray for the Lord to fill us with the Holy Spirit and to enable us to speak in tongue. Unlike some Christians thinking the gift of speaking in tongues was in the past, after reading that book, Yishan and I were convinced that God was still giving that gift to His children who sought it.

That night Yishan prayed, "Lord, in December, we're going to Taiwan to bring the gospel to my parents. Please fill me with Your Holy Spirit so that I may receive the power to witness to them."

Once he mentioned the word *power,* he felt a surge of power pouring down on his head and going through his whole body, and he began to shake uncontrollably. He shook in such great force that the bed was also shaking. At that point I heard his prayer change, and he began to say very quickly, "Hallelujah, hallelujah, hallelu, hallelu, lu, lu, lu." This was then followed by utterances I could not understand. Until then, I had never heard him use the word *hallelujah* in his prayer.

Both Yishan and I knew at that moment he was filled with the Holy Spirit and was speaking in tongue. Honestly, I should have been happy for him, but I was not. Instead I felt dismayed. I felt God did not like me. *I* was the one who initiated the seeking of spiritual filling and also the one who gave that book to Yishan to read. In my lack of fully understanding the Bible at that time, I thought I had displeased God and therefore failed to receive what I had asked for. So instead of rejoicing, I began to weep.

Yishan went on in his ecstatic utterance (or tongue, as usually is called) for twenty or thirty minutes. Finally, I could tell the power was waning because he was moving less forcibly and his prayer slowed down and reversed into "Lu, lu, lu, hallelu, hallelu, hallelujah, hallelujah." Then everything stopped.

(Although I did receive this gift of special filling a year later and it has since become almost daily experiences for me, even to this day I still do not consider myself charismatic. If possible, I shall explain. Suffice it to say that I have strong reasons that I cannot identify myself as charismatic.)

When Yishan stopped, both of us got up. He was so excited that he was unaware I had wept. He began to tell me what *he* had experienced and how wonderful it was. I was tired and had to sit down. So we both sat at the head of the bed. He did the most talking, and I tried to go along. I had to admit God had done something wonderful, and I totally agreed with Yishan. But I was tired and told him I had to go to bed. He said he was full of energy and wanted to read the Bible. So he went to his study, and I went to sleep.

Sometime later he wrote an article about that wonderful experience and its impact on him. (That article was included in the first issue of my magazine, *Fish and Loaves*, the only article that was not written by me in that issue. That article had caused a few people to label me and Yishan as charismatic and even forbid the distribution of my magazine in their churches, which was very unfortunate.) He said he slept very little that night. From that day on, he began to read the Bible day and night. At least it seemed so to me.

Two nights later, four or five hours after my obstetrician broke my water, I went into labor and checked into the hospital. Yishan drove me there. Once I was admitted, they put me on a hospital bed and hooked me to a baby monitor.

At first, I tried to bear the pain and prayed silently whenever I felt the pain become unbearable. Eventually, the pain was too great to bear, and I let out a yell. The nurse pulled up the railing on both sides of the bed to prevent any possible accident. I looked across the room at Yishan who was sitting less than ten feet away, completely absorbed in reading the Bible. Immediately, my memory took me back eleven years earlier to Holden Hospital, where I had labored hard for Angela's birth. Back then Yishan told me when he saw me in such great pain, he shed tears for me. Yet right in front of me now was the same husband, but he now seemed totally oblivious to what I was going through. I could not help but call out to him, "Yi, don't you care that I'm in great pain?"

He looked up at me and said, "What can I do to help you? I can only pray for you."

He did not even try to get up. He just sat there and continued in his Bible reading.

What I needed was his love and sympathy. If I could just hold his hand, I was sure I would at least feel better mentally. Yet he continued to sit where he was, never once again looking in my direction. I felt crushed by the lack of emotion I saw in Yishan. What a vast difference between now and then!

With rails up on all sides around me, I felt like I was being shut up in a cage. Lying helplessly all alone, I felt as if I were being crucified, and I began to think how much Jesus suffered when He was on the cross. I prayed silently, "Lord Jesus, please forgive my weakness. I thank You for allowing me to go through such great pain now so that I can understand at least to some degree how much You suffered on the cross for my sin. I now understand how lonely You must have felt when You were on the cross and no one could give You a helping hand."

I believe God had allowed all that to happen so that I could have a better understanding of the love of Christ. Had I not felt so desperately alone, despite the fact that both Yishan and a nurse were not too far away from me, it would have been very hard for me to grasp the essence of Christ's loneliness on the cross. No wonder He cried, "My God, My God, why hast Thou forsaken Me?"

By 1:00 a.m., the nurse told me that my dilation had reached five centimeters, and I felt better. I thought that the baby would soon come out and that the pain would be all over. However, as time went on, there was no further progress in my dilation. I was not informed of that, however, until many hours later.

As time dragged on and with sleep coming and going, I became groggy and did not remember much of what went on. All that I remembered was the pain that would never go away and my desperate feeling of loneliness despite my best effort in attempting to praise the Lord in the midst of all this.

Morning came, and my situation was still the same. Around 9:00 a.m., my doctor gave me a shot, and then Corrie was born about thirty minutes later. This was what my doctor told me when she came to see me still much later, "At 6:00 a.m., I came to look at you, and your dilation was still at five centimeters. So I went back to sleep. At 9:00 a.m., I gave you a shot to induce the dilation and *zoom*. It opened up, and the baby came out."

When she told me that, I felt like rebuking her, "If you had known that my dilation had stayed at five centimeters, why didn't you give me the drug earlier instead of letting me suffer so many more hours?" I knew it was useless to argue, and so I just kept silent.

Back when Angela and Leslie were born, hospital policy did not allow the father to stay in the delivery room. By 1978, the rules had changed, and so when Corrie was born, Yishan was standing right by me.

At the births of Angela and Leslie, I remembered, after the doctor gave the baby to the nurses, it took the nurses only a few minutes to weigh them and get them cleaned. Then they were wrapped in blankets and handed over to me. However, when Corrie was born, I was puzzled by a few things. First, I did not hear the usual cry from the baby. Then there was a long delay in getting the baby to me. I did not know what had happened; so I asked Yishan. He said there seemed to be some problem with the baby.

"What problem?" I asked.

He pointed a finger at his own lip and said, "Cleft lip."

At that moment I felt the whole world had caved in on me.

I don't remember what I said, but obviously, Yishan saw my disappointment and tried to comfort me. He said, "Well, we still have to thank the Lord for giving us this baby."

At that moment I knew why the Lord had let Yishan experience that special filling two nights earlier. He had filled Yishan with His Spirit and the fullness of joy so that Yishan could withstand the onslaught of disappointment. (In hindsight, now I understand why Yishan was so aloof earlier in the night when I was so helplessly lying in bed and why he said, "I could only pray for you," and did not try to get up or hold my hand. It must be the Lord's will that He was purifying me so that I could learn to look up to Him rather than to my husband. He had changed Yishan when He filled him with His Holy Spirit two nights before, and Yishan began to be interested in absorbing himself in the Lord's Word in the Bible and less interested in anything else in the world. From the article he wrote about that first filling experience, I realize now he became a changed person overnight.)

While talking to Yishan, I heard some commotion among the doctor and the nurses.

"Get Dr. Pum to come quickly." The tone of the person's voice told me there was an emergency.

Dr. Pum was the pediatrician I had wanted for the new baby. A year before, I had taken Leslie to see her when Leslie had developed some rash on her right arm. Dr. Pum prescribed an ointment that soon cured Leslie's rash.

Originally, I had only picked up Dr. Pum's name from the Yellow Pages. I did not know how competent she was. When I was asked to pick a pediatrician for the newborn, naturally, I wrote down Dr. Pum's name.

When Corrie was born, I learned later, something was stuck in her throat, and that was why I did not hear the usual first cry of the baby. By law, I was told later, once the baby was delivered, it was the pediatrician's job to take care of the baby. The obstetrician could no longer touch the baby. Since Dr. Pum was not around, a Dr. Z was called in to take care of the emergency. It was actually an easy solution. With a suction ball, Dr. Z easily sucked out the mucus that was stuck in Corrie's throat.

It was a real emergency though. During the time it took to get the pediatrician to come, the newborn almost died for lack of oxygen. By the time Dr. Z arrived, the baby's face had turned purple since the mucus in her throat had prevented her from taking her first breath. (Of course, I already knew the importance of the baby's first cry.) Dr. Z really arrived at the critical moment. After he used the suction ball to suck the mucus out of the baby's throat, I heard him say, "It's okay now." Not too long after that, the baby was handed to me.

When I took a look at the new baby, I thought she was the ugliest baby I had seen. The color of her face was purplish white, and her cleft lip had left a big gaping hole in her mouth. I felt heartbroken, and a sinful thought told me to reject this baby.

I was very disappointed at what the Lord had given me. He did not give me a son as I had wanted, and what's worse was that He had given me a baby with a birth defect.

In my own frail condition, not only did I fail to appreciate the fact that the baby had just been saved from certain death, but I had also failed to thank the Lord for answering my prayers for a baby. I did not realize I had greatly sinned then; however, the Lord surely took notice of that, and He had a way of correcting my sinful mistake.

Actually, the thought of rejecting the baby only flickered momentarily through my mind, and very quickly, I chided myself for having had that thought at all. In my heart I immediately asked the Lord to forgive me for having sinned. Yishan and I prayed together, thanking the Lord for giving us another baby. Then the nurse took the baby away, and sometime after that, a nurse wheeled me away from the delivery room.

On the way to my room, I asked the nurse to stop by the nursery window so that I could take another look at the new baby. By that time she had been completely cleaned. Her full head of black hair had been combed toward the back, and her pink color had returned to her face. When I looked at her, I thought that despite her cleft lip, she looked very much like Angela at birth, and I marveled at how two babies eleven years apart could look so much alike. *How wonderful God's creation is*, I thought. At that moment I knew the Lord had given me another beautiful baby, and I just could not wait to hold her and kiss her.

Once I was settled in my hospital room, I told Yishan to go home for some sleep, and then I waited for the nurse to bring me the new baby to nurse. I waited and waited. Lunch hour came and left, but no baby.

While I was still in the delivery room, my doctor told me, "I'd like to tell you about an unspoken rule among the physicians. Once a baby is attended to by a doctor at birth, we let him take care of the baby throughout the baby's entire hospital stay. So I recommend that you let Dr. Z take care of your baby until she is discharged."

That was fine with me, I told the doctor. In fact, I never told Dr. Pum I had picked her to be the new baby's doctor, so I was not expecting any trouble. What I did not know was that a certain nurse knew about my choice of Dr. Pum and had called her to come. Once Dr. Pum saw Corrie's cleft lip, she was eager to find out the cause.

(As I look back now, I'm quite certain that if that nurse had not told Dr. Pum of my decision and if Dr. Z had been able to remain as Corrie's pediatrician, then many things that followed would not have taken place, and it would have saved me a lot of trouble.)

Later that afternoon Dr. Pum came to ask me about our family history. Had anyone in my family or my husband's side been born with a cleft lip? No. Had anyone in our family been born with a birth defect? No. Was there anyone in our family who had died right after birth? No. I knew only one brother who died at the age of three, but not right after birth.

She asked a lot more questions.

Since I answered no to all her questions, she said, "If the cleft lip is not hereditary, then maybe there's some irregularity with the baby's chromosome at conception. We'll have to run some tests to find out the cause."

I had no idea what she was going to do with the new baby. All that I knew was that I waited in my hospital room for two days without getting to see my newborn daughter. The feeling was awful. While all the mothers got to hold and feed their babies and bond with them, each time I was the only mother with empty arms. The feeling was even worse on the second evening when Yishan was with me during the visiting hour. There was a tornado warning, and all the patients were ordered to evacuate the rooms. All the mothers with their husbands congregated in the corridor away from windows. Then when the babies were brought to their mothers for feeding, Yishan and I could only look at each other without our baby. (Today I think I can understand with my own experience then why childless couples struggle and try to have babies. That empty feeling was very awful.)

By that night before I went to sleep, I had been informed that Corrie was going to be sent to the Holy Family Hospital for a brain scan the next day. When Dr. Pum came to talk to me earlier, she had told me, "Your baby is listless," and she made a gesture of drooping her head to one side. "She has water in her brain. She also has a heart murmur. There's a hole in her heart. When she eats, she throws up. There's a hole in her esophagus. And she doesn't urinate. She has no urinary tract."

When I heard that, I thought I had gotten a baby with Down's syndrome, and the doctor's words made me feel as if my baby were a monster. *Oh, God, what hast Thou given me?* The doctor's words also gave me a sense that my new baby was not going to make it at all.

That night after the nurse had given us the sleeping pills for the night and my roommate was sound asleep, I stayed up writing a letter to a cousin who was also a Christian with whom I had reconnected only a few months earlier. I could not sleep. My heart was full of pain and complaints. So with tears streaming down my face, I wrote to my cousin these words: "I don't understand this. If God is going to take away my baby so soon after birth, why did He let me go through nine months of pregnancy and suffering in the first place? I'm praying and asking Him to spare the baby and let her live. Even if she indeed had Down's syndrome, I would still keep her."

The next morning before the scheduled time came for Corrie to be taken to the Holy Family Hospital for her brain scan, I was determined to walk to the nursery to see my baby. Dr. Pum had given me the impression that once she was taken to that hospital, she would never come back. I had not seen her since birth, and if I did not go to the nursery in time, I might never get to see her again. Therefore, I was determined to go see her at least one more time.

Several years later Yishan and I returned a few more times to that hospital to visit church members during their hospital stays, and I realized that the corridor of that hospital was actually not very long. That morning, however, in my frail postpartum body, as I held my hand against the wall for support and haltingly walked down the corridor by myself, that corridor seemed to be almost as long as the Great Wall of China.

When finally I reached the nursery door and walked inside, I saw and learned for the first time that Corrie had been kept in an incubator! Two nurses were working on her. One of them quickly pulled a high stool for me to sit on. The other held a small piece of sharp, curved metal in her hand and poked it into the bottom of one of Corrie's tiny heels and quickly held a tiny glass tube to catch the blood. When she had two or three tubes filled, she placed a bandage over the cut wound to stop the bleeding. Then the other nurse asked me, "Would you like to touch the baby?"

I said yes, and she opened one of the two hatches of the incubator so that my hand could reach through it to touch the baby.

While the nurse was poking the bottom of Corrie's heel, I noticed that whole area, more than one-third of her tiny sole, was almost covered with cut marks where nurses had poked her to take blood samples. Oh, my poor baby! I wished I had known earlier so that I could have asked them not to take so much blood from her.

As I sat there and watched the nurse working on Corrie, I noticed her eyes blinked, her brows narrowed, and her forehead wrinkled as if in pain when the nurse poked the sharp metal into the bottom of her tiny heel. At that moment, red flags of doubt came up in my head.

Up until then, I had never had a chance to hold Corrie or to observe her reaction to a stimulus. Until then I had totally relied on and believed in the information given by Dr. Pum. She told me my baby was listless and did not show any reaction. However, right in front of me, for the first time I saw with my own eyes that my baby reacted strongly to the pain in her tiny heel. So for the first time, I doubted whether Dr. Pum had told me the truth about my baby.

From my own past experience, I knew that when the mother's nipple touched one side of the baby's face, the baby would react by turning his or her mouth to that side and simultaneously begin a sucking motion until the nipple was found. Once I had doubts about Dr. Pum, I wanted to find out whether Corrie would react to stimulus as a regular newborn or not. So I did a simple experiment of my own. I slightly tapped one of Corrie's cheeks with my right middle finger. Immediately, she turned her face toward the side of my finger and simultaneously started a sucking motion as if to find the nipple.

Again, I lightly touched her other cheek with my finger, and similarly, she turned her face toward *that* side and also began a sucking motion.

Praise the Lord! My baby is not as hopeless as the doctor had told me. With great satisfaction, I withdrew my hand, closed the incubator hatch, and left the nursery. I kept my findings to myself and did not tell it to the nurse.

I was beginning to doubt whether Corrie truly did not have

urinary tract as the doctor had said. I also doubted whether Corrie had all the other monstrous defects described by Dr. Pum.

That afternoon Dr. Pum came to see me again. She said, "Your baby has too many problems. This hospital is not well equipped to treat her. I'm going to send her to the ABC (name withheld) Hospital in XYZ Town (name changed)."

When I heard that, I was not upset anymore. Since I did my own experiments on Corrie and had my own findings, I no longer believed my baby was as hopeless as the doctor had said. I was in fact happy to hear that my baby was going to a better hospital and would be in better hands. Nevertheless, I was very anxious to find out how my baby was going to be treated and how much longer I would have to wait before I could take her home.

Later I learned that ABC Hospital in XYZ Town was very well known. Many difficult cases were referred or transferred there. People came from as far as Europe to this hospital to have their children treated.

Early that evening around dinnertime, four adults in uniforms arrived at my room, two male paramedics and two female nurses. They arrived pushing a portable motorized incubator from ABC Hospital. They told me they had come to take my baby there for treatment.

When I saw them, I felt like crying and laughing. Oh, my baby must have been a very severe case to warrant such a pageantry of care! Yet it was a comical sight to see that four uniformed adults had come for a tiny baby.

One of the two nurses had a writing pad in her hand and started asking me questions. Right away I told her my earlier findings and observations about Corrie and my thoughts and doubts about Dr. Pum.

"Very good," said the nurse, writing everything down. "I'm going to report all these to the doctors at ABC hospital." She also informed me to call ABC hospital before twelve that night to inquire about Corrie's condition. Then the four adults left my room to take Corrie from the nursery.

I did call ABC Hospital before twelve that night. "Your baby is doing fine," I was told.

Still, I had no idea what her real condition was. So the next morning when Yishan came to visit, I sent him to XYZ Town to see how Corrie was doing.

Around noontime Yishan called me from ABC Hospital. He talked in great excitement, "When the doctor saw me, he immediately said, 'Your baby is very normal. The only thing abnormal about her is this,' and he pointed at his own lip."

What great relief! What great chastisement I had received from the Lord for my sin of ungratefulness!

Two days later our whole family went to XYZ Town to bring our new baby home. Although it was very hard taking care of a baby with cleft lip and cleft palate, with many surgeries to come and more difficulties to overcome, the Lord had brought me to learn many precious lessons through those difficult experiences.

Best of all, from the literature given by the doctors at ABC Hospital, I learned that only 20 percent of cleft-lip/cleft-palate conditions were hereditary. I learned that my new baby's birth defect was only due to some interruption during the respective formative stages of the lip and palate between one month and three months.

My sufferings were not in vain after all. With each of Corrie's corrective surgeries—except the last one, which was outpatient—and with each hospital stay, I experienced a lot of inconvenience because I had to stay with Corrie throughout that whole period, but *I was able to see those sufferings were really blessings in disguise.* Compared to the other babies with more severe cases, including heart conditions, I learned that my new baby was born only with minor defects that were correctable. What the apostle Paul said in 2 Corinthians 1:3–4 turned out to be true for me as well. "Blessed be God, even the Father of our Lord Jesus Christ, the Father of mercies and God of all comfort; who comforts us in all our tribulation, that we may be able to comfort them which are in any trouble, by the comfort wherewith we ourselves are comforted of God."

There was an added blessing for me from the birth of the new baby.

Back in 1973, three weeks after we moved into our new home in Schaumburg, I received a concussion when a carpenter from the builder came to fix our front door. He opened the door with such great force that the door hit me and left a bruise about one inch long and an eighth of an inch wide on the center of my forehead. Although the hospital X-ray showed no fracture, my brain in the back of my head was injured, which was where the real impact had occurred.

I could have sued the carpenter and would have succeeded in receiving compensation since my doctor was willing to provide the medical proof. However, I thought of my own mother, who had had a head injury at age nineteen, and she became a weather station for her whole life. Every time there was a change in the weather, she would know it because she *always* had a headache.

I did not sue the carpenter, but I prayed to the Lord instead, "Lord, I do not want to sue the carpenter. He did not mean to hurt me, although he was careless and caused my injury. What does the monetary compensation mean to me if I become another weather station for the rest of my life like my own mother? Please do not make me a weather station."

Although I prayed that prayer repeatedly, at that time it seemed the Lord did not hear my prayer because I *did* become a weather station after that. Every time there was a change in the weather, I would *always* feel pain in the back of my head. That went on for almost five years.

However, sometime after the new baby was born, I realized the Lord *had* delivered me from being a weather station, and weather changes had no more effect on me. It was then I knew the Lord had mercifully allowed me to experience what the apostle Paul said in 1 Timothy 2:15 (NASB). "But women shall be preserved through the bearing of children if they continue in faith and love and sanctity with self-restraint."

With the birth of the new baby, the Lord *did* bless me with the suffering to learn of His comfort as well as the added blessing of *deliverance through childbirth.* My heavenly Father is always wise and worthy to be praised!

Corrie wearing dress made by Angela

Chapter 11

Fish and Loaves

In 1977, the church that grew from our home Bible study group had its first Sunday worship service. I'll called it the NW Church. More than a year later, the church got its first pastor. When his name was mentioned, I considered objecting because I had heard him preach before, and his sermon was so disorganized that it was the only time I ever fell asleep during a sermon in those years. In the end, however, I didn't say anything.

Sometime after the arrival of the new pastor, the church decided to publish a church magazine titled *The Sheepfold*, and I became its editor. *The Sheepfold* was really my brainchild, but it was a church publication. Two issues were published. All the articles in both issues were handwritten since Chinese typing was not available or affordable to us then. Although only two hundred copies were printed and distributed for each issue, the response was overwhelmingly good. I praised the Lord for the result and gave Him all the credit.

A few months after the arrival of the new pastor, church members began to grumble about him, especially concerning his sermons. Yishan and I were once again caught in an unpleasant situation because people grumbled to us, but no one wanted to confront the pastor. To make a long story short, after much prayer and consultation and ascertaining the Lord's will, we decided to leave that church, and we went to an American church.

While attending the American church, I felt a burden to continue publishing *The Sheepfold*. Knowing that none of the people remaining in that church would be interested in picking up the reins of editorship and having seen the response of friends to the publication of the two previous issues, I felt it would be wasting a good effort if *The Sheepfold* was not continued. Yet for a period of six months, despite my continuous prayers and seeking the Lord's will, I did not sense that the Lord was giving me a nod of consent.

Then it dawned on me that *The Sheepfold* was not an appropriate name for a magazine I was going to publish single-handedly. It definitely was well named for a church publication, but I would have to come up with something else for *my* magazine.

Thus, I prayed, "Lord, if *The Sheepfold* is inappropriate for my magazine, please give me another title."

One afternoon as I was leafing through a Christian publication, I came to an advertisement page of a well-known publishing company. As I saw the five loaves and two fishes in the center of the page, the words *fish* and *loaves* leaped out of my head, and I was overjoyed. Right then I knew it was an appropriate name. Just as the Lord used the five loaves and two fishes from a little boy and blessed them and multiplied them to feed thousands of people, I was sure the Lord was going to use me as He had used that little boy. Then when I had a chance, I asked a pastor from Taiwan if he knew of any Chinese Christian magazines published there bearing the same name.

"Not that I know of," he said.

Once I was certain about naming my magazine, the Lord seemed to make each subsequent step clear to me. A few months later on a Thanksgiving weekend, a friend invited us to a winter retreat held in Southern Illinois. A Chinese pastor and his wife from St. Louis were the featured speakers. At the dinner table our family sat with the pastor and his wife. When I casually mentioned my intention of publishing *Fish and Loaves,* the pastor's wife promised to send me two articles. Thus, I received the first contribution of articles.

A few months later, the Lord made His will very clear to me and Yishan that He wanted us to go back to the Chinese church (NW Church) that we had left behind. At first, I tried to ignore the Lord's urging. Finally, when it was inevitable, Yishan and I bowed our heads to the Lord and went back to NW Church, exactly eleven months after we had left it. At the first Sunday service there, I picked up a program with Chinese typing. After some inquiry, we found that it was printed by a brother who owned a print shop. When we had left that church eleven months earlier, he did only English typesetting. Now he also did Chinese. Thus, I learned that by commanding me to go back to that Chinese church, the Lord really had intended to bless my magazine so that it could have a more appealing format to its potential readers. It would *not* be handwritten as *The Sheepfold* had been.

Yishan and I talked about creating a nonprofit organization to publish *Fish and Loaves*. In order to incorporate this organization with the state of Illinois, we would need three US citizens. Yishan and I made two, but we still needed a third person. We put the whole matter in the Lord's hand and prayed daily for the brother who owned the print shop. If we talked to him, we were sure he would not refuse us. Yet we wanted it to be the Lord's will and let Him pick the right one.

By that time I had already written several articles, and Yishan gave them to the brother to do the Chinese typing. One Sunday as Yishan handed him two more articles to type, he asked Yishan, "Why don't you put up these articles into a magazine?"

"That's exactly what we plan to do," answered Yishan.

"Then I would like to join you in your publication effort," said that brother.

Thus, Yishan explained to that brother our intention of incorporation, and immediately, he asked to have a part in it. Praise the Lord! He did pick His own man to be our partner.

Then one day I received a phone call from an American friend saying that she had a houseguest from Taiwan who spoke no English. I told the friend to send her guest over. She was very glad to be relieved of a burden and brought the guest to my house.

The guest turned out to be a lady minister who worked in a

church in Taipei where twenty years earlier my friend Esther used to work.

I called up Esther, and immediately, she and her husband, Daniel, drove all the way from Carbondale to Schaumburg. All of us had a happy reunion and very good sharing. I shared with them how the Lord was giving me the burden to publish *Fish and Loaves*, and I showed them the articles that were already typed. When the lady minister finished reading them, she commented that they were very inspirational.

Two days later Esther and Daniel left, taking the guest to the airport. Before they left, the guest gave me an envelope marked, "Offering for *Fish and Loaves*." I opened the envelope and found forty-five dollars inside. Thus, the Lord provided the first contribution to the funds of *Fish and Loaves* even *before* its official publication.

Two or three weeks later when all the typing and editing work was done, I ordered a printing of fifteen hundred copies for the debut issue. Very quickly, all the copies were distributed, and I had to order another fifteen hundred copies.

With the printing of the next and several subsequent issues, circulation increased. By December 1989, when the twenty-second issue came out, eight thousand copies were printed and sent to thirteen countries throughout the world.

From the very beginning, the Lord impressed upon me that the content of *Fish and Loaves* was to consist of "the gospel, testimonies, and songs." By then the Lord had given me many songs to write, and I was able to include one or two of my songs in each issue.

A number of pastors or pastors' wives gave me articles to publish. Some laymen also contributed to the articles. Whenever Yishan got the inspiration, he would also write for the magazine. Above all, I myself was the major contributor, sometimes using my real name, sometimes using aliases.

Of all the manuscripts I received from different sources, except for one or two authors, most of them required a lot of editing. One of the frequent contributors was a pastor's wife. She was the one who gave me the first two articles I accepted for the magazine. Her articles had been published somewhere else where editors had modified her writing, and both were touching stories that were well written.

It is interesting how the Lord had used that pastor's wife to help me get the magazine started since she was the one who provided the first contribution of articles. Yet the Lord had deliberately withheld from me knowledge of the true nature of her writing. If I had known it then, I might have turned down her contribution on the spot. Her stories were interesting, but her writing style gave me a tremendous headache every time I had to edit her articles. In her effort to beautify her writing, she added a lot of embellishments to the sentences, and many of them were either redundant or simply awkward! Many times I had to stop and pray, asking the Lord for patience and wisdom, while I was working on those articles. Her subsequent contribution proved that the Lord used her to a certain degree, but it was at my expense.

Of course, my effort was richly rewarded when each issue came out and the readers told me how much they enjoyed reading *Fish and Loaves.*

Thank God that people enjoyed reading *Fish and Loaves.* However, the magazine was not meant to please the readers only. It was aimed at reaching nonbelievers as well as Christians. Surely, the Lord has used *Fish and Loaves* in this respect. A woman told me that someone gave her a copy while she was still a nonbeliever. She took it home and read it. The Lord used it as a bridge to reach her, she said. Not only was she converted and baptized, but she became an avid supporter of the magazine too.

From time to time, I was told by Christians either directly or through Yishan or via the mail that they were encouraged or their faith was strengthened by *Fish and Loaves.* No wonder pastors recommended it to their members. Churches sent for copies to replenish their libraries, and frequently, we received requests by new subscribers or for gift subscription to friends or relatives. However, through all those years, *Fish and Loaves* was *always distributed free* to its readers. We never charged a dime either for the cost of printing or mailing.

I believe that the Lord used *Fish and Loaves* to bring about much good. But as its founding editor and publisher, I myself received much benefit throughout those years of working on this magazine. Of course, I'm not talking about financial benefit. I never received a dime for myself, but on the contrary, the first series of major monetary contribution to *Fish and Loaves* came from our own funds.

As a mother of two teenage daughters and one preschool girl, I had my hands full just to take care of my own family. Besides, I was taking some correspondence studies from Moody Correspondence School and also attending Moody Evening School in the suburbs together with Yishan. Almost every night I had to stay up late, long after Yishan and the girls had gone to bed, so that I could have my own time for devotion and Bible study and doing homework. As I look back now, I have to say that without the Lord's grace and mercy, I could not have done all that *plus* editing and publishing *Fish and Loaves*.

I tried to publish this magazine as a periodical, but I did not have much success. With all the time and energy spent on my family and the Bible, I have to confess that I did *not* have much left for the magazine. It was as if the Lord had to nudge me each time so that I would then turn my attention to writing and editing. Once in a few months when finally I had delayed long enough, I would spend a few days concentrating on putting up a new issue of the magazine. When boxes of new copies arrived from the printer, the whole family (and later some church members) would pitch in and help with stapling and fixing mailing labels. Yishan and I would finish up sorting and sending them out through the post office.

Though the writing and editing work was challenging enough, the time and physical strength involved with mailing were also daunting. As if all this was not enough to discourage me, Satan would invent new ways to frustrate me. Once a sister in the church chided me about the magazine. Why? Well, the printer's wife had a sister in Taiwan who typed the articles for the magazine. At first, the printer sent out those articles to Taiwan after we gave them to him. Later on his wife told me to send those articles directly to Taiwan. Of course, I would include a few words of appreciation each time I sent them out. Since the printer's wife had asked us to pray for her family members in Taiwan who were all Buddhists, I would also use this opportunity to encourage the typist to turn to Jesus since the articles she typed were all about Jesus and the Bible.

Even though we did pay the printer for all the typing cost, I took it as a courtesy to include a few words with the articles when I sent them to Taiwan, thanking her for typing the articles and sometimes encouraging her to turn to Jesus Christ in faith, not knowing that the typist was infuriated, accusing me for cursing her father. The typist told her sister, the printer's wife, who in turn told a woman in the church, and the latter came to chide me.

Nothing could be further from the truth. Why would I curse a man I had neither known nor met? There was nothing whatsoever in those articles that had any personal reference to the typist or her father. Then I realized that *the devil*, who is the *accuser*, had inflamed the typist against the articles she typed *and* the person who had sent those articles, me. A few of them did talk about the necessity of believing in Jesus Christ and the consequence in the lake of fire, which is all true according to the Bible.

If I did not believe in the whole Bible and *if* I did not desire souls to be saved from eternal damnation, I would not be publishing *Fish and Loaves*, and then the devil would be happy. Yet I had to continue. The printer's sister-in-law refused to type my articles after that, but then my youngest sister (in Taiwan) recommended her sister-in-law (also in Taiwan) to me. The latter turned out to be a much more competent typist than the previous one. (That means it saved me a whole lot of editing time.) Praise the Lord! (I've always told people that the devil is actually very dumb. In this case, he inflamed the typist so that she quit the job, but in the end, I got a better typist instead without having to pay more. When we are on the Lord's side, He guarantees us the victory, doesn't He?)

It was the Lord who had carried me through those years of publishing *Fish and Loaves*. Otherwise I would have thrown in the towel long ago. To be honest, quite a few times I was thinking of doing *that*. There were no committee or board members to share the burden with or to cheer me on. However, each time I felt disheartened and thought about quitting, I would immediately pray, asking the Lord if it was worthwhile to continue publishing. The Lord answered by way of the readers' mail. Either I would receive a letter thanking us for the help through the magazine articles, or a check of appreciation and support would come. Sometimes the mail came two or three days later, sometimes on the very same day I prayed. Maybe most of them had not come in answer to my prayer, but once in a while, the Lord moved the writers' hearts to write those letters even *before* I prayed, knowing I would need them for encouragement. Once or twice when I prayed in the morning, asking the Lord to move some readers' heart to send us support fund, that very afternoon I received a letter containing a check.

Another time I asked the Lord to move someone to send us some money because we were publishing another issue. We were not exactly short of funds, but I asked the Lord for $300 to show me that it was His will to have me continue publishing the magazine. The very next day, I received a check of $300 from a man living in a town closer to Chicago than Schaumburg. This man was in his late fifties. For about a year, he and his wife drove a long way every Sunday to attend our church in Schaumburg. When he and his wife decided to hold a Bible study in their home on Saturday night, Yishan and I drove there to lead them in the Bible study.

When I received that check, I called that man to thank him, and he told me a wonderful story. Two or three days before that when he woke up and was still in bed, he heard a man's voice speaking loudly to him, "*Fish and Loaves* needs $300. Send it soon!" He knew it could not be his wife since it was a man's voice. However, after he got up and got busy in other things, he soon forgot about it.

The next morning the very same thing happened. It was the same voice only more urgently saying the very same words. He told his wife God was speaking to him, telling him to send a contribution to *Fish and Loaves*. That day he wrote that check and immediately sent it out.

Obviously, the Lord had moved into action even *before* I opened my mouth to ask Him. What a wonderful God we serve!

Once a woman in the church came to my house. Yishan and I used to call this woman "Little Mrs. Yellow," so named because her husband's last name, Wong, means yellow, and her husband's younger brother had a wife who also went to that church. The younger brother's wife was much bigger in size, and so we called one woman "Little Mrs. Yellow" and the other "Big Mrs. Yellow." Both brothers worked as chefs in different Chinese restaurants. Little Mrs. Yellow worked alongside her husband as a waitress.

She began attending the church that started from our home Bible study soon after the church began. She had migrated from Hong Kong and spoke primarily Cantonese. Her English ability was very limited, and she began coming to my home whenever she needed assistance with English, whether with a bill she received or with a call to someone who spoke only English. Of course, I could talk to her only in Mandarin. Half of our conversation would go on by way of my trying to figure out her Cantonese. She would correct me if I had misunderstood her. She understood Mandarin with much less difficulty compared to my knowledge of Cantonese.

When *Fish and Loaves* came out, she became a regular reader and loved the magazine, but she was not a contributor. She was a Buddhist. Despite the fact that I used every opportunity to witness to her and to tell her about the Bible, she remained steadfastly committed to Buddhism, saying that she had made vows to the Buddha for something while in Hong Kong. She was afraid she would receive a curse by converting to Christianity. I gave her Romans 8:1, which says, "There is no condemnation for those in Christ Jesus," and Galatians 3:13, which says, "Christ redeemed us from the curse of the Law, having become a curse for us."

Eventually, the Holy Spirit did enough work on her, allowing her to see many answered prayers in her own life and others. She was then convinced that Jesus was the only true God, and she was no longer afraid of any curse that could befall her. Finally, she was baptized in the name of Jesus Christ, and Yishan had the privilege of baptizing her in yet another church, which I'll call the Cedar Church. (I'll talk about it in a later chapter.)

Now I don't remember whether it was before or after Little Mrs. Yellow received baptism. I just remember that day she came to my house with money in her hand. She gave the money to me and said, "This is an offering for *Fish and Loaves*." She then related the following story about the money.

"Last Friday night I was working at the restaurant," she said. "There were not many customers around 9:00, and I suddenly said out aloud to myself, 'I have never given to *Fish and Loaves*. I'll give $50.' I myself was surprised for having said that, but then I thought, *Well, $50. Sure, it'll be $50.* I then counted the total of tips, and it was less than $30. At 9:30 p.m., two people came in, and five more at 9:50. The restaurant was supposed to close in ten minutes, but I waited on them anyway. When all the customers left, I found more tips, and the total came to be $51. So here, this is all that I received last Friday night. I'm very happy the Lord enabled me to give."

"Praise the Lord! He gives us more than what we asked," I told Little Mrs. Yellow.

"I was really not thinking about how much I would give when I blurted out, 'I'll give $50,'" she said rather reflectively. Obviously, $50 was not a small amount to her, but she was willing to sacrifice it for the Lord's work. So the Lord blessed it and gave her more than that amount. "My cup runneth over." Surely, that's how the Lord works. Little Mrs. Yellow learned it that time, and that's what I learned during those years of working on *Fish and Loaves*. Praise the Lord! He is always so good.

Chapter 12

Taiwanese Church

When *Fish and Loaves* was first published, Yishan gave several copies to a Taiwanese colleague who often visited a Taiwanese church, the only Taiwanese church in the greater Chicago area at that time. This Taiwanese colleague of Yishan's was not a Christian, but he took those copies of *Fish and Loaves* to that Taiwanese church and distributed them. (A year later Yishan was able to lead this colleague to the Lord.)

A certain Mrs. Lee received a copy of the premiere issue. When she read one of my articles titled "A Wilderness Trip," she was greatly touched. She called and talked to me over the phone for two hours. Later she arranged for Yishan to speak at the Taiwanese church. Her husband was a deacon in that church.

Two weeks later Mrs. Lee called me again. This time she asked me and Yishan to pray for a Mrs. Wang who had terminal cancer.

When we arrived at Mrs. Wang's home, her husband received us into their living room. They had a nice home located in an upscale suburban neighborhood. Mr. Wang was a civil engineer manager. He told us how he and his wife used to turn down invitations to go to church since he had an advancing career and neither he nor his wife felt the need for God. He said that his wife had terminal cancer that had spread from the uterus to the ovaries. On the day she was to receive surgery, she held her husband's hand and asked, "If I do not wake up from the surgery, where will I be?"

So after Mrs. Wang's surgery, she and her husband began seeking the Lord, and only two weeks before Yishan and I met them, they had been baptized in a Chinese church.

That day seven or eight other Taiwanese also went there and joined me and Yishan as we prayed for Mrs. Wang. It was not until a few weeks later that we learned they actually were there to observe how we prayed. They told me then, "We are Presbyterians. We have never seen a patient being prayed for. So we went there to watch you and your husband pray."

That prayer meeting turned out to be a manifestation of the Holy Spirit working in a wonderful way. When we were praying for the patient, she was filled with the Holy Spirit. Although she was very frail and despite the fact that she was only a two-week-old Christian, she spontaneously began to praise the Lord and said repeatedly, "Hallelujah, thanks to the Lord." Her voice being barely audible, she said to a woman standing by her headboard, "I'm filled with the Holy Spirit." Then she started to cough and became exhausted and fell asleep.

Although God did not heal Mrs. Wang, He did honor *my* specific request to remove her pain. Whereas she was constantly in great pain before and could not fall asleep, she was able to sleep as peacefully as a baby from that day on, and two weeks later she slipped into eternity in her sleep without any more pain.

As those Taiwanese Christians joined me and Yishan in praying for Mrs. Wang, they were very impressed and invited us to join their biweekly Bible study, which was meeting that very evening.

Actually, one of those present at the prayer meeting was an exception. She was not a Christian, but she told me two weeks later when she joined the Bible study, "You are very different."

"No," I said, "we're not different. My husband and I are Christians just as all the others."

"Oh, yes, you are very different from the other Christians," said that woman. Her name was also Mrs. Lin. She then explained why she thought Yishan and I were different.

Mrs. Wang was home alone during the daytime when her husband was at work, and her two children were in college. Mrs. Lin happened to live across the street from the Wangs. So Mrs. Lin usually went over to take care of Mrs. Wang during the daytime.

"Mrs. Wang was in such pain that she could not sleep at all," Mrs. Lin told us. "In addition to that, she could not eat or hold down anything in her stomach. She could only drink a little 7 Up, but even that she would throw up as well."

In fact, Mrs. Lin saw such difference our prayers made on Mrs. Wang that she herself became a Christian and was baptized about two months later.

During the week following our first encounter with the Taiwanese Christians, two women from that Bible study group called me. They were also present at the prayer meeting at Mr. and Mrs. Wang's home. They wanted to find out how to start a church. They knew a church had grown out of Bible study started at my home.

I told them first they had to start praying and seeking the Lord's will. I told them the Bible study that started at my home had been the result of many prayers and that the church just naturally grew from it. It was the Lord's leading rather than my own will in starting a church.

Those women seemed very anxious to get a church started. They said they had been meeting more than a year, and all they lacked was someone to lead them. They saw in Yishan and me the leadership they had been looking for. Within a week they called for a meeting on the following Sunday. During that meeting they discussed the first worship service for a new Evangelical Formosan Church. They were going to use the facilities of a nearby Presbyterian church. And they asked Yishan to deliver the first sermon on the very next Sunday. Yishan felt obliged to accept the responsibility.

Once we got home, Yishan began to prepare the sermon, but he really had no idea. I suggested the title "The Church Began" using the text of Acts 2:41–47.

Since Yishan was then working full-time as a microbiologist, he had only evenings and lunchtime hours to prepare the sermon. By Wednesday evening he had spent three evenings and three lunch hours preparing that message. I said to him, "You have never preached

111

a sermon. Would you like to practice what you have prepared so that I can see how it sounds?"

When he began to practice, I timed him. It was only five minutes long. He had used up half of the week and prepared a sermon only five minutes long! It was supposed to be forty minutes. How would he ever find enough time to prepare the whole sermon since he only had three more days left?

Once I finished listening to his five-minute sermon, I wanted to say, "Boring and dry." However, I was afraid of frustrating him and only said, "Boring." Then I commented, "You need to be filled with the Holy Spirit."

Since Yishan had his first spirit-filled experience two nights before Corrie's birth, he had another similar experience when we left the Chinese church the year before. He had not had any more such experiences since then. On the other hand, I had had similar experiences almost on a daily basis since then.

So I held Yishan's hand and both of us knelt down by the couch on the family room floor and prayed. Very quickly, Yishan was filled with the Spirit and started the ecstatic utterances of which he had experienced two times before. While Yishan was thus being filled by the Holy Spirit, nothing specific happened to me. How wonderfully the Spirit was manifesting His power and sovereignty! It was Yishan who needed His filling, not me.

When the prayer ended, both of us were very excited. I knew the Lord was going to give Yishan His message for a soon-to-begin Evangelical Formosan Church. Yishan felt empowered and set aside the sermon he had written and began writing a new one. The next day, which was Thursday, he went to work and continued to write. On Friday, he took the day off and stayed home to concentrate on his writing.

When it was near noontime, I asked him how he had been doing. He said that words had been coming out like a spring. When I picked up his manuscript and read it, I was satisfied. I knew it was going to be a powerful sermon.

By Sunday, November 1, 1982, Yishan had his sermon ready to

launch a new ministry at a new church. Thirty-two adults attended the worship. When the service was over, the man who was responsible for inviting speakers said excitedly to Yishan, "We don't need to invite other speakers. You may preach every Sunday."

Yishan answered, "Oh, no, out of the whole Bible, this is the only sermon I can preach."

A month later when it was time for Yishan to preach his second sermon, he had that Spirit-filled experience again two weekends in a row. The third month when he preached his third sermon, he received that spirit-filled experience only on the Saturday before he actually preached. Obviously, the Holy Spirit Himself knew how to prepare His servant for service. By the time Yishan prepared his fourth monthly sermon, he did not receive that supernatural experience again, but the Lord still gave him the message to speak.

From then on, Yishan experienced that special filling only sporadically, usually when there was special need. Other times he just prayed, and the Lord would give him the necessary words to preach.

Since that new church did not yet have a pastor, most of the members looked up to me and Yishan as their spiritual leaders, especially when it came to evangelism. The sad fact was that none of them really knew how to talk to people about believing in Jesus. And yet they were very effective in inviting nonbelievers to church. Naturally, they would arrange for me and Yishan to go visiting these people in their homes to talk about Jesus.

Yishan and I emphasized the importance of prayer support when doing evangelism. Each time as Yishan and I visited people for evangelism, usually on Sunday afternoons, a group of brothers and sisters would stay at church to cover us with their prayers. We also stressed the necessity of praying ahead for the person(s) to be evangelized, preferably weeks ahead or at least several days ahead.

During the eleven months of our ministry with the Taiwanese church, we did a total of seventeen evangelistic visitations. With the exception of one visitation, all the others ended successfully with those we visited making decisions to receive Jesus as their Lord and Savior and later to be baptized.

That one exception with no conversion really came as no surprise to me or Yishan. We had believed in the Holy Spirit doing the conviction and also in the necessity of praying ahead for the Holy Spirit to prepare those people's hearts. However, that couple we visited that afternoon happened to come to the Taiwanese church for the first time that morning. For that reason, Yishan and I had not meant to visit them that afternoon. Yet because of the enthusiasm of some of the Taiwanese Christians in arranging for us to do the visitation, we gave in and consented to go, bowing to pressure rather than being led by the Holy Spirit. No wonder that visitation turned out to be a failure.

During our eleven months of ministry with the Taiwanese church, we saw repeatedly the work of the Holy Spirit. We saw many lives turned around for the better.

Once we visited a woman in her early sixties who had Parkinson's. We took two or three other women with us when we did that visitation. We learned that her husband had died in a car accident in Africa. He was a member of an agricultural aid team sent by the Taiwan government. Then one day she was informed that her nineteen-year-old son was a drug user when the police came to search her house. The revelation gravely upset her and triggered the onset of Parkinson's. During our conversation I saw her hands and body shaking terribly.

As Yishan and I talked to the hostess about the need for repentance of one's own sin, we came to an impasse because she could not see her own need for repentance. I mentioned the fact that sometimes we may not be aware of any sin in ourselves, but the Holy Spirit will always reveal it to us.

As if the Holy Spirit was coming to our aid, one of the women there shared a story from her earlier life. I'll call her Tammy here.

"When I was in the first grade," said Tammy, "I was the class monitor and was responsible for collecting a dollar from each student for the class fund. Since my family was poor, I did not bother to ask Mother for the dollar. I found two half pieces of the same side of dollar bills and pasted them together. After I had collected all the dollar bills from my classmates, I secretly slipped the no-good dollar bill into the pile and handed the pile to the teacher. The teacher, however, was not fooled. He found the no-good bill and was angry. He demanded confession from the culprit. As the culprit, I did not confess, and of course, no one else did. The teacher was enraged and determined to find out. He went on to feel the heartbeats of every student. One boy possibly had a faster heartbeat. He was pulled out for a beating. I was very scared and tried very hard to forget it.

"Eventually, I was able to forget about it completely," Tammy went on. "Then I graduated from junior high with very good grades and was promoted to the tenth grade without having to pass a highly competitive exam for entrance to high school. That summer I had plenty of leisure time and went hiking to the mountain with some friends. My face, however, was scratched by tree branches and sustained an infection that would not heal. My mother took me to many doctors, but none of their prescriptions worked. She even bought snake soup for me to drink. The snake soup was supposed to work wonders, but even that failed. I was desperate. A beautiful face was very important to a teenage girl like me, and I refused to go out. I even began to contemplate suicide.

"Fortunately, a friend had taken me to church a few times prior to that. When the pastor found me missing at church, he came to my home. I stayed in my room and would not go out. He, on the other hand, insisted on seeing me, or he would not leave. I finally gave in and went to meet him in the living room. Upon seeing me, he made no comments except saying, 'Confess your sin to the Lord.'

"When the pastor left, I prayed, 'Lord, I do not know what sin I have, but the pastor told me to confess my sin. So I confess it to you now.'

"At that moment," Tammy said, "what I did in the first grade came back to me, and I felt deep regrets and sorrow for the pain I had caused to that boy. I then prayed to ask for God's forgiveness. After I confessed my sin to the Lord, my face began to heal without any medication."

Well, this story was a very good example of the lack of awareness of sin's presence in many people's lives and of the Holy Spirit's convicting power (John 16:8). It also helped our hostess to see her own need of repentance. She conceded that she was very angry with her son and was still holding resentment in her heart.

At our urging she prayed to receive Jesus Christ as her Lord and Savior. We then prayed for her, asking the Lord to help her deal with her anger so that she would be able to forgive her son.

The following Sunday somebody drove that woman to church. She came in walking with great difficulty. In fact, she had to be supported by someone else as she walked. Throughout the worship service, I saw her hands and body shaking uncontrollably just as before. As days and weeks went by, however, I noticed the tightness of her muscles loosening, and gradually, I saw smiles on her face. Her tremors greatly diminished too. Obviously, the Lord had healed her *both physically and spiritually.*

In November, someone brought a Mrs. Tsai to church. The coworkers tried to arrange a date for me and Yishan to visit her, but she kept saying, "Wait until February." She had been a nurse in Taiwan, and she had an important exam coming up in February, one that would determine if she could have a nurse license in Illinois or not.

Then another woman hosted a Christmas dinner on December 16 and invited a lot of people who had been going to the church, including Yishan, me, and also Mrs. Tsai.

We had been praying hard for Mrs. Tsai by the day we went to the dinner. When we got there, the hostess had an apron on and was busy in the kitchen. We were led to the living room, and sometime later Mrs. Tsai and her three children arrived. During the ensuing conversation, Yishan and I actually tried not to push the topic of Christian faith since it had seemed to us that she was probably not interested. However, surprisingly enough, she told us stories about herself, how she went to Texas first, where a former colleague from Taiwan coaxed her into buying a house and some appliances, and eventually, she realized the former colleague had in fact acted for her own benefit. As a result, Mrs. Tsai lost a lot of money. Then when she moved north to Chicago, where she did not know anybody, she happened to have a Chinese woman as a neighbor. The neighbor, a Christian, was kind to her and took her to a Chinese church that she regularly attended. Compared to her former acquaintance, Mrs. Tsai said, the Christians who were total strangers actually were a lot nicer to her.

As our conversation went on, I realized our topics had actually centered around Christianity and Christians, and I found Mrs. Tsai began to shed tears. I knew the Holy Spirit was touching her heart. I then asked her, "Mrs. Tsai, would you like to receive Jesus Christ as your Lord and Savior?"

Instead of answering yes or no, however, Mrs. Tsai turned the topic around and began to talk about a relative who was totally unrelated to our conversation. As she did that, strangely, her tears stopped. I was afraid it would result in the quenching of the Holy Spirit, and I immediately brought our topic back and asked her the second time, "Mrs. Tsai, would you like to receive Jesus Christ as your Lord and Savior?"

Interestingly, as soon as I brought back the conversation (mentally pleading for the Holy Spirit's help), tears came to Mrs. Tsai's eyes again. But just as the first time, Mrs. Tsai changed the topic again, and her tears stopped as well. Not willing to give up, I took back the control of the conversation and asked the same question the third time. Instead of shying away from my question, this time she cried out in tears, almost wailing, and said, "Yes, I'm very weak! I need Jesus!"

All of us there rejoiced greatly as Yishan led Mrs. Tsai in praying to receive Jesus. She then went on to tell us (me and Yishan), "I've been going to church quite some time now. I first went to FC Church (the church where Yishan was baptized), and then someone brought me to this church. I have had many questions about Christianity, but no one has been able to answer them for me until now. You have answered all my questions."

What a surprise! Neither Yishan nor I had any inkling what

questions she had. Obviously, it was the Holy Spirit who was in charge of the whole conversation. Praise the Lord!

In fact, this was not the only time I saw the leading of the Holy Spirit in our talks. In many other conversations, the person we were visiting would suddenly bring up a question about the Christian faith or the Bible. Almost every time that person would turn toward Yishan as he or she asked the question, obviously expecting Yishan to answer it. However, since Yishan had not received any seminary training then, when that happened, a lot of the times he had no idea how to answer the question, and he would simply look at me. A few times I was able to answer those questions for him, but other times I would feel panic inside because *I* did not know the answer either. I tried to stay calm and mentally sent out an SOS to the Lord, and without any exception, the right answer would instantly pop into my head. I was able to give a satisfactory answer. Time and again I was surprised and relieved and found that the Holy Spirit was always our best teacher.

Two weeks after Mrs. Tsai prayed to receive Jesus, the wife of her husband's older brother came from Taiwan and Mrs. Tsai brought her to church. When the service was over, Mrs. Tsai invited me and Yishan to have lunch with them at a Chinese restaurant in order that Yishan and I might witness to the senior Mrs. Tsai. When lunch was over and our talk was nowhere near the end, Mrs. Tsai invited us to her home so that we could continue to talk to her sister-in-law. As the afternoon wore on, Mrs. Tsai detected that Yishan and I needed more time, and she invited us to stay for dinner.

Yishan and I did not want Mrs. Tsai to go through the inconvenience of cooking for us, but she insisted on it and immediately began to prepare dinner. I could tell she really wanted her sister-in-law to convert to Christianity. She came to join our conversation sometime later and began to witness.

"At first, I thought my upcoming nurse exam in February was the most important," said Mrs. Tsai. "Now that I have accepted Jesus Christ as my Lord and Savior, I realize that believing in Jesus *is* the utmost important thing in life. I used to study five subjects for the nurse exam, but now I'm also studying a sixth subject, the Bible. Whenever I felt tired from studying the five subjects, I just picked up the Bible to read, and I would feel energized."

Mrs. Tsai's testimony gave us an opportunity to urge the senior Mrs. Tsai to accept Jesus, but she said, "This is the first time I attended a church service and heard about Jesus. I think what you have said is good. But I need time to know more and think."

Well, this was another unscheduled visit and not enough preparatory time was spent on prayers. Obviously, the soil was not loosened beforehand, and so the gospel seed could not sprout quickly. Yet Yishan and I rejoiced to see in Mrs. Tsai the power of the Holy Spirit changing her life. Years later we heard that she moved and went to another church where she was elected to be a deacon and led many people to Christ.

The best example of how the Holy Spirit was working in that Taiwanese church was perhaps what happened to Mr. and Mrs. Sun (name changed), who were at the brink of a divorce. Sometime after the Taiwanese church started, coworkers tried to invite Mrs. Sun to church. Actually, Mr. Sun had been attending the worship services. It was Mrs. Sun who refused to come. Yishan and I soon found out why. One Sunday afternoon they arranged for me and Yishan to visit that couple, and the rest of them stayed at church to pray for us.

When we arrived at their home, Mr. Sun introduced us to his wife, and we exchanged greetings. Then pretty soon Mrs. Sun began to tell how she had suffered in her marriage. First, she had an interfering mother-in-law. Then her husband left for another country to study, leaving her alone to take care of their daughter in Taiwan a number of years. Later on she joined her husband in that other country, and then they immigrated to the United States. Later they had another child, a son, but instead of improving, their marriage began to deteriorate. They quarreled often, and one time Mr. Sun was so angry that he slapped her and tried to choke her. She thought she had had enough, and she began seeking an attorney for divorce. That was when Yishan and I were told about them.

Yishan and I sat there and watched them bicker, not knowing

what to do. I actually felt embarrassed watching a pair of almost total strangers quarreling. I prayed inwardly, and I was sure Yishan did too, asking for words to say. I remember I began to witness how some years back Yishan and I were at a low point of our marriage and how I was contemplating suicide. I assured them there was hope in Jesus. We told them that their marriage might not improve right away, but there was always the chance it could if both of them were willing to try trusting in Jesus for help.

Eventually, Mrs. Sun said she was willing to follow Yishan in praying to receive Jesus as her Lord and Savior. Before the prayer began, however, I interrupted. "Mrs. Sun," I said. "I need to let you know that your decision to accept Jesus must be sincere. Don't do that just because we are asking you to and you feel obligated. It won't work if you're not praying out of a genuine heart."

Mrs. Sun said she really wanted it. Then Yishan began leading her in praying to receive Jesus as her Lord and Savior. When that was over, I gave a prayer of thanks and asked the Lord to manifest His power in this couple's life so that their marriage could be improved.

After I finished my prayer, Yishan addressed Mrs. Sun again, "Congratulations. You are a Christian now."

Well, before long, Mrs. Sun began to complain about her husband again, and of course, Mr. Sun responded quickly in defense of himself. Again, almost an embarrassing situation was in front of us.

This time Yishan was quick to act like a referee. "Well," he said. "your marriage has been full of unhappiness, and it's not going to improve overnight. Now that Mrs. Sun has accepted Jesus and both of you are Christians, it's important that you ask Jesus to help you. I'd recommend that you read the Bible every day, and whenever possible, the two of you can pray together."

In the end, both of them promised that they would try, and we headed for home.

Shortly after we were home, the phone rang. On the other end of the line was Mrs. Lee, the woman who had called me months earlier after she read my article and had eventually gotten the Taiwanese church started. She called to ask about the result of our visitation. I told her that Mrs. Sun had accepted Christ. "Praise the Lord!" Mrs. Lee was excited and hung up.

A few minutes later, however, Mrs. Lee called back. "Are you sure that Mrs. Sun has truly accepted Jesus?" asked the eager caller. "When I called to congratulate her over the phone, she immediately began to broadcast her husband's faults. She has not changed at all. I wonder if she has truly trusted in Jesus."

"I don't know if Mrs. Sun has truly accepted Jesus or not. Only God knows that. But I *did* tell her that her prayer had to be genuine in order for it to work." I continued, "Well, she has accepted Christ only a short while ago. Did your own life change right away after you believed in Jesus? Give her time for God to work in her life."

A few days later, Yishan called Mrs. Sun during his lunch hour to check if she was reading the Bible and praying daily. She was. He also used the opportunity to answer her questions about the Bible and to encourage her in continuing her spiritual pursuit. He told me that he called her almost weekly.

About a month or two later while at church, Mrs. Lee happened to stand next to me. She took a look at Mrs. Sun and commented, "This lady surely looks much younger and prettier now."

I totally agreed to that. Whereas Mrs. Sun was full of bitterness and hated her husband before, she was now happier and naturally looked younger. Almost every time Yishan called her, Yishan informed me, she would thank him for having helped her and her husband. One day she told Yishan over the phone, "Last Sunday it snowed, and I got up very early to shovel the snow. I did that so that my husband did not have to get up so early before going to church. I even made his favorite breakfast, whereas I would not do that before. I then waited for the last minute to wake him up. After he ate breakfast, our whole family then went to church."

Of course, Yishan said that every time Mrs. Sun thanked him, he would always say, "Don't thank me. Thank God."

And she would always reply, "Yes, I thank God, but I also need to thank man."

And Mrs. Sun was not the only person to thank Yishan. Her

husband also told Yishan, "Thank you for helping me and my wife. Our family is much happier now."

Praise the Lord! Surely, the Suns' lives had been turned around, and it was a very good example of how the Holy Spirit was working in that new Taiwanese church. Yishan and I were excited and almost felt like seeing the early church in the book of Acts. The early disciples obeyed the Lord's command and loved one another. The Bible says, "And the Lord added to the church daily such as should be saved" (Acts 2:47). We saw that happening in that new Taiwanese church. Wow! The Lord is to be praised. He is still working miracles today.

Chapter 13

Callings and Training

In chapter 7, I told of how I experienced my first miraculous healing and heard the Lord say, "Compose music. Compose music." Shortly after that, I began to think about entering a Christian college to study the Bible and music. However, Yishan was not enthusiastic about that at all. In fact, I could tell he was trying to stop me from receiving Christian seminary training at all cost. Almost every excuse he gave when opposing me was obviously unreasonable. Years later after he became a pastor, he admitted in one of his own sermons that he was at that time objecting to my receiving training with pretexts.

Earlier in the spring of 1974, our church began a monthly fellowship meeting for women, and I was invited. During the first meeting as we were electing officers, I talked about how we women could arrange a bazaar to raise funds for our church building project. Unexpectedly, I was elected the president of the women's fellowship, obviously as a result of my brief casual talk. Personally, though, I thought another woman, Mrs. Chou, who was a lot older than me, should have been elected.

I then asked the pastor's wife to be our speaker for the next monthly meeting. I gave her thirty minutes, but she far extended her time to forty-five minutes. That meeting was held at the home of another woman about four or five blocks (large city blocks) away from where Yishan was attending a baptismal class taught by the pastor. I had taken our car to drive to the fellowship meeting and told Yishan I would come back for him when our meeting ended. Since I had given the pastor's wife thirty minutes to talk, I was sure our meeting would end long before Yishan's class was over. I waited anxiously for the pastor's wife to end her talk, and when the meeting was over, I walked hurriedly to our car. When I got to the door on the driver's side, I was startled to find a man sitting there. It was Yishan! He angrily chided me for not picking him up at the end of the class.

Well, I had to go to Mrs. Chou and asked her to take over the president's job. She had been elected to be the devotional leader. I exchanged my position with her, and I was supposed to lead the group in devotional studies during the fellowship meetings. However, because of Yishan's hostility, I ended up not attending the fellowship half of the time.

The next spring in 1975, when the fellowship was up for another election, I was elected president again. By that time, Yishan had been baptized, became the choir director, and had been elected a deacon. It was easier for me to serve, but I felt I had failed in my devotional role the previous year. I asked to serve as devotional leader and suggested keeping Mrs. Chou as the president. Both she and the group consented. That year I served *very* faithfully in my role of leading devotions. (God actually rewarded me for keeping this role. In my preparation for leading the devotions, the Holy Spirit opened up my eyes to the hidden treasures in His Word. I was the one who gained most from these preparations.) It was not until the following year, 1976, when I was elected president the third time that I did finally serve in that position.

I have told this story to illustrate how hard if not impossible it was for me to serve the church in any role at all before Yishan himself was involved in church service. (Singing in the choir was the only exception.)

Eventually, I received a total of seven callings from the Lord before I was able to stand up and say yes to the Lord. Seven is the perfect number, and of course, we know that God is perfect, and I really do not know if God wants me to see He is the perfect God so that He called me seven times, but I do know He stopped calling me after I made up my mind to stand up in public to show my determination in serving Him when he called me the seventh time. I was so ignorant in understanding His calling that He had to again and again call me until I fully understood it and responded properly. At least I understand Him to be the perfectly patient God in dealing with a very ignorant child.

Let me tell the sixth calling here since it was very significant to me. It was the summer of the American bicentennial year, 1976. Our family of four visited several national parks during our two-week vacation. On the night of June 17, we stayed at a cabin in Grand Canyon National Park. Around 1:00 a.m., I woke up from a dream, crying. When Yishan was awakened by my crying and asked me about it, I refused to tell him.

In this dream I was saddened by an affair Yishan had with another woman in the church. *Then* in the dream Yishan began to spread a rumor that *I* had had an affair. And the worst of all was that everybody in the church believed in him and nobody believed in me—that is, nobody except Mr. and Mrs. Hall, who of course did not belong in that church. Instead in the dream I felt they represented God, who was the only one who understood me. They stood in the distance, watching me with eyes full of compassion.

At that point I began to cry and woke up Yishan and Leslie. I told Leslie to go back to sleep, and she did. I refused to tell Yishan about the dream and continued to shed tears, so sad from the dream. After a little while Yishan went back to sleep, but I lay there a long time, tears still in my eyes. Suddenly, words came and startled me. "Only one life, which will come to pass, but in Christ it shall last."

Even to this day I still remember those words and feel the sadness of that dream.

As those words came, I began to contemplate in my heart. "One day if the dream should become a reality, what am I to do? If the one whom I love so much betrays me, what do I have to live for?"

Those words I heard after the dream really got to my heart. I thought then, *Jesus is the only one I should love and serve. I want to devote my life to serve Him.*

When I recorded that dream in my journal, I wrote down these words (in Chinese): "In the dream Mr. and Mrs. Hall seemed to represent Christ. Only they (i.e., only Christ) truly understand me, the only true friend for me when everyone else left. Thank God for having shown to me while I'm still young that Jesus is the only hope that will never change. He is the only one I should live for."

Despite my firm decision to give my life to serve the Lord, I had never stood up in the public at any meeting in answer to a call. Since I never told Yishan of all these callings from the Lord, he had no knowledge of my decision and thereby continued to misunderstand why I spent the whole day around the house doing nothing. So my uphill battle continued as described in an earlier chapter.

By the summer of the following year (1977), the Bible study that began at our home had turned into a church. Once the church started, Yishan again was pushed to the forefront of the worship service, and I assumed the supportive role instead of being the leader of the Bible study as before.

During the Thanksgiving weekend of that year, we had a three-day retreat at Lake Geneva, Wisconsin. To me it was a weekend to be remembered. The singing, the messages, and a special presentation together all served to fan the flames that were already burning in my heart. At the end of that special presentation, the main speaker had us bow our heads and close our eyes, and then he gave a call for those willing to give their lives to serve the Lord to stand up.

A sister and a brother responded to the call and stood up. I knew this from the words of the speaker who was waiting for others to respond. Again, for the seventh time, I felt the Lord was calling me, and I hesitated at first. I really lacked the courage to stand up. I struggled for a while and reasoned within myself, "Perhaps it was my lack of resolution to stand for the Lord in public that made me so weak in my daily life." I then made up my mind and stood up.

Too late. By that time the speaker had said, "Let's pray." Obviously, he did not see me stand up.

Someone else did, however. It was Yishan. He peeked while the rest of us had our eyes closed. From then on, I had a more difficult time at home. If I should have any disagreement with him or if I did something to displease him, he would shame me with these words, "You who stood up to give your life to the Lord."

It hurt me greatly. Yet his words were very effective in silencing me. As I look back now, I know the Lord was using all that as part of the process of purifying me.

It was not until Yishan began to receive his own calls from the Lord that he stopped saying those words to me.

One day around 1977–78, two pastors unexpectedly came to visit us. The elderly pastor that I invited once to our Bible study brought another Chinese pastor who had a church in Columbus, Ohio. By that time Yishan had already had his first charismatic experience of ecstatic utterance. Both of us exchanged very good sharing with the two pastors.

Before our visitors left, the elderly pastor suggested that we pray together. The three men stood in our living room, and I alone knelt by their feet on the carpeted floor while praying. As usual, I was soon touched by the Spirit and was in tears.

When the elderly pastor prayed, he surprised us in the middle of his prayer by saying, "Brother Lin, the Lord wants to use you. He wants you to dedicate your life to serve Him."

That time Yishan considered the elderly pastor was "talking nonsense." However, it was indeed one of the Lord's callings to Yishan, but in the beginning neither of us recognized it. Yishan was, as he himself had said repeatedly, "dull in feelings," and for quite a while, the Lord seemed to have a hard time getting His message across to Yishan.

The Lord, of course, is mighty in power, and nothing is impossible for him. For years Yishan had a stony heart and refused to acknowledge Jesus Christ as his Lord and Savior. Once he did, the Lord began to show His lordship in Yishan's life. Twice this was manifested most clearly to Yishan as I have described when both times he was moved into tears uncontrollably. Then the Lord began to call Yishan to preach and eventually into full-time Christian ministry.

I'm not going to describe every detail of all the instances in which the Lord spoke to Yishan. However, I'll mention the two or three times when He did make His callings clear to Yishan.

In chapter 10, I mentioned how the Lord led us away from the Chinese (NW) church that started as Bible study at my home. Eleven months later the Lord led us back to that church. During that eleven-month period, we went to a Baptist church for five months and then to an Evangelical Free Church for six months. Later when I published *Fish and Loaves*, I included in the first issue an article titled "A Wilderness Trip" describing our experience during that period. It was a period the Lord greatly manifested His presence with us just as He did with the Israelites during their forty years in the wilderness.

Since Yishan did not feel comfortable discussing Bible in English, we did not join much fellowship except in adult Sunday school and Sunday evening prayer/Bible study. He was not as active in those two churches as he used to be in the Chinese church. As a result, he had more leisure time and spent a lot of that in reading the Chinese Bible.

During his Bible reading in that period, he found a lot of connections among different Bible passages. The more he read the Bible, the more interested he was, and the Bible became alive to him. Of all the years of his studying the Bible, he told me, this was the period when he learned the most, even more than what he later received in the seminary. I compared this period of his life to the forty years Moses spent in the Median desert as a shepherd. It was the Lord Himself who taught Yishan and prepared him to preach even before he began formal seminary training.

Sometime during that eleven-month period we received a letter from a pastor in Taiwan. In it, he inquired about the situation of the Chinese church we had left behind. To that question Yishan replied, "We have heard that every sheep in church is spiritually undernourished."

The next day on his bus ride to work, Yishan took the finished letter out of his briefcase and read it one more time. When he came to that previously mentioned sentence, he experienced uncontrollable tears again. For ten minutes his tears came out freely, and he wondered, *Why? How come reading that sentence would bring me tears? The malnutrition of the flock is the responsibility of the pastor. What does it have to do with me?*

Perplexed, he read that letter a second time, and coming to that sentence, the same phenomenon occurred. Suddenly, it dawned on him that the Lord was calling him to shepherd the flock as he recalled something similar he had read in a story. In that story a certain pastor had uncontrollable tears while reading a news story involving some youth gang members in New York and the Lord used that to call that pastor to preach to many gang members and saved quite a lot of them.

Yishan's reaction to this calling? He said to the Lord, "Lord, I'm not suitable to be a shepherd. Please call someone else." Up to that time, he had heard a number of stories how pastors and their families had suffered insufficient financial support among church members. He had concluded only fools would turn into preachers, and he was not going to be one of them.

Shortly after the eleven-month period when the Lord led us back to the Chinese church, Yishan had a tremendously clear and meaningful dream. In the dream he saw himself standing in a living room with a sister from the church standing on the other side. Yishan considered that sister very spiritual, but in the dream she said to him, "Our pastor is incapable of shepherding our church, and I'm at the brink of spiritual bankruptcy."

As soon as Yishan heard her confession, he replied, "Since our pastor is incapable, let me do the shepherding."

At that point Yishan woke up from the dream, and according to his own writing, his heart was thumping wildly. He prayed and asked for God's forgiveness, "Lord, how could I shepherd the church? Please forgive me for being so proud in the dream. You know I'm not interested in becoming a pastor."

Another time he read Colossians 4:2–4. The Lord used that passage to impress Yishan, and he began to ask God to open the door

129

for him to preach. But almost always he would add, "Lord, I still do not want to be a preacher."

It was during that time my publication, *Fish and Loaves*, came out, and invitations began to come for Yishan to preach. It eventually launched Yishan's role in monthly preaching for eleven months in the Taiwanese church as mentioned in chapter 7.

For years I had wanted to receive Bible training, and Yishan kept standing in the way. I wanted to go to Moody in downtown Chicago, but in Yishan's eyes it was a forbidden place—too far and too dangerous. I kept pleading with the Lord, and He answered my prayers by moving Moody nearer to us. A new extension of evening school in the northwestern suburbs about a twenty-five-minute drive from our home opened up.

I suggested to Yishan that both of us take classes there. He replied, "Unless God speaks to me through three people in seven days, I do not think He wants me to take seminary classes."

I felt exasperated and said, "You're really challenging God to do the impossible."

That exchange between us occurred on a Friday evening. Two days later on Sunday, we went to church. Once inside the church, Yishan met a retired pastor from Malaysia who was regularly attending the church along with his wife. Upon seeing Yishan, that retired pastor said to him, "Brother Lin, I think you should take seminary classes."

When the worship service was over, Yishan left that room and was walking down the hallway where he saw the wife of that retired pastor. Not knowing what her husband had said to Yishan before the worship service, she also said, "Brother Lin, I think you should take seminary classes."

At home later that evening, Yishan told me what had transpired at church. I commented, "See? I've told you God wants you to receive seminary training."

Immediately, he retorted, "Don't rejoice too soon. Only two people have spoken to me. I still need to hear a third person for the confirmation of God's will."

It was only after Yishan went home to be with the Lord that I realized Yishan was a man typical of most males in those days. He was not willing to show weakness in front of his wife, and it was not easy for him to concede to me. This realization brought me back vividly to an incident that took place six days after our odyssey to the American churches began.

This incident was recorded in my journal. The date was April 26, 1980. On that Saturday evening, I invited three charismatic American friends to our home for dinner. I served them some sumptuous Chinese food I cooked. After dinner we had an unplanned prayer meeting. During the prayer one of my guests had me sit on a chair, and the rest of the company (the three guests plus Yishan) laid their hands on me and prayed for me to receive the gift of speaking in tongue.

Since all the three guests were charismatic, they immediately began praying in tongues. Although Yishan had had that experience of ecstatic utterance two nights before Corrie was born, he had not since had that experience again. So he and I both prayed in Chinese.

However, that evening's meeting turned out to be another manifestation of God's sovereignty in our lives. Instead of my receiving that specified gift, Yishan had another experience similar to what had happened before Corrie's birth. It stunned all my three guests.

I was not surprised at all, but this second occurrence of Yishan unexpectedly receiving such a peculiar gift led me to think that maybe the Lord had a special will in Yishan's life. Thus, I wrote down these words in my journal as a conclusion of recording that special event. "If God is going to call Yishan to be a preacher, I'm willing to offer him for the Lord's use. However, my dedication of Yishan may not count, for I cannot decide for him. May the Lord's will be done."

Surprisingly, Yishan was very curious about my journal, and one afternoon I found him reading it without my permission. I never kept my journal a secret. I left it in one of the storage areas of the living room tables, and everyone in our house had free access to it. However, I expected anyone wanting to read my journal would ask for my permission first. I was upset with what Yishan was doing, and I yanked the journal out of his hand.

It was too late. He had read my entry, and he began to laugh at me. "Ha, I'm still not sure of God's will, and you have already dedicated me! I think you are just interested in being a pastor's wife."

As sinners, both of us had our share of sneaky acts, and I soon forgave him. But his words again stung me for some time. Of course, the Lord vindicated me when my assumption of the Lord's calling for Yishan became a reality.

As I look back now, I think possibly Yishan was being cautious and did not want to plunge ahead into a vocation he considered to be foolish. That was why he was not willing to concede that indeed the Lord was calling him.

Now let me get back to that Sunday evening when Yishan still doubted if the Lord had truly spoken to him through that retired pastor and his wife. I was a little annoyed at his remarks and commented, "You're really stone-hearted. You have to wait for the end of the full week to find out God's will!" I really thought he was giving God a hard time.

Of course, nothing is too hard for our God. At the end of that week on the seventh day, Friday, while Yishan was secretly rejoicing that he was finally off the hook, a letter arrived from Taiwan from the pastor who had written earlier. In the letter its author casually wrote these words, "By the way, Brother Lin, I think you should take seminary classes."

By then Yishan knew he had no escape and had no more excuses to oppose my receiving Bible training. One evening each week, we attended classes together. It went on for five years for Yishan and one more semester for me.

During my time of waiting for the Lord's answer, I had taken a course in the local adult education class, an easy shorthand course. Thus, I was able to take good notes when I entered Moody evening school as well as Moody summer school (one summer only) on the main downtown campus. Yishan, however, took very few notes during class. He mostly just listened and reviewed my notes later on.

Those evenings when we went to classes together were always very enjoyable to me, and they went by very quickly.

Because of his language limitation, Yishan did not take in so much as I did from those classes. I'm very thankful that I had been an English major in college. I'm also amazed at how the Lord had led me to major in *Teaching English as a Second Language* rather than in music as I was originally interested in. *If* I had majored in music, I would have been *limited* in my capacity for serving the Lord. I would have been able to serve only in the area of music. As it turned out, I was able to continue singing in the choir for many years as well as sing solos on many occasions, but more importantly, I was also able to preach in Chinese, English, and sometimes in Taiwanese. And I was also able to do side-by-side sermon translation for many years for Yishan and other speakers.

Although Yishan was limited in his English ability, he made it up by reviewing my notes and reading the Bible diligently. Once he encountered a problem in a test given by a professor. The answer to the question is to give the names of the two spies who had faith in God in entering the land of Canaan. The two names are, of course, Caleb and Joshua. At that time Yishan did not know the name of Caleb in English, so he wrote down the Chinese name in the test for answer. When the professor handed the tests back to us, he told Yishan, "I took your paper to a Chinese student on campus, and he said the answer was correct. So I am giving you credit for that. You're wise in doing that."

The week after the midterm exam of our first semester at Moody evening school, someone (in the class on Genesis) asked the professor how many got A's. He said he graded on curves, and there was one or two A's. (Later I was told by a classmate there was actually only one A.) When I heard that, my heart sank. Surely, I could not have got an A, and yet how much I wanted to have an A! When I was in grade school, except for the first semester in the fifth grade after our family moved to Taipei, I was always on top of the class and even the best of the whole school. When I entered Taiwan Normal University, I found that I had the top score of the university from the lists announced in the newspapers. (In order to enter a college/university, in those days you had to pass a very tough entrance exam for all colleges/ universities in Taiwan. Every student had to take the exam, with no exception. When the official lists of students accepted into each college/university were announced in the newspapers, they listed the top and the bottom scores of each department in three groups— science majors in the first group, liberal arts and business/law schools major in the second group, and biology and medicine schools in the third group—and I found my scores to be the top score of all three groups for that university. We had to take tests for six subjects, and the test scores were added up to decide each student's eligibility.)

Toward the end of that Genesis class, the professor began to hand out the midterm exam papers. Yishan and I were the only students left in class by the time we received ours since ours were the last ones to be handed back. The professor said to Yishan, "Your family is doing very well."

I looked at my paper. I had an "A." I was relieved, but I felt incredulous. Except for that shorthand class I took in adult education, this was the first time in more than fifteen years that I was a student again. Yishan and I were among the older students in class. So it was natural I had been very nervous. I wanted to do well, but being a wife and a mother of three, my time for studying was rather limited. I did my best in studying, and I also prayed that the Lord would help me do well. I can only say, "Surely, the Lord has answered my prayers."

In still another class, I think the instructor was probably very impressed by Yishan and me. At first, I was not aware of that. However, one week that instructor was not able to teach the class, and he asked someone to teach in his stead. When the substitute instructor came and saw Yishan and me, he immediately blurted out, "You must be that couple they were talking about!" Who were *they*? Did he mean the other professors? To this day I still have no idea why or what those Moody professors were saying about me or Yishan.

I'm not telling these stories to brag about myself or Yishan. I'm only very thankful that the Lord gave me very pleasant experiences while I was attending Moody. More importantly, He gave me the necessary biblical and theological training during that period. I was so absorbed in the joy of learning that I did not pay much attention to the fact that Yishan was not taking in as much as I was. (He told me that fact years later.) Of course, the Lord knew that, and when the time came, He would move us to the San Francisco Bay Area where He would have further training for us, especially for Yishan's sake.

Just as the apostle Paul said to the Philippians, "He which hath begun a good work in you will perform it until the day of Jesus Christ" (Philippians 1:6), I saw that in our own lives as well. Our Lord is so patient with us that He will not stop polishing us while we are doing His work. He will keep doing that until we see Him. At least I know the Lord will keep polishing me "until the day of Jesus Christ." He really should be praised!

Chapter 14

The Cedar Church

In an earlier chapter, I talked about how the Lord used Yishan and me to help start a Taiwanese church. Toward the end of that eleven-month period, the Lord began to speak to Yishan through Genesis 31:2–3, which says, "And Jacob beheld the countenance of Laban, it was not toward him as before. And the Lord said unto Jacob, 'Return unto the land of thy fathers, and to thy kindred, and I will be with thee.'"

Yishan understood that the Lord was saying to him, "It is time to leave the Taiwanese church. Go back to Schaumburg, and start a new church."

At that time I happened to hear of a Chinese language school meeting on Sundays in our local high school. A lot of the parents just gathered there with nothing to do while waiting for their children. The person who told me of this said that she wished somebody could bring the gospel to those parents.

When I heard that, I promised to pray about it. I passed the information onto Yishan, and some words kept ringing in his head, "Chinese school meets on Sunday. Chinese school meets on Sunday."

Yishan was convinced that the Lord wanted him to start a Chinese church right there in that high school.

"Will you be able to preach every Sunday?" I asked Yishan. He was still working as a microbiologist. I wondered if he would be able to shoulder the responsibility of a new church all by himself.

"Of course not. I need your help."

That was how the Cedar church started its first Sunday worship service on October 16, 1982, with Yishan preaching the first sermon and me teaching adult Sunday school while Angela played the piano and Leslie took care of the children. From then on, Yishan and I exchanged our roles every Sunday, and our two daughters rotated theirs as well. This continued for probably two years until Yishan was capable of preaching more frequently each month, and then I taught children's Sunday school whenever I did not have to preach.

A year later we found a Baptist church not too far from the high school, and we moved our meetings to that church.

Not too long after the new church started, one Sunday somebody brought a sixty-two-year-old Mr. Wang to church. He had retired from the army while in Taiwan and had newly immigrated to the United States to join his eldest daughter. The latter held two jobs and was working almost 24-7. Yishan visited him at his daughter's home that very afternoon, and he prayed to accept Jesus after hearing the way of salvation.

Mr. Wang told Yishan that his wife had passed away, and here in the States, he felt lonely since his daughter was rarely home. His house in Taiwan was situated near a cemetery, and while living there, he quite frequently experienced demonic oppression at night. Usually, when he was falling asleep, he would feel something furry creeping up his legs and body until he felt choked. He had come to the United States in the hopes that he would be able to get away from the demonic oppression.

However, the demon had followed him to the United States. He experienced the same kind of oppression again at night. Yishan told him to pray in the name of Jesus to cast it away when it happened again. Well, the first time it occurred after that, Mr. Wang was not prepared. By the time the furry thing crept to his throat, it was too late when he remembered Yishan's words. He felt choked and had a hard time opening his mouth. When he was finally able to utter the words, "In the name of Lord Jesus," the furry thing instantly fled. Another night when he felt the furry thing creeping up his feet, he was prepared and quickly said, "In the name of Lord Jesus, I cast you away." Immediately, the furry thing left and never came back to bother him again.

Naturally, when we held our first baptismal service, Mr. Wang gladly received baptism along with eight or nine other men and women only a little more than a month after the Cedar church started.

Sometime later we were told of an elderly couple who were both Christians but did not attend church. They had friends who came to play mah-jongg with them on Sundays. Was mah-jongg more important than Jesus to them?

When Yishan and I heard that, we began to pray that the Lord would break up the mah-jongg party so that this elderly couple could come to worship with us.

Sure enough, a few months later, we heard that one of the mah-jongg players moved away, and with only three left, they stopped playing the game.

Yishan then called to invite that elderly couple to church, and they consented. However, they needed transportation, and we began to pick them up. We had two cars, so Yishan and I each drove one. The following week their two grandchildren also came. It was a first-time church experience for them. These two children never stopped attending church all those years we were in Schaumburg. In fact, both of them were baptized a few years later.

The two elderly people were in their early eighties and late seventies respectively. The first Sunday they came to church, I saw that old man walking with a cane, taking difficult steps. However, with time he seemed to improve, and a few months later, he forgot about that cane and went home without it. That day someone else happened to take them home. If Yishan or I had taken them home, we would have helped that old man remember to take that cane, and this probably would not have occurred. God surely had His own way of working things out for those who love Him. Anyway, after that old man got home, he realized he had left his cane behind and immediately called the church. Fortunately, Yishan and I were still at church. After Yishan answered that call, he went to the place where that old man had left his cane. Yes, the cane was there. We took that cane home for him. From that day on, that old man did not need that walking stick again. This was one of the wonderful things we saw the Lord working in the Cedar church.

As I have mentioned, we had adult Sunday school from day one of the Cedar church. One of those who attended that first class was a seventy-year-old woman. After attending the Sunday school for some time, she said during the class one Sunday, "I have been a Christian over thirty years, but now I realize that I am only a babe in the Lord. And not only that, I'm actually undernourished spiritually."

As one might expect, this woman's husband was still not a Christian, but he was also one of the attendants on the first Sunday. As his wife began to grow in the Lord, he also began to feel the conviction of the Holy Spirit. He accepted Jesus as his Lord and Savior, but he was hesitant about receiving baptism when Yishan approached him. Why the hesitation? He had been a smoker for the better part of his life. Now with his newfound faith, he wanted to kick the smoking habit before receiving baptism so as to prove his faith. Although Yishan told him it was okay to receive baptism first, he would not be persuaded otherwise. So Yishan and I prayed diligently for this man (who was in his midseventies) to be delivered from the bondage of cigarette smoking. The Lord granted this wish, and within a month this man was able to stop smoking without any pain. Needless to say, he was among those to receive the first baptism of the Cedar church.

Can you guess why this man and his wife attended our first worship service in the local high school? It so happened that this elderly couple lived with their daughter and her husband. While their two young granddaughters attended the Chinese language school, this elderly couple stayed with other parents who waited there. It was really the Lord's good will to raise the Cedar church right there in the high school. Not only did this elderly man get saved and kick his smoking habit, but their daughter and the two granddaughters also began attending church a year later when we moved to the Baptist church since we also moved the worship time to Sunday afternoons.

Thus, they were able to come after the Chinese language school was over. Still some time later, their daughter also put her trust in Jesus Christ and was baptized. Their son-in-law also began attending church, and in the end *he* was also saved and later on became a steadfast believer. In the end, the whole family was saved.

A pair of sisters also joined our worship on the first day. To introduce this pair of sisters, I need to backtrack to the time about a year and half earlier when the Lord told me and Yishan to leave the Evangelical Free Church and to go back to the NW church that had begun as a Bible study at my home. When we went back to that church, it had been eleven months since we left, and we saw many new faces there. This pair of sisters, one married and the other divorced, was among them. Both were believers, and they lived together. I'll call the older sister Amy.

Around that time the Lord showed Yishan five different ways of reading the book of Galatians. Yishan was so excited from this new gift that he was eagerly looking around for people to share. During his lunch hour at work each day, he called five or six people. One of those who showed interest in Yishan's sharing was Amy.

Amy said she had been a Christian almost twenty years, but she still did not understand the Bible. So Yishan and I visited her and her sister at her home and led them in weekly Bible studies. Before we began that first meeting, Yishan suggested that each of us take turns to pray. Amy said, "I can pray only silently. I'm not good at praying out loud."

To that Yishan replied, "Now it's a good chance for you to practice praying out loud."

The moment Amy opened up her mouth to pray, she began to cry and continued to do so as she prayed intermittently, asking God to forgive her sins. She prayed for quite a while, and her life was transformed from then on. The Bible became meaningful to her, and she began to spend time each day in Bible reading. One evening she confessed to us during our sharing, "I'm hot-tempered, but my husband is actually very nice. It's only lately I began to realize I've been taking advantage of him over the decade we have been married.

My husband is working two jobs in order to support our family. Now that I realize how hard he has to work, I have changed my attitude toward him. I'm much nicer to him now."

One evening our discussion went on longer during Bible study, and it took longer to answer those questions. Anyway, when we were ready to leave, Amy's husband came home from his second job. Yishan apologized for staying so late and for any disturbance to him.

"No problem," said Amy's husband, smiling. "As long as it pleases my wife, it doesn't matter how late you stay for Bible study."

Since Amy was pretty much a baby believer when we started leading her and her sister in Bible study, her husband was still not saved, and up till then he had never been to a church. But a year or two later, he began attending Sunday worship at the Cedar church, and after some time (probably two or three years), he was baptized in the name of Jesus Christ.

It was during the next few months after we began Bible study with Amy and her sister that Yishan and I came in contact with a group of Taiwanese Christians and very soon started the Taiwanese church (see chapter 12). However, we continued our weekly Bible study with Amy and her sister while carrying on our ministry with the Taiwanese Christians. Amy wanted to follow us along to the Taiwanese church, but Yishan told her no. Since both she and her sister understood very little Taiwanese, it would not profit her to be present there. Plus we considered it too far for them to drive. Instead Yishan encouraged them to stay on in the NW church, and they did; however, we continued the Bible study with them every Friday night.

Eleven months later when the Lord gave us the burden to start the Cedar church, Yishan and I shared the news with Amy and her sister, and immediately, she wanted to come to the church.

By that time the pastor of the NW church had left that church and started a new church in a nearby town. His wife was working at the same place where Amy worked. Amy had followed that pastor to his new church, not that she really wanted to go there. Rather his wife's tears had stirred up Amy's pity, and she felt obliged to go with them.

However, Amy repeatedly told me and Yishan that she was not

receiving spiritual nourishment at that church. That was why she wanted to go with us to the Taiwanese church in the first place. Now that we were starting a brand-new church, she wanted to come.

Amy and her sister came to the very first worship service of the Cedar church, primarily to take part in an inaugural service. On the second Sunday, however, Yishan told her to go back to the other church where the pastor's wife was her colleague at work. She did, but she felt miserable. Her own senses told her the Cedar was the church where she could get spiritually fed, yet her sentiment was disturbed every time that pastor's wife implored her with tears.

Amy kept pleading with Yishan to let her come to our church. "Just tell me yes," Amy was almost begging Yishan, "and I'll come to your church immediately."

"No," Yishan said seriously, "I don't want to decide it for you. I want you to pray earnestly and ask God to guide you."

The problem with Amy was, according to her own words, no matter how hard she prayed, she just did not know what God's will was. But I assured her, "If you pray hard enough, God will make His will clear to you."

So one Friday evening, as we were told later, Amy made up her mind to go to her colleague's church one more time, and then she would come to the Cedar church every Sunday.

The Sunday following that Friday, Amy asked her husband to write a check for her colleague's church, and then she left home. As she drove to a stop sign, she stopped as usual, but what happened next completely caught her by surprise. Her steering wheel seemed to have a mind of its own that morning. Instead of going straight after the stop, the car made a left turn, the direction for the Cedar church.

It's weird, Amy thought, *but that's okay. At the next stop, I'll make a right turn, and then I'll still go to my colleague's church.*

At the next stop, however, to her surprise, the wheel would not make a right turn. It went forward instead toward the direction of the Cedar church.

At that moment Amy understood perfectly God's will. Not only was she very happy, but we rejoiced as well when she told us this story later that morning. It was the Lord who brought Amy to the Cedar church, not through any human manipulation but because of God's own direct guidance. A seeking heart will surely find out God's will!

That morning Amy experienced some extra wonderful working of the Lord as well. As she sat there singing the hymn "My God, How Wonderful Thou Art," Amy told us when the service was over, she heard to her left some beautiful voice singing loudly.

Our congregating was still very small at that time, not even twenty. As usual, I was sitting on the right side. To Amy's left were a few elderly ladies whose singing was quite feeble. Since I still had a strong singing voice at that time, my singing could usually be heard over the rest of the congregation.

"It was *not* your voice," Amy told me when she was sharing this story. "Nevertheless, it was so beautiful that I was very touched and my tears came out."

I'm sure an angel choir or just one angel was singing with our small congregation that morning to celebrate the wonderful thing God had just done, leading one wayward sheep back to the fold. And quite consequentially, "My God, How Wonderful Thou Art" has remained one of my favorite hymns. Even to this day, almost every time I sang this hymn, I would be brought to tears. I cannot help but be touched whenever I think how wonderful our God really is.

More than a year later, sometime after we moved to the Baptist church, Amy began bringing her eldest daughter to church as well, not just her two younger children. Her daughter was a sixth-grader, but it was a first-time church experience for her.

By that time we had more than one Sunday school class for children, and I was teaching the oldest class, one that included a fifth-grader, a sixth-grader (Amy's daughter), and a few high-schoolers, including my two older daughters.

When Amy's daughter sat in my class that first Sunday, she showed no smile whatsoever. In fact, you could see anger and unwillingness written all over her face. Since the other children were mostly familiar with the Bible, Amy's daughter being the only exception, I began teaching Genesis 1:1, telling them it was God who created the universe, which was contrary to what was taught in school about evolution.

From that day on, I prayed very hard each day for Amy's daughter, asking the Holy Spirit to work in her life. Gradually, I saw her hostility lessened, and two or three Sundays later, smiles even crept up on her face. And if my memory was not wrong, I think she was baptized a few years later. Praise the Lord! He never disappoints us.

At Cedar church's picnic

Remember the sixty-two-year-old Mr. Wang? Soon after coming to the Cedar church, he also joined our Friday night Bible study. Each Friday it rotated to different homes, and the hostess usually served refreshments after each meeting. I still remember the first Friday night Mr. Wang joined us. When the refreshments were served, he said, "No, thanks." We asked him why, and he answered, "I have a weak stomach. I cannot eat sweet stuff." However, as months went by, Mr. Wang's stomach seemed to get stronger. A year or two later, he could eat sweet food without any problem and was able to enjoy the refreshments with the rest of us.

Something similar had happened a few years earlier to a young man in his early thirties. When my home Bible study group became the NW church, we sent out two hundred flyers to the Chinese people in the surrounding suburbs. This young man (let me call him Jeff) came to the first worship service of the NW church in response to that flyer. Later Yishan and I invited him to our home for dinner. I still remember one of the dishes I cooked for that dinner was rice noodles. However, I was surprised and felt sorry when he said he could not eat rice noodles because he had a stomach problem.

As Jeff continued to attend Sunday worship services and Friday night Bible studies, His health seemed to improve and a year (if not months) later, he could eat rice noodles!

In both cases of Jeff and Mr. Wang, it seemed to me there was a correlation between the spiritual and the physical realms. When one comes to Jesus Christ and receives the spiritual nourishment, it often seems that the Lord heals that person both physically as well as spiritually. With that elderly man who forgot his walking stick, I believe the same principle was also at work.

Each of our Friday night Bible studies began with hymn singing followed by prayers. Pretty soon Mr. Wang asked us to pray for his two unmarried daughters, who were staying in Taiwan in order to sell their house there. His prayer requests included selling his house, facilitating the immigration process of these two daughters, and them finding their salvation in the Lord.

Week after week we prayed for Mr. Wang's house to be sold for a good price. We asked the Lord to bring his two daughters to our church to be saved. Eventually, the Lord answered all these requests. I'll always remember how the elder daughter was saved. (This was actually Mr. Wang's third daughter since his second daughter was married and stayed in Taiwan. His eldest daughter was the one who worked on two jobs.)

This third daughter was in her midtwenties when she came from Taiwan. Let me call her Susan. She quickly learned to drive a car within a few months, and every Sunday she was able to bring her father and her younger sister (Mr. Wang's youngest daughter) to church in her own car. Her younger sister attended high school and was able to attend church on Sunday only, but Susan came to Friday night Bible study as well as Sunday worship service.

Before long we were sharing with Susan how the Lord had answered our prayers in bringing her and her sister from Taiwan. She seemed to agree with us by saying that the housing market in Taiwan actually was very slow and prices were usually not good, but they were able to sell their house for a pretty good price.

By the time Susan and her sister arrived from Taiwan, Yishan had been leading a fellowship meeting for the elderly every Wednesday evening at Mr. Wang's place since his eldest daughter bought a large house with a spacious living room and a separate family room. We named that Wednesday evening meeting "The Palm Tree Fellowship" based on Psalm 92:12–14.

About six months after Susan had been attending meetings with us, I felt a special burden for her and said to Yishan one Wednesday evening before he left home for the Palm Tree Fellowship, "Please tell Mr. Wang and Susan that next Wednesday I'll come to their home to talk to Susan." Ever since Mr. Wang told us the names of his two daughters, Yishan and I had not stopped praying for their coming to know the Lord.

The following Wednesday I rode with Yishan to Mr. Wang's home. When Yishan conducted the fellowship meeting in the family room, I sat with Susan in the living room. I showed her from the Bible, beginning with Genesis and ending with Revelation, how God created the world for His creatures to live, how man fell and needed salvation, and how Jesus would come back to reign in the future. I went through the whole Bible with Susan, supplementing with scientific and archaeological findings as well as personal testimonies. I had never been so thorough with anyone before as far as the gospel was concerned. By the end, I believed Susan had no reason to reject the gospel. Yet when I asked her if she would like to receive Jesus as her Lord and Savior, she thought for a second and answered, "I think it is still better to worship Buddha."

I was very disappointed, to say the least, but I was not daunted. I knew Satan was holding her back, and I was not willing to lose the fight. I knew I could not force Susan to accept Jesus, but I believed God could do the impossible. When I went home, I doubled my effort of praying for Susan.

Daily I prayed for her. Three weeks later I felt a burden again, and I told Yishan, "Please call Mr. Wang and invite him and his daughters to our home for a barbecue."

The day came when Mr. Wang and his daughters arrived for the Chinese-style barbecue. When food was served, we sat in the living room and talked. Inevitably, we came to the point of asking if Susan would like to receive Jesus, and she told us quite an amazing story.

"When Mr. Lin called, I asked Dad, 'Why are Mr. and Mrs. Lin inviting us?'

"Dad said, 'The Lins are ministers. Naturally, they want you to believe in Jesus.'

"Actually, before Mr. Lin called, early that very morning, I woke up from a nightmare. First, I dreamed I was in a room where there were nine or ten coffins. Every one of those coffins had a dead body inside, and all the lids were open. I was very scared when I woke up, but I went back to sleep right away.

"Then I had another dream. I dreamed I was driving a car with the windows rolled down, and I was wearing a red cape. All of a sudden, the wind blew up my red cape, and it covered my face. I could not see where I was driving, and I began to panic. At that point I woke up and found myself very much afraid, and my heart was pounding wildly. Immediately, I prayed to Jesus, 'Jesus, if you are truly God, please give me peace, and I'll trust You to be my Lord and Savior.'

"As soon as I prayed that, I felt great peace, and then I heard some music. At first, I thought Dad had woken up and turned on the radio. So I went to his room, but he was asleep. Then I thought probably my neighbor's radio was on, but it was about three in the morning. My neighbors were all sleeping. So where did the music come from?"

I then told Susan I believed that she probably had heard the angel choir singing. Jesus said, "There is joy in the presence of the angels of God over one sinner who repents" (Luke 15:10).

Indeed, *that* sinner repented by God's grace. The Lord did show

His sovereignty and mighty power in Susan's life. He used those two dreams to save Susan. I believe that both dreams were meaningful. In the first dream, Susan said she was in a room where she saw nine or ten caskets with dead bodies inside of each. It was pretty much her spiritual condition since she had not accepted Christ, and she was in the company of the dead. In the second dream, she was wearing a red cape. I think it showed the Lord Jesus was covering her with His shed blood. He was the one to deliver Susan from the horror of eternal death.

So there in our living room, Yishan led Susan in praying to receive Jesus. But before she prayed, she confessed to me (and to everyone present there as well), "That Wednesday evening when you asked me to receive Jesus, my heart was actually convinced, but my mouth was not."

Praise the Lord! Our God is so wonderful, and His word is so true! "With men this is impossible, but with God all things are possible" (Matthew 19:26). "Things which eye has not seen and ear has not heard, and which have not entered the heart of man, all that God has prepared for those who love Him" (1 Corinthians 2:9). Truly, the Lord has done more wonderful things than what we have asked or anticipated. I really cannot stop thanking Him or praising Him.

Shortly after the Cedar church moved to the Baptist church, someone brought a Polish neighbor to join our Sunday worship, and we began translating the sermon side by side so that she could understand. After I had done the translation several months, a sister commented to me, "Your translation is very good. I can also learn English by listening to your translation."

Whenever it was my turn to preach, who would do the translation? Well, I still wrote out the sermon in Chinese. Then when I was preaching, I spoke by translating it into English, and Yishan just read my manuscript. Everybody thought that I was preaching in English and Yishan was translating my sermon into Chinese. The end result was the same.

A year later the Lord brought a couple who had moved from Indiana. The husband had a PhD and spoke very fluent English.

From then on, that brother shared the translation work, and my burden was lightened.

The Polish woman who came to the Cedar church was actually a Catholic. Let me call her Joan. Her neighbor had been taking her to a Baptist church for some time before bringing her to the Cedar church. Her neighbor told us that Joan had trusted Jesus to be her Lord and Savior.

We were also told that Joan had two daughters who were in their twenties and that both were suffering from schizophrenia. Joan had a heavy burden in her heart because of her two daughters. One or the other would often leave home in the middle of the night and wander around in the neighborhood. Many a time the police would bring the daughter home.

Yishan and I often prayed for Joan and her two daughters. Quite frequently, the Lord gave us messages that we knew would help Joan (and others) to trust God more.

Yet Joan's faith was being tested all the time, and she would have collapsed if it were not for the grace of God. One Sunday she shared with us the following story.

Late one Friday afternoon, Joan was driving home after work. The setting sun was on her face, and she felt tired from her work, especially from the burden of her two daughters. As she was driving, she thought, *Can God really be trusted? How come He did not help me? Will my two daughters ever be healed?*

At that moment Joan figured that if her daughters' situation did not improve, she would not go to church on Sunday anymore. There was no point in continuing to trust God, she reasoned.

Later that evening Joan still felt depressed when she went to bed. After she put her head to the pillow, however, she heard an audible voice saying, "Read 1 Corinthians 1:9."

Joan's neighbor had given her a Good News Bible. She got up and read that Bible. She found that verse, "God is to be trusted, the God who called you to have fellowship with His Son Jesus Christ, our Lord."

God surely knows how to give us His Word. That same verse in my NASB says, "God is faithful, through whom you were called into fellowship with His Son, Jesus Christ our Lord."

If Joan had had my NASB, I think that verse would not have meant so much to her. Yet when she was doubting whether God really could be trusted, the Lord gave her His Word so overwhelmingly straightforward. *Yes, God is to be trusted.*

Praise the Lord! Once again He gave His Word to strengthen the faith of one who needed it.

Doubtlessly, our Lord is the good and great Shepherd who knows how to lead His sheep.

When the Cedar church first began, an elderly woman in her seventies who had been a widow and had served as a devout Christian most of her life came to us. She asked me and Yishan to pray for her son. Let's call her Mrs. Chan and her son Billy.

Mrs. Chan said, "Billy has married a church elder's daughter. He and his wife go to an English-speaking Methodist church. Every Sunday they are fifteen minutes late, and he never reads his Bible. I believe his Bible is collecting dust. I'm not sure if he is born again or not. Oh, Mr. and Mrs. Lin, please pray for Billy. I don't want him to go to hell."

Yishan and I promised to pray for Billy, and we did faithfully and daily.

A week or two after we began praying for Billy, we heard that he was sick. God answered our prayers in quite an unexpected way, and ouch, it was painful. At first, they thought Billy had flu, but he continued to cough. Finally, he was found to have fungal infection in his lungs.

However, before the final diagnosis came, X-rays showed that Billy had spots in his lung, and he was really scared. At first, doctors thought he had cancer and would have to operate on him to remove it. That night Billy could not sleep, and at midnight he went to his mother's room to ask for prayers. That night, he told us later, he "covenanted with God" that he would serve God if he was healed.

Doctors had to make an eighteen-inch incision on Billy's right side through his rib cage in order to remove the cancer from the lung. When they opened him up, they found fungus, not cancer, and they immediately sewed him up. When Yishan and I later visited him in the hospital, he showed us his incision. It went diagonally from his chest to his back. Even now, I still remember Billy's beaming face when I saw him in his hospital room. Despite the big cut he'd received, he was obviously very happy.

Both Billy and his wife (I'll call her Irene) were relieved. Irene was a nurse, and she told us, "If my husband had had this illness fifteen years earlier, he would have no cure." By then medication was available to bring Billy back to health, and they both were grateful that God had spared Billy's life.

Still it was a painful process. Billy had to go through a series of treatments somewhat like chemotherapy. It would take three to six months since the strength of the dosage and the interval between treatments would have to be adjusted depending on how well Billy could tolerate each.

As it turned out, Billy's treatment lasted six months. Sometimes, according to his own words, he felt so nauseous that he could not eat much. Sometimes he would crave some special food as some women did during pregnancy, and Mrs. Chan would cook it for him.

During those six months, Yishan visited Billy each week to pray for him and read the Bible with him. Billy was very appreciative. As he recalled this experience later, he said he felt as if he had gained a brother who went through the illness with him.

Yishan and I often thanked the Lord that He was sovereign and merciful. Through that illness, not only did the Lord bring back a prodigal son, but He also made Billy a changed person. After he was recovered, his family was no longer late but always one of the first to arrive at the Cedar church. He became an important coworker, and both he and his wife pitched in as Sunday school teachers. For our Christmas celebration that year, Irene made two large trays of cookies and very tasty jellied rolls. They were both showing in their lives their thankfulness to the Lord and their willingness to serve.

Praise the Lord that He is our Shepherd. It was truly His good will to start the Cedar church. In the Cedar church as well as in the Taiwanese church, we were seeing the Lord fulfill His promise (actually a command at the time it was given) to Yishan during our *wilderness trip.*

It happened a few weeks after we went to the Evangelical Free Church. On a Saturday Yishan and I had decided to join that church, and he was going to tell an elder of our decision the next day. The next day, Sunday, when Yishan woke up, the Lord gave him words (in Chinese), "I want you [the plural *you*, not singular] to build up the Chinese church. Why do you want to join the American church?"

When I woke up later, Yishan told me this, and I asked him, "Are you sure the Lord spoke to you and it was not your own imagination?"

"I don't know."

When both of us prayed together, Yishan said, "Lord, I'm not sure if the words I heard were truly from You. We have decided to join the American church, and I'm going to talk to the elder this morning. If it's *not* your will for us to join the church, please stop it then."

Yishan did talk to the elder that morning, and he was very happy, promising to give us the church constitution that evening. Well, suffice it to say, the Lord did stop it that evening, and He did lead us back to the Chinese church months later.

So it was the Lord's will for us to help start the Taiwanese church and later the Cedar church. During those years *Fish and Loaves* was published, and Yishan and I went to classes at Moody. Both of us were happy that the Lord was using us to build up the Chinese church while Yishan was still working as a microbiologist. However, it was not the Lord's will for us to stay there forever. He is our Shepherd, and He was going to lead us away from the Cedar church.

"For my thoughts are not your thoughts, neither are your ways my ways, saith the Lord. For as the heavens are higher than the earth, so are my ways higher than your ways, and my thoughts than your thoughts. For … my word … shall accomplish that which I please" (Isaiah 55:8–11) In all the years Yishan and I served together, I saw the Lord guiding us exactly as He has promised in the Bible again and again. He indeed is faithful to His own Word and to His children as well.

Chapter 15

A Difficult Move

*I*n 1988, the Cedar church held a retreat during the Memorial Day weekend at Cedar Lake, Indiana. Rev. Hsieh, a seminary professor, was our speaker. Actually, he was the same speaker for the 1977 Thanksgiving Retreat at Lake Geneva, Wisconsin. (I mentioned that in chapter 7.)

I was the song leader at the retreat. While I was standing in the front and leading the singing, I could hear Yishan's voice, but I could not see his face. He was sitting in the back row, and his face was hidden by the high back of the sofa in front of him. During the singing I noticed that twice Yishan stopped singing for a while before I heard him again, but I did not know why.

That night when both of us returned to our room, he told me what had happened that afternoon. While he was singing heartily, words came to his head, "*You* should study theology at CW Seminary." (When Chinese people talk about receiving seminary training, they usually say "study theology.") As soon as the words came, Yishan felt greatly touched, and tears came to his eyes. However, he did not feel any sadness at all but great joy in his heart instead. The tears kept him from continuing to sing, but once the tears stopped, he resumed singing with the rest of the attendants. (The word *you* here is singular in Chinese, referencing Yishan. The other time when the Lord said to Yishan, "I want you to build up the Chinese church. Why do you want to join the American Church?" the two words *you* were both plural in Chinese, referring to me and Yishan.)

Then while he was singing heartily, the same thing happened a second time—same words, same reaction, tears and joy. Likewise he was not able to continue singing for a while.

Both of us recalled how the Lord had called Yishan to preach and the one occasion a few years back when a pastor in Taiwan wrote to Yishan and said, "Brother Lin, I think you should give up everything now to enter a seminary." At that time Yishan prayed during his lunch hour at work the day after he received that letter. He prayed, "Lord, Rev. Chang said I should enter a seminary. Should I resign from work now?"

Yishan did not hear any answer right away, but he picked up a book to read after he finished praying. Later he told me the Lord answered him through that book because there he read these words, "Wait quietly. Do not rush into things."

All those years Yishan and I waited quietly when we ministered at the Taiwanese church and then at the Cedar church while at the same time attending Moody. By 1988, Yishan and I had stopped taking classes at Moody. Yet we were still waiting for the appropriate time to resume our training again. Both of us had expected to stay in Schaumburg for the rest of our lives. The Cedar church was still not big enough to support a full-time pastor. The members of the congregation and the two of us were waiting for the time when Yishan could retire from his job and become the full-time pastor of the church.

So that evening at Cedar Lake when Yishan and I talked in our room, we knew the Lord's time had come for Yishan to quit his job. I said to him, "Now that the Lord wants you to go to that seminary, we should be obedient to Him. We'll have to move to California. Let's talk to Rev. Hsieh tomorrow at breakfast to find out more about that seminary." Rev. Hsieh had come to our retreat from Berkeley. He was then teaching at that seminary.

After we talked to Rev. Hsieh, we decided to move a year later, and we knew God had good timing for us. It was the end of May then. There was no way we could sell our house and move in three months, and it was also too late to apply for the fall entry that year. Plus, our two older daughters still had one more year of college to go, Angela at University of Illinois in Champaign-Urbana and Leslie at MIT in Cambridge, Massachusetts, and they still needed our financial support. A year later when Angela and Leslie both graduated from college, they would become financially independent. We only had to take Corrie along with us (she would enter sixth grade), and we would be able to attend the seminary without much worry. What perfect timing!

After we came home from the retreat, Yishan returned to work, but I began to worry. I thought of how all through our twenty-plus years of marriage, we had been pretty financially stable, especially after he began his job as a microbiologist. Granted, almost every year from May to September, I had to struggle because of inflation and had to dip into our savings, but almost every year I found it easier to breathe by October when Yishan's salary was raised. What would happen once Yishan quit his job and there was no more steady income? We had heard of stories of hardships some seminary students and pastors' families had suffered. As a Chinese saying goes, "A skillful wife cannot cook meals without rice." What could I do if it should happen to us? Had God really told Yishan to go to the seminary, or was it just his own imagination? Could he have been so moved by the singing that he just thought God was talking to him?

That night I was really worried. The more I thought about it, the more afraid I was. I could not help but pray to the Lord before I went to bed, "Lord, please let me understand Your will. Please let me know that You truly had talked to Yishan. Otherwise, I'm afraid to step ahead into full-time Christian ministry."

It was not that I was afraid of full-time Christian ministry. I knew God would be responsible for those whom He had called. What worried me was the possibility Yishan had imagined God talking to him, in which case I did not think God would be responsible for us.

The following morning I had a dream before waking up. In the dream I clearly saw a very large hall with a shining granite floor, and scattered all over the floor were jade objects of all sizes and colors—red, blue, green, white, yellow, orange. (I had never before seen so many colors of jade.) There were rings, earrings, bangles, ornamental objects like bookends, and things carved into shapes of different animals. In the dream I clearly saw many of those items were perfect in shape, but some others were broken.

Then my dream ended. When I woke up, I thought this dream was significant. I had had several experiences in which God talked to me through dreams. I was going to pray for the meaning of the dream. Before I began to pray, however, eight Chinese words came into my head, which translated word for word are equivalent to "Rather be broken for jade than be whole for clay."

These eight Chinese words actually constitute a rather well-known Chinese saying. However, I've found out not everyone knows it. A year later when an older brother questioned why we had to move to California and I explained to him by telling this dream, he immediately understood.

At that moment I understood why God gave me this dream. He was telling me that sacrificing for the sake of the gospel is more worthwhile than maintaining a financially wholesome living just as jade is more valuable than clay. In other words, God was saying to me, "Sacrifice yourself for My sake."

Praise the Lord! He gave me the confirmation it was truly His will for Yishan to quit his job. From then on, I had no more doubt, and every day I was full of joy, praying for our move a year away.

Then Yishan and I thought of another problem that needed to be solved. It had been six years since we began the Cedar church. How were we to tell the brothers and sisters that we were going to move? They surely would feel shocked and disappointed that Yishan would not be their pastor after all.

After Yishan and I prayed and talked, we decided to keep it a secret for the time being. Then Yishan would gradually let on that we would move away, and at the proper time he would make the formal announcement of our decision.

We made this decision for the sake of the church so that the congregation would not be too shocked by the impact. However, our

God is a surprising God, and very quickly, Yishan and I were actually the ones to be shocked.

The Wednesday following the retreat, a brother unexpectedly showed up at our Wednesday night prayer meeting. This brother lived very far, almost an hour's drive away from church. He usually came to church only on Sundays.

As soon as I saw that brother that evening, I asked him, "What wind has blown you here?" (It was another way of saying "What has brought you here?")

That brother replied, "I had a dream this morning. I was greatly touched when I woke up. So I decided to come to the prayer meeting."

"What dream did you have that made you so touched?" Yishan asked him.

"I dreamed that you [plural in Chinese, referring to me and Yishan] were attending a certain denominational [he actually named the denomination] seminary, and you kept it a secret from people of our church."

Yishan and I both were greatly shocked. How did this brother know our secret? When I heard that brother's answer, my first reaction was to deny it so that our secret decision would not be made known. However, I did not want to lie. Happily, I thought, it was definitely a seminary Yishan and I would never attend since it was a denomination we would not want to be associated with. It did give me an excuse to deny that brother's dream, and I said, "It's impossible. I'll never attend that seminary." What I said was true.

As soon as I heard that brother, of course, I also thought of the book of Daniel, especially chapter 2 of that book, where God revealed to Daniel the content of King Nebuchadnezzar's dream. I certainly believed that just as God had revealed the king's dream to Daniel, God also had revealed our secret decision to this brother in his dream.

But why did God give this dream to this brother instead of anyone else in the church? Immediately, I knew the reason. This brother was different from anyone else in the church. This brother had graduated from a Bible college and was pursuing a graduate degree in music. The theological training he received was "God's revelation is complete when the Bible was written. Today there are no more dreams or visions from God."

Yishan and I could say, "Amen," only to the first half but not the second half of this teaching. In our sermons or Bible studies, we have taught that all the principles that God wants us to know are written in the Bible and that is why it forbids additions to or subtractions from the Word (Deuteronomy 4:2, 12:32; Proverbs 30:6; Revelation 22:18–19). Yet we also believed—and I still do—that in our seeking God's will, sometimes specific situations necessitate God's giving His specific directive through dreams or visions. Yishan and I had both our own experiences of dreams and visions. Yet when we so taught in the Cedar church, all the brothers and sisters could accept our teaching, except this brother.

I believed God had given this dream to this brother for his own benefit. I was also confident that this brother could have our trust to keep this secret for the time being. Therefore, I talked to Yishan and suggested that he talk to this brother at church on Sunday to share with him our decision.

At church the following Sunday, Yishan took this brother to a very small room where there were only two sofas and one lamp on a table with the sofa on each side of the table arranged into an "L" shape. When Yishan and this brother were in this room, each sitting in a sofa, Yishan shared our decision, which of course differed a little from this brother's dream in the name of the seminary.

After Yishan finished talking, this brother said, "What I saw in my dream was exactly what we are doing here, you sitting there and I sitting here."

Wow! How awesome! What a great God we serve! He is all-knowing and capable of doing whatever He chooses to do. We are His workmanship, and none of us can escape His will. Yet when we choose to follow Him, He can accomplish His will for us. Amen!

Well, this brother did keep our trust and did not reveal the secret to anyone else until a few weeks later when Yishan made the announcement in church.

A few days later, a woman said to me over the phone, "Wow, I think you and your husband surely have great faith just like Abraham's. The Lord told Abraham to leave his hometown Ur of the Chaldees, and you are obeying the Lord's command to move to California."

Honestly, Yishan and I never considered us to have great faith as Abraham's. To me, it was natural to obey the Lord's command when we knew it was His will. (As I think about this now, this is even more emphatically so. Today we have the whole Bible to guide us, but Abraham did not have this advantage. Yet he obeyed God exactly as he was told. We can never compare our faith to that of Abraham, and that is why he is called the father of faith.)

When the coworkers heard the announcement, they banded together for a meeting and came to me and Yishan. They said, "We are going to need a pastor after you move. It means we have to learn from now on how to get ready to support a full-time pastor. So we have decided to give you $1,000 a month until you move. You have to let us learn to grow financially independent."

Yishan and I were almost speechless. We had not anticipated them to take this move. Except for a brief period of two or three months in the past, we had not received any financial payment from the Cedar church. During those two or three months, we were paid a monthly stipend of $200 as a transportation allowance. However, after a small misunderstanding, we decided to return that month's stipend to the treasury and never took any more payment from the church.

To be frank, we had been very tight financially ever since our two daughters entered college at the same time.

However, the fact Angela and Leslie entered college at the same time was not the main factor of our financial stress. They both graduated from high school with a lot of scholarships. Leslie had $7,200, and Angela had more than $6,000. When they first entered college, we did not have much burden. However, that very fall, the Illinois State Assembly made a big cut in the budget for state colleges and universities, which of course included University of Illinois, Champaign-Urbana. Because of the budget cut, Angela's scholarship was eliminated, and we as parents had to shoulder every penny of her whole college education, although we were not prepared to do so.

Our financial burden was also complicated by a wage freeze announced by Yishan's company and by a church building fund drive.

The Cedar church began a building fund drive when our two daughters were still in high school. At one prayer meeting, we took a pledge from the coworkers to see if we would have the potential to start the drive. At the time our family was in fairly good financial shape, so Yishan and I decided to pledge a sizable amount. After we collected the sheets of paper each family wrote out, we found we had enough basic funds to start a drive for the whole church.

By the time the church building fund drive officially kicked off, all the original pledged amounts had been collected, and our two daughters had gone to college. Then each family had to pledge another amount again. This time, I told Yishan, our family's financial situation was not as good as before, and we could not pledge as much as we did the first time. But Yishan would not listen.

"As leaders of the church, we have to pledge the same amount if not more. We cannot pledge less. We have to set a good example," he told me.

Maybe my faith was not stretched far enough, but I did not believe God would want us to pledge an amount *far beyond* our ability. I thought a pledge was really between God and us, not for men to see. Yet Yishan would not accept any arguments from me, and since the Bible says, "Wives, submit yourselves unto your own husbands, as unto the Lord" (Ephesians 5:22), that settled it. The original amount of $2,000 was pledged once more. (I have always believed in what Jesus said in Matthew 6:3–4. Please forgive me for disclosing this amount here. Otherwise, I would not be able to tell the following story.)

Almost as soon as the pledge was handed in, then the testing came. After I wrote a check for $1,000 to the church, the following month when Yishan's salary would receive the annual raise, his company announced a wage freeze. Of course, it meant not only Yishan's salary was not raised, but we immediately were headed for a very tight monetary year too. At that moment I felt I could hear

Satan laughing and saying, "How are you going to meet your pledge and pay the other $1,000?"

I knew I could not. It was impossible. For a whole year, we struggled financially and barely survived. During the following Christmas, Yishan brought home a $500 bonus, and I immediately gave it to the building fund. I did not use even a single cent for our own family.

One Saturday evening about a month or two after that wage-freeze news, Yishan asked me when I was washing dishes after dinner, "How much money do we still owe the church building fund?"

"Five hundred dollars," I answered without raising my eyes to look at him.

"Then we'd better pay it soon," Yishan said it matter-of-factly.

At that moment I felt anger rising inside of me, and I was going to chide Yishan for not knowing anything about our financial situation when I felt the Lord was nudging at me and saying, "How about the $303 from MIT?"

Earlier in November we had received a letter from MIT informing we had some $600 surplus (I do not remember the exact amount) in Leslie's account for the coming spring semester. I was confused when I saw that letter. Usually around that time, the letter would indicate an amount we still had to pay MIT for the coming semester. How come there was a surplus this time instead of an amount to pay? I knew we had not paid anything. Had Leslie paid it? I held the letter until Leslie came home for Thanksgiving. When I showed her the letter, she was confused as well. After she returned to MIT and inquired at the bursar's office (financial office), she was told the letter was correct, but she still had to pay some $300 for meal tickets. That meant we would receive a $303 refund check in a few weeks, and we did.

When I received that $303 check from MIT, I immediately deposited it into the bank and thought, *Although we do not have to pay MIT this semester, we still have another year to go. This money is still needed for next year.*

Quite coincidentally around that same week I had also received another check from my younger sister in Taiwan. It was actually a check I wrote to her for $192 to cover the cost for Chinese typing for my *Fish and Loaves* articles. Usually when I sent a check to my sister for that purpose, she would cash it. However, that time—and that single time only—when my sister received the check, she did not cash it, but only signed her name on the back and sent it back to me. Probably she suspected our financial situation was tight. (Actually, I had not told her anything specific.) I thought she had given the check back to help me. (Now I believe it was really the Lord who moved her heart to do so.)

Well, that Saturday evening by the sink, the Lord reminded me of the $303 check from MIT plus the $192 my sister had given me. Together, they amounted to $495, and I knew the Lord had helped us to meet the pledge. He had asked me to give only five dollars, *one percent* of the $500, which we could not originally afford.

Although I saw clearly at that time it was a miracle the Lord had performed for us, actually I did not see the whole picture until much later. After Leslie graduated from MIT, she went on to Harvard University for one year to get a master's degree. Since MIT and Harvard are geographically quite close, she was able to visit MIT quite frequently when she was at Harvard. One day when she was visiting at MIT, her curiosity was aroused, and she inquired at the bursar's office. Well, our suspicion was confirmed. Indeed, they had made a mistake when they sent us that $600 surplus letter. However, they assured Leslie that since she had already graduated, they did not require her to pay it back. (As it turned out, Leslie went back to MIT to get a second master's degree after receiving one from Harvard. And still a few years later, Leslie was asked to represent MIT in interviewing its future students, a service Leslie still performed in 2014. I believe MIT has been more than compensated for its kindness in helping our family.)

Well, if MIT had not made that mistake, not only would there be no building fund miracle, but we would have had a hard time paying MIT for that semester and also fulfilling our building fund pledge.

Indeed, our God is merciful and knows us much better than we do ourselves. He does not ask us to do what we can't but only asks us to do our best. What Apostle Paul said in 2 Corinthians 8:12 is totally true. "For if there be first a willing mind, it is accepted according to that a man hath, and not according to that he hath not."

Now let me get back to the decision made by the Cedar church coworkers to give me and Yishan $1,000 each month when they heard that we were going to attend the seminary in Berkeley. Yishan and I believed that the Lord had seen the tight financial condition we were in, and He had moved the hearts of the coworkers to give us that support. As a result, for the final year of our two daughters' college education, we had no more difficulty paying their bills. Praise the Lord! He is really merciful.

(The reason we were so tight financially was, of course, due to the fact that I had quit my last job in obedience to the Lord's call and had not worked since 1977. If I had been working and our family had had a second income, we would have been much better off financially. That was one of the tests of the Lord before He finally led us into full-time Christian service.)

Christmas in Schaumburg home

The Memorial Day weekend of 1989 came around and the Cedar church was going to have another retreat. This time, I told Yishan, I could not attend the retreat because I was going to stay home to clean windows in order to prepare for our move to California. Since I was going to be home alone during the retreat, it was about the best opportunity for me to get this job done.

All my life I have never been a great house cleaner, especially when I was living in Schaumburg. What with my time spent in personal Bible study and correspondence courses and cooking meals and washing dishes plus keeping dozens and dozens of house plants and conducting Bible studies as well as preparing sermons and Sunday school class lessons *and* publishing *Fish and Loaves*, I was not left with much time to do a lot of housecleaning, let alone window washing. Although I had done some window cleaning before, deep down I knew I owed those windows a good amount of washing. (As I look back more than thirty years later, I realize the Lord's arm really had upheld me then. Otherwise, I could not have been such a superwoman!)

So that Memorial Day weekend when Yishan and the girls were away, off I went—not to the retreat but to every window of my house to give it a good scrub. Armed with the knowledge I had gleaned from the Moody radio program and *Better Home and Garden* articles, I found out that ammonia was the best cleaning agent for washing windows and other household objects. I also found out I really enjoyed washing windows. While I scrubbed the screens and the windowpanes, I meditated on how spiritually I was cleansed by the blood of Jesus sprinkled from the cross. While I washed physical windows, my spiritual window was cleansed as well. Sometime later I was able to write down an article about the spiritual truth I gleaned from that window washing.

Of course, it also meant that when Yishan and the girls came home from the retreat, I was physically exhausted from washing those windows. But what an accomplishment! Everybody, especially Yishan, was happy to see those shiny windows.

On June 22, 1989, I flew out to California alone for house hunting.

I had wanted Yishan to come with me, but he had to stay home in Schaumburg to sell the house.

I came to California at the worst time. Housing prices were on the rise and every house was overpriced. I was in California only a week, and I had to find a house during those seven days. With the price of my Schaumburg home, I would not be able to find a decent home of comparable size. I ended up buying a much smaller house ten years older than my Schaumburg home and one and a half times more costly than the latter.

I cried when I was in California. My tears came out when I prayed, "Lord, why are You giving me and Yishan such a difficult task to move out here? Not only are the houses here more expensive, but my Schaumburg home is still not sold. I have no cash to buy a house here. I'll have to borrow money from my brother, and Lord, You know I don't want to borrow from him. He is so proud!"

This brother of mine was financially the most successful among my siblings. He and his wife came to visit in 1984. When I shared the gospel with him, he said, "I don't need God. I am God."

Naturally, I did not call him. I called my younger brother instead, but he told me that he had just bought a house and that he had no money to lend me. "Call Second Brother," he urged me, and I told him why I did not want to call.

"That's okay. I'll tell him," he assured me.

A little later my other brother called to tell me he would lend me the total amount for that house. I could not wait for my Schaumburg home to sell because I wanted to settle down in California right away so that I could concentrate on seminary study. Otherwise, I would have to rent first and move later after we got the money.

In a few days after I returned to Schaumburg, I had to get busy again. Leslie was getting engaged on July 2, and I wanted a public ceremony at church. Since we were moving away and Leslie was planning to be married at MIT the following year, this was the only opportunity for us to share the joy with our friends in Schaumburg.

Actually, I had to get busy right after I returned to Schaumburg.

Our house was put on the market, and I had a lot of work to do, sorting things out and putting things into boxes plus getting new carpets for our house. My hands were already full before I went to California. I was naturally busier when I got back home, even without an engagement ceremony.

Fortunately, Yishan met me at the airport with the good news. The church coworkers were helping out, taking care of all the decorations and provision, and I did not have to worry about anything. Come Sunday, July 2, I only had to sing a song and translate what Yishan said for the ceremony. That happy occasion was beautifully carried out and even recorded on video by a brother. Besides thanking God, I was really grateful for the generosity and tender loving care of these brothers and sisters.

By that time, of course, Angela had graduated from the University of Illinois. Besides some part-time job and occasionally going out for job hunting, she was actually home some of the time. One day while I was packing, I looked at some old stuffed animals and asked Angela, "What should I do with these?"

Those stuffed animals had been given to Angela when she was a baby, and in more than twenty years' time, they had grown old through being handled and caressed. But Corrie had claimed them to be her own, although she also had quite a few new stuffed animals given to her.

Angela knew that I was trying to cut the cost of moving by giving or throwing things away since this move was on our own and no company was going to pay the moving expenses for us.

"Throw it away now that Corrie is still in school," Angela urged me. Well, she was the rightful owner of those old stuffed animals, and she had given me the permission to throw them away. So I did.

When Corrie came home and found those stuffed animals missing, she did not say a single word, and I did not suspect anything wrong. Actually, I was *too* busy to pay attention to the fact that she stopped talking to me from that day on. I did not realize that *until* much later after we had moved.

In order to save the cost of moving, it also meant I had to call many movers to come in for estimates before finally deciding on one. That took a lot of my time. And Yishan had to continue working until only a few days before the move. All taken together, besides the help from Angela plus Yishan lending a hand in the evening after he came home from work, it meant I was the sole packer of boxes most of the time. No wonder by the time moving day came I was still not able to get everything done.

Come moving day, August 10, 1989, the moving company's big truck arrived at our house, but I was not ready. While the movers were busy at their job, I still had a few boxes to pack, and I had to clean my kitchen floor. I had planned to have all the boxes packed and the kitchen completely cleaned by that day so that when the movers' truck left, our family could leave the house behind as well. No way!

By the time the mover left, which was long past dinner hour, the house was pretty empty, and I felt empty inside too, not much strength left.

In fact, at that time I felt mixed emotions. I remembered when I was in the fifth grade, my family moved from Kaohsiung (in southern Taiwan) to Taipei (in northern Taiwan). When our train passed by the elementary school, which I had attended ever since kindergarten, I felt very sad, and my tears flowed for a long time.

That moving day as my childhood moving scene came into mind, I thought, *This is another big move, another milestone in my life.* On the one hand, I was excited, thinking God was leading me and Yishan on an adventure. Yet on the other, I felt nostalgic and a little sad too because we had lived there since November 1973, almost sixteen years. This is the place where Corrie was born (although she was actually born in a hospital in a neighboring town), the place my two older daughters grew up, growing from elementary/kindergarten through college. This was also the place where Yishan became a believer and those Bible studies happened and a lot of other occasions when God felt so close to me. There were a lot of memories packed into this place.

The next morning, August 11, when I woke up, I felt exhausted, and I wondered how I was going to clean the kitchen floor and those cupboards. I still remember I prayed, "Lord, how am I to tackle such a formidable task? I'm so tired. Could you please send an angel to help me?"

As I prayed, I thought of all the women in the church. Everyone was working outside the home except Laurie. She was the only one who could help me. Yet how could I call her and say, "Laurie, could you come over to help me?"

I remember I did pray, "Lord, if You see fit, could you move Laurie's heart to help me?" Yet neither because of unbelief in God nor because of disbelief in human kindness, I still felt uneasy asking for Laurie's help. I did honestly expect God to literally send me one of His angels to appear at my door.

About an hour later while I was dragging my fatigued body around the kitchen, the phone rang. Laurie was on the line. She said, "Carmen, this morning as I was praying during my devotion time, I thought of the waxing machine I have. I would like to come to your house to wash the floor for you. I'll also bring a fried chicken dinner so that you don't have to cook lunch. You can have some rest."

I was almost in tears. God was so good. He did send His angel, a loving sister in the Lord who obeyed God's prompting.

I don't have much recollection of what I did the rest of that day. I do remember I cleaned the cupboards while Laurie washed the floor. And the other thing I remember is that we did not leave that house until the following morning since it was pretty late by the time all the cleaning was done.

And still the house was not repainted when we left it. Our budgets did not allow us to hire a painter to do the job for us. Yishan and I had originally planned to do it ourselves, but for lack of proper training, we encountered some problems. And since we were depleted of time and energy, we had to leave the house to the coworkers of the church to tackle the problem for us. I'm forever grateful for those brothers and sisters who helped us so much. Between the time we moved away and the time when the house was sold, which was several months later, the colored glass panel of the storm door in the front was broken by a vandal. Then the outside faucet caused some flooding in one room when it was turned on. It was those brothers and sisters who took care of all the problems for us. It was as if Satan was so furious at our obeying the Lord's command that he launched an all-out attack on our house. Thank God for those loving brothers and sisters who helped us out so much. I know I'll never be able to repay them. It's all on the Lord's account.

When we finally said good-bye to Schaumburg, we drove away in two cars, Yishan and I in a small Toyota, Angela with Corrie in a still smaller Hyundai. Partly because Angela was young and energetic and maybe because the Lord was watching over her, she was able to drive alone all the way to California without any mishap. (Corrie was sleeping a lot. Angela added here, "Ha-ha, I was actually falling asleep half the time! God protected us!")

With me, it was a different story. I had originally agreed to take turns with Yishan to be at the wheel during the trip. However, I was so exhausted from the whole summer's work that each day I was at the wheel for only five minutes before I began to feel drowsy. I had to keep praying to fight sleepiness. Well, I ended up driving only fifteen minutes each day and had to leave the rest of the driving to Yishan.

Usually, whenever we traveled, I had to *serve* Yishan, such as handing him a towel to clean his face or to feed him food in order to keep him awake. *Not so* in that trip when we moved to California. Whenever I tried to keep him company, I would end up falling asleep. That showed how fatigued I was.

We had planned to take five days driving. We tried to do a little sightseeing whenever there was a place of particular interest not too far from the route we took. However, early afternoon of the fourth day, when I was still taking a long nap while Yishan was driving, I woke up and heard him say, "We have arrived in California." It was the Nevada-California border. Yishan rolled down the window, and a border inspector said, "Welcome to California."

Thank God that we arrived one day ahead of schedule. It was August 15, 1989. When we arrived in our Pinole home, it was before

4:00 p.m. Thank God for keeping us safe all the way. (Here I can only quote a hymn that says, "All the way my Savior leads me!")

We were all happy and thankful, even though it was a difficult move. We had obeyed the Lord in moving all the way to California, and I was looking forward to whatever excitement the Lord had in store for us. Nevertheless, that afternoon I did not know that more difficulties were waiting ahead for me.

Chapter 16

Seminary Days

*A*ctually, God did more to help us in our move to California than what I have mentioned. We had expected our bank account to be depleted when we arrived in California, but the Lord did not allow that to happen.

On the last Sunday afternoon in Schaumburg when the Cedar church gave us a farewell party, an elderly brother took Yishan to the men's room. This elderly man was the one who had left his walking stick at church and went home without it. He, too, like Mr. Wang, had a house in Taiwan that was still not sold. For a long time, we prayed for it to be sold.

That afternoon in the men's room, he handed Yishan two envelopes, one with $5,000 for church building fund and another with $2,000 for Yishan. He said that he just sold his house in Taiwan, thanks to our prayers.

Yishan accepted on behalf of the church the envelope with $5,000 but refused to take the other. He reasoned that the elderly brother needed to keep the money for his own living expenses.

"Don't worry about me," said that elderly brother. "I've got enough for my own. You're moving to California. This is to help with your moving expenses."

"We've got enough to pay for that."

"Well then, count it as a scholarship for your seminary tuition."

Yishan found no reason to refuse such a kind offer. He thanked that elderly brother and took that other envelope. It was money we never expected to receive. The Lord *and* that brother surprised us.

Well, we were surprised again in another way the morning following our arrival in our Pinole home.

That morning Yishan went to the kitchen to boil hot water for breakfast noodles. When he turned on the stove, he found two burners were out. One was just warm, and only one burner actually worked.

I immediately called our realtor, who in turn called the seller's agent. Our realtor had purchased a home warranty for us, but there was a $35 deductible, for which I thought the seller should be responsible. However, in the return call, we were told that the seller refused to pay the $35 deductible, and his agent felt so bad that she was willing to pay it for us.

The next day Yishan as well as Angela and Corrie told me that they all got many mosquito bites. A few days later when I was hanging clothes out in the side yard, I saw fleas jumping. *That* was what they thought were mosquitoes! Our house as well as the yard was infested with fleas! The previous owner had a dog.

I had to call an exterminator. He advised me to sign a contract for a monthly spray for a whole year in order to ensure those fleas would never return. The monthly service cost was $77 each time.

Then on Thanksgiving Day, I invited some people over for a turkey dinner. It was cold, and I turned on the heater for the first time. Guess what? The furnace did not work. So I had to call Home Warranty Service. Another $35 deductible, this time out of our own pocket.

One day two or three months later, Yishan opened the garage door. It went up as usual. A few minutes later when he tried to close it, the garage door just stayed there and refused to come down. There was no compromise, absolutely no way to coax it down. Well, an acquaintance recommended a handyman to install a new garage door for us. It cost $725.

A few months later, the water heater broke. Water was everywhere on the garage floor. At least we were fortunate that nobody was nearby to get injured. I don't remember how much it cost us to replace that broken one, but it was several hundred dollars.

You think that's all? Nope. I forgot to mention this at the very beginning. When I came to California to house-hunt and decided on this house, I only saw its plus side and did not see anything wrong. Not even the realtor who took me there saw anything wrong. In fact, I hate to say this, but it's true. Both the realtor and I were duped by the seller. He had removed all the screens from the windows and did not show them. That was why we did not see anything wrong. After we moved in, we saw that all the windows had screens, but all the bottom halves of the screens were missing. They were all broken. I had been told that the seller was a handyman and that he had done some remodeling to the house. What I found out much later was that he was no handyman at all. He just tried to do those things himself to save the money. When I saw the new kitchen counter, I did not suspect anything wrong until three years later when we were trying to sell the house to move to F City. That day as a realtor I had called in was talking to me in the kitchen, he checked the kitchen counter to see if it was glued down. He just lightly tried to move it, and he did!

I'll spare you all the other defects we found. We really should have sued the seller for failing to disclose all those defects. Well, we were too busy pursuing seminary studies and doing God's work to spend our precious time on that matter.

It was not until much later when I got to meet my new neighbor, and she told me this house had been a rental home for many years. Our seller was an immigrant from Vietnam who purchased this house from that previous owner and made a fortune when he sold it to us.

Then there was the big shock. On October 17, 1989, two months after we came to California, the Bay Area was hit with a big jolt, the 7.1 Loma Prieta earthquake. When it hit, I was standing right between our dining room and the living room, and I felt as if the floor was going to melt. I immediately cried out, "Earthquake!"

Yishan was at his desk in Corrie's room studying. When he heard my cry, he ran out and asked, "Earthquake? Where?"

I pointed out the moving chandelier to him and said, "If this is not an earthquake, what is it?" That showed how concentrated Yishan was on his studies. (Maybe it was proof of what he had said of himself, namely that he was not very sensitive.)

Immediately, I turned on the TV. The station was broadcasting the World Series game going on at the Candlestick Park. Very quickly, that station was out, and the TV screen went black. I turned to another station that said, "There was just an earthquake." As the real life drama unfolded on the screen, I got to watch tragedy after tragedy, one of which being the woman meeting her death when her car came to the section of the upper deck Bay bridge that had just collapsed.

All the problems concerning the house were really nothing compared to the heartache I encountered. After all, money problems never really make me feel daunted since I believe my heavenly Father has plenty in supply.

Almost as soon as we arrived in the Bay area, I encountered two other problems.

One was with the seminary. While we were still in Schaumburg, I was promised by an acting president (the president was on a health leave) that all my Moody credits would be honored for a master's degree at the seminary. However, when Yishan and I went through the registration process, the president of the seminary who had returned refused to approve of my credits from Moody. "They are not graduate-level courses," he said.

Okay. He was correct in saying that. I could not deny it. "Then the classes I'm going to take should offer me learning to surpass that at Moody," I reasoned, and I expected it. So I enrolled in *NT Greek*, *life of Christ*, and *systematic theology*, three courses altogether.

After I went to the first classes of *life of Christ* and *systematic theology*, I dropped both of them. I did not want to waste my time going to classes where I learned very little or nothing at all. I guessed I did not need a master's degree in order to be used by God. After all, it was Yishan who wanted me to take classes with him. When the Lord told Yishan to come to this seminary, it was a singular *you*, not a plural *you*. I reasoned that the Lord had not expected me to take all those courses from the seminary that He had told Yishan to attend (see chapter 15).

I had always wanted to learn biblical Greek and Hebrew, but I had never had a chance until I was at this seminary. That was why I did not drop the NT Greek course. Later I went on to take Hebrew as well. I'm thankful to the Lord for having grounded me in English training because it helped me tremendously in learning Greek and Hebrew.

My disappointment in the seminary was compensated by other opportunities to serve. I soon found out that, with our Moody training and pastoral experiences in the past, we both were ahead of practically all the other students. Almost daily we had opportunities to share with them in fellowship and to help them in biblical understanding as well as in some of their personal areas. I was asked to teach an English class (with no credits) to those students who needed it. Being an instrument in the hand of the Lord to help others always brings me great joy. One English-speaking professor always asked me to translate for him whenever he spoke at the morning chapel. Then during a weeklong series of messages given by the vice president of a very well-known seminary in Texas, I had the honor of translating his messages into Mandarin. He jokingly said to me that I was his "interrupter."

Still later, after I completed the New Testament Greek classes, the president of the seminary asked me to offer a Greek class parallel to the regular New Testament Greek to some students who were otherwise hampered from taking it for lack of English ability. One of them actually had flunked that course. Thank God for giving me the experience of teaching English as a second language. As a result, I was able to apply some principles of English teaching to teaching Greek and helping those students successfully learn New Testament Greek and earn those credits.

Even Yishan had problems with the Greek class and had a hard time working on some of the required exercises. Thank God that He used me to help Yishan overcome those obstacles as well.

Of course, all these opportunities to serve did not bring me any extra income, but being able to help was enough to give me a sense of achievement. It was more than enough to compensate for the disappointment of not being able to earn a master's degree.

The other problem I encountered right after I arrived in the Bay Area was my relationship with Corrie. *She would not talk to me.* Every time I tried to talk to her, she would turn her head away. Leslie was in Boston, too far to help me. So I turned to Angela, but she said, "Corrie won't tell me anything. Sorry I cannot help."

Was Yishan able to help? No, he said the same thing as Angela did. Plus it was obvious to me that he was so engrossed in his own seminary studies that he had no time to even try to help.

I felt heartbroken. I had always considered Corrie a lovely girl. She seemed to have a personality that was magnetic to other girls of her age. While in Schaumburg, girls always gathered around her. After we enrolled her in the sixth grade of a neighborhood school in Pinole, she quickly made several friends. But now *I* had become her enemy.

I felt all my prayers concerning Corrie had bounced back from the ceiling and never reached God's throne of grace. And since I had encountered so many problems after moving to California, I even began to question whether we had correctly followed God's guidance in the first place. Was it because Yishan and I were too zealous that we had misunderstood God's will? I was in a place of predicament, feeling like Job, trying to figure out God's way but unable to hear anything from Him.

Although Greek was the only course I took, it was enough to keep me busy since I wanted to learn it well. (I have since realized Greek and Hebrew to be the hardest languages in the world, having heard so much from people who had taken either one or both classes about their own experience.)

A lot of my Greek studies included memorization of its very complicated conjugation. Sometimes I wondered why God had led me to study Greek and Hebrew only when I was nearly fifty years of age when my memory was only half as good as it had been when I was in my teens and twenties or even thirties. (Well, I should not blame God. After all, it was Yishan who stood in the way for many years and delayed my time of receiving seminary training.)

Since Yishan and I had only one car (Angela had the other), I had to commute with him to Berkeley practically every day. Although most of the time I concentrated on my studies, sometimes I could not help being distracted by the thought of Corrie. I was agonized by my failure to get through to her.

One day the seminary held a one-day retreat in a large Chinese church in Saratoga in the South Bay, which was very far from Pinole where we lived. We had to get up early so that we could reach there in time. On the way there it was no problem for me since Yishan always drove when we traveled together.

On the way back, it was different. Since the thought of Corrie was heavy in my heart, I told Yishan I wanted to go home after the lunch break. (In those days whenever there was a meeting at the seminary, usually Yishan was asked to lead the singing, and if an interpreter was needed, I would have to translate the message into Chinese. There were no English speakers for the retreat, and so I was free to go.)

I remember it was overcast sky when I left that church, and it began to drizzle not too long after I got to the freeway. Can you imagine its effect on me? No sun, and I soon began to feel drowsy. Sure, I had the radio on so that I could listen to message while driving, but the speaker began to sound more like singing lullabies than preaching on God's solemn words. I kept praying, but it did not help. However, the Lord was faithful, and He probably was holding me in one of His arms while His other arm was holding the driving wheel for me. In that half-sleepy and half-driving condition, I found myself on the part of the freeway between Hilltop on the left side and the hill on the right side, and it was sunny and bright with some wisps of white clouds below a very beautiful lapis lazuli sky. When it was time to take an exit, I turned left as usual on Appian Way and began a downward descent toward San Pablo Avenue, where I would turn left again to get home.

Once I was on the downward descent on Appian Way, I found right in front of me a gigantic rainbow (the largest rainbow I had ever seen in my whole life) almost encompassing my whole frontal view except a little part of the right side where I saw the end of the rainbow descend into the San Pablo Bay. (At the end of the rainbow is a pot of gold!)

Such a magnificent rainbow! I immediately thought of the words in Genesis where God promised to Noah that He would never again flood the whole earth. At that moment I felt it was also a promise from the Lord that He would give me peace and solve my problem.

The first breakthrough came one Friday almost six months after we moved to Pinole. I had no class that afternoon and was working on Greek conjugation in the seminary library. Yishan was still in class. When I felt a little tired, I got up for a stretch and walked up to a section of the library where on the shelves were books that had not been organized or cataloged. All of a sudden, I thought, *Although I have brought up two daughters, I'm totally thrown off course by Corrie. Maybe I need to read a book on child education that can give me some fresh ideas on how to deal with Corrie.*

Lo and behold, at that moment I saw right in front of my eyes a book title that attracted me, *Happily Ever After.* When I pulled it out, I saw on the cover a picture drawn by a child, and it *was* a book on child education. Maybe the Lord was going to show me the way out. I read some pages, put a piece of blank paper as a bookmark, and took the book home.

That evening after washing the dishes, I continued my reading of the book. When I turned to the pages where I had left the bookmark, I forgot I had actually almost finished both pages, and I began to read the page on the left side. Well, that must be the way the Lord drew my attention to it. As I continued to read the pages, I realized the author was telling the story of a time when she went through tests somewhat similar to what I was going through. She said one evening when she and God were not on friendly terms, she did not want to attend a church meeting, and as her husband left home, he threw her a dirty look. Once he left, she began to watch a TV program with her two children, a son and a daughter. Since her mind was not on it, she forgot that it was her turn to pick the program. By the time she realized it, it was too late. Her children had picked *The Wonderful World of Disney*, and they were watching it intently. It was a movie about an Indian girl and her horse. She had entered a horse race on a bet. If the horse won the race, her tribe would be able to keep their land. Otherwise, they would have to forfeit it. So the Indian girl trained her horse to do all sorts of impossible tricks.

It was a tear-jerking movie, the author said. Her children's tears were for the horse, for they pitied that horse. Theirs were also tears of joy, for the horse won the race in the end. But the author said her tears were shed more for herself because she felt she was like that horse enduring so many hardships. But then she said that she suddenly felt the Lord telling her, "*You* are that horse. If you can persevere, you will come out a winner."

Well, all of a sudden, I felt the Lord *was* talking to me too through that book. *I hear Him loud and clear*, I thought.

A day or two later, I was washing dishes one evening, and a sister from the seminary called. I began to share with her all the sufferings I was going through, and I was soon in tears. When I finished the dishes, I left the kitchen and was going back to the master bedroom, which was also my study. It was then near Easter, and Yishan and Corrie were sitting on the living room couch, watching NBC's *Jesus of Nazareth*. As I walked, Yishan gestured to me to sit with him and watch the movie. I shook my head and continued to walk toward the bedroom. However, as I passed in front of the TV, I could not avoid catching the scene of Jesus hanging on the cross—His bloody face with the crown of thorn on His head and both His hands stretched out and nailed to the cross. It was a speechless scene, but at that moment I felt Jesus was saying to me, "See how much I suffered for you? Can't you suffer a little for My sake?" My tears came out like a broken dam. I asked the Lord to forgive my weakness.

Then on the following Friday afternoon, since I had no class, I felt an urge and said to Yishan, "I'm going home early this afternoon. I think I should not leave Corrie alone so often. You can get a ride from Carl (another student)."

Yishan consented, and I left. However, I needed to go to the bank first, and I took one exit earlier than the one I usually took to get home. After I left the bank, I continued to drive northbound on San

Pablo Avenue, where otherwise I would be driving southbound if I had taken the other exit from the freeway. I believe this was the way the Lord worked it out for me. Otherwise, what followed would not have taken place.

As I continued driving, I saw Corrie walking on the sidewalk on her way home from school. I stopped the car for her. She hopped in, and I continued to drive. As soon as I got to our driveway and parked the car, she opened the door and ran into the house without saying a word.

I felt furious. Such a rude and thankless child! Had I given the ride to a stranger, at least that person would have said, "Thank you," before she left. However, I immediately prayed and asked the Lord to help me calm my anger.

Once inside the house, I found Corrie had shut herself in Angela's room. I uttered another word of prayer and knocked. No answer. I opened the door and saw Corrie sitting on Angela's bed.

I was determined to dig to the bottom that day to find out why she would not talk to me. I began by asking her, "Do you know why Mommy gave you a ride?" No answer, so I continued, "It was because I love you. Otherwise, I could have just driven home by myself without giving you a ride. If I had given the ride to a stranger, at least she would have said, 'Thank you,' before leaving. You didn't even say a word and just banged the car door and left. Why don't you want to talk to Mommy? What's wrong?"

All that time there was absolutely no answer, just complete silence. As I continued to press her, she began to sob but continued in silence.

Then suddenly, she blurted out something. She talked so fast without taking any breath. Those words were almost garbled, but fortunately, I was able to figure out what she said, "You threw away my stuffed animals!"

So *that* was the reason! I was able then to explain to her what happened in Schaumburg and why I did that. "You know it was God's will for us to move to California, and Mommy had to try to save money. It does not mean that Mommy doesn't love you."

Then she said, "You don't hug me anymore!" (It's funny to think

180

back how she complained. There was absolutely no way I could have hugged her up to that time since every time I tried to talk to her, she would immediately turn away from me.)

By then I was in tears as well, and the two of us hugged each other and cried together. And then she said, sounding like a complaint, "You don't read the Bible with me anymore!"

I used to read the Bible with Corrie back in Schaumburg, and she enjoyed it. After moving to Pinole, partly because she refused to talk to me and partly because I was so busy with seminary study and church work, I had not been able to pick it up again. That afternoon I happily resumed my reading of the Bible with her.

Until now I have not had a chance to talk about church work after our arrival in the Bay Area. So let me go into more details here.

While still in Schaumburg, we were informed of HG Church. I visited that church the Sunday I was in the Bay Area house-hunting. My realtor took me there, and then he let me roam around. However, nobody greeted me, none whatsoever. As I walked down the hallway, I saw an elderly woman, and *I* had to initiate the greeting. Later I told Yishan I felt it was an icy-cold church, and it gave him a great burden to want to help. Prior to that, we had been told HG Church had been without a pastor for three years, and such was the condition we found that church to be in when we began serving there. It was not until many months later when we learned that once during those three years some of the deacons actually thought about closing down the church for good. Both Yishan and I believed the Lord had moved us to the Bay Area at a critical time to meet the needs of that church.

It was Rev. Hsieh who recommended me and Yishan to that church. However, by the time we came, another seminary student had beaten us to that church. This particular student had been a pastor in Southeast Asia and was on leave pursuing a master's degree at the seminary. Since he had a title of reverend and the church had been without a pastor for three years, they welcomed him when he found his way there.

When I was in the Bay Area house-hunting, one evening my realtor took me to his home to meet his wife. As I asked questions about the church, I was told this reverend had been coming to their Friday night Bible study.

"How was his Bible study?" I asked.

My realtor kept silent, not answering my question, but his wife said, "It's only so-so."

"Then it's not good," I said, "because my husband is good in preaching as well as in Bible studies, and people will compare."

I was not trying to brag about my own husband and degrade another man. I was simply stating the fact.

Of course, this man had an edge over Yishan. He had the title of "the Reverend," and Yishan did not. I'll call his name Jay.

As it turned out, HG Church decided to keep both Jay and Yishan as "seminary students in practical training," and each would receive $400 per month. However, for lack of financial ability, they could not give me the same status.

They did not inform us of this decision until two or three weeks after we began attending HG Church. By that time I had been serving the church on my own initiative. The very first Sunday we went to HG Church, I saw several kids running around before the hour of worship service, and no one taught them while their parents were in adult Sunday school. Immediately, I gathered those kids and began to teach them singing and Bible stories. I could not sit there and watch them goofing around. I did not wait until I was told to teach a class.

However, soon after we came to Pinole, I found out, to my dismay, that the cost of living in the Bay Area was much higher than what I had been used to in the Chicago area. I also quickly figured out how much we would need each month to meet all the basic necessities. Leslie and her then fiancé Ling-Yi had decided to give us their combined monthly tithe of $500. One or two churches plus a few individuals had also pledged to support us—$50 or $100 from each. A month after we moved, the Cedar church surprised us with a monthly gift of $500. With the $400 for Yishan from HG Church, I realized—unfortunately—we still did not have enough to meet our monthly needs. Yishan and I prayed hard to the Lord, but I did inform Rev. Hsieh of HG's decision to keep Jay and Yishan but not me. He immediately said, "Then we'll refer you to another church."

As we continued praying and putting the matter in the Lord's hand and while Rev. Hsieh was still trying to find another church for me to go, we were invited to a banquet held in a fancy Chinese restaurant. I was surprised to see not only some deacons of the church but three important faculty members from the seminary as well. During the banquet the host said to those three faculty members, "Thank you for referring Mr. and Mrs. Lin to our church."

So I was retained as another seminary student in practical training, and I figured out why. When Yishan preached his first sermon, I served as his interpreter and translated it into English. I was probably considered an asset that the church definitely needed. Well, I was very thankful not only that the Lord answered our prayers for our financial need but that Yishan and I could serve in the same church as well.

Not only did I teach children on Sunday and serve as an interpreter when Yishan preached, I also helped on Friday night at youth fellowship meetings. Two college students were leading the meeting, and two adults were serving as advisers. During the meetings I tried to just listen and pray. I would open my mouth only when I considered it necessary, such as to help answer a difficult question none of them knew how to answer or to share some biblical insight that I considered helpful to them. Since I was the oldest person in that group, I did not want to make myself unwelcome.

Six months after we served at HG Church, I found very few of the youth attending the worship service even though sermons were translated into English for their sake. I even found that one or two of them had been invited to other Chinese churches. After praying about it, I told Yishan of my concern of the need for a separate English worship. I was afraid the church might eventually lose most if not all of its younger generation.

Yishan informed the deacons of my concern, and it was included in the agenda for the upcoming deacons' board meeting. After some debates and discussion, they decided to give me the responsibility to start an English worship service with those two adult advisers helping. On April 1, 1990, we had our first English worship service.

I preached on that first service, but I waited a few weeks before I preached again, *not* because I needed that much time to prepare the second message but because I did not want the young people to feel I was forcing it down on them. I tried to invite different speakers from outside. Only when I had no other speakers available would I put my own name down as the speaker.

Whenever the English church had an outside speaker, I usually joined the adult choir in the Chinese worship service. I seldom sat with the English church, but I was still able to know what was going on there for one of the adult counselors usually filled me in on it.

A few months later, I was informed of two things. First, I was told of something that happened during one worship service. An elderly retired missionary was the speaker that day. I was told he was a pretty good speaker, but he seemed unable to hold the attention of two teenagers. Those two young men played with a dollar bill they passed around. However, their novelty did not escape the attention of the senior speaker, who then stopped speaking and spent some time lecturing on the fun-loving young men.

At that time I had observed with my own eyes what some of the teens were doing during Friday night youth fellowship meetings, and I had pretty much figured out what spiritual conditions these young people were in, even without being told of this money-playing incident during the worship. I had been praying for them, and after this, I pleaded with the Lord even more earnestly for their lives to be turned around.

The second thing I learned was actually told by a father. He and another father did not speak Mandarin, and both attended the English worship service together with their children every Sunday. Several months after the start of the English worship service, this man startled me by saying, "You should know that some of the speakers you invited are not so good."

It so happened by that time that most of those speakers I had invited began to decline my invitation to come again. So it seemed to be a signal from the Lord that it was time for me to begin preaching more frequently.

For every sermon I preached, I prayed very hard and made sure it was a message from the Lord. And personally I believe the Lord had given me those messages. Otherwise, they would not have shown such life-changing effect on those young people. By the end of August 1992, when Yishan and I completed our three-year ministry among the congregation of HG Church (actually only two and half years with the English congregation), every single one of those young people (a dozen or more of them) was converted and baptized.

By nature, I was not a funny person and was not good at telling or making up jokes. However, in my sermons the Lord often gave me humorous words to speak. Quite a number of times, He seemed to be guiding my attention to some interesting but fitting stories to use as illustrations, or He would also give some thought-provoking ideas that would challenge those listening.

Looking back now at those three years at HG Church, I can say with confidence that I'm full of thanksgiving to the Lord that He gave me three years of a fruitful ministry with no regrets whatsoever. Once I was somewhat under the influence of the weather and coughing quite a bit. I remember that Wednesday evening at the prayer meeting, a deacon prayed for me, "Lord, we pray that you'll keep Mrs. Lin healthy. She's very important to our church." I'd like to say I felt very much pampered by that church, especially since it is the only church where I never heard a single word of criticism about me. (Well, there was one time when one woman criticized me to another woman because of some misunderstanding about me. But the Lord corrected them shortly after that by giving one of them a dream, and the one who had the dream later called me and told me about this. Otherwise, I would not have known about this incident. The Lord Himself had corrected this problem, and that was why I never counted it to be against me.)

Yes, those were three years of joy but not without difficulties or challenges. A lot of times, I actually considered the job very challenging since there was such a big gap between my age and those young people. As a result, I had no confidence in myself, but I had to totally depend upon the Lord for wisdom and love and patience to work among that group.

It was unfortunate that I had no means to do any follow-up work for those young people after I moved away. By that time I was busy with another church, and HGC had another pastor of its own. I thought I had ended my work with HGC and the Lord had given me another ministry. All that I could do for those young people was to pray for them, and I left them in the Lord's hands. After all, He is the chief Shepherd, and He will be responsible for their safekeeping.

During those three years of ministry mixed with seminary studies, Yishan and I saw the Lord's hand in a lot of our daily living.

Back when we were in Schaumburg, I had the habit of stocking up on sale items. By the time we moved from Illinois to California, we still had two or three gallons of vegetable oil and Yishan just stuck them into whatever crevices he could find in the car or in the trunk. A few months after we moved to Pinole, I found we were down to the last gallon of vegetable oil, and I told that to Yishan.

If we were still back in Schaumburg, I would not have done that. I would simply have driven to the grocery store and bought one myself. However, in California, it was different. We had only one car then, and usually, we did our major grocery shopping in Oakland's Chinatown. At that time I was still not used to driving on the freeway to Oakland all by myself. Yishan usually did the driving.

"Okay, we'll get it when we go to Oakland," Yishan answered when I told him that.

The Saturday after I told Yishan of the need to buy vegetable oil, we got a call from an elderly lady who told Yishan over the phone that she was going to give us four brand-new folding chairs.

"Oh, we've got chairs," said Yishan.

"I've already bought the chairs. You are a minister and often have meetings at home. You can always use them."

Yishan found it hard to decline such a kind offer. So he thanked that lady, and he went on to inform her that the next day he was not going to be at HGC since he was going to preach at another church.

"Please give the chairs to my wife," said Yishan.

Well, the next day, Sunday, that lady did not come to me. She went to Corrie, and the latter came to ask for my car key. That elderly lady knew I was usually busy, she told me later. She just put those chairs in the trunk of my car without bothering me.

After I drove home with Corrie, I opened the trunk to get the chairs and got a surprise. There were two gallons of vegetable oil together with the four chairs. When Yishan came home and I told him about those two gallons of vegetable oil, he mused, "People in Chicago give you chocolate, but here in California they give you vegetable oil."

Another time I found that I had opened the last jar of black mushrooms. Back in Schaumburg when Yishan was working as a microbiologist, those who came from Taiwan to receive the eleven-week training at his company usually brought black mushrooms to us as gifts. Black mushrooms were a lot more expensive in those days. Over the years I had so many of those given to us that I just put away the unused ones in tea cans or jars, and I never had to buy them. After we moved to California, those jars of black mushrooms were used one by one, and finally, I told Yishan. He said, "We'll buy them when we go to Oakland."

A few days later, we went to visit a deacon's family. Once we were inside the house, the deacon's wife came out from the kitchen and gave me a package and said, "I just came back from Hong Kong. I brought back two packages of black mushrooms, and this one is for you."

Yishan jokingly commented that in both cases these two women overheard our conversation from their homes (2 Kings 6:8–12). But earnestly, both of us believed the Lord had known our needs and moved the hearts of those two women to give us those unusual gifts.

Still another time I was given an unexpected gift. It happened around my birthday. Here in the States we use solar calendars. However, my mother used to celebrate my birthday according to the lunar calendar, which was the seventh day of the fifth month, two days after the fifth day of the fifth month, a Chinese festive day when people usually wrap sweet rice in palm leaves (called *tsong-tse* in Chinese).

That year as that festive day approached, I remember I was lamenting to myself, "Too bad I'm so busy that I have no time to make tsong-tse anymore." It was rather a wish than a lament. In fact, over the years when we were living in Schaumburg, I had become lax in observing Chinese festive days, and I really did not care too much about them. As a Christian, I usually paid more attention to the traditional Christian holidays such as Thanksgiving and Christmas.

Anyway, that Sunday after I had that wishful thought, I went to church as usual. The church parking lot was in the back, and we usually entered the church through the back door, which was right by the kitchen. That morning as soon as I entered the church, I met an elderly brother in his late seventies who was usually working in the kitchen. He came up to me and gave me a small brown bag package and said in Cantonese, "Mrs. Lin, here are some tsong-tse I have made."

Wow, I did not even ask the Lord for this. And here at this church nobody knew its connection with my birthday at all. At that moment I felt as if the Lord was telling me, "Even though you did not ask for it, I'm still giving it to you. You don't have to worry about your needs. I know your heart." At that moment I thought of Psalm 37:4, "Delight yourself in the Lord, and He will give you the desires of your heart." Praise the Lord!

During our last year of ministry with HGC, Yishan began leading a Bible study at a senior citizens residence in Oakland. Sometimes I accompanied him there, and sometimes he drove there by himself. Once or twice I had to drive there by myself to lead the Bible study when Yishan was not able to go. The Bible study usually began at 7:00 p.m after those senior residents had their dinner.

One evening in May, Yishan drove there alone several months after he began leading that Bible study. That time while he was driving, he told me later, he was feeling dry in his throat, and he said to himself, "Oh no, I forgot to bring water along. Surely during the

Bible study, I'll begin coughing after I talk for a while. What shall I do?"

Well, when Yishan arrived in that hall and sat down, he found a cup of hot tea on the table right in front of him. It was the *first time* ever that somebody had prepared a cup of hot tea for him. He could not help asking who had done this, and an elderly brother in his late seventies or early eighties said, "This evening as I was ready to leave my room and come down here, I suddenly thought, *Pastor Lin has been leading us in these Bible studies, and yet we have not given him anything to drink. I guess I'll pour him a cup of tea.* And so I brought this cup here."

Yishan was greatly touched by that. He was very thankful that the Lord had once again met his need and moved in a special way. Of all the days of his leading Bible studies, he said, that evening *was* the time he especially needed that. After that time, that elderly brother began taking the whole canteen downstairs and left it on the table for Yishan.

While we were living in Pinole, we not only saw God's provision again and again, but we also saw His *one special protection*. That day was Tuesday, April 29, 1992, a very hot day, so warm that by midnight I still left the back patio door open.

Around 1:30 a.m., I just finished wrapping my last batch of curry pastry, put them in oven to bake, and began to wash pots and pans at the sink.

While I was standing in front of the sink washing dishes, I was praying for something that the Lord had burdened me to pray for. Naturally, I should be looking at the window shutter right in front of my eyes rather than what was going on outside the patio to my left side. However, it must be the Holy Spirit who suddenly drew my attention to some bright light and also some human sound beyond our backyard fence. At that moment I decided to walk over to the other side of the kitchen and pull the patio door shutter at least to partially cover the door. While I was standing there, I heard something moving on the patio not too far from where I was standing but about five or six feet away from the left side of the patio door, which was open. Although I could hear the movement, I really could not see anything outside except for a flicker of green or blue color. (It must be the color of an eye in the dark reflecting the light from inside of the house.) A few weeks back, a large black dog happened to wonder into our backyard, and I had to chase it away. So at that moment I thought it was some dog or other animal there, and I just stepped over a pot of poinsettia plant and calmly walked to the left side of the door and switched on the patio light in order to see what was actually out there on the patio.

The light I turned on was a very bright 500-watt halogen bulb, which immediately flooded the whole backyard with its white light. I still felt very calm since I thought it was only a dog or another animal. At that moment that animal ran away toward the wooden gate. (It was a double-sided gate and the hinge of one side had been broken, but Yishan had propped it up with two concrete blocks.) Then I heard the sound of pottery fallen to the ground. Whatever was running away had run with such a force that it had bumped that broken side of the gate down and the two concrete blocks had also fallen down, which I later found out.

"Well, whatever is there has run away," I said to myself and went back to wash dishes, still leaving the patio door open.

A few minutes later, I noticed a bright light outside the kitchen window in front of me. I assumed our next-door neighbor, whose house was higher than ours, had heard the commotion and had turned on their side light and came out. Curiosity made me walk outside to the gate where I saw two policemen coming toward me, and one of them asked, "Did you see the guy?"

"What guy? I didn't see a man. I saw an animal."

"No," he said, "it's not an animal. It's a guy. He jumped into your yard."

I then said, "He broke my gate too."

That gate had completely fallen down. It was lying on the ground, but none of the concrete blocks were broken.

Both the police officers went into my backyard and looked around and then left. I also came inside the house and locked the patio door and pulled the shutter completely closed.

It was then I realized what could have happened to me! Someone being chased by the police had jumped into my backyard and was stealthily trying to get into my house, and I had taken it to be an animal! He saw me, a lone woman in the kitchen, and my patio door was open. What an invitation for him to sneak into the house to rob or to harm me! When the Holy Spirit prompted me to walk over to the door, that guy was obviously crouching on the patio right next to a yellow bucket. He touched it and made a noise, and that was how I was able to judge his distance. It was my turning on the bright light that scared him off. The sudden bright light obviously had temporarily blinded him, and that was why he had to flee.

At that point I felt it necessary to wake up Yishan, who was soundly asleep in our bedroom.

"You need to get up and pray with me to thank the Lord for having kept me safe from harm."

After telling Yishan what had happened and praying together to thank the Lord, I went back to the kitchen to continue washing the dishes, but my heart kept beating wildly now that I realized what could have happened. So I also kept thanking God in continuous prayer.

However, I was not able to concentrate for long because I was also wondering what was happening to that thief. Were the police able to catch him? So I went out the front door and saw the same police officer walking down the street toward me, and I asked him if he was able to get hold of the thief. Unfortunately, he answered no. I then came back inside, locked the front door, and continued my dish washing. I continued to thank the Lord while washing the dishes.

Just then the doorbell rang, and Yishan cried out from the bedroom, "Do not open the door!" It was then I realized he was still awake. I went to the front door and asked, "Who is it?"

"Police department."

I turned on the front light, and from the peephole I could see a policeman (another one) in uniform, so I opened the door.

"There is a prowler around here," he said. "Could I come to your backyard and look?"

"You're welcome," I answered. "Would you like me to turn on the back light for you?"

"If you don't mind," he said.

I then turned on the patio light and saw the policeman shining a flashlight on a tree in the backyard. He kept looking up into the tree, obviously trying to see if anybody was hiding up there. He was there a long time before he left. I let the halogen lamp on for a while before turning it off.

By this time Yishan was up sitting by his desk, studying. I then knelt down with him by our bed to pray and thank the Lord again. Then I went back to the kitchen to continue the unfinished dishes. When I finally finished washing those dishes, I went to the bedroom to take a shower. By this time Yishan was asleep again, but my mind was still much occupied. It was impossible to fall asleep. I then opened up the Bible to Psalm 91. I read the Chinese version and then the NASB. After that, I also read Psalm 27. I read both psalms a few times, and then meditated on Psalm 91. This psalm became very personal to me because of that night's experience. I felt as if the whole psalm was meant for me, especially when I thought of the disaster that had come so close to me. My life was almost endangered. My heart would beat much faster thinking about it. Then I would begin to praise and thank God again. And so it went on the whole night, and I did not really go to bed until sometime after 6:00 a.m.

Sometime around 2:00 p.m., I went to knock at the door of my next-door neighbor. I told her what had happened during the night before. Upon hearing that, she picked up her phone and called the Pinole Police Department. They told her there were *two* car thieves on one of the higher-up streets who were pursued by the police down to the road outside my backyard fence and then jumped into my backyard.

It was actually more dangerous than I thought the night before! No wonder those policemen kept coming to my yard. What if the second thief had continued to hide in my yard?

Then later that Wednesday evening when I watched the TV news, I heard that very same day a policeman who was pursuing a car thief in another Bay Area had been shot in the leg by that car thief and had died.

Wow! Car thieves are armed! They are dangerous! The Lord certainly had great mercy on me and had protected me from all the possible dangers lurking in the dark that night! I am *so* thankful!

I have one more story to share with you of the Lord's faithfulness in keeping us in His care before I move on to another chapter.

This happened during the second year of our ministry with HGC. By that time the man I called Jay had finished his seminary studies and returned to Southeast Asia, and HGC was in need of someone to function as a pastor. Very quickly, HGC decided to ordain Yishan as its pastor and invitations were sent out to various churches and friends, including those who had been supporting us after we moved to the SF Bay Area.

Shortly after the ordination ceremony, however, some of our friends and churches stopped sending us the support checks, probably assuming that Yishan had become a full-time pastor receiving full salary. In fact, Yishan was only pastor in name while the monetary support we received from HGC remained the same. As a result of the stop of most outside support, our income was drastically reduced, and we were in financial trouble.

Nevertheless, Yishan and I stood steadfast in our reliance on the Lord. We made our needs known only to Him and would not mention it to any human soul.

I remembered once back in Schaumburg when Leslie asked me that question, "Mommy, Boppy is the sole breadwinner in our family, and you do not have an income. In the future when both Angela and I go to college at the same time, who is going to provide the tuition money?"

At that time I assured Leslie that God and I had sort of an unwritten agreement when He called me into the ministry that He would be responsible for my needs, and if He should *ever* let me suffer financial lacks, it would be a signal that He had no more need of me. Then I could be free to find a secular job.

So in 1991 when I looked at our tight financial situation after Yishan's ordination, I was beginning to think, *Maybe the Lord has no more use of me, and it is time for me to look for another job.*

It was another trying time for me and Yishan. I repeatedly told the Lord that I would rather serve Him than any secular employer, and unless He made His will clear to me, I was not going to take any move.

Just then I happened to think we should invite a specific deacon's family to have dinner with us. This deacon's daughter, being one year younger than Corrie, was very close to Corrie, and I thought it would be especially beneficial for Corrie to have that family over. By then we still had not revealed our special financial needs to anyone else.

I still vividly remember that late afternoon as that deacon and his wife were sitting with me and Yishan at the dinner table. In the middle of the conversation, that deacon suddenly mentioned, "By the way, we had a deacons' meeting at church the other day, and we decided to give you a raise in salary."

When he told us the amount of the salary, Yishan and I felt relieved, and we also believed the Lord had once again heard our prayers. I was especially grateful because I knew the Lord was still going to use me.

Our God is faithful indeed, and His word is always true. "O taste and see that the Lord is good: blessed is the man that trusteth in him. O fear the Lord, ye his saints: for there is no want to them that fear him. The young lions do lack, and suffer hunger: but they that seek the Lord shall not want any good thing" (Psalm 34:8–10)

Yes, those seminary days were full of trials and tests, but we saw also plenty of God's grace. Would I have moved to the Bay Area if I had known I would be going through so many trials? Absolutely. There is no turning back when we follow Jesus. Plus, I would not have exchanged those trials and God's grace for any amount of silver or gold. God's way is always the best way, and those seminary days have become part of God's blessings to me.

Chapter 17

Our Fathers

From the very beginning, I have mentioned Yishan and I had a common background. Both our fathers had squandered the family inheritance and made our families poor. As far as I could remember, I was never fond of my own father.

With Yishan's father, it was a little different. He never mistreated me. When he and Yishan's mother came to live with us in Chicago, although his smoking irked me, I tried to be a dutiful daughter as I mentioned in chapter 3. Then in 1974, when I received the miraculous healing on my toothache and felt the wonderful touch of the Lord and experienced His power, my life was greatly changed, and I began to pray for the salvation of all my loved ones and acquaintances, including Yishan's parents, my own father being the only exception.

In December 1978, six months after Yishan and I prayed daily for our visit to Taiwan and for our relatives' salvation, we made the trip to Taiwan but did not have much success in our evangelistic effort. Yishan talked to his parents, especially his father, but they seemed very aloof.

In February 1982, we made our second trip to Taiwan. Within a week Yishan led his second sister to the Lord, and he was able to convince his mother and both sisters to attend a Taiwanese-speaking church where he was asked to give his personal testimony.

However, Yishan was not able to improve on his father. The latter was as immovable as the Rock of Gibraltar as far as his faith was concerned. Every time Yishan tried to talk to him about the Christian faith, he would soon walk away to the second-story balcony to work on his orchids, or as Yishan continued to talk to his mother, his father from time to time would shoot back a few words at his son because he had inevitably listened to the whole thing his son had said to his wife.

Across the street from Yishan's parents' home, there was a Catholic church. To my father-in-law, Catholics and Protestants were not much different. All were believers of Jesus Christ. He retorted to Yishan by saying, "I have watched those Catholic nuns and priests a long time, and I am convinced that people came to believe in Jesus either because they had survived grave illnesses to the point of death or because they had been losers in love affairs. You can ask those Catholic nuns and priests if you don't believe me."

Yishan was able to correct his father by saying, "Well, I am a Christian, and neither of those scenarios you mentioned applies to me."

After that trip both Yishan and I came to our conclusion that his father, being a Taiwanese male of an older generation, would not easily yield himself to take his son's faith. It would take a special act of God for this old man to submit himself to the Lordship of Jesus Christ.

On December 14 (a Tuesday) of that same year, 1982, I received an unexpected phone call in the evening. Yishan was still at work that evening, attending a special meeting held at his company. The phone call came from his second sister, who had received Christ earlier that year.

"Father is ill," she said. "He has been hospitalized here in Hsinchu for two months. Doctors are not able to tell us what's wrong. He has been vomiting, even vomiting blood now. He is crying for Yishan and keeps saying, 'Too late, too late.'"

I prayed as soon as I hung up the phone. As I prayed, I felt great peace, knowing this was God's way of working for my father-in-law's salvation. Until he was told he was going to die, he would not worry about going to hell, which was what Yishan had told him would be the consequence of rejecting Jesus Christ. That was why he was crying.

He wanted his son to come to lead him to Christ now, but he thought it was too late.

When Yishan came home later that evening, I informed him about the phone call as well as my prayer and my own conviction. Later he prayed, and he felt the same conviction I had.

The next day Yishan called the same travel agent from whom we had purchased tickets for our both trips to Taiwan. The agent answered, "There are no more tickets available since it is so close to Christmas now." I still remember a month earlier before that somebody at church had told about being unable to get a ticket when planning to go to Taiwan.

Yishan was about to hang up the phone when the agent asked, "How many tickets do you need?"

"Only one," answered Yishan, and that agent said, "Somebody just returned a ticket thirty minutes ago." Praise the Lord! He always supplied our need.

That Saturday, December 18, Yishan left for Taiwan. Before he left, we both prayed together daily, asking the Lord to intervene. We asked the Lord to give doctors the wisdom so as to be able to diagnose my in-law's illness. We also asked the Lord to help Yishan's mother and sisters so that they would know what to do in every situation.

When Yishan arrived in Taipei, his eldest sister met him at the airport and said, "Relax. Father is not going to die."

She then went on to tell him how around the time when Yishan and I were praying, his mother and sisters decided that they should once again send his father back to veteran's hospital in Taipei, where he was initially admitted. When the doctors *there* could not find out what was wrong,then he was transferred to Hsinchu Hospital to be near home. When he was taken back to the veteran's hospital, his wife and daughters had also prepared burial clothes for him in case he could not make it. In fact, doctors had already informed his family that he would not survive and that they had better be prepared for a funeral and burial.

Once back at veteran's hospital, however, the doctors were able to find gallstones in him. They gave him medication to arrest the pain, and he was out of immediate danger.

It was rather unusual that during the first two plus months doctors of both hospitals failed to pinpoint the cause of his illness since gallstones were not that hard to detect. Yishan and I both saw the Lord's hand in his father's illness since he was the kind of person that unless his life was endangered, he would not capitulate easily.

When Yishan arrived at the hospital and saw his father, he said, "Pa, all my Christian friends in the States are praying for you."

Yishan said his father was greatly moved when hearing that, his eyes becoming moist, and he said, "All seventy-plus years of my life, I have been a Buddhist, and I have never prayed for people other than my own family. Your Christian friends do not know me, and yet they're praying for me. Christians are so loving and selfless. Oh, I'm greatly touched."

Yishan told me he had never before seen his father shed tears, and he believed the latter was really touched by Christian love. Thus, Yishan was able to go one step further in leading his father in praying to receive Jesus Christ as his Lord and Savior.

It seemed that Yishan's father really opened his heart to Christ because he immediately showed a hunger for the Word of God. While still in the hospital in his weak condition, he would try to hold up a heavy Bible to read. After he was discharged from the hospital and went home, he started attending Sunday worship at a Taiwanese church with his wife, the same church where Yishan gave a testimony before.

(Let me interject a comment here, not mine but that of Yishan on the situation under which his father became a believer in Jesus Christ. "His own prediction about surviving grave illness even to the point of death before turning himself in to Jesus Christ was literally fulfilled on himself." Nevertheless, it was still something for us to thank and praise the Lord for!)

Back then overseas telephone calls were quite expensive. Communications were kept mostly by way of letter writing. About six months after Yishan's father accepted Christ, Yishan wrote to his father and said, "Now that you have believed in the Christian faith for some time, I think you can begin considering receiving baptism."

The old man wrote back and sternly scolded his son, "I know how to handle my own affairs. Don't meddle with me. I don't want to be baptized until I have a thorough understanding of the Bible. I don't want to be like your sister [Yishan's second] who went ahead to receive baptism without fully understanding the Bible. Ha, she has even been elected a deacon at church!"

Yishan wrote back to his father, "Nobody can thoroughly understand the Bible in his lifetime. Even *I* myself still have not been able to do that." It was useless urging his father to take one more step further. We knew the Holy Spirit had to do the work. We just continued to pray for him that he would receive baptism soon.

Sometime later around January or February of 1984, while Yishan was attending a conference in Las Vegas and visiting some friends near LA, I got another unexpected phone call from Yishan's sister who had become a deacon at her church.

"Father is gravely ill again."

I was greatly concerned and asked, "Has he been baptized yet?"

"No," was the reply.

I prayed before I had a chance to call Yishan to relay the news to him. As I prayed for Yishan's father, I had a strong ominous feeling that this illness was not going to improve and that it was about time for him to be taken. Still, I prayed that the Lord would give him an opportunity to be baptized before taking him.

After Yishan returned from the West Coast, he kept in close contact with his sister. Every so often he would call her to ask about his father's condition and whether he had been baptized. Both answers were in the negative.

Then one day we were told that he slipped into a coma. We almost became frantic and desperately pleaded with the Lord: "Lord, please don't take him. He is not baptized yet. Please let him wake up to receive baptism. Then You can take him."

The Lord mercifully answered our prayers. Sometime later my father-in-law woke up from his coma and asked to be baptized. His wife and daughters hurriedly called the pastor to come and baptize him. The following day he went home to be with the Lord. What a faithful God! What a marvelous Savior!

Now let me focus on my own father.

Throughout my years growing up and most of my adult life, I was never fond of him. The reason? My family was poor because of Father's irresponsibility. Every semester during my six years of junior and senior high, I always had a hard time paying tuition. It was not a tuition-free education then. As a result, I became severely pessimistic and felt a strong sense of social injustice. I resented my father and disliked his presence at home whenever he was not living with another woman.

When I was born, my mother later told me a number of times that my father was living with another woman and did not bring money home. We were so poor and Mother was so lack in nutrition that she did not produce enough milk to nurse me. As a result, I cried a lot as a baby!

What does our modern psychology tell us about a baby crying a lot during her infancy because of hunger? No wonder I was pessimistic and feeling lonely a lot of times during my teenage years. It was really by God's grace that I did not become an emotional wreck.

Another reason I disliked Father was because I thought he was an atheist. Mother was a devout Buddhist and often sacrificed to her gods. Whenever Father was home and saw Mother burning incense and offering sacrifices, he would snicker at her superstition. It only intensified my resentment toward him.

In 1974, when I experienced the miraculous healing of my tooth and was convinced of the literal reliability of the Bible, I began to pray for the salvation of all my acquaintances with one exception. I believed Father deserved hell and refused to pray for him.

As I began to witness for the Lord and led Bible studies and even preached sermons, the Holy Spirit began to convict me of my need to forgive my father (John 16:8; Matthew 18:35). I would simply turn a deaf ear to the Holy Spirit, or I would bargain with Him, "Lord, I have been so deeply hurt by Father that I cannot forgive him. You'll have to heal me *first* before I can pray for his salvation."

For almost ten years, I held on to that tug-of-war with the Lord. Of course, the Lord never yielded to me, but then I would not budge. I was really stone-hearted without realizing it.

In an earlier chapter, I mentioned my friend Juliet, although not by name. She is a dear sister in the Lord to me. When I was still in Schaumburg, she once joined a short-term mission team taking the gospel to Taiwan. Around Thanksgiving of 1990, she called me, "Carmen, pray for me. I feel the Lord wants me to go to Taiwan next spring."

"Are you going with that mission team again?" I asked.

"Probably not."

"Then how will you be able to speak to the people about Jesus since you will not have an interpreter?"

"I don't know. Just pray for me."

I also asked Juliet what month she had in mind of going, and she said April.

I began to pray earnestly for Juliet's trip. As I prayed more, I began to feel a conviction that I should accompany Juliet on this trip. Being a Caucasian and knowing neither the Chinese nor Taiwanese language, she was willing to obey the Lord in taking the gospel to Taiwan. It would be my obligation to help her in fulfilling the great commission.

I also asked Yishan to pray for this. Somehow he had a different idea and began praying, "Lord, please help us so that next summer Carmen and I can go to Taiwan to preach the gospel."

At that time, you probably recall, Yishan and I were both seminary students living in Pinole and pastoring HGC. I was thinking of skipping one semester so that I could accompany Juliet to Taiwan in April. Yishan, however, was a full-time student, and only summer was convenient for him. Although we often prayed together for the trip, he was not happy that I wanted to go in April. He thought I was being selfish, trying to go by myself and depriving him of a chance.

That Christmas someone from church gave Corrie a gift, a very nice sweater bought at Macy's. Five minutes after she put it on, however, the bottom edge unraveled. Since the store was not open on Christmas Day, I had to wait until December 26 to take Corrie there for an exchange. When I came home, Yishan told me, "Juliet called."

"What did she say?"

Instead of answering my question directly, Yishan asked me, "What month did you say Juliet wanted to go?"

"April."

Yishan could be sneaky when he chose to. He then went on to tell me he had asked Juliet that very question, and she had given the same answer.

Well, for Yishan, it was a confirmation from the Lord. From then on, he began to pray with me that I might be able to take the gospel to Taiwan in the coming April.

However, as I continued to pray, the Holy Spirit began to deal with me again. "If you are taking the gospel to Taiwan, you should tell it to your own father first. He is eighty-five years old. There is not much time left for him."

By then I had been told that Father could no longer take care of himself and had been taken to a nursing home. None of my sisters had visited him there, and they knew only the general area rather than the specific location of that place.

Yes, I was convinced of the need to witness to Father, and I began to pray for the April trip and also for Father's salvation.

As I prayed more, I began to feel accompanying Juliet would be a hindrance to me. Thus, I began to pray that I might go alone and dedicate the whole trip to bring Father to the salvation of the Lord.

It was interesting (and awe-inspiring) to see how the Lord led me on this trip step by step. Although I never told Yishan how I felt, one day he said to me, "I think you should go to Taiwan by yourself. If you accompany Juliet, how are you going to have enough time to help your father to know the Lord?"

So Yishan and I began to pray that Juliet would change her mind so that I could go to Taiwan alone.

On January 14, someone I had asked to pray for my trip called, "Carmen, have you purchased a ticket for your Taiwan trip yet? I've heard that starting tomorrow Northwest Airline is going to raise the airfare."

"No, I have not heard from my friend in Chicago, and I don't know if she has bought the ticket or not. I'll call her right away."

Immediately, I called Juliet, and she answered, "No, Carmen, I have not purchased a ticket. In fact, to tell you the truth, since I made that phone call asking you to pray, I seemed to have lost my burden, and I no longer want to go to Taiwan."

Praise the Lord! If He had not touched Juliet's heart to call me in the first place, I would never have initiated that thought of taking the gospel to my father. Surely, our Lord is sovereign and merciful. He truly is "not wishing for any to perish but for all to come to repentance" (2 Peter 3:9).

So I made the trip to Taiwan in April 1991 and two of my sisters accompanied me on the first visit to see my father. Since neither of my sisters knew the exact location of that nursing home, we had to ask the neighbors around that area before we were able to locate it. I still remember that the day was a Tuesday.

Once we were inside that building, we had difficulty finding Father. It was not an awfully large building, only somewhat larger than an average two-story house in the United States. At the entrance downstairs, there was a small reception booth, only there was no attendant there. So we began looking around, trying to find Father among those old men.

As soon as we entered that place, my second sister actually said, "That old man sitting in front of the TV looks like Father."

My other sister and I took a look, and we both said, "No, it couldn't be. Father has long hair, and that old man's head is shaved."

Someone there asked, "Who are you looking for?"

We said Father's name, and that man said, "No, he is not here. He is on the second floor."

The three of us began climbing the stairs. Halfway up, we met a man going down, obviously an attendant there, and he asked, "Who are you looking for?"

When we told him Father's name, he said Father was on the first floor, not the second floor, and he pointed out the old man sitting in front of the TV.

Second Sister walked over to Father and called him, "Father." However, he seemed to have dementia and had a hard time recognizing who was talking to Him. When he finally recognized his second daughter, the latter said, "Carmen is back." Again, Father seemed lost.

By that time I had begun walking toward the entrance. A sudden anger rose in me, and I thought, *If Father has a hard time hearing and understanding, what's the use of my coming back all the way from the States to bring the gospel to him?*

Stopping at the entrance, however, I prayed and immediately recognized Satan's tactic. I asked the Lord for patience and wisdom, and a thought came, *Since I have come all the way from the States, why not give it a try?*

By the time I walked over to Father, he seemed to have regained his senses. He not only recognized me but also said, "Carmen, you are back! Is ... back also?" I knew he was asking about Yishan, but he was not able to recall his son-in-law's name.

So I said, "I came back all alone. Yishan did not come back. He stays in the United States with the girls."

Then he asked me, "When are you going back to the United States?"

I answered, "April 28."

In the short ensuing conversation, he asked me the same question two more times, and each time I gave him the date. Immediately, I realized that Father had a problem with short-term memory. So I cut short the formalities and went directly to the purpose of my visit and simply said, "Father, you need Jesus."

His answer totally surprised me. He said, "Yes, I know."

Curiously, I could not help asking him, "How did you know?"

"At my age I know I need a heavenly home where I can go."

He went on to tell me that when he was sixteen years old, Mrs. Lee, his next-door neighbor, took him to a Taiwanese church for a whole year, and there he learned of the Creator of the heavens and the earth. "That is why your mother's religion and mine are different."

For the first time in my life, it dawned on me that Father was not an atheist. Still, I wanted to make sure he understood the gospel, the true meaning of salvation.

"Do you know why you need Jesus?" I asked.

He stammered as he tried to find words to answer. Then the words of John 17:3 came to my mind. "And this is eternal life, that they may know Thee, the only true God, and Jesus Christ whom Thou has sent." And then I realized why the Lord wanted me to take this trip. Father knew only the first half of the eternal life ("knowing Thee, the only true God") but he was still ignorant of the second half ("and Jesus Christ whom Thou has sent"). Right there I also saw clearly God's mercy and my own disobedience. God was willing to deliver Father from the damnation of hell and give him the gift of eternal life, but Father needed to know the second half of the truth, the knowledge of the salvation provided through Jesus Christ. And yet I had so adamantly refused to bring the gospel to Father until this moment. *I was ashamed of my own sin*, and inwardly, I prayed for the Lord to forgive me.

Therefore, I explained the way of salvation to Father and asked, "Do you believe you are a sinner?"

"Yes," he answered without any hesitation.

"Do you want to pray and ask Jesus to forgive your sins and receive Him as your Lord and Savior?"

Thank God. Not only was I able to be straightforward in asking Father these questions, but he also gladly answered in the affirmative and prayed the sinner's prayer. Then I prayed to thank the Lord and asked him to bless Father.

Around that moment an attendant brought Father a lunch box, and he opened it and began to eat. His hands were a little shaky, and he dropped some rice on the bed. I was thinking of helping him, but he seemed to read my mind and said, "That's okay. I can do it myself." He was able to pick up the rice without difficulty.

As I sat there watching Father eating his lunch, unable to do anything to help him, for the first time in my life, I felt the love of a daughter for her father ebbing out from my heart.

The Lord had healed my hurt!

It was then I realized how sinful I had been all those years in holding on to that tug-of-war with the Lord. I had insisted He heal me first so that I could forgive Father. And yet the Lord had meant to heal me once I had been obedient to His command! Not only was I ashamed of myself, but my heart was also full of thanksgiving that the Lord was so gracious in giving me the joy of bringing Father to salvation in His Son, Jesus Christ. What a sovereign and merciful God!

The next day, Wednesday, I went to a Christian bookstore and bought a large-print Chinese New Testament Bible. I then took it to Father as I visited him for the second time. I wanted to be sure his repentance was genuine, and I asked, "Did you mean it when you prayed to receive Jesus yesterday?"

"Yes, I was serious," he said.

I asked him if he would like to be baptized and explained to him the meaning of baptism. As I talked, I opened the Bible and read several passages of important doctrine. Again, Father's reply was in the affirmative.

I then called my eldest sister, the only Christian among my three sisters, to ask her pastor to baptize Father. However, since her pastor did not know Father, he said he needed to talk to Father first. So on my third visit to the nursing home, I witnessed the conversation Father had with that pastor and an elder from his church whom the pastor had brought along.

At the beginning the pastor practically examined Father's faith and eventually led Father to pray the sinner's prayer one more time. I rejoiced the Lord was allowing me to witness the confirmation of Father's genuine repentance. Furthermore, I was able to see the Lord's hand of blessing on Father. It seemed to me that once Father received Jesus into his heart, his dementia seemed to lessen. He was able to carry on a very lively conversation with the church elder in Japanese that was so fluent that the elder commented to my eldest sister, who was also listening on the side, "Your father's memory is still very good. He remembers so many things from long ago, and he has not forgotten his Japanese." (My eldest sister was also fluent in Japanese.)

Father was baptized on Saturday, April 27, 1991. What a joyous occasion! His younger brother, my uncle, who was also an elder of that pastor's church, and my uncle's wife both came for the occasion. Together with my younger brother and my eldest sister, both Christians, we celebrated the addition of a fourth Christian in our family. As I held the bowl of holy water, the pastor sprinkled water on Father and baptized him in the name of the Father, the Son, and the Holy Spirit. My mission was accomplished.

Nearly four years later on January 30, 1995, I received a phone call from Taiwan saying that Father had gone home to be with the Lord. That day was the lunar calendar's New Year's Eve.

According to the Taiwanese custom, Father's funeral would not take place until more than three weeks later. I was thus able to purchase an airline ticket and prepare for the funeral.

However, disputes ensued among my three brothers regarding the funeral. Everyone in the family agreed, except one brother, that Father should have a Christian funeral. Even my eldest brother and his wife, both devout Buddhists, agreed to this since Father had been baptized. Yet that lone brother insisted having a Buddhist ceremony for Father.

By Taiwanese customs, girls once married are out of the family and thus have no right in the decision-making process. However, I believe the Lord reigns supreme. I prayed and prayed. Finally, a compromise was reached. There would be a Buddhist ceremony for Father in the funeral home on Sunday afternoon followed by cremation. The next day on Monday morning, his ashes would be picked up and the urn brought to the church for a memorial service.

I believe in the power of Jesus to keep His believers saved until the end, and I had no doubt in the genuine repentance of Father. However, I was not able to go back to Taiwan to visit Father again after that trip in 1991, and although I faithfully prayed for Father during that period (nearly four years), I did not know if Father was able to have any fellowship with other Christians. He had made himself so odious to his children that my eldest sister did not visit Father again after his baptism. I was also unsure if Father ever picked up that Bible again after the baptism. Without God's Word or Christian fellowship to grow on, I could not be assured if Father had been firm in his faith.

Before I flew to Taiwan for Father's memorial service, I prayed daily, asking the Lord to give me a sign that Father was with Him. I have always believed in the doctrine of salvation by grace through faith in Jesus Christ and His keeping power. Deep down in my heart, I was sure Father was saved, but my uncertainty about Father's spiritual condition after his baptism plus the arrangement of the Buddhist ceremony cast a long shadow on my firm belief.

The night I arrived in Taiwan, several days before the funeral, my eldest sister and younger brother came to meet me at the airport. I was to stay at this brother's place. As he was driving toward my sister's home to drop her off, she told me she had a dream the night before.

"I dreamed Father's urn was glowing in the church."

I knew the Lord had given me the sign I asked for. Of course, Father was safe with Jesus.

Still, four years later in 1999, when my eldest sister and her husband together with my youngest sister came to visit, the former told me of another dream she had some time earlier. Keep in mind that my eldest sister and her husband were both baptized Christians, but my other two sisters are Buddhists.

"I dreamed that you [referring to me] were leading me, Chung [her husband's name], and Hwa [my youngest sister] on a journey to the heavenly kingdom. Halfway through the journey, you said to Hwa, 'You still do not know the way of the heavenly kingdom. You cannot come with us yet. You can join us later.' Then when we arrived, I saw a big mansion, and I asked to see Father. As we stood at the entrance, I saw Father in a handsome white suit walking downstairs. A girl at the entrance told me, 'This man is the chairman of the board of our company.' And then I woke up."

I believe the Lord gave my sister these two dreams so that I could be assured of Father's salvation as well as his reward in heaven. Although Father *never* lived a life of a victorious Christian, the Lord *did* receive glory through Father's salvation *and* his death. For that day in church during the memorial service as I delivered the eulogy for Father, I was able to tell how the Lord had graciously led me to bring His salvation to Father and assured me of Father's place in heaven by my sister's dream of the urn glowing in the church. The Lord was glorified during that funeral service.

Besides these two dreams the Lord gave my eldest sister, my youngest sister, who was not a Christian, told me something else when I was in Taiwan during another trip after the time I attended Father's memorial service, and that was also very important to me, knowing the true repentance of Father and his salvation. About two or three months before Father went home to be with the Lord, I was told that twice Father cried and said, "I have done wrong. I have done wrong" (a literal translation from Taiwanese). In telling me this, my youngest sister emphasized the fact that Father was truly sorry when he said those words, crying with a lot of tears. Father was not a man who cried easily. I never saw him shed tears in my whole life. Surely, under the conviction of the Holy Spirit, Father was repenting all the wrongs he had done to his family, and I'm sure by God's grace he had been forgiven because of his confession of faith in our Lord, Jesus Christ.

Recently, I had a chance to ask my sister again about Father's crying and repentance, and she said more specifically that Father repented of his wrongs to Mother and to our whole family. Praise God!

Our God is really good and gracious. He mercifully saved both our fathers, Yishan's and mine, two men who otherwise would deserve hell.

Chapter 18

Children and Grandchildren

*I*n September 1992, Yishan and I were still living in Pinole when we began ministry with the church in F City. Earlier in July of that summer, we put our house on the market. Since the big Loma Prietta earthquake of October 17, 1989, the housing market in the San Francisco Bay Area had been sluggish, and by September 1992, when we began new ministry in F City, our Pinole home was still waiting for a good offer.

We did some house-hunting in F City in the summer, and the picture looked bleak to us. We were told the M District had the best schools. (Corrie would begin high school in September.) But all the houses we looked at cost more than three hundred thousand dollars, which very uncomfortable for us since our Pinole home was priced for less than $170,000, and we had not been able to get an offer close to that. There was no way we could bridge the gap to get a decent home in the M District. The only thing we could do was pray.

By September when we began our new ministry in F City, we had to commute forty-five minutes to an hour one way. Once on a rainy day, it took even longer, somewhat more than an hour, and it happened that I had to drive alone that day. By November, I was beginning to feel weary from the almost daily commute, and I prayed, "Lord, if you see fit, could You please get our house sold by the end of this year?"

Finally, when we got an offer that was accepted and the buyer signed the contract, it was December 31, 1992. The Lord pitied me and answered my prayer exactly as I had asked. Although we lost twenty thousand dollars on that house, the Lord more than made it up for us in our next purchase. In the five or six months' time when our Pinole home was waiting for an acceptable offer, home prices in the M District were also tumbling, even more than those in the Pinole area. Since we were able to accumulate some savings during these months, by the time we were ready to make an offer in F City, a home was within our reach, and thus, Corrie was able to transfer to M S J High School later as a sophomore.

The house we purchased in F City is situated on the M Hill. Interestingly enough, during those months when Yishan and I were commuting from Pinole to F City, I used to look at that area where those houses looked so high on the hill, especially since you could see that area as soon as you exited from the freeway. As soon as I saw those houses, I would think, *They're too high for us to reach.* To me at that time, high meant both literally and figuratively. Almost every time I had that thought, I would also ask in my heart, "Lord, are those houses too high for us to reach? All things are possible with You."

Indeed, once again the Lord proved nothing was impossible for Him.

However, we encountered another problem that we had to ask the Lord to solve for us. Since it was not good to transfer Corrie to a new school in the middle of the semester, we asked the Lord to provide a family for Corrie to stay with in the Pinole area until summer. I asked the Lord for three specific things. First, it had to be a Christian family. Second, there would be no older boy(s) in that family. Third, I wanted the room and board asked by that family to be within our means.

One day Corrie told us a girl named Lianne had talked to her parents about Corrie's need, and they wanted to talk to me and Yishan. This was really another answer to prayer. Lianne, you see, was a sophomore, and since Corrie was a freshman, they would not have known each other. However, Lianne had not taken biology when she was a freshman and ended up in the same biology class with Corrie. It also happened that both girls liked to go to the library

211

after school, and they had spent some time together. When Yishan and I went to Lianne's home, her parents graciously received us. As it turned out, her parents were new Christians and were going to be baptized shortly on that upcoming Easter. Lianne had a younger brother in the sixth grade, and when I saw him, I knew he was too young for me to worry about. Then we asked Lianne's parents how much we would have to pay for Corrie's room and board.

When I heard the figure, I thought it was too little, and I asked them, "Are you sure it's enough?"

"Yes, we have thought it over and figured it out," answered Lianne's father.

Thus, the Lord solved our problem, but moreover, at the end of that semester when Corrie came home for the summer, she seemed a changed person. She had become much more agreeable to me after staying with Lianne's family for less than three months! It seemed to me the Lord had performed another miracle.

In less than a year after we moved to F City, we heard the good news that Angela was pregnant, and later we learned it was going to be a boy. She and her husband, Albert, decided to name him Daniel. She also told me they wanted Albert's father to give Daniel a Chinese name and use it for his middle name. "When we have a second child, then we want *you* to give the baby a Chinese name," Angela said to me.

It was welcome news because it meant that I would not have to worry about naming a baby for the time being. As a matter of fact, after I learned of Angela's pregnancy, I began to feel something like a panic attack. Since we were very busy in our ministry, I was rather worried that I would not have time to enjoy being a grandmother.

Daniel was born on the day before we had to leave for a church retreat. However, we did not get to see him until we returned. Since Angela developed gestational diabetics during the pregnancy, the birth had to be induced. That afternoon Yishan and I hurried to the hospital to pray for Angela and the soon-to-be-born baby, and then we had to leave. When we returned from the retreat, Angela and baby Daniel had already gone home.

Amazingly, I found that in spite of my duties at church and home, I was still able to find time to help Angela with bathing the baby and cooking some special food for her. Thank God that I *was* able to enjoy being a grandmother, and I realized that a grandson was a tremendous joy. Yishan showed no less joy in being a grandfather, although he was not able to go over to Angela's house as frequently as I was.

Sometime after Daniel was born, I asked Angela what Chinese name his other grandfather had given him. When Angela showed me the name Albert's father had written, I told Angela it was not so good, and Angela replied, "Too late. It's already been registered with the county."

Let me explain a little here. Albert's parents speak Cantonese, and his dad chose that name only thinking in Cantonese, not in Mandarin. The name written in Chinese was fine, but when it was sounded out in Mandarin, it also sounded like the words for cunning or traitor. Later I asked several friends, and they all felt the same. Yet when I told this to Yishan, he said, "Don't bother. Daniel is an American. How often does an American kid use a Chinese name?"

Maybe I was stubborn, but this Chinese name of Daniel's really bothered me, so I put the matter before the Lord. "Lord, move Albert and Angela's hearts so that they'll do something about it. Give Daniel a good Chinese name."

At the time when Angela said to me, "Too late," Albert was not home. He was away in Japan on a business trip. When he came home, Angela did tell him, and he called his dad. A few days later, she informed me that the problematic word had been changed. When I heard it, I praised the Lord because it was a perfect solution. Although the meaning of the name was basically the same, its Mandarin pronunciation was different (same sound but different tones). They were as different as heaven and hell when compared to the original name. The best of it was that its Cantonese spelling for the middle name could remain the same, and thus, there was no need to change registration.

This whole thing later prompted me to write an article about giving names. "If giving a baby a suitable name was so complicated," I wrote, "how much more difficult it was for Adam to name all the animals! Surely, Adam must have possessed super high intelligence, and thus, we can also understand why early man's history exemplified high intellect such as in the pyramid and other ancient civilizations." (I had read some archaeological books that contained a lot of evidences for the advanced human mind in ancient civilizations.)

Two years after Daniel's birth, we got two more grandchildren. Leslie gave birth to Ethan, and six weeks later Megan was born to Angela and Albert, both in 1996. Megan actually had the same due date as Daniel's birthday, and she could have been born on that same date. But Albert and Angela chose a date earlier than that so that they could avoid celebrating two kid's birthday together, afraid one would not receive as much attention as the other. Well, for many years they ended up celebrating the birthday together! What an irony. For me, it was good since we would not have to spend so much time just traveling to celebrations. I could kill two birds with one stone!

A little earlier than that, one morning about more than a month before Ethan was born, I woke up with a word in my head, "Stillborn!" Although Angela and Leslie were both expecting at that time, when I woke up, I thought of only Leslie's baby, not Angela's, and I knew the Lord had given me a warning.

At that moment I thought of a woman back in Chicago more than a decade earlier. She was a nurse, and her pregnancy was in full term when one day she realized the baby in her womb had not moved for more than twenty-four hours. She immediately went to the doctor, but it was too late. The doctor told her to go to the hospital to have the birth induced. Since the baby was already dead, she had to push extra hard by herself, and she finally delivered a stillborn baby boy. The umbilical cord was wrapped around his neck, and he had choked to death.

That morning Yishan also woke up about the same time I did. Without telling him anything, I asked him, "Would you like to pray with me?"

"Sure," he said. Both of us knelt by the bed, and I began to pray.

"Lord, You are omniscient, and all things are possible with you. If the word I just heard was from You, I asked You to prevent the umbilical cord from wrapping around Ethan's neck or endangering him. However, Lord, if the wrapping is bound to occur, then I ask You to let Ethan be born ahead of his due date so that his life will not be endangered."

I think it was only when I prayed those words that Yishan learned of what was on my mind, and he kept saying, "Amen." His concern was no less intensified than mine.

After both of us rose from our prayers, I called Leslie. When I finished talking, even though I could not see her face, I knew she was horrified.

"What should I do?" Her voice was full of tension, and I tried to ease her.

"Do not be afraid. I think the Lord wants us to be diligent in prayer, and it will be okay."

Then I told her the story of the woman back in Chicago since Leslie never heard of it. And I also told her of something that occurred before she turned ten. It took place on a Sunday afternoon during my eighth month pregnancy with Corrie. My tummy was very large by that time. When I woke up that Sunday morning, Yishan said to me, "This morning when I woke up, I felt words in my tummy saying, 'Beware of a car accident.'" Then when we prayed together, Yishan said, "Lord, if You were warning me this morning of a potential car accident, we ask you to prevent it. When we go to church this afternoon, please watch over us and do not allow any car accident to occur." However, by the time the worship service was over, I had totally forgotten about the warning and our prayer that morning.

We were going to the NWC at that time. After leaving the church, our family got into the car, and Yishan was driving. After he passed an intersection with traffic lights, there was on the right side of the road a large shopping center with an empty parking lot since stores were closed on Sunday in those days. However, when Yishan came to that parking lot, a car that was waiting at the entrance suddenly came out and headed toward my side. Yishan, as I have mentioned, was usually not very sensitive, and by nature, his reaction was slow. However, at that critical moment, he turned his wheel to the left and went two lanes over to the other direction of the traffic. It was a four-lane street with two lanes on each direction. There was only a double-yellow dividing line and no middle island or divider. Fortunately, there was no coming traffic on that lane.

Around that time there were some accidents in the Chicago area involving people in old beat-up cars stopping suddenly in front of newer models to get hit, and then they would sue for compensation. Obviously, that was the purpose of that car that suddenly came out because it was full of passengers, and with more passengers, they could have sued for more compensation. If Yishan had hit that car, our loss would have been astronomical. However, it came out a little bit late, and it would have hit our car instead of ours hitting it. If an accident had occurred, I would have been hit first, and who knows what would have happened? However, the Lord enabled Yishan to avoid an accident, and all those people inside that car roared out in laughter as its driver sped away. (Obviously, there were some wicked people in that car with a wicked purpose, but the Lord did not allow them to harm us.) By then, of course, both Yishan and I remembered the Lord's warning that morning, and we were so thankful for the Lord's mercy in keeping us safe.

Leslie was ten when Corrie was born. She said she did not remember that incident, and I said, "Share this with Ling-Yi and pray with him every day. Boppy and I will pray for you also."

From that day on, Yishan and I prayed daily for Ethan, the same way I prayed that morning. Not only that, but we covered Angela and Megan in our prayer as well. I wanted no mishaps to happen to either Angela's or Leslie's pregnancy.

Ethan was born eleven days ahead of the due date, but I was so busy that I did not get to ask about the umbilical cord. That year from July 22 to 29, some members of our church and I were going to Anchorage, Alaska, for short-term mission, and Yishan had already left for Anchorage three weeks ahead of us. The Chinese church there was without a pastor, and he was helping with their ministry. I was busy with our own church while he was gone.

Yishan and I were together in Anchorage only two or three days, and then he had to fly back to California. I came back on July 29 and flew out to Boston the very next day to help with Leslie. It was not until two days after I was there when I remembered to ask Leslie that question.

"Oh, yes," said Leslie. "The umbilical cord *was* wrapped around Ethan's neck two times, but the nurse said it was all right because the umbilical cord was long."

"No," I corrected Leslie. "It's *not* because the umbilical cord was long. It *was because* God had answered our prayers. Everybody's umbilical cord was long, but the baby of that woman in Chicago did not make it because the umbilical cord had chocked him. Don't you think it was the Lord's mercy that He had let Ethan be born eleven days ahead so that he would not be choked?"

Later I learned that throughout the course of pregnancy, sometimes a baby could get entangled in the umbilical cord and was later able to untangle himself, but sometimes tragedies still struck when the baby failed to get him or herself out of the tangle.

When still later I told Ethan's story to my eldest sister who was ten years my senior (she is with the Lord now), she said that *I* was wrapped in the umbilical cord two and half turns when I was born. Did that mean that it was hereditary and ran in my family? I don't know, but I know one thing to be certain. God's mercy is plentiful in my life.

It was not until I began to edit this book that it dawned on me that I had been chosen by the Lord from my mother's womb. He had protected me from being harmed by the umbilical cord that had wrapped itself around my neck. Wow! No wonder early on in my childhood, I knew that I detested going into the Buddhist temple. I hated it because the inside looked so gloomy and terrifying to me. Then when I was in high school, whenever I accompanied my mother going to another one of those detestable places, it was even worse. I was simply disgusted in seeing those men and women burning incense (I was allergic to smoke of any kind) and bobbing their heads up and down while mumbling something in their mouths. To me at that time, that was the utmost form of superstition. (I must explain that I did not look down upon the Buddhist religion since it was the only religion I knew back then. It simply was the way I felt toward it. Especially when I was a child, I never heard of anything about the gospel, and Buddhism was the only religion in my world.) And of course, from then on, I refused to accompany my mother in going there again.

Then when I remembered what happened during my fifth- and sixth-grade years, I understood it was because the Lord had called me when I was still in my mother's womb. My family moved to Taipei City two weeks after I went into fifth grade. At the suggestion of my uncle's wife (we lived with their family at that time), my younger brother and I were enrolled at Chungsan Elementary School, which was not in our district. Chungsan School was a much better school than the one in our district. My uncle's wife asked a friend of hers who lived in that district to move my brother's name and mine into the latter's household so that the two of us could attend the better school. Sometimes my brother and I had to walk to school if we left early enough. If we were late, then we would have to take a bus.

In many of those late afternoons when I was walking home—my younger brother's class ended earlier, and he had left for home—I would always pass a church, a concrete Gothic-style building with a tall steeple, its door in the middle and a glass window on each side. Inside the left window was always displayed a picture of Jesus dressed as a shepherd with a flock of sheep behind Him and green meadow and deep blue sky and wisps of white cloud in the background. Whenever I was not in a hurry to go home, I would always stop at that window, look at the picture, and wish I were one of those sheep!

Still later when I was in junior high, whenever I had enough time, I would take the long way home. (On the shorter way, I would have to pay for a ticket to cross the platforms of Taipei Railway Station.) And I would pass a Catholic bookstore. There was also always a picture of Jesus (only the head, the traditional picture of Jesus I have seen in a lot of books or magazines) in the display window, and I would stand there and look at that picture for a long time. As I remember now, I must have loved Jesus even before I truly knew Him!

Those times in my younger years when I stood in front of those pictures of Jesus and looked for a long time, to me, really witness to the truthfulness of the words of Jesus as He says in John 12:32, "And I, if I be lifted up from the earth, will draw all men unto me." He indeed is the living Savior who has risen from the dead and is drawing all to Himself, even me at a tender young age, a girl who still did not truly know who He was!

I used to think I was one of the most unfortunate persons in the world. Well, now I know I have been blessed without realizing it. What can I say? God certainly is working mysteriously, and He does not have to consult with us for what He is going to do. But I can say, whatever He does, He does it beautifully!

When Megan was born, I was inspired by a card I bought and wrote a poem. I have written quite a number of Chinese poems, but I do not think I'm very good at English poetry. I have written a few in English, and in college two of them even won me prizes. But writing poetry in English has always seemed a lot harder for me. However, I did pray when I saw that card with baby handprints, asking the Lord to give me words, and this is what I wrote:

For My Grandchild

Ten tiny little fingers
that were wondrously made,
Do the work to God's command,
always a tribute to Him paid.
Two tiny hands and little feet
that were made by the awesome God,
May the Good Shepherd guide them
all the days of their life with His rod.

Leslie got two more children, Marisa and Jonathan, respectively in 1998 and 1999. They have both turned out to be fairly good gymnasts. Since they were together a lot, some thought they were twins, same as Angela and Leslie when they were in high school. That was interesting.

My sixth grandchild, Leslie's third son, Joshua, was born a few years after Yishan went home to be with the Lord.

Earlier that year someone at church told me that she was going to join a tour to China, and she suggested that I go with her. At first, I was told of a wrong return date, which made me very hesitant to join the trip. Joshua was due only a few days after our return from the trip. I had promised Leslie to go to Boston to help her when Joshua was born, and I was afraid I would not be back in time. On the other hand, I yearned to be on this tour. Since Yishan was with the Lord, when would I have a chance again to go on a tour with someone whom I will feel comfortable with?

As usual, I put this matter in the Lord's hand and fervently prayed about it. Later I was able to find out the exact return date. I would have two more days for housework in between the two trips. After I prayed about it some more time, I decided to join the tour. Thereafter, I daily prayed, "Lord, keep Joshua in Leslie's womb until I'm able to go to Boston. Please don't let him come out too soon."

Leslie used her frequent-flyer mileage to reserve a ticket for me. The date I decided on was a holiday since Leslie said the flight would not be so crowded on that holiday. She also said that we could change the date anytime without any penalty if necessary. Deep down in my heart, though, I did not want to change the date. At my age I've learned it's more convenient to have an aisle seat. If I should change the date at the last minute, chances were I would have to lose my aisle seat. Therefore, I fervently prayed that the Lord would see to my plight and help me.

Well, on the very day I returned from China, I received a call from Leslie, "Mommy, I'm starting to bleed."

Leslie was not distressed though. She was hopeful because she thought I could change the date whenever it was necessary.

I did not want to change the date, however, and I kept pleading with the Lord, "Please stop Leslie's bleeding and keep Joshua in Leslie's womb until I'm ready to go." The truth was that it was difficult for me to go any date earlier than the day originally planned. Since I had just come back from a long trip, I had quite a lot of housework to catch up before I could leave. And with only a few days between the two trips, any date earlier was just impossible for me.

I kept in daily contact with Leslie, and then she told me her doctor said she was beginning to dilate. I almost panicked, but I had confidence the Lord would answer my prayer.

The day before I left for Boston, Leslie called, "Mommy, I have just remembered this morning that tomorrow night when you come in, Ling-Yi might have difficulty picking you up. There will be a parade and fireworks in Boston, and they are probably going to begin at that time."

Goodness, there was one more thing to be worried about. Well, it was just one more item to go into prayer. "Lord, I would like to watch the fireworks tomorrow night. I have not watched a good fireworks display in ten years. If You see it fit, please give me a chance to see the fireworks, but please do not let the parade interfere with Ling-Yi's driving."

Well, Joshua could not wait for me to arrive, and he came out early that morning before I left. Since I had returned from my China trip in only four days, I was not able to get everything done in time, and I was up almost the whole night before the flight. I was able to go to bed and sleep only two or three hours when the night was almost over. When I woke up, I found a message on my answering machine. Leslie had called, "Mommy, my water broke early this morning, and we had to call and wait for our babysitter to come over because the kids were all sleeping. Then Ling-Yi rushed me to the birthing center, and Joshua was born at 6:30 a.m. Boston time."

All was well in the end. I was able to catch up on some sleep on the airplane, and when I arrived at Logan International Airport, it seemed the fireworks had just started. (It could not start until after dark.) So I was able to see the fantastic outbursts of colors from my airplane window. By the time I retrieved my bag and called Ling-Yi on my cellular phone, he was already in the airport, and I soon saw his car. When we passed through Boston downtown area, the fireworks were still in full display, and thus, I was able to see some more. The parade obviously would not start until at the end of the fireworks, and we arrived at Leslie and Ling-Yi's home without any delay.

Oh, yes, since Leslie gave birth in a birthing center, not a hospital, she stayed in the birthing center, recuperating only eight hours, and then she had to go home at 3:00 or 4:00 p.m. However, Ling-Yi was able to stay home and took care of her and Joshua until I arrived.

Praise the Lord! He is merciful, and He answers prayers according to our needs. I don't think I deserve His many mercies, but I know He is always faithful to those who look up to Him. "Indeed, none of those who wait for Thee will be ashamed" (Psalm 25:3a NASB). "They looked to Him and were radiant, and their faces shall never be ashamed" (Psalm 34:5, NASB). "The Lord is my strength and my shield; my heart trusted in Him, and I am helped: therefore my heart greatly rejoiceth; and with my song will I praise Him" (Psalm 28:7 KJV).

I think another note about Joshua is worth sharing here. During the Christmas holidays of that year when Leslie's family came to California, one morning she told me she had a dream about Yishan. In the dream she said, "Boppy was dying in the hospital, and you said to me, 'Quick, bring Joshua to Boppy so that he can see him.'" After saying that, she began to cry, saying "Too bad Boppy didn't get to see Joshua."

Since Leslie was the only daughter who did not get a chance to participate at the bedside vigil during Yishan's final hours, I reasoned, she still had a void deep down in her heart, and that was why she began to cry. However, I also believe that by giving her this dream, God was actually bringing a closure to her, and I said, "Even though Joshua was born after Boppy was gone, don't you think he knows about Joshua's birth and is actually able to see Joshua now?"

Leslie nodded and said, "I guess you are right." And she was comforted.

In 2008, Steven Jacob was born to Steve and Corrie, my seventh grandchild. Seven is the perfect number, signifying completion. I thought having seven grandchildren was enough, a complete number to satisfy me. However, it seems God was not satisfied to stop there. In 2010, Steve and Corrie gave me the eighth grandchild, their second son, Matthew.

I was living in U City then, and Angela and Albert had moved away to join Corrie and Steve in another city, leaving me alone in the Bay Area. I drove there several times in order to visit them. Although they also drove down to the Bay Area to visit me, I was the one who had to drive more often since they were mostly busy with their work. So I began praying for the Lord's direction concerning where and when to move, primarily because in June 2008, I misstepped and fell and broke my left ankle bone while I was accompanying my younger sister shopping in San Francisco. By the Lord's grace, my ankle bone was completely healed in less than three weeks.

When Corrie's second son, Matthew, was born, I also went there to help her. Unfortunately, because of some remarks I made when I saw her that first time at her home (commenting on her still protruding stomach, having forgotten that was how postpartum mothers looked), she misunderstood and thought it was my disapproval of her look. She became very angry and refused to have me help anymore. I was disappointed and had to return to U City many days before I had originally planned. Why did I make that comment to her? It was because of the fact I had no one to help me after the births of Leslie and Corrie, and as a result, my uterus was never able to shrink back to its normal size. It pressed against my urine bladder and caused me severe back pains for many years. In the end, I had to go through a hysterectomy to have it removed. I was concerned for my youngest daughter, and yet she totally misunderstood me. What was I to do? I prayed for her for many years, and eventually, the Lord did solve our problems. I'm always thankful to the Lord for helping me.

Later that year in November, I joined my former high school classmates in Taiwan on a round-island tour to celebrate our fifty years after high school graduation. In the bus someone raised a question,

"Which one of us has the highest number of grandchildren?" I said I had eight. Another classmate and I tied on that. It was an honor I had never anticipated receiving.

For a number of years, I had been agonized by the question whether to move eastward to Boston to be near Leslie or to move northward to join Angela and Corrie. Living alone and getting older each year, I knew I had to move sooner or later to be closer to my children, although deep down in my heart, I really did not want to move out of the Bay Area, where I had friends and opportunities of preaching and leading Bible studies.

Eventually, the Lord made His will clear to me to join Angela and Corrie, but my faith was again greatly tested, seeing the housing price tumble to the lowest when I moved. I had no choice but one available house to move into. I thought I had gone through enough tests, but it seems the Lord spares no time on testing and purifying His children. It was almost as if the testing I went through after moving to Pinole was being repeated again. I had learned enough of God's sovereignty to know not to complain but still praise Him in the midst of the most difficult circumstances, yet it was not easy, just to say the least. I felt as if the Lord was saying, "Christians are not shielded from ordinary testing just because of your faith in the Lord Jesus Christ." We still have to encounter difficulties and solve problems, but God will show His grace to be sufficient for us.

I finally moved to the current place toward the end of June 2011, after a long year of trying to sell my U City home. While I knew I had to downsize, moving from a house with more than 2,300 square feet to one that was almost a thousand square feet smaller, I also had to move in a hurry (with only two weeks to find a suitable house and move) and did not have enough time to sort through everything to properly dispose of them. Soon after I moved into the current place, I realized I did not have enough space to organize everything, and I just gave up, allowing myself to live in a congested, disorganized home. What else could I do? The Lord is still teaching me how to get rid of things in preparation for my final move to my heavenly home when I'll have to leave everything behind.

So in the midst of trying to get used to living in a much smaller house, I got the joy of seeing the arrival of another grandchild, my ninth, Corrie's third son, Benjamin Justice.

Nine is the number of the fruit of the Holy Spirit. After Benjamin was born, I thought, God has given me nine grandchildren to tell me I have a fruitful life." I was certainly very grateful for that.

Well, God's way is always higher than our way. One evening while I was babysitting for Corrie's three boys, her house phone rang, and I picked it up. It was Leslie on the other end, and I thought she wanted to talk to her younger sister. "No," she said, "I want to talk to you."

She went on to say, "Mommy, you're going to have your tenth grandchild."

"You're kidding," I said.

"No, it's an accident."

I was more concerned than feeling excited. From the due date, I figured by then Joshua would have celebrated his eighth birthday, and Leslie herself would be more than forty-five. So I told her I would be there to help when she gave birth. She would definitely need someone there to take care of her and the baby.

Unexpectedly, I became quite sick by the end of February 2013. In fact, one night during the middle of that month, I was so sick that I had to call and wake up Steve and asked him to take me to the ER.

However, none of the doctors I saw following that could properly help me. I ended up making two medical trips to Taiwan in that year with an interval of four months in between them, and I saw a total of seven doctors!

My mind was primarily concerned with Leslie's postpartum need. When Leslie heard of my illness, she said, "Mommy, I think my three older children are old enough to help. It's okay if you cannot come to help me." However, I was not convinced that Leslie's three older children would be able to provide all the needs of Leslie and the new baby. So before and during my first trip, I kept asking the Lord, "Please heal me so that I'll be well enough to help Leslie and the baby." I also sent out a prayer request to friends, asking them to storm the gate of heaven on my behalf.

Once again, God's grace was sufficient, and by the end of my first trip, I was well enough to return home, although quite a number of the symptoms still remained. The medication and acupuncture treatments I received from a TCM (traditional Chinese medicine) doctor had enabled me to be free from the prickly pains on the skins of my four limbs, and my ability to walk greatly improved. But the damages from a medication I had taken since 2009 for treating osteoporosis had seemed mostly irreversible. So a little more than a month after returning home, I was able to go to Leslie's place to help a week after Xavier was born.

On the first day of my arrival in Leslie's place, Leslie's three older kids were very willing to help. On the second day, they were not so eager, and I had to call them a lot of times. By the third day, none of them could be moved, and I just did all the things on my own. Wow! God knew all this ahead of the time, and He was so gracious in allowing me to be well enough to go to help Leslie. If I had not been able to go, I wonder what would have been the result for Leslie and the baby. She might not have been able to get so much rest after all!

Ten is a perfect number, and I know God has shown me His perfect grace in giving me ten grandchildren. However, I have also learned none of God's grace is to be taken for granted. We definitely have to be humble in our total dependence on our Lord in all the ways as He has said in Proverbs 3:5–6, which says, "Trust in the Lord with all thine heart; and lean not unto thine own understanding. In all thy ways acknowledge him, and he shall direct thy paths." In enjoying my tenth grandchild, I definitely learned the importance of the total dependence on our Lord in all the ways.

"Lo, children are an heritage of the Lord: and the fruit of the womb is his reward" (Psalm 127:4).

I think both children and grandchildren are heritage of the Lord, and I'm very thankful to Him for giving them to me. However, I've learned that it takes a lot of prayers to keep myself in tune with the leading of the Holy Spirit so that we can experience the full blessings from the Lord.

Chapter 19

Spiritual Warfare

I'd like to begin with the theological question whether Satan is a real person or not. Some think that Satan is just an evil force or influence. I cannot agree. The Bible mentions Satan numerous times, and Jesus Himself said, "I beheld Satan as lightening fall from heaven" (Luke 10:18). The book of Job twice mentions Satan as one of the angels ("sons of God") appearing in front of the throne of God (Job 1:6; 2:1), and both times he had dialogues with God. He must be a real person to have dialogues with God. A force or influence could not have done that. Apostle John states most clearly, "And the great dragon was cast out, that old serpent, called the Devil, and Satan, which deceived the whole world; he was cast out into the earth, and his angels were cast out with him … for the accuser of our brethren is cast down, which accused them before our God day and night" (Revelation 12:9–10).

The Bible clearly teaches that Satan is a fallen angel, and he is the deceiver who deceived Adam and Eve in the garden of Eden. He tempted Jesus in the wilderness, and he is the archenemy of God's kingdom. Apostle Paul has said, "For Satan himself is transformed into an angel of light" (2 Corinthians 11:14). I think I can say that Satan is the master masquerader, and if we are not careful, we may fall into his trap just as Adam and Eve did long ago.

Twice in his epistles, Paul mentions that we as followers of Jesus Christ are involved in a spiritual warfare. "For though we walk in the flesh, we do not war after the flesh. For the weapons of our warfare are not carnal, but mighty through God to the pulling down of strongholds, casting down imaginations, and every high thing that exalteth itself against the knowledge of God, and bringing into captivity every thought to the obedience of Christ" (2 Corinthians 10:3–5). "Put on the whole armour of God, that ye may be able to stand against the wiles of the devil. For we wrestle not against flesh and blood, but against principalities, against powers, against the rulers of the darkness of this world, against spiritual wickedness in high places" (Ephesians 6:11–12).

I have been keenly aware that as Yishan and I were called by the Lord into the ministry we were often standing in the front line, withstanding the onslaught of Satan and his followers or whoever was willing to be used by him. However, for some reason or another, usually I was attacked more often than Yishan was. Sometimes the attack came by way of a certain person or people. Other times we were so attacked that we became physically ill.

The very first attack came to me during a church board meeting. I was so unduly criticized that I broke down in tears immediately in front of everybody. Yet the grace of God was such that He gave us endurance, and in the end, not only were we toughened, but we learned the wisdom knowing how to deal with attacks.

A few years later, I was attacked again. This time I was attending another church board meeting (at the church which had grown out of the Bible study I started) on behalf of Yishan, who was away on a conference in New Jersey. (I had been targets of so many attacks that I tried to avoid board meetings whenever possible.) As that meeting started, one began to speak after another, and before long, I realized they were all aiming their criticism against me. I was stunned, to say the least, but I tried to remain calm. Thank God I did not break down in tears. I was sad nevertheless.

That evening Yishan called home from his motel room in New Jersey to ask me about that afternoon's church board meeting. I told him what had happened. When he hung up the phone at the end of our conversation, he told me later when he was home, he felt so hurt to hear what I had gone through on his behalf that his heart was very heavy. He then prayed, but he felt no relief. Then he picked up the Bible to read, as his usual habit, the portion of Scripture for that day. It was Matthew 5, and he read the words of Jesus, "Blessed are ye, when men shall revile you, and persecute you, and shall say all manner of evil against you falsely, for my sake. Rejoice, and be exceeding glad; for great is your reward in heaven; for so persecuted they the prophets which were before you" (Matthew 5:11–12).

All of a sudden, Yishan felt the boulder in his heart lifted. Praise God for the comforting power of His words!

Still a few more years later, I preached a series of three messages on giving and tithing on three separate Sundays. The timing seemed to be coincidental, but on that Sunday when I finished my third message, we had our monthly coworkers' meeting. (This was at still another church.) Sometime during the meeting, one coworker began to criticize me for having preached that message. I had a clear conscience concerning those three messages. I had prayed and received those messages from the Lord, and I knew I had no selfish motive whatsoever. The Lord knows that during the process of preparing those three messages, I did not at any one single moment even consider that brother at all.

Praise the Lord that there was no need for self-defense. I remained silent all those awkward minutes when I listened to those words of accusation. I just kept praying in my heart, "Lord, You who are all-knowing, please help me and speak up for me." The beauty of the working of the Holy Spirit was such that at least two other coworkers, one brother and one sister, spoke in my defense by saying, "This kind of teaching is biblical and necessary for our church."

There was a period of time when the working of the Holy Spirit was so strong in our lives that Satan also wanted to have a hand. During that period Corrie was very young and I was taking some correspondence courses from Moody. I could only do my course study and homework as well as my devotion and Bible study during the night when everyone else in the family was asleep.

It also happened that I had put a picture of a cheetah in front of

229

the fireplace in the family room where I did my study and devotion at night. That picture was one of Angela's junior high art projects, and she did so well that I liked it and left it there for everyone to see.

In the beginning I did not see anything wrong with that picture. After some time, however, I began to feel fear in my heart every time I saw that cheetah when I walked into the family room at night to do my devotion. That picture was so well-done that the cheetah looked real and very mean.

The irony about the situation was that I could not effectively deal with the fear at first, although I knew the biblical teaching about spiritual warfare and I also knew how to pray. As soon as I began to fear, I would kneel down at the couch and pray, "Lord Jesus, I thank You for Your love, which was manifested when You were hung on the cross for *my* sake. You have said that 'perfect love casteth out fear' (1 John 4:18), and I know I have been made perfect through Your blood, which was shed on the cross. In Your perfect love, I know I should have no fear, and in Your name, I reject the fear. In the name of Jesus, I command Satan to leave."

I did not understand then, but now I know that I was far from perfect, and God had a good purpose for me to learn a valuable lesson. It seemed that my prayer was going nowhere, and yet I knew the Lord was with me. Every time I prayed I was filled with the Spirit and experienced His anointing, and yet the fear seemed to refuse to leave. It went on for a few weeks until one night. That night I suddenly woke up from sleep. My journal entry says it was 3:30 a.m. when I woke up. Then I went to the family room, my usual spot, to pray. While I was praying, I again felt the fear. The strange thing was that again I was filled with the Spirit and even began to sing in the Spirit. (It was actually a rather uncontrollable singing.)

When I finished praying, I came to the living room and sat by the clock radio. The clock said 4:05, and I turned on the radio because I knew this was the time for the program *The Living Word* by Radio Pastor Donald Cole on WMBI FM. It was one of my favorite program on that station. Since the rest of my family was still asleep, I turned down the volume of the radio as low as possible so that it would not wake up my family.

At first, I sat on the carpet so that my ear could be close to the radio. However, after a few minutes, I felt uncomfortable sitting on the carpet without any support for my back. So I got up and sat on the sofa. In this position I was actually farther away from the radio than in my former position on the carpet. The volume of the radio was so low that it certainly was not going to produce any effect on my eardrum.

As I sat on the sofa and listened to Donald Cole talking about "the fear of the Lord is the healthy fear, not terror," I began to wonder why I was feeling fear of the dark again a while ago when I was praying in the family room. "Perfect love casteth out fear. Probably I was not filled with the Spirit when I was praying. I need the filling of the Spirit to cast out the fear." As I was thus thinking in my heart, the *sound wave* coming out of the radio suddenly seemed to have been amplified, and it entered my right ear with such great pressure that it almost felt unbearable, while my left ear felt perfectly normal. When I had this feeling in my right ear, I found that power entered my whole body, and I felt hot. And at the same time, I could also clearly feel the fear literally going out of my body.

Then while Donald Cole continued to speak, the sound wave of his words entering my right ear became streams of heat that went through my body, and I felt I was bathed in the love of the Lord. My heart was filled with joy, and the darkness in the room totally had no effect on me.

At that moment I thought of Luke 1:37, which says, "For with God nothing is impossible," and Hebrews 4:12, which says, "For the word of God is living and powerful." What had just happened to me was really the fulfillment of these two verses. The Word of God was transformed into power entering my body and casting out the fear. Praise the Lord for His faithfulness in fulfilling His promise and for His love in taking care of me!

Sometime after that, I began to search the reason for that fear to have entered me. I finally got the answer when I opened a box in the closet and found some incense sticks inside. The incense sticks (the kind Buddhists use) had innocently come to me back in 1972 when my in-laws brought them from Taiwan. At that time I was working in a company in Chicago and one of the fads among the coworkers in the office was burning incense for its aroma. I had asked my in-laws to bring those incense sticks from Taiwan, and as a favor, I gave each coworker some. There were still some leftover. I did not use those incense sticks myself. They were left in that box until I remembered. By that time I had learned of the spiritual warfare between the kingdom of darkness and God's kingdom of light. At that point I also realized it was a mistake (one might even say it was a dangerous decision) for me to have asked my in-laws to bring those incense sticks. They were clearly associated with idol worship, and my initiation to bring them into my home had involuntarily yielded an opening for the power of darkness to attack me. That day I prayed for God's forgiveness for my own ignorance and prayed once again for His protection for myself and my whole family while I broke those sticks of incense and threw them into the trash.

The fear never came back.

A few months after that was my fortieth birthday. In my memory it was the only birthday that was ever spent in illness.

A week before my birthday, I became sick with fever, and two days later, I was so sick that I could not get up. Yishan had to take off from work and stay home to take care of me. When Yishan took me to the doctor, the latter diagnosed it as a case of pneumonia (my left lung was infected), and he prescribed antibiotics for me. A week later, two days after my birthday, I was still coughing and feeling weak even after I had taken antibiotics for a whole week.

I slept a lot during those days. One afternoon I woke up from a long nap and felt much better. Immediately, I got out of bed and went to the family room. Yishan was there reading the Bible. As soon as he saw me, he told me something that had just happened.

"As I was sitting on the carpet, reading the Bible, and listening to the music simultaneously," said Yishan, "I felt a little tired. So I closed my eyes for a moment and just listened to the music. All of a sudden,

I saw a gray-colored screen (like a cardboard or a TV screen) right in my front and a large, ugly black spider crawling on the screen. I was surprised and opened my eyes. The screen and the spider were still there. That ugly spider crawled slowly and suddenly went outside of the screen and disappeared. I tilted my head, trying to find the spider. The screen was left alone there, and then it, too, disappeared. I was just pondering what all this meant and prayed. Then you came here."

"What does it mean?" I asked.

"Yes," said Yishan, "I prayed, and I think this is the answer. That cardboard or screen represented your body. That ugly spider represented Satan or a demon that caused the illness. As long as the spider crawled on the cardboard/screen, it meant the illness lingered in your body to make you sick. Now that the spider disappeared, it means the illness has left you."

Indeed, not only did I feel much better, but I was completely well, well enough to stay up late that night to make a dress for Corrie.

The second Sunday after I got pneumonia (the day before my birthday), Yishan also came down with a fever (though he seldom got sick). Corrie began to cough as well. She was two months away from being three.

Since Corrie was born with a cleft lip and cleft palate and had difficulty feeding as a baby, she was never as heavy or strong as her two sisters as a young child. Comparatively, she got sick more easily, and she always had high fever when she was sick.

I was worried when Corrie coughed and had a fever around 103 and 104 degrees. I called her pediatrician right away, and he told me to give her medication to bring down the temperature, alternating between baby Tylenol and Bayer baby aspirin every other two hours. Sure enough, twenty minutes after taking the medicine, her temperature came down, but never below 101 degrees. Before the next turn for the other medicine, the temperature would rise again. I also put an ice pack on her forehead, but nothing seemed to work.

On Tuesday night as I prayed for Corrie, I was filled with the Spirit and began to sing uncontrollably. I knew the Lord was with me and comforting me, and yet my worry for Corrie was not alleviated.

My spirit and my intellect were comforted, but my soul and my body were still cumbered with worries.

On Wednesday morning I was thinking of praying for Corrie again while I was still in bed. Suddenly, I was filled with the Spirit and felt a powerful energy entering my body, and very distinctively, a feeling of peace was securely lodged in my bosom while at the same time all the worries and the original desire to pray and petition completely disappeared. At that moment the peace of the Holy Spirit was solidly in my bosom, and it stayed there for quite a while. It was like a physical thing that I could literally feel. Instantly, I thought of the plague of darkness in Egypt, darkness for three days, and the Bible says that it "could be felt." (At least that is what KJV and the Chinese Bible say.)

After a while, that feeling of solidness in my bosom disappeared and was replaced with unlimited thankfulness, praises, and complete peace and faith. I was able to completely rest in peace and faith, and I worried no more about Corrie's high fevers.

Later that day Yishan and I took Corrie to her pediatrician. He listened to Corrie's chest and said he could not detect pneumonia yet, but he was going to treat it as pneumonia. He prescribed antibiotics for her.

During dinnertime Corrie slept over the time for antibiotics, and I did not wake her up. When she woke up later in the evening, her fever reached 104.4 degrees. Leslie was scared and asked Angela, "What's the temperature that one dies at?"

Angela answered, "Don't ask!"

(Keep in mind that they were thirteen and fourteen years old respectively.)

However, I was not worried because I knew we were all in the hands of the almighty, sovereign God, who was in perfect control. Praise the Lord, for He had given me complete peace and rest. My body, soul, and spirit had been comforted.

A few days later on Sunday, Corrie seemed to be getting better. Her temperature went down to 99 degrees. Yet the very next day on Monday, her fever suddenly went up to 105 degrees. I was scared and called Yishan at work and asked him to come home immediately. Meanwhile, I put an ice pack on Corrie's forehead, trying to bring down her temperature. After Yishan came home, we took her to the pediatrician immediately. He said indeed it was pneumonia. Her right lung was infected. He told me to double the amount of antibiotics for her.

After several doses of the doubled amount of antibiotics for Corrie, her fever significantly went down, and she seemed to be back to normal. I was confident that we were out of the woods, so we took her with us to attend Angela and Leslie's junior high commencement the following evening (Tuesday).

The commencement exercises were held in a gym, and they still had the heat on. (Remember, this was in Schaumburg, outside of Chicago.) Possibly because the air in the gym was too dry, Corrie kept coughing the whole evening. At midnight her temperature shot up to 103 degrees. I gave her an ice pack and dared not go to sleep until her temperature was not as threatening. I brought her to our bed and let her sleep between me and Yishan. (Since I myself had just recovered from pneumonia, I did not want the trouble of having to get up and leave my bed in the middle of the night.)

In the middle of the night, possibly around two or three o'clock, Corrie suddenly awoke and sat up. I tried to make her lie down and go back to sleep, but she pointed her finger to the opposite side of the room where the closet door and the ceiling met and asked, "Mommy, what's that?" Her voice sounded like she was in fear.

I looked at the place where she had pointed her finger, and I could only see a tiny red glow reflected from the night-light. Other than that, I saw only darkness. I thought possibly Corrie was in delirium from her fever. So again, I told her to lie down because I could see nothing there.

Corrie would not lie down but asked again, "Mommy, what's that?"

I still could see nothing, and I told her so. Yet I was beginning to think maybe she *did* see something that I could not see. So I prayed silently in the name of Jesus if there was something there, it would be revealed and could no longer remain hidden.

The reason I prayed in this way was because I recalled something that had occurred almost six weeks earlier.

That morning more than five weeks earlier, I was making sandwiches for Angela and Leslie's lunches after Yishan had left for work when I heard Corrie suddenly wailed in her room as if she had woken up from a nightmare. I sent Leslie to Corrie's room, and Leslie came back and said, "Corrie said there was 'ho-ho' in her room. I did not understand what she said."

I told Leslie, "Possibly she was saying *bug* since she is afraid of bugs." There was a moth that flew into the house two nights before, and Corrie wailed when she saw it. (A few days later, I found a dead moth in the bathroom's medicine cabinet.) Leslie probably had difficulty understanding Corrie because the latter was crying and talking at the same time.

A few moments later, Corrie walked into the kitchen, still crying loudly. I asked Angela to hold her, and she stopped crying. Then after Angela and Leslie left for school, I took Corrie and laid her down on the hallway carpet outside the bathroom to change her diaper. At that very moment, I remembered the check I had left half-written on the kitchen table. So I left Corrie there on the carpet and went back to the kitchen to finish writing that check. It was for mortgage payment, and I was afraid I might forget if I did not finish that job right away. While I was still in the kitchen writing that check, Corrie started crying again. I said, "Corrie, Mommy is here in the kitchen. Come here." Usually that would be enough to calm her down, and she would come to me by herself.

But not that morning. She cried even louder and almost made me angry. I thought she was crying for no reason. I poked my head in the hallway. What was going on here?

I saw Corrie standing in the hallway as if in great fear. In fact, she was backing up until she reached the end of the hallway, her eyes looking straight into the living room, and she kept saying, "Bug! Bug!"

I saw nothing in the living room, but she insisted there was a bug.

I never saw such an expression of terror on her face! At that moment I prayed silently, asking the Lord for help. All of a sudden, I thought of the Chinese word for *snake* or *serpent*, which has the word *bug* on its left side, and I was also reminded of the words in Revelation 12:9 which says, "And the great dragon was cast out, that old serpent [the word *serpent* in the Chinese translation is *snake*], called the Devil, and Satan." So I realized at that moment that either Satan himself or a demon must have transformed into a bug to frighten my little girl.

Immediately, I said to Corrie, "Corrie, follow Mommy and say, 'Lord Jesus loves me. I'm not afraid.'" I had her repeat those words a second time.

After she had said that twice, she calmed down, and her fear obviously was gone. I then drew apart the living room drapes to let the light in and asked her, "Is the bug still there?"

She shook her head, and you could clearly see a puzzling expression on her face. She must have thought, *I did see the bug there a moment ago. How come it is gone now?*

So that night after Corrie repeated that same question, "Mommy, what's that?" and I prayed in the name of Jesus for that thing or person hidden there to be revealed, Corrie continued to look at the ceiling and then suddenly asked, "Mommy, who is that person?" Her voice was as fearful as that earlier time when she cried, "Bug! Bug!"

At that moment I knew Corrie indeed was seeing someone there in the form of a person. I then placed my hand in her back, closed my eyes, and had her pray with me, "Lord Jesus loves me. I'm not afraid." Then I led her to pray that prayer the second time, and again, I saw the same result of that prayer—a simple prayer but with a powerful result.

I then prayed for myself, asking the Lord to cover me with the blood of Jesus and commanded Satan to leave. Then I asked Corrie, "Is the person still there?" She shook her head and lay down with me and was fast asleep.

In the morning when Corrie woke up, her fever was gone, and she was soon fully recovered. In both cases of my own pneumonia and

Corrie's, it was not simply a physical battle, but it involved spiritual warfare as well.

When we were still in Schaumburg, once Yishan and I were invited to minister to a Catholic fellowship group that met once every other month on Saturdays. Both Yishan and I considered this invitation an important opportunity to witness for the Lord, so we vigilantly prayed about it.

On the morning of the Saturday of that meeting, I asked Yishan to go to the grocery store for me. When he parked the car at the store, he found the car was leaking oil. He checked it and was able to add more oil. If I had gone to the store myself, I would not have noticed anything wrong with the car, and we could have suffered some dire consequence later.

Well, *something* did happen. Since there was going to be a potluck dinner after the fellowship meeting, I prepared a dish to take with us. I did not want to go to that meeting empty-handed. The dish I prepared was deep-fried vegetable balls, always popular among the Chinese whenever I served it. While I was cooking, I began to feel stomach cramps. I tried to endure the pain and continued dropping vegetable balls into the pot of oil. After a while when I saw the pain was not going away, I realized that it was very possible that I had been attacked again by the enemy. I immediately began praying in the name of Jesus. I practically had to be engaged in a spiritual battle while continuing my cooking much like what Nehemiah and his fellow Jewish people had to do while they were trying to finish up building the walls of Jerusalem (Nehemiah 4:13).

Finally, I put all the vegetable balls into the oil, and feeling I could no longer endure the pain, I asked Yishan to help finish the cooking job. (He only had to take out the cooked ones.) I went to lie down on the family room couch, and I continued to pray while lying there.

When Yishan took the last vegetable ball out of the oil and turned off the burner, he came over and laid his hand on me and began to pray for me. When he finished praying and saw me still in pain, he said, "I think I'll go by myself and let you stay home and rest."

Although the intense cramp did not lessen a bit, I knew we were involved in the spiritual warfare, and I did not want to back down. I knew when we had enough faith in the Lord, the victory would always be ours.

"No," I said, "I want to go with you. I'll get up and get dressed now."

We then both went into our bedroom and opened the closet doors. While I was putting on my dress, I began to feel the cramp losing power, and very quickly, it was completely gone. Victory through our faith in the power of our risen Lord! The sweetness of victory in Jesus!

Truly as Jesus said, "All power is given unto me in heaven and in earth" (Matthew 28:18). I'm so thankful that by our faith in Jesus we can always invoke His name and overcome the enemy.

In Schaumburg, Yishan led a Taiwanese couple to the Lord. The husband, a retired pharmacist in his midsixties, and the wife, a woman in her late fifties, had both believed in the traditional Taiwanese religion for their whole life. A few months after they came to the Lord, the wife's mother came from Taiwan to join them. The wife's father had died of cancer more than a year before the aged widow came to Schaumburg. Her husband used to be a practitioner (an equivalent of a witch doctor) of that religion, one that usually involved demonic power in his practice. (I came to this conclusion through quite a few true stories I had heard, not that I had any personal prejudice against that religion. A story told by a Taiwanese Christian friend will serve to illustrate my point. This Christian friend said once he was in a crowd, watching such a man doing his religious practice. Usually at the beginning such a man would look normal, but after he did a few rituals, he would start to jump or dance almost like he was crazy and would a lot of times be able to do some supernatural feats. One could certainly tell the change in that man because his eyes would look different as if glazed over. On that occasion when our friend was present, that religious practitioner asked if there was any Christian among the crowd. Although our friend was a Christian, he kept his mouth shut and said nothing. He knew that man would have stopped his ritual right there had he known of any Christian around. Our friend said he was young and curious, and he wanted to watch that practitioner do his tricks; that was why he kept silent. Well, since our friend said nothing and there was supposedly no Christian presence, that man began his rituals, and after some time when he thought he had got his demonic or magic connection, he began to run. He tried to jump through a rather small hole in a brick wall. Usually, our friend said, that man was able to supernaturally jump through that small hole without any difficulty. However, on that occasion, obviously because of the Christian presence, that man's demonic connection lost its power, and that man's head was hit against the brick wall, so he bled profusely.)

We were told that this elderly widow was seventy-five, and she had brought a wooden plaque that bore her dead husband's name. (The Taiwanese who believe in this religion usually worship the dead by burning incense to this kind of wooden plaque and offering food to the dead on his birthday and on the day of his death as well as on other religious festive days.)

When Yishan and I heard of the coming of this elderly widow, we both went to visit her at her daughter and son-in-law's home. After we were seated in the living room and while we were still exchanging pleasantries with the host couple, we suddenly caught a glimpse of the wife's aged widow-mother when she came out of one room and passed through the hallway and went into another (possibly from the bathroom to a bedroom). Although it was a fleeting glimpse, I was able to see her face and somehow felt that I saw evil on that face or in her eyes. It does not mean that I thought she was evil, not at all. Possibly because of her late husband's lifelong demonic connection, the power of darkness cast a long shadow over her and her daughter's family. Later when I shared my feeling with Yishan after we were home, he said that he had the same feeling as well.

We didn't get to talk to that elderly widow that day. They were in the process of moving to another apartment and so our next visit to them was halted for some time. About a month later, we heard that she had become ill. Yishan went to visit that family and led her in praying to accept Jesus. He then set up a time with them for him to go back the next evening to baptize her. Since she was gravely ill and also because of her age, we both thought it was better to baptize her as soon as possible.

Unfortunately, she was not able to wait to be baptized. I went to pray for her the next afternoon. Her daughter and granddaughter told me her stools were black, and I knew she was suffering from internal bleeding. Not too long after I came home in late afternoon around 5:00 p.m., while I was washing dishes at the sink, I heard the siren of an ambulance wailing, and although I could not see any ambulance from where I stood, I *knew* it was an ambulance going to that family, which was only about three blocks away from our home, to take that elderly widow to the hospital. (I'm sure it was the Holy Spirit who enabled me to have that kind of knowledge.)

When Yishan came home from work, I informed him of what I had seen and heard. He immediately called them. The ambulance I heard indeed had gone to their home to take that elderly widow to the hospital, and sadly, it was too late.

So instead of going to that family, we went to the hospital and found the daughter and son-in-law of the elderly widow in an exclusive, quiet area. The wife sat there with teary eyes, and her husband sat silently with her, not knowing how to console her. They tried to tell us what had happened, which we actually had already known. However, their words were really inadequate in describing either the unfortunate event or the new grief that was added to their overloaded sadness not only from the loss of the wife's father in the not-so-distant past but also from a recent loss of their own son-in-law about a month before that.

Yishan and I tried to comfort them with the Word of God. And then I realized that they were beset with plenty of grief and also rather helpless. Since they were new immigrants in a new place and spoke very little English, the sudden death of the wife's mother had left them completely lost as far as the funeral service was concerned.

Although I had no previous experience dealing with a funeral home, I volunteered to find a suitable one for them. Once they heard the final word from the hospital, they then came home with us so that I could call funeral homes for them.

After some calls and after they picked a certain funeral home, they called their daughter to take them home. It was decided that the body of the deceased would be cremated the next day (Tuesday), and Yishan would conduct a memorial service that evening.

Up to that time, Yishan had never conducted any funeral service, and because it was on such a short notice, he seemed to have difficulty deciding on what scriptural text to use for a message for the memorial service. (He had less than twenty-four hours to prepare that message.) I knew he needed time to pray about it, but I suggested he use the text of 1 Thessalonians 4:13–18. He thought it was an appropriate one, and he sat down at his desk and began to prepare the message.

Around 11:15 p.m., about an hour or so after that couple had gone home, Yishan was busy writing the message for the next evening's memorial service. Our phone rang, and I answered it. It was the husband of that woman who had just lost her mother. (I'll call the husband Mr. Yang.)

"Oh, Mrs. Lin, please help us," said Mr. Yang. "My wife seemed to have lost consciousness a while ago. Her two arms went stiff, and her eyes looked glazed. And something was in her throat going up and down. Oh, Mrs. Lin, I'm a pharmacist, but I've never been so terrified in my life."

Yishan and I decided it was a case of demon possession or demonic oppression, and we immediately drove over to their apartment. We then heard about what had transpired in greater detail.

When Mr. and Mrs. Yang got home, their daughters had already had the dinner made, but Mrs. Yang, being sad at the sudden death of her mother, said she did not feel like eating. She lit up a cigarette and wanted a puff first. (She, being a new Christian, had not given up her smoking habit.)

Yishan and I both thought that her father's lifelong demonic connection and her mother's having brought that wooden plaque used in idol worship had left them vulnerable to satanic influence. Personally, I also believe Mrs. Yang's lighting up the cigarette was an act of uncleanness, be it an ignorant act, and it had especially opened up an involuntary invitation for demonic attacks.

After Mrs. Yang had taken a puff, she lost her consciousness, and her two arms went straight on the table and became stiff. Her eyes seemed to become glazed over, and her husband saw a lump in her throat moving up and down.

"Get your mother and wake her up," Mr. Yang commanded his daughters. One of them slapped her mother's arm, and she woke up.

Mr. and Mrs. Yang's second daughter, the one who had just lost her husband a month before the sudden death of her elderly grandmother, had two young sons sleeping on the sofa at that moment, their ages being five and three. The demon seemed to have left Mrs. Yang and temporarily bothered the younger grandson before leaving them all. The latter suddenly cried out at that moment, "Mom!" They said that cry sounded very loud and terrifying.

(Bear in mind that Mr. and Mrs. Yang were the only Christians in the family. And out of their religious background, they had no idea of what the Bible taught about demons.)

We then told them the stories of how Jesus cast out demons and why idol worships often involved demons and invited demonic attacks. We prayed for them, but we encouraged them to do a thorough renouncement of demonic connections and to burn everything involved in demonic worship.

At that point the second daughter opened up a suitcase in one bedroom and showed us a bunch of incense sticks and some foiled paper (usually burned for the deceased to use as paper money in the underworld) that her late husband's mother had sent her to be sacrificed to him. She told us she also had a silver necklace given by her mother-in-law, which the latter had placed more than a year on her family altar of idol worship.

We told her she also needed to bring that necklace to be burned. We set up the time with them for Wednesday evening to burn those items of idol worship. I also warned them that Satan could try to thwart their effort of following the Lord's command, and because of the Lord's promise in the Bible, they would have to invoke the name of Jesus for spiritual victory.

On that following Tuesday evening when Yishan delivered the

memorial service message from 1 Thessalonians 4:13–18, two of the granddaughters of the deceased raised hands to accept Jesus as their Lord and Savior. A grain of corn buried had indeed yielded more seeds.

Still the next evening, Wednesday, when we were burning the items involved in idol worship, the Yangs' second daughter told us the following story about the silver necklace, which we also put in the fire.

"Yesterday morning at ten, I went to the bank to retrieve the necklace from the safety deposit box, but I could not get the door of the safety deposit box to open. In the end I had to ask a teller for help, but even *she* had difficulty opening that door. When she went to get another bank personnel for help, I then remembered your words of warning about Satan. So I prayed in the name of Jesus to rebuke Satan. When the bank personnel returned, she found the door was already open. 'It's just opened like that,' said that bank personnel. Oh, Mrs. Lin, I experienced it myself."

Praise the Lord for His wonderful work! Not only is He so faithful, but from time to time, He even authenticates our message from His Word.

Back when we were in Schaumburg, once a young woman (Susan in chapter 14) brought a friend, a nonbeliever, to church. This woman had come from LA to visit Susan. She was angry with her husband because she had found out he was divorced before marrying her and had not told her the truth, and she had left home without informing him.

That very Sunday when Susan's friend came to the Cedar church, I happened to be the preacher. While I was preaching, I learned later, Susan's friend saw my hair glowing as if a three-inch-thick cap of yellow light covered my whole hair. Later Yishan went to visit her at Susan's home, and she prayed to accept Jesus as her Lord and Savior. I don't remember if she came on the second Sunday or not, but she rejoiced so much after receiving Jesus that she soon forgave her husband and went home.

The same thing happened again during another Sunday worship

service about seven or eight years later at THC. It so happened that I was also the preacher on that Sunday. (I did not preach as often at THC as I did at the Cedar church.)

That second time it happened to a woman in her midsixties. Although she was a believer, she was often prevented from sitting in the sanctuary with the congregation during the worship service. She had a grandson about a year old who was born with Down's syndrome and could not sit up by himself, and she often sacrificed herself by taking care of the grandson in the fellowship hall outside the sanctuary so that her son and daughter-in-law could enjoy worship inside the sanctuary. Although there was a loudspeaker installed in the fellowship hall, she practically could never listen to a full message since she had to spend most of the time paying attention to the grandson.

That Sunday, this woman's son said, "Mom, this morning you sit in the sanctuary during the worship, and I'll take care of the baby."

While I was preaching during that worship service, this woman also saw my hair covered in a gently glowing yellow light. At first, she thought everyone else was seeing the same sight. But after looking at the persons to her left and right, she realized they were not seeing the same special sight. When the worship service was over and she told her son of what she had experienced, he exclaimed, "Mom, you have seen a halo!"

Yishan once commented about the glowing yellow light those two women saw on my hair. "If I had been the preacher that day," he said, "it would have been no big deal, for my head is bald and reflects light easily. Yet the preacher that day was my wife, who has a full head of black hair."

When I first wrote this chapter, I thought it was too long, and I left out a few other stories. However, I realize now there is a story that is really important that needs to be included. So here it is.

One Sunday night around midnight after Yishan had gone to bed, I was still sitting at my desk and working when the phone rang. It was a man from church.

"Mrs. Lin, I just woke up from a dream. In the dream I saw two people praying for me to cast out demons."

When I heard those words, I felt as if I had been shocked by electricity, and all the hairs on my body stood up.

As I listened a little more, I knew this man was troubled by demons, and he was in great fear. Since Yishan said from the bedroom that he was awake, I said to this man, "Pastor Lin and I will be right over to pray for you. In the meanwhile before we arrive, if you feel fear, take the Bible and hold it with you."

Yishan got dressed faster than I did, and he was downstairs in a few minutes while I was still getting dressed. I then remembered something and said to Yishan, "Take some hymnbooks with us."

We were in such a great hurry that I remembered to ask Yishan if he had taken the hymnbooks only when we were already on the freeway, more than ten minutes after leaving home. "No," he said, "I could not hear what you said then." I sighed, knowing we failed to bring a very important weapon with us.

Once we got to this brother's home, his door was open to the left, and he was standing on the right side at the left end of a three-seat living room couch. He was a big tall man, but his back humped a little, showing that he was in fear. He had the Bible clutched tightly in front of his chest.

"Long time no see," said this brother. It was late Sunday night, and we just saw him at church that afternoon. I praise the Lord because He was in control. Because of these words, Yishan and I were both alerted of a demonic source in this man, and we both (or just Yishan, I do not remember) said, "In the name of Jesus, what is your name?" (Yishan and I had both taken a course in Moody evening school where we had learned that in dealing with demons, the first thing to ask was the person or the demon's name. That's based on Mark 5:9.)

The brother seemed to be still in control of himself because he answered his own name. However, as soon as he said his name, he lost control and fell over into the couch with his head landing on the middle cushion and his two legs and feet dangling from the left arm of the couch. Then he began to laugh, and he wiggled all over like what is said in Mark 9: 18, 20, 26. While this was going on, Yishan and I prayed in the name of Jesus, telling the demon(s) to get out of him. We also tried to sing hymns by memory, but I knew we were short of one important weapon. I also knew why the demons were laughing at us. We failed to bring the hymnbooks with us. It was definitely not the same singing the hymns by memory, not with the full force we could have when singing with a hymnbook.

Since we commanded the demon(s) to get out of the man in the name of Jesus, the man stopped after wiggling for a while, and foam immediately came out of a corner of his mouth. I thought that was it. So I stopped praying. But very quickly, he started laughing and wiggling again just as before. So Yishan and I started praying again, commanding the demon(s) to get out.

Sometime during the process of praying, the man kept moving his left hand to the left as if to point something. Yishan must have been annoyed by that gesture, and he said, "In the name of Jesus, I command the demon to leave and go to that direction." Yishan pointed his hand to the same direction that hand was moving. However, the hand kept moving without stopping.

Since Yishan had been busy preparing to go to Alaska to help a Chinese church in Anchorage on the following Tuesday (actually, only one day away) and he must have been physically tired and probably was not so alert spiritually (I've found there is a correlation between the physical and spiritual strength to a certain degree), I sensed that Yishan had been tricked by the demon, and so I immediately said, "In the name of Jesus, I command the demon to go to *that* direction," pointing my hand to the opposite direction, and that man's hand immediately stopped moving.

This went on for a total of two hours, and eventually, the brother stopped laughing, wiggling, and foaming completely and woke up, but I suspected that might not be the end.

The brother seemed dazed right after he woke up, but after a while, he was able to carry on a normal conversation, and we shared with him all the passages from the Bible on how Jesus dealt with the demons that troubled people and also Bible passages on how to fight the spiritual warfare. We also asked that brother questions concerning his family background trying to find out the cause for the demonic possession or oppression. We learned that his father passed away when he was quite young and his mother remarried, and he was brought up by grandparents, who worshipped spirits. He said when he was eight years old, he got very sick, and his grandparents took his name to the local Buddhist temple and gave his name to one of the gods there to be an adopted son. *There* we found the cause, an unfortunate vow that people oftentimes committed without realizing that having traffic with the demonic world was very dangerous and could cause harm to them in their later lives, such as that experienced by this brother.

By the time we left that brother's house, it was already daybreak. We had spent about six hours in his house! Since I suspected there might still be some demons remaining there, I invited that brother to come to our home for prayers that afternoon around four and then to have dinner together, and later we would go to his house to pray in the evening. (Our learning and experiences told us cases like this often occurred in the nighttime.) That brother took off from work early and came to our house later as I had asked. I also called up a sister and asked her to come at the same time to pray and have dinner together.

When we prayed, that brother changed as if he had become a frightened little kitten, barely able to utter very soft sounds when he prayed. Looking at that brother, I knew we definitely had to go to his house that evening and pray again.

We went to his home after dinner, and this time we remembered to take hymnbooks. I also took a three-inch cross with me, my silvery cross pendant, which I held in my hand. I had heard from a radio program that a cross was very powerful when used in praying for demon-possessed people.

After we got to that brother's home, I read some Bible passages concerning spiritual warfare, and then we began singing hymns. I stood next to the brother while we were singing, and I noticed he was singing completely out of tune. Nobody would sing out of tune like that, and I knew the demon was affecting him.

After singing a few hymns of praise to God, we positioned ourselves so that the brother remained in front of the sofa and the three of us stood facing him, and we continued to sing a few hymns that we knew would help us in bring victory in the fight. While we were singing, I held the cross in my hand toward the brother, and a few minutes later, he said, "Please stop singing, for I'm hearing some noise and I need quietness so that I can know what it is." All of us stopped singing, but then the brother went on to say, "Only Mrs. Lin needs to stop, and the rest of you can continue to sing."

How interesting! What a self-revealing demon! Only I had a cross and the demons were afraid of the cross in my hand. Of course, all of us resumed singing, and very quickly, the demon could not stand it. Then that brother fell on the sofa again. (That night we were in the family room.) Immediately, he began shaking as the night before and laughing as well, but this time the demons were obviously weaker. The brother's force in shaking was not as strong, and the laughing was not as loud as the night before. (This time we were well prepared, and there was nothing for the demon to laugh at us about. It just showed how disrespectful the demons were toward us and was even mocking our Lord Jesus Christ.)

By that time we stopped singing and prayed out loud, commanding the demons (in Chinese, the word *demon* is the same for plural as for singular) to leave, and sometimes one or two of us would sing hymns while one was praying for that brother. After just a short while, the brother stopped shaking and laughing. Foam came out of his mouth, but the amount was not as much as the night before. This scenario repeated again and again that night, with foam coming out of the mouth at the end of each round. Each time the force of moving and laughing was getting weaker, and the amount of foam was becoming less as well. Then about two hours later, the brother completely stopped moving with only tiny amount of foams coming out, and he became still as if he were dead.

We continued praying for some time, and then the brother woke up. At first, he seemed dazed, and then he said he could not remember anything. We had to tell him what had happened, and he seemed to be still in a little fear. We shared with him Scripture verses again, some of which we probably read for the third time since the night before. We then prayed more with him so as to give him encouragement. By the time we left, we had spent probably more than four hours there, and it was midnight. The next day I took Yishan to San Francisco Airport for him to catch the flight to Alaska.

I was not sure if all the demons had completely left that brother or not. So I decided to call more brothers and sisters to go to that brother's house again on Saturday afternoon to do one more round of spiritual fight and to ensure a total victory, and I also decided to do a five-day fast ending at Sunday afternoon.

I knew my physical condition would not allow me to do without food for many days (I knew this from previous fasting), and I drank one cup of milk each day. But otherwise, I drank only water without taking any solid food during that period. Saturday afternoon when we went to that brother's home, nothing special happened, and we knew it was a total victory by the power of our Lord.

The next day, Sunday afternoon, when I preached an English sermon to the young congregation (someone else preached at the Chinese side), I experienced great power that I never felt before. Like rivers of living water coming out of the bosom, words just poured out easily without any snags. Wow, it was power that came as a result of the five-day fasting! I praise the Lord for giving me that bonus reward. Although I had known great power comes with fasting, yet because of my own weakness, I had not been able to experience it until then. Praise the Lord, for His Word is always true!

From that experience of dealing with demonic beings, I was most impressed with the power of the hymns when we engaged in spiritual warfare, and I wish I could have all the space to mention the many other times when I saw the power of hymns in myself or other people. Because of what I learned from those other times and this time, I can conclude that many churches today are probably forfeiting a powerful weapon since they no longer sing hymns in worship. I'm sure Satan is very happy that many churches are no longer using hymns in worship but have replaced them with contemporary music. I strongly believe it is not a matter of personal taste concerning what kind of music to sing in church. Rather I think we should consider *what God wants* us to sing while worshipping Him. I have strong reasons to believe we would sing hymns when we gather in heaven.

Although we are often weak and frail, I praise God because He loves us and will not abandon us. We are engaged in a spiritual warfare against a formidable adversary of whom the human flesh and blood seem to be no match, but the Bible tells us greater than the enemy is the Lord our God (1 John 5:19). When we follow the Lord and serve Him faithfully, He does all sorts of wonderful things to ensure our victory in the spiritual warfare. "Now thanks be unto God, which always causeth us to triumph in Christ, and maketh manifest the Saviour of his knowledge by us in every place" (2 Corinthians 2:14).

Chapter 20

Dreams and Visions

*I*n some previous chapters, I have mentioned some special dreams Yishan and I or others had through which the Lord communicated to us. I'm keenly aware there are theologians who think God does not give dreams or visions today just as one brother was taught as I mentioned in chapter 15.

I still remember one specific class Yishan and I took while attending the seminary. That class was taught by a professor who happened to hold that view. However, once in class he was asked to share the story of his calling, and he answered by telling us about a dream he had. "I dreamed I was standing by a seashore. I saw many people drowning in the sea. I wanted to go rescue them. But I felt my feet were glued to the sand, and I could not free myself. Then I saw my mother among those drowning, and all of a sudden, I was able to free myself. And I flew to her, but then I woke up."

So the Lord called this professor to rescue souls through a dream! Therefore, I said to him, "See, the Lord used a dream to call you into the ministry. Doesn't it mean He still talks through dreams?"

The professor answered, "That's an exception, not the norm."

Maybe he was correct in this theological thinking, but in my own experience as well as the experiences of those I have heard or read about, *exceptions* are so plenty that they have become *norms* to me.

I know I am no theologian, but I *know when* the Lord is present with me and talks to me either through words or dreams, sometimes

252

even through visions. (I have to explain here why I can be sure when the Lord is speaking to me. It is *not* a natural intuition that made me so sure. Rather it requires the discipline of keeping an intimate relationship with the Lord, and through the understanding of His Word, I've learned how to discern whether He is speaking to me. When He is speaking to me, I feel complete peace. If it is something that gives me uneasiness or lack of peace or even fear, I can tell its source. It is definitely not from God.)

Of course, I've heard some who claim there are no more miracles today. I used to hold that view myself until 1974 when I experienced the miraculous healing of my toothache. The Lord has changed my thinking since then.

Both Yishan and I have experienced the Lord's working so many times I just cannot agree that there are no more miracles, dreams, or visions.

In July 1978, when Corrie was born with cleft lip and cleft palate, I began to doubt whether God loved me, and the Lord proved His love for me through a miracle.

When Yishan and I were at ABC Hospital in XYZ Town and going to bring Corrie home, they gave me a bottle with a special long nipple to feed Corrie. After I brought her home, however, every time I tried to feed her, she would end up choking herself and start to cry. After a few times, whenever she cried, I would cry as well. I began to think that God did not love me because He was punishing me by giving me such a hard-to-feed baby. So too, two nights before I went to the hospital for Corrie's birth when Yishan and I both prayed together, he began to speak in tongues, but I did not. At that time I thought I had displeased God, and I began to weep. Of course, I had also prayed for a baby boy, but God had given me a girl instead ... and such a hard-to-care-for baby!

Make no mistake. I loved my baby. After all those wrong diagnoses given by that stupid pediatrician, I had learned to cherish my baby despite her birth defects. Yet every time when I held her in my arms and gave her the bottle and she choked, she would stop feeding and begin to cry. It was heart-wrenching for me. Fortunately, she quickly learned how to take in the baby formula, and in a few days, she stopped choking.

When I nursed Angela and Leslie while they were babies, I never knew normal babies were actually miracles and were to be thankful for. When I came home from ABC Hospital with Corrie, I began to read the literature they gave me on cleft lips and cleft palates. "Babies begin to form their lips and palates during the second and the third month of pregnancy. If there is any disturbance, the growth of lips and palates will stop and result in cleft lips and cleft palates."

So *I learned then* that throughout the nine months of pregnancy, any disturbance could interfere with the forming or growth of a certain body part or organ and abnormalities could result. Therefore, a normal baby is actually the result of countless miracles (since nothing happened to disturb his or her growth), and everybody, especially the parents, should thank God for their normal babies. It was *then* I realized how much gratitude I had owed the Lord, for He had given me two beautiful and *normal* girls, and I had taken them for granted and never thanked the Lord for them.

A few days after Corrie had learned to feed without choking, we took her to an orthodontist as instructed. He took a molding of her cleft palate and made a plastic plate to fill the hole in the palate. This turned out to be disastrous for me, however, for Corrie *had to learn* how to *feed all over again.*

We normal people who don't have holes in the palate probably never thought about our *blessings.* When we eat, our tongues send the food directly down the throat without any problem. Cleft-palate babies are different. They have holes in the *roofs* of their mouths. When their tongues try to send the food or drink down the throats, the food or drink ends up going through the holes in the roofs and into the nostrils. This, of course, would interfere with their breathing, and they would choke themselves.

The orthodontist's intention of filling the hole in the palate was good, of course. In Corrie's case, however, it was hard on her. After all, she was only a newborn, and I myself really had no idea how to help her. With the plastic plate on her palate, she must have felt different, and yet she could not talk. When I gave her the bottle, she sucked a few seconds and began to cry. It was really a struggle. One time the plastic plate fell off but I did not know. I continued to try feeding, and she continued to refuse the bottle. The struggle went on a while, and then I saw blood coming out of her mouth. The upper side of the plastic plate that fit into the hole was actually jagged and very sharp.

So during those days when Corrie *learned and relearned* to feed on that special nipple, she cried a lot. It was hard for me not to feel sad, and I would cry too. In the end, I began to think God did not love me and He was punishing me. (At that time I had not learned enough from the Bible about God's love, and that was why I had this wrong thought.)

Before the first month was over, the Lord corrected my thinking. During that first month, I usually took an afternoon nap since my body was still recovering. One afternoon I was awakened from my nap by a loud bang.

For decoration purpose I had two pictures hung on the bedroom wall right above the headboard of our bed. On the right side where I slept was "Pinky," and on the left was "Blue Boy," both reprints of famous paintings. Each picture was hung in a heavy frame of hard, pressed wood particles.

More than a foot away from my side of the bed stood a nightstand and a table lamp. That afternoon when I was awakened by the loud bang, I saw the bottom of "Pinky" sitting on the nightstand, right side up with the upper end barely resting on the bed by my side, almost touching my arm.

The picture was hung on the wall by a hooked hanger with glue secured to the wall, but the years of moisture in the air possibly had caused the original glue on the hanger to become loose. It should have fallen directly on my head or on the headboard and then down on my body. Either way I would have been hurt, perhaps seriously.

However, it looked as if someone had turned that picture 90 degrees and pushed it away from the bed and let it drop on the nightstand so that its upper end would rest on the bed but not touch me at all.

I then picked up the picture and found one side of the frame cracked. Such was the impact of the fall! The force was so great that I surely would have been hurt had it fallen directly on me.

At that moment when I realized I had been protected by an unseen hand, I knew God loved me after all, and I cried out, "Lord, thank You for protecting me. Forgive me for having doubted Your love."

A year or two after Corrie was born, Yishan experienced a healing miracle of his own. The year was 1980 or 1981. That year he was attending a convention in New Orleans.

Back when Yishan was a graduate student, a few months after he began his PhD studies, he began to complain of discomfort in the chest (actually heartburn, a term I learned many years later). Since we both were quite ignorant at that time, neither of us thought of taking any action. Our student insurance covered only hospital stays, and we never thought of seeking any medical help until he began working as a microbiologist. Probably because of the strain of driving he had to endure during the daily commute, his heartburn became more frequent, and he soon found a doctor. His company insurance had a much better coverage than the old student insurance.

The doctor ran a test on Yishan's stomach but found nothing wrong. Therefore, he suggested taking some liquid antacid. Yishan followed his advice, and the antacid worked. From then on, he would have a bottle of antacid packed in his suitcase whenever he traveled.

That year when he attended the convention in New Orleans, I forgot about the antacid when I packed his clothes in the suitcase, and he himself also forgot to check it. By the time he realized he needed the medication, it was already too late. It was 4:00 a.m., and he was in a hotel room in downtown New Orleans. But he did not know where the pharmacy was, and it was doubtful any store was open.

When it was getting unbearable for him, Yishan prayed, "In the name of Jesus, I command my stomach pain to leave right away." Even before he said, "Amen," the pain instantly stopped, and he was fine.

He was overjoyed and jumped down from the bed and began

to jump and dance on the room floor, praising the Lord just as the healed lame man did at the gate called "Beautiful" (Acts 2).

Yishan and I experienced more healing miracles than I am able to mention. As for visions, each of us had also one experience of our own. I'm going to tell mine here and Yishan's in a later chapter. (After I wrote the previous part, I then remembered I actually had more experiences over the years, but this one I'm going to tell is the most dramatic.)

In the summer of 1990, while we were ministering at HGC, we also helped with another church. Our responsibilities at HGC ended each Sunday once lunch was over, and Yishan and I would drive fifteen or twenty minutes to a Taiwanese church. This Taiwanese church was without a pastor, and the Lord gave us the opportunity to minister there on Sunday afternoons. Yishan and I took turns preaching sermons. We also led prayer meetings and Bible studies. We pretty much filled in the pastoral needs.

Midway through the summer, we were informed of a special need. One of the church members was a surgeon, and he had a patient in the area's hospital. This patient (I'll call him Horace) had the same family name as ours, Lin. His home was in Seattle, Washington. He was diagnosed with terminal liver cancer and had been referred to the surgeon who was a member of the Taiwanese church.

Horace's wife and mother came to take care of him at the hospital. At night they stayed in a small room in a nearby motel. On Sunday afternoon, through the recommendation of the surgeon, his wife and mother came to the worship service at the Taiwanese church.

Yishan and I began visiting Horace in the hospital and prayed for his healing. We learned that Horace's mother had been a widow for many years, since when she was still young and her children were small, and Horace still had an older brother and a younger sister in Taiwan.

Horace was probably between forty-five and fifty years of age. I felt burdened to pray for his healing lest his wife would be widowed as well. However, the Lord chose not to answer our prayers, and within a month, Horace went home to be with the Lord on August 23, 1990.

The day Horace passed away, Yishan and I still went to the hospital to visit him and prayed for him in the morning. We were told they were expecting Horace's older brother and younger sister to fly in from Taiwan that afternoon.

As Yishan and I prayed for Horace that late morning, my heart was heavy. Throughout our prayer that whole time, Horace uttered not a single word, not even "Amen." He did not even open his eyes when his wife told him, "Mr. and Mrs. Lin are here to pray for you." I was sure he knew it, but he seemed to have gone into a coma. I knew it might be the last day on earth for Horace unless the Lord performed a miracle.

When Yishan and I went home, it was already past noon. We had a simple lunch and then went to our separate studies, Yishan to his desk in Corrie's room and me to mine in the master bedroom, which had a large window facing the backyard.

My mind was still preoccupied with the thought of Horace's condition and the possibility of two widows in his family. I could not concentrate on books or the Bible. And instead of sitting down, I remained standing at my desk a long time, brooding.

I don't remember for how long I stood there, but I do remember at one point my head was somewhat bowed, and my eyes were really not looking at anything specific. All of a sudden, out of the corner of my eye, I caught sight of a man running past the window in front of me. I immediately cried out, "Yi, someone was in our backyard and has just passed outside our window."

Immediately, Yishan ran to the kitchen, out through the sliding patio door, and into the backyard. Moments later he came in and said, "You must have seen a vision. No one could have run past the window. The gate on the other side is securely locked."

When I heard those words, I thought indeed I had to have seen a vision. What I saw was clear and genuine. There could be no mistake, but it was a "black-and-white picture." I saw the profile of a man with full black hair who had a black umbrella over his head and quickly passed outside the window, but I heard no sound. It was like a black-and-white silent movie.

Our home had a crawl space about three feet high, and most of the crawl space was underground. The level of our bedroom floor was somewhat higher than the ground in the backyard. Usually, when Yishan stood outside our master bedroom window, I could see the top of his bald head but not his face. Yet the profile of the man I saw from the top of his head to a good portion below his shoulder was more than a foot long. That man would have to be more than six feet tall! (Yishan was five-foot-seven.)

One more thing about the vision. That backyard right outside the window was full of gravel (one more defect of our Pinole home!), and I had been digging those gravel stones out for days. There were a shovel and a small bucket lying right there on the ground. If someone had tried to run outside the window at that speed, he surely would have tripped and should have fallen down instead of running!

The time I saw the vision was almost exactly 3:00 p.m. I had no idea why all of a sudden I was allowed to see that vision, and I felt more disturbed. So instead of sitting down to study, I went out to the backyard. I went to the spot where that man in the vision would have been, and there I saw the small bucket and the shovel lying on the ground. I picked up the small shovel and began to dig the gravel.

While digging gravel and moving around in the backyard for more rocks, I tried to figure out the meaning of the vision and prayed more for Horace. I was lost in thoughts and prayers, and unknowingly, I spent about an hour digging and praying.

My reverie was finally stopped by Yishan around 4:00 p.m. He said somebody from the Taiwanese church had called to inform us that Horace had just passed on. When I heard the news, I kept asking the Lord, "Why, Lord? I don't understand why You chose not to heal Horace. Now You have made his wife a widow just the same as his mother. I don't understand why our prayers have met a dead end just as I don't understand the meaning of the vision I saw earlier."

For the rest of that day, I heard no answer from the Lord.

The next morning Yishan and I drove to the motel where Horace's mother and widow were staying. When we walked into their small room where a double bed was in the middle against the wall, I saw his mother sitting with her back against the headboard and her legs spread straight lengthwise over the middle of the bed.

As soon as the elder Mrs. Lin saw us, she began to ask in English, "Why? Why? Why?"

Immediately, I tried to comfort her, saying, "Mrs. Lin, we have been praying hard for the Lord to heal your son, and we don't know why God did not answer our prayers. I think in this life we have many questions for which we'll have no answers until we see the Lord just as what I experienced yesterday afternoon." And I began to tell of what I saw at 3:00 p.m. the day before.

The other Mrs. Lin, Horace's widow, who had been squatting on the floor by the other side of the bed and working over an open suitcase, had neither stood up nor said anything since Yishan and I went in but had been listening. All of a sudden, she raised her head, looked at us, and spoke up, "Now I know."

I was puzzled and asked, "What did you know?" She stood up and began to tell what happened in the hospital room around 3:00 p.m. the day earlier.

"We were expecting my husband's elder brother and younger sister to come to the hospital around 3:15 p.m. So at 3:00 p.m., I was looking out the window of the room and was looking down at the people entering the hospital when suddenly I heard my husband muttering something. I didn't catch what he just said, and I asked, 'What did you say?' He said something that sounded to me like 'Let them come,' and I replied, 'Yes, your brother and sister are coming here soon.' Now I know he was actually not saying, 'Let them come,' but rather he had said, 'It's raining.'"

In Taiwanese, "Let them come" and "It's raining" are both composed of three words and two of them sound the same while actually only one word is the same—*Ho yin lai* and *Ho lai la*. The word *lai* is the only one that is the same (meaning come or coming). The literal three-word translation for the Taiwanese meaning "It's raining" is "rain is coming." So the same word in both phrases is come or coming.

Then instead of *my* offering condolences, the younger Mrs. Lin began to encourage me by saying, "He knew you cared and had been praying for him. That was why he appeared to you yesterday afternoon."

Praise the Lord. Horace's wife understood the meaning of my vision, and the Lord had used that vision to give her hope and comfort in time of great sorrow.

From many testimonies I have read, some even written by medical doctors and nurses, I have learned that the spirit (or soul) of a near-death patient could often go in and out of his or her body at any moment, especially in the case of a Christian believer. In the state of coma, the patient sometimes heard and said something that might sound puzzling to us, while actually, his spirit was probably *somewhere else*, experiencing something we could not see.

In Horace's case, his home was in Seattle, a place with a lot of rain. That afternoon when his wife heard him say, "It's raining," his spirit obviously was instantly out of his body and ran to Seattle with an umbrella outside of my window. (Keep in mind the speed of the spirit running is awfully fast.)

Whether this was what actually had taken place, I cannot be dogmatic; only God knows. However, the Lord in His great mercy and wisdom had given me that vision not only to console Horace's widow but also to show me His sovereignty. Whether in our life or death, *He is Lord*, and we always have to trust Him. But His love will never depart from us (Romans 8:28, 37–38).

Why does God choose to answer one prayer but not another? I don't know. I do know that occasionally the Lord does choose to perform a healing miracle, maybe to remind us He still loves us and cares for us and He still runs the universe.

On the evening of November 10, 1998, Yishan's mother and two sisters together with a friend came from Taiwan, and we had dinner very late. After the dinner I drank some special fruit juice in order to help digestion. Someone had given Yishan a jar of homemade preserved plums with juice. We had eaten all the plums and some of the juice still remained in the jar and was kept in the refrigerator.

For more than twenty years since 1965, I had been tormented by heart burns and pain in the right side of my back. Although I had gone to doctors and had tests done, the pain remained a mystery. In December 1987, the Lord prompted me to check a medical encyclopedia in answer to my prayer, and I finally realized I was probably bothered by gallstones. A subsequent appointment with a surgeon and an ultrasound test confirmed my own diagnosis, and in April of 1988, my gallbladder was removed. (I have briefly mentioned this in chapter 2.)

After the surgery I was told to be careful about my diet. I tried to avoid greasy food, but occasionally, I could still feel something funny in my back where I had enormous pain before.

Since we ate dinner very late that evening of November 10, 1998, I deliberately drank some juice from that jar of preserved plum in hope that it would help my digestion. It was not until many days later that I realized the juice had probably fermented with live yeast, and it was actually detrimental that I drank that juice. (I had heard from a man who was working at a brewery where he once tasted some live yeast and began to have a bloated feeling, and only later he took some medication to kill the live yeast and found relief.) I had ignorantly drunk that juice that evening, and it caused me great trouble.

By midnight of November 10, 1998, when I was ready to go to bed, I felt bloated, and I could not lie down or sleep. I had to sit up in a sofa downstairs all night, while Yishan and all the guests were sleeping soundly upstairs. I was able to doze off finally when I was too tired to stay awake, but twenty minutes later, a sharp pain kept me awake again.

By next morning, Wednesday, I felt I could not stand it anymore. I had tried two kinds of antacids, some Chinese medication, and even a mixture of water and baking soda. Each time I burped, I released a little gas and felt slightly relieved, but quickly, the pain would begin to feel uncomfortable again.

I called the 800 number of my medical insurance in Florida and was able to talk to a doctor. He advised me to take something, but I did not know where to get it (I never heard of that stuff before) and therefore did not follow through with his advice. Probably I was so uncomfortable that I was getting confused.

By Friday morning, I decided to see a doctor. I called my clinic and got to see Dr. Wu, a young internist in his thirties. He examined me and had some tests done on me. When the results were in, he told me, "I'm sorry. We don't know what's the cause."

The pain went on. By Saturday night I was suffering tremendously. No amount of prayer or any remedy was able to alleviate my pain, and yet I still had to prepare a sermon for the next day's English worship. God seemed to have totally forsaken me. I was not able to eat or sleep much.

Early Sunday morning at 4:20, I was awakened by sharp pains, and I woke up Yishan. "You'd better take me to the ER," I told him.

He got me to the ER in record time. My case was not life-threatening, so they let me sit there, waiting and waiting. Finally, I was admitted into a room. I looked at my watch. It was 5:30 a.m. Still I had to wait for three more hours before finally a doctor came into my room. I told him what had happened, and he had several tests done on me, all the possibly necessary tests that Dr. Wu had not ordered. Sometime after 11:00 a.m., that emergency doctor came to pronounce his diagnosis, "My diagnosis is the same as that of Dr. Wu. Sorry. We don't know what the cause is either."

I continued to suffer for another week. By the time the next Sunday rolled along, I was even more miserable and desperate. That Sunday afternoon I had to first preach an English sermon and later teach a Chinese adult Sunday school class, and later in that afternoon, Yishan and I were scheduled to conduct Sunday school teachers' training in a nearby Taiwanese church. Yishan was to teach a Taiwanese class, and I was to teach an English class.

That Sunday afternoon, November 22, 1998, I arrived at the church practically empty-handed. I had to have one message and two lessons ready, and yet I had very little prepared. As I sat down in the empty room with chairs arranged for worship service and knowing I was actually not ready with the message to be delivered, I cried out silently to the Lord, "Lord, You know what I have been going through these past two weeks. In a few minutes, the young people are coming in for the English worship service, and yet I do not have a message for them. Lord, give me words to speak as You have promised in John 7:35, 'In that day those who believe in me shall have rivers of living water flow out of their bosom.'"

At that very moment, I felt very clearly something three inches from the top of my head, some covering like a hat in the shape of an upside-down bowl (or a wok without its handles), its diameter being exactly the same as my body width from one shoulder to the other. Although my eyes were closed, I could feel distinctively the covering on my head began to move downward in front of me, and as it moved, it began to shrink smaller and smaller until finally it went into my bosom. This may sound very strange to an outsider, yet the feeling was real and unmistakable. (Quite interestingly, there is an old Chinese saying that says, "God is three inches above your head.")

When this occurred, I was so moved that tears came out, but I was relieved. I knew the Lord had given me His word as He had promised in John 7:35. So the English worship service went by, and I was able to deliver a message without a hitch. In fact, almost none of the young congregation members, except a couple of them, knew the struggle I went through that whole week. Then the Chinese adult Sunday school also moved along smoothly as well.

Right after that Yishan and I drove to the nearby Taiwanese church. When we arrived, their worship service was still in progress. Somebody directed us to their fellowship hall, where later they would have a potluck dinner to celebrate Thanksgiving. I deliberately picked a seat at the far end of the long roll of tables so that I would be away from the tables of food. The past two weeks I had eaten very little. I had been feeling bloated on an empty stomach. I was definitely not going to touch any of that food.

I sat there trying to utilize the precious time to prepare my talk. I tried to think and write down the main points, knowing I would not have enough time to write down everything. I wrote and paused, and I prayed very hard in between. However, I felt very tense and found it hard to concentrate.

Once their worship service was over, people began to move into the fellowship hall. Somebody greeted Yishan and me, inviting us to take food. Yishan went along, but I remained in my seat, trying to avoid food. However, a little later somebody brought me a plateful of food. Fortunately, it was not a big pile, and I ate everything since I thought it might be considered rude to refuse the offer. I quickly went back to prepare the talk.

When the time came, Yishan and I went to separate designated rooms, and the training session began. By that time I already had a pretty good list of main points ready, and I felt more at ease and said a short prayer of thanks to the Lord.

I was able to give each point of the talk with ample examples, and then it was time for them to ask questions. When my talk was over and I went to look for Yishan, he was just wrapping up his talk as well.

That evening, about 10:30 p.m., as I sat in front of my bathroom mirror, getting ready for a bath, I suddenly remembered that my bloated feeling had gone and the whole evening I had not had any single pain despite the fact I had eaten all that food offered on that plate. The Lord had performed a miracle of healing on me when the power of His Spirit went into my bosom that afternoon! It's an understatement to say I was so thankful!

Now I'm going to talk about dreams. Yishan and I differed from the professor I mentioned earlier in this chapter in our views on this subject. Over the years the Lord has used many dreams to speak to me and Yishan. I'll just mention one here—one that *saved* me in a way.

Once when Yishan was out of town, he asked me to lead a Wednesday night prayer meeting. I only functioned as a facilitator, and I just had to control the timing of everything.

That evening Yishan had an outside speaker scheduled to give a short talk before the session was to disperse into separate small groups for prayer. The speaker was a Charismatic pastor, and Yishan had scheduled him to be the featured speaker at the suggestion of a retired pastor who was a regular attendant at the prayer meeting.

I was aware of the fact that a number of deacons and one elder of the church were against some views of the charismatic movement, such as laying on of hands to pray for charismatic gifts. Although Yishan and I did not promote this kind of practice ourselves, we did not see anything wrong with inviting such a speaker to share at a prayer meeting, especially when it had been suggested by the retired pastor.

Usually when Yishan scheduled someone to speak, he would inform that person the time allotted for him to speak. That evening, however, that pastor went overly long in his talk, and worse yet, as soon as he stopped talking, he began to walk around, laying hands on everybody to pray for him or her.

I felt very bad when I saw what that speaker was doing. *However, I did not know how to stop him.* I was sure either Yishan or the retired pastor had told him how long he was supposed to talk when they invited him. When he dragged on in his talk, I wanted to stop him, but I thought it would be rude since he was a guest speaker. I felt helpless, and I could only silently ask the Lord to help.

By the time that charismatic speaker stopped his rounds of laying hand and praying, there was no time left for small group prayers. So I called the prayer meeting to end. I knew there were quite a few unhappy elders and deacons, but I did not know what to do. I felt as if my hands were tied.

A week later on the following Wednesday, Yishan was to come home, and I was to pick him up at the San Francisco International Airport. That morning, however, before I woke up, I had a vivid dream. In the dream I saw Yishan and me putting out fires in a room. In the room were two large open barrels with fires burning and rising, and Yishan and I each had a hose in our hands, trying to dowse the flames. Then I woke up, and words came into my head, "Go apologize at the prayer meeting." Immediately, I knew the Lord was instructing me what to do.

When I met Yishan at the airport, I told him what had transpired at the previous Wednesday night's prayer meeting, and I also told him the dream I had that morning. I said, "Tonight at the beginning of the prayer meeting, let me apologize first."

That evening I told the group, "I have to apologize for last Wednesday night's prayer meeting since I did not do a good job of controlling the time." And I went on to explain why I did not stop the speaker when he went over his time.

As I did that, I saw two tense and hostile faces break up into smiles. One of them, a deacon, satisfactorily said in agreement, "Yes, it went over so long that we had no time for small group prayers."

Praise the Lord. He who knows every human heart gave me that dream to know how to mend a situation that had gone wrong. He knew there were burning barrels that needed to be quenched.

I must say that Yishan and I were not the only *lucky* people to have received these special gifts of tongues or dreams and visions in our own times. Other people around us had also told of stories of people who had received these gifts. Then there were the Armenian Christians (I learned from a book I read in the 1990s) who were able to escape to the United States because of the prophecy given by some gifted people who had received God's revelation through dreams and visions. Thus, they were able to avoid the atrocities, persecutions, and massacres committed against the Armenian people! In that book it is also mentioned some people who had the gift of tongues as well.

I think it is most unfortunate that the wrong theology taught by some scholars has hampered many Christians from embracing the whole teaching of the Bible to seek the gifts of the Holy Spirit to the fullest extent! It is only when we can fully embrace all of those that our witnessing will be most effective. This is probably the main reason why in the churches Yishan and I founded together, we were able to see people coming to the Lord in much greater percentages compared to the many much larger churches where you do not see so many people receiving baptism each year. Please keep in mind I'm not bragging about me or Yishan. I'm fully aware it was all the work of the Holy Spirit, but I'm also firmly aware that what we believe in does make a lot of difference.

I also think it is really our common enemy Satan's scheme to cause those scholars to have that kind of misunderstanding of the Bible, and as a result, many believers have been misled simply because Satan has been trying to thwart God's plan and to prevent believers from receiving the full power of the Holy Spirit to be effective witnesses! It is so unfortunate there is such a great division among Christians into two different camps—Evangelicals and Charismatics! *There should never have been such a division!* If you study the Bible carefully, you'll find the early believers in the book of Acts to be *evangelical as well as charismatic!* The great apostle Paul says that about himself.

I could go on telling more dreams and healing miracles, but I think enough has been said to illustrate my point. However, before I end this section, I would like to tell one special story that I recorded on a small piece of paper and placed in my Bible. That day was Friday, January 28, 2005. Around 10:35 a.m., I heard the host of a classical radio station say, "From where I sit it's difficult to see what's beginning to look like fiction to me. The weather forecast says it's going to be partly cloudy and scattered shower for the Bay Area this afternoon. If those of you out there see it rain, any of you, call me to let me know."

When I heard that, I thought it to be ridiculous. His office was in downtown San Francisco, where he could only see clouds and no rain, and so he doubted the truthfulness of the weather forecast. At that time I was reminded of what a brother thought to be "no dreams, no vision, no tongues today" (chapter 15) because of the teaching he received.

This is really not that brother's problem only. It seems to be quite prevalent among a lot of Christians and even pastors or some theologians. Their faith system or understanding of the Bible is limited by their own physical sight or personal experiences. Just because they have never experienced it, they'd say, "It's no longer here today."

That day after that radio host said that, he played a piece of music, and then he said, "Someone (the name of a woman) just called from Walnut Creek saying it was raining there and a patch of blue. Well, microclimate. That's what Bay Area is known for." Then after another piece of music, he said, "Somebody (another listener's name) also called from North Fremont saying it was pouring rain out there, and another one said it rained in Concord as well and even hailed."

During that time I was going to call and tell that host that it rained heavily in U City. However, I was still looking for that station's phone number when so many had already called. It saved me a phone call.

Still, after one more piece of music, a different host (a woman this time) said, "Weather forecast said it was going to be partly cloudy and scattered shower for the Bay Area this afternoon. Obviously, microclimate was shown everywhere in the Bay Area today. Some places it rained and even hailed, while some other places it was only cloudy."

I hope this story serves as a reminder for us to be careful about our own understanding of the Bible. Some ways of looking at the Bible are obviously wrong when one limits it only to his or her own understanding or lack of experience just as the mistake made by that first radio host.

Jesus says in John 5:17 (NASB) "My Father is working until now, and I Myself am working." I believe the God who worked miracles and gave dreams to His children in the past is still working today. Although His revelation through the Bible is complete, sometimes His specific guidance for our individual circumstances still warrants the giving of a dream or vision or even a healing miracle. *Nobody* has ever been able to put God in a box, and if we need His dreams and visions for help, why would He refrain Himself from giving those miracles? His thoughts are higher than our thoughts, and His ways are higher than our ways. I'm very thankful that the Lord has not limited Himself to rules but has allowed me and Yishan to experience dreams and visions in our time of special needs. Praise the Lord!

Chapter 21

Decision, Decision

A year before Yishan completed his three-year seminary training, we began praying for the Lord's guidance as to where we should go after Yishan graduated from the seminary. Although we were enjoying a fruitful ministry at HGC, one evening while we were visiting a member's family we encountered unexpected difficulty.

That evening we visited a woman who spoke Cantonese and a little Mandarin. At church I usually conducted conversation with her in partial Mandarin and partial English. Her husband usually drove her to church, dropped her, and went home alone. I was told that he spoke only Tai-San (another Cantonese dialect but totally different from Cantonese) and was still not a believer. When I found that out, I told Yishan and suggested we visit that family.

When we arrived at that home, the wife introduced us to her husband and his mother. As we talked, I realized it was impossible for us to give the son and his aged mother (she was in her nineties) the gospel. That evening for the first time, I found that the conversation between that husband and wife was conducted in English since the wife did not know Tai-San and the husband did not speak Cantonese. And I also found out that husband's understanding of English was rather limited. As to his mother, there was no means by which we could communicate to her. She knew no English at all.

As we were trying to carry on the conversation, I felt like Baalam's donkey. I had a mouth, but I really could not talk. How could we convey the gospel message to them? We had to cut short the visit.

That night I had a strong conviction HGC needed a pastor who could speak Cantonese. Yishan felt the same too. From then on, we began to seek the Lord's direction for our future and the church's as well.

Around that time a friend called us from a town in Indiana. He told us he and his wife were part of a Chinese Bible study group that was turning into a church, and he invited us to speak there. We flew to Indiana, spoke to the group, enjoyed some sweet fellowship with our friends, and came back to the Bay Area. When they invited us to go there the second time, only I was able to go since Yishan had to stay behind for his seminary classes.

My solo trip turned out to be even better. Not only was I able to minister God's Word to them, but I also enjoyed some relaxed time with a few of those couples. We wrapped Chinese dumplings together, and the occasion also served as a time for personal sharing as well as a good Q and A session. When I came back to California, I knew my heart was still in the Midwest, and I yearned to be able to move to Indiana to minister to that group again.

Yishan did not share my sentiment, however. He said to me, "If you want me to do ministry in Indiana, I might as well retire." What he meant was that the Chinese population there was too small. He wanted to minister to a larger Chinese population.

Of course, there was also a third member in our family—Corrie. Her heart was in California. She did not care for Indiana. So two against one, the Midwest was out despite the fact that all ten coworkers of that group unanimously invited us to shepherd them.

Then another friend called from Southern California, north of the LA area. He and his wife were members of a fairly large Chinese church. He asked Yishan to speak at his church. Then they invited Yishan a second time and asked me to go as well. Both Yishan and I knew their intention. They were considering to invite Yishan to be their pastor. Someone at the seminary whose daughter was also a member of that church told me and Yishan repeatedly, "They really like you both."

However, Yishan did not feel confident enough to pastor that church. He told me, "They have too many PhDs."

Still another Taiwanese church in the approximate vicinity of that Chinese church invited Yishan to conduct a series of three evangelistic meetings over a weekend. Before he flew there, he asked the Lord for ten people to make decisions for Jesus during those three meetings. When he arrived there, he was led to a dinner party at a restaurant. There would be no meeting until the next day, Saturday morning.

At the dinner table, Yishan found a number of MDs. One of them, a nonbeliever, was seated across the table from Yishan, and another who was a believer was seated right next to Yishan. For convenience's sake, I'll call the former Dr. N and the latter Dr. B.

A lively conversation ensued during the course of the dinner, according to Yishan's description. Dr. N kept saying, "There is no such real person as the historical Jesus. You Christians only made him up to be a symbol. And there could be no resurrection of Jesus either. Christians have made up that story as well. They are all myths."

Hearing such outrageous claims Yishan made no answer. He just smiled, knowing Dr. N was trying to provoke him to a debate. However, Dr. B could not keep his silence, and the conversation turned into a heated debate between Dr. B and Dr. N.

In the end, Yishan told Dr. N, "This is your opinion only, but that is not what the Bible says. Wait until you hear my talk tomorrow."

Actually, Dr. N also made some other remarks at the dinner. "My wife goes to church," he said. "However, I'll never become a Christian when I see how she behaves."

Yishan told me Mrs. N blushed profusely when she heard her husband's remarks, and she looked as if she would like to find a hole in the ground to hide herself.

The first meeting on Saturday morning was attended by forty or so people. At the end of his message, Yishan asked the congregation to bow their heads and close their eyes, and then he invited those willing to trust in Jesus as their Lord and Savior to raise their hands.

"The first two hands that shot up almost simultaneously right after my invitation were those of Dr. and Mrs. N," Yishan told me. "And it was only after the meeting was over that they knew of each other's decision."

At the lunch that followed the first meeting, Yishan saw a marked change in the attitude of Dr. N. He became very humble when he talked to Yishan, and Yishan asked him, "Didn't you say last night that you'd never become a Christian? How come you raised your hand?"

"Oh, that's very marvelous," answered Dr. N. "I didn't mean to raise my hand. But there was a force that just pushed my hand up, and I couldn't help raising it. Now I know that Jesus is truly God. I also believe in His bodily resurrection now."

And Mrs. N told Yishan a story that was no less remarkable. "When I bowed my head, my heart began to pound wildly. I knew Jesus was knocking at the door of my heart, and I had to open my heart to let Him in. I raised my hand, and I was full of joy."

Dr. and Mrs. N were very joyful to find that each of them had accepted Jesus to be their Lord and Savior.

The second meeting was held in the afternoon of that Saturday, and the third meeting *was* the worship service on Sunday. At the end of his sermon, Yishan gave the third invitation to the congregation, and more hands were raised.

"There was a total of nine people who raised hands by the end of the third meeting," said Yishan. "And when the worship service was over, a woman came to talk to me. She said she didn't get to attend yesterday's meetings and only heard my message this morning. She was interested in accepting Jesus, and I asked why she failed to raise her hand a while ago. She said she did not know how to accept Jesus. So I led her in praying to receive Jesus. So the total number of people who accepted Jesus in those three meetings came to be ten, exactly as I had asked the Lord."

I must admit Yishan had a lot more faith than I did, at least in this case. When he told me he asked for ten people to make decisions, I thought he was a bit too ambitious. If he could get half a dozen, he should be satisfied. Yet the Lord answered his prayer exactly as he had asked. The Lord really rewarded us according to our faith.

That Taiwanese church was interested in having Yishan as their pastor, but Yishan told me he had no interest, and he explained to me why. I could not quite agree with his thinking, but then I could not make him decide against his own heart.

Another church in the San Francisco Bay Area was also looking for a pastor, and Yishan and I had been repeatedly asked to lead meetings—Friday night fellowship, special sessions, Sunday worship, etc. At one of their yearly retreats, we were even asked to be their speakers. A reliable source had told us more than once that they were interested in us. Yishan and I could sense it even without being told. Yet for some reason Yishan was reluctant to receive that call. Yes, he did tell me why, but there is no need for me to disclose it here.

Around that time our daughter Leslie and her husband, Ling-Yi, were living in White Plains, New York. Both were working in nearby towns and attending a Chinese church in that area. One day they informed us of their church's searching for a pastor and asked if Yishan would be interested. Actually, Leslie was very enthusiastic in getting Yishan to be a candidate, and she gave Yishan's name to their pastoral search committee. They asked her if Yishan had any recorded messages. Yishan sent them two cassette tapes containing two Sunday sermons.

Pretty soon they were asking Yishan to send his resumes. I can't recall if Yishan did or not. I guess either it was difficult to move Yishan out to a time zone with a three-hour difference, or the Lord just saw it fit to keep him in California. Anyway, by that time Yishan had pretty much settled his mind and felt he was called to another church in the Bay Area. Let me call this church, THC.

Perhaps I should go back to the previous year when it all started. Around the time when Yishan and I made that fateful evening visit to that Cantonese-Taisan family and began praying for the Lord's guidance, one day I received a phone call from a woman whom I had led to the Lord some years back when we were living in Schaumburg. She and her husband had moved to the Bay Area a number of years ahead of us. She said she had heard Yishan was attending CW Seminary, and she suggested to an elder of her church to invite Yishan to preach there. Since her church, THC, was about forty-five-minutes to an hour's drive from our Pinole home and my heart was yearning to go back to the Midwest, her invitation for Yishan to preach at that church really did not register much in my heart. To me it was just another invitation for Yishan to preach.

Two months later, however, Yishan was invited back again, and still, a third invitation came for a Sunday in October. That Sunday turned out to be the day of the big wildfire in the Oakland Hills in which more than two thousand homes were burned down, so I'll always remember it. When Yishan came home in the afternoon (he stayed for the fellowship lunch provided after the worship service), he told me about the dense smoke he saw from the freeway, and he also said, "THC seems to be very interested in me, and the elder has asked me to bring you along next time I go there."

Upon hearing Yishan's words, I was more concerned about the fire than THC's interest in Yishan, and I remember I retorted by saying, "Why should I go to that church? I'm not interested in moving to F City."

Indeed, I was very concerned about the fire in the Oakland Hills. Immediately, I turned on the TV and spent the rest of the whole afternoon watching that big fire on TV. A retired missionary and his wife were living in that area. He was one of the speakers I had invited to preach at the HGC English worship services, and he and his wife had invited me and another sister to spend an afternoon and early evening in their home, which had a beautiful commanding view of the night scene of the Bay Area.

While I was watching that fire on the TV, I kept praying for that retired couple. I asked the Lord to protect them and to spare their house, and I also asked the Lord to turn back the fire by shifting the wind because I knew in that way the fire would burn itself out.

The Lord answered part of my prayer but not the other. Later that evening I heard on the TV that the wind began to shift direction, and the fire eventually was out. But the next day I heard the bad news that the retired missionary's house was not spared, although he and his wife were safe.

Why did the Lord answer one prayer but not the other? I don't have the answer, but I do know one good out of that tragedy. At that time that retired missionary was serving as a pastor of the elderly ministry at a very large church in Berkeley. That church had many pastors, and it also had many members who lost their homes in that big fire. That Sunday following that big fire, I was told none of the pastors dared to stand in front of the congregation to preach because none of those pastors lost their homes. The retired missionary was the only pastor who had suffered the loss of his home, and thus, *only he* was able to stand at the podium to preach a message of hope and consolation to the congregation. And in about a month after that, when I invited him to preach at HGC English worship service, he did deliver a very moving message to the predominantly young congregation. He brought a ceramic pot that had survived the fire, and he said, "This pot survived the fire because it had been burned in a furnace before, and thus, the fire had no more effect on it. Likewise Jesus Christ had been 'burned' for us when He was crucified on the cross. If we trust in Him as the Lord and Savior, no hellfire will have power on us in the future."

The day after the Oakland fire, I still remember, among the extensive coverage of the fire in the newspaper, I saw an eerie picture of the aftermath of the fire—fireplace chimneys dotted a total ruined landscape. Those chimneys were made of bricks that had been burned in kilns and thus were the almost exclusive remnants of the two thousand or more homes.

Well, enough is said about the Oakland fire. Now let me get back to THC's interest in Yishan and his words that I was supposed to go with him to that church the next time. Although I felt reluctant to move to another part of the Bay Area, I did begin to pray in unison with Yishan, asking the Lord to show us His will in this matter.

I asked the Lord for two things as signs of His leading. First, Corrie would show her willingness—instead of rebellion—in moving to F City. Secondly, I asked the Lord that He would enable me to strongly like that church the first time I went there.

To me, the second sign would be more difficult to obtain, although up to that time, Corrie's obstinacy was enough of a stumbling block to me. The reason I asked for this second sign was based on my own past experience to be able to strongly like a church on my first visit, especially a church to which I was a total stranger, would be something amounting to a miracle.

Here, either I had deluded myself, or something miraculous had occurred, for I did have a strong pleasant feeling of THC that Friday night when we both went there about a month after they gave Yishan that invitation. That evening Yishan spoke briefly first, and then he gave me the remaining time to speak. Of the whole congregation, that woman whom I had led to the Lord and her husband were the only familiar faces to me. Yet quite a number of women and also a few men came to speak to me after the meeting. Usually, Chinese people were reserved and seldom gave me compliments when I spoke. Yet that night quite a few made me feel very welcome. When I came home, I felt quite elated. The elation was less for the positive reaction from the congregation but more for the realization of the sure guidance of the Lord. I could also tell Yishan was just elated as I was.

About this time Yishan and I were surprised one day at the seminary when the president invited us to his office to talk. He said he was having problem with his health, and he had been looking for someone to take over his job. Since Yishan had a PhD, he believed Yishan was the best person for the position and would be able to represent the seminary well.

Yishan and I should have felt flattered. Yet after we prayed, we did not feel led to take this offer. We both felt he should take the pastorate of THC rather than the presidency of the seminary. (At the time when we accepted the offer from THC, we did not know it was probably the largest Chinese church in the SF Bay Area.)

In the meanwhile, we had also been praying for someone to take over Yishan's job as pastor of HGC. When we prayed, I thought of someone back in Illinois. Although Yishan could not see eye to eye with me at first, he did eventually give his consent and let me recommend that person to the church.

Within a matter of three or four months, our decision making was settled. THC voted unanimously to call Yishan to be its pastor, and we presented our resignation at the next board meeting of HGC.

At the meeting when Yishan finished speaking, it was as if he had thrown a bombshell or an earthquake had occurred. The deacons and others present were shocked, to say the least. Their unwillingness to relinquish their pastor to another church was obvious, but someone began to remark that Yishan resigned for the reason of a better pay since THC was a much bigger church. The reason for resignation was not such, as I had to explain to the deacons, for we had *not* received a contract, and we had not been told how much we would be paid. It was because we had been praying and seeking the Lord's guidance, and I told them all that we had felt and experienced. I also went ahead to give them our recommendation for a new pastor. Eventually, one of the deacons said, "If you recommend him, we believe that will be good for our church."

Truly, we had not been told how much monthly salary we would receive from THC. In fact, one day I asked Yishan, "How much do you think THC will give us?"

He answered, "I have no idea."

"What if they do not give us much? Will you still accept the offer even if it is not high enough?" I continued to probe.

"Of course, we'll have to accept it since it's the Lord's will."

This showed not only Yishan's attitude, but it had always been our guiding principle in serving the Lord.

Eventually, we did receive contracts from THC, one for each of us, his for the senior pastor and mine to head the women and children's ministries. The figure was a little higher than what we received from HGC but comparatively lower than what would be expected from a larger church. Yet we both signed the contracts unequivocally. We believed in the Lord to be our real employer, and He would reward us when we rendered Him faithful service.

As I look back now, I know the Lord has always been faithful, but sometimes the way He leads us seems quite puzzling to me.

Officially, our ministry began with that church in September, but almost from the start, disaster seemed to strike us. Even before that, about six months prior to our official start, I was asked to help lead a woman's fellowship once every other month, and almost every time it gave me a mixed feeling. While some women made me feel welcome, a few others seemed strangely hostile or indifferent to me. It was a subtle attitude that you had to be sensitive—or should I say spiritually alert?—enough to be able to discern it. Unfortunately, subsequent months after our official start proved my discernment to be correct. It was not just a feeling.

The Saturday of our first official week, we were invited to attend a home Bible study (one of three of the church at that time plus several other fellowship groups), and I was asked to lead the singing at the beginning. I took the church hymnal (not one I was familiar with) ahead of time and picked out a few numbers and asked Yishan to play on the keyboard while I led the congregation singing.

At that meeting neither Yishan nor I saw anything wrong. Yet the following Wednesday when I was at church, the phone rang during the lunch hour. I picked up the phone and a man who had come to that meeting said over the phone, "Mrs. Lin, I don't know if I should say this or not, but I think last Saturday evening at the singing your notes were too high and sustained too long for us to follow."

When I hung up the phone, I felt stung. My first official week and such comments! Honestly, I did not know if I should laugh or cry.

I prayed and prayed, and then I took out *Today in the Word*, a monthly devotional booklet published by Moody Bible Institute. I had used it since 1988.

I turned to that day's entry (September 8, 1992), and the Lord used the first two paragraphs to speak to me.

> British landscape painter Joseph Turner used such brilliant colors in his works that other artists hated having their paintings hung next to his art exhibitions.

Turner's colors made their works appeal dull. Portrait artist Sir William Lawrence once complained so bitterly about having one of Turner's paintings hung between two of his that Turner changed the golden sky in his work to a duller hue. "What have you done to your picture?" a horrified friend asked Turner.

"Well, poor Lawrence was so unhappy," Turner explained good-naturedly: "It's only lampblack. It'll wash off after the exhibition."

I felt that day the Lord clearly showed me that my work for Him was like Turner's use of colors: brilliant and outstanding. I can only say that Satan hated my work for the Lord so much that he launched his attack from the very start. Did I feel daunted? If I did, I would have to go "lampblack" and resign, just as Turner did by darkening his painting. I wrote down these words on the margin of that devotional page, "God has prepared this devotion for my need today!"

In fact, the first sentence following those two quoted paragraphs was no less remarkable to me. "If David's brilliance had been visible the day he appeared before Samuel in Bethlehem, no doubt his brothers would have complained bitterly about being outshone so badly."

To me, the most remarkable thing about this devotion was that it was prepared at least two or three months ahead of time, and yet God had used it in time for my need. Praise the Lord! He indeed is sovereign, almighty, and omniscient.

This *complaint* incident not only foreshadowed what was to come in our ministry with that church but also served well to illustrate why our ministry there lasted only two years and four months.

Ours was by no means an unfruitful ministry. On the contrary, it was so effective that the church was practically doubled by the time we left. Both Yishan's teaching and mine were very well received by most of the congregation. Yet Satan was so bent on wrecking havocs that a handful became his henchmen. Yishan was in his mid to late fifties at that time, and he felt frustrated that he had to waste a good amount of his time dealing with senseless disturbances.

Visiting Monterey Aquarium

Six months before we gave our resignation, we began to pray again for the Lord's guidance. One night the Lord spoke to Yishan in his dream, "Go start your own." And six months after that, the Lord pressed it on my mind to name the new church we would start, but I'll just give its initials here—SCC.

I still remember that last Sunday in October when Yishan announced at the end of his sermon. "I'm going to leave this church in two months." (That church's constitution required giving a notice two months ahead of time.)

I was sitting among the congregation, and I saw with my own eyes quite a number of people began to shed tears right after hearing Yishan's words.

Almost a hundred members signed an oversized petition card imploring us to stay. "Please continue to shepherd us," it said. Yet the Lord knew this, and He had told me ahead of time. One day before that while I was sitting at my desk at home, out of the blue the words of 1 Kings 13:9 came into my head, and this was stressed upon me, "Even if they try to persuade you, you should not stay."

For a long time I was tormented with the question, "Why did the Lord lead us to this church?" Once I even discussed it with Yishan, but he was not able to give me an answer. At that time I was not able to see that he was even more hurt than I was. Eventually, it was the Lord who led me to think, *God's way is the best way, but not all men obeyed His will. When He sent His Son to be Savior for this world, He was crucified on the cross instead of being crowned on the throne.*

Decisions, decisions. Life is full of struggles, and sometimes it takes not only faith but great patience and humility and even courage to discern God's will. In the end, we can say, "All's well." The cross turned out to be victory, not defeat, after all.

I think I need to address the issue of speaking in tongues here. I know it is an issue that has caused a lot of confusion in churches and even church splits. It was also part of the reason that caused Yishan and me difficulty with this church since some leaders of that church labeled me and Yishan as Charismatics.

I consider it very important to address this issue here. From all that I have read and all that I have experienced, I think this should never have been an issue in the first place if theologians had been able to properly understand it all the time, and all the church splits and denominational differences could have been minimized.

God has given me and Yishan the gift of speaking in tongue, but it was not a gift automatically given to us. We prayed for it. Paul encourages Christians to seek spiritual gifts. The Bible never forbids us. Yishan and I read a book titled *They Speak with Other Tongues* (chapter 10), and we were convinced that it was a gift we should seek and that was why we prayed for it.

This was a book I checked out from Schaumburg public library, and so there is no way I can turn to it today. Yet I remember at least two stories from that book that happened during late nineteenth or early twentieth centuries in the United States. In one story a man was filled with the Holy Spirit and began to speak Polish (but he did not know it), while in the other a woman at a church spoke the Hebrew language to a Jewish man, rebuking him since he had entered the church and tried to disturb the worship. Nobody there knew him or his intent. As a result of being rebuked, this Jewish man stood up in the service and confessed his malicious intent of trying to disturb the service and was converted, knowing Jesus to be truly the Messiah.

The way Yishan and I were filled with the Holy Spirit and spoke in tongue has led us to believe that speaking in tongues is a gift that is still being given to us today when we seek it just as that book has said. According to what Jesus says in Luke 11:10–13, if we sincerely seek to be filled with the Holy Spirit, God will fill us with His spirit and not deny us. However, I'd caution about praying for the gift. I've read of testimonies of people who sought the gift of tongue and got evil spirit instead. God is holy. Before we seek any gift, we need to be sure we do not have any unconfessed sin standing between us and God. It is dangerous to seek any gift at all when we are hiding any sin within us since it is a chance to invite the evil spirit to come in.

Yishan and I never considered us to be Charismatics, although we did receive the gift of tongue. (Again, as I have just mentioned, there should have been no differentiation between Charismatic or non-Charismatic at all if this issue had been properly understood. All Christians, according to the exhortation in the New Testament, should be charismatic, being filled with the Holy Spirit and receiving gifts of the spirit.) Yishan and I prayed for it, but it was the Lord who gave it to us. I believe the Lord gave it to us so that we could know that it is a gift that's still given out when the Lord sees fit to give it to whoever asked for it. If the leaders of THC had understood this correctly, we would have been spared a lot of trouble.

It was my own understanding when we were filled with the Spirit, we saw great power in our ministry as I have described with all those churches where we served. Whether speaking in tongue would make the difference, I cannot be dogmatic, but it was my own personal experience. When I began to speak in tongue, I did feel it was greater power working in me than the previous times before I received this gift. Unfortunately, because of the close connection between being filled with the Spirit and speaking in tongue, churches today seem to have stopped encouraging believers to seek these two altogether, and thus, it is very hard to see whether it is the power of the Holy Spirit working or only human activity. I cannot say whether a certain church is only depending on human activity or not, but I certainly believe if the power of the Holy Spirit is strongly working in a church, the church should be able to see many, many people coming to the Lord. Why are some churches stagnant today? I can say with certainty that if more believers are exhorted to seek being filled with the Holy Spirit as the Bible commands us to, then revival will come as a result. I cannot guarantee it, but I'm sure we can expect it since I know God will not let us down.

Well, God is sovereign. We cannot tell Him to do anything one way or another. We just need to be humble so that Satan will not hinder us in understanding God's Word or His will. I'm only thankful for the way God led me and Yishan in His will.

Yosemite National Park

Chapter 22

Hidden Rocks

$\mathcal{L}$ ate January of 1995, my father passed away. In an earlier chapter, I mentioned the dispute concerning my father's funeral. When I was in Taiwan, I was told of how one lone brother dissented with all the other siblings concerning Father's funeral. In the end, it was conducted with a compromise among my three brothers—a Buddhist service followed by cremation and then a memorial service in the church the next morning. After the memorial service, all of us took the urn to a special place outside the city. That brother was the only sibling who did not attend Father's memorial service, but he joined us outside the church for the trip to that place. When I saw him outside the church after the memorial service, I could see anger written all over his face.

After the funeral and the memorial service were over, I was ready to fly back to the States. My younger brother drove me and my second sister to the airport. After the check-in, as the two of them sat with me in a waiting area, we were reminiscing and talking. All of a sudden, I said to them, "You know, Second Brother must have thought that I stole his money."

When I was living in Schaumburg, this brother trusted me with his money in the bank. Once his savings totaled more than $320,000, and he used to trust me back then. I never had any inkling that he ever suspected me to be stealing his money. It must have been the Holy Spirit who prompted me to say those words, for at that moment

285

my sister said, "Yes, he already told me *that* a year ago, but I have never told you this because I'm afraid you'll feel hurt."

That was the first time in my life somebody accused me of stealing and by my own brother!

Upon hearing my sister's words, my younger brother immediately said something in my defense, "Third Sister cannot be that type of person. I totally trust in her. She is not one who cares for money." And he went on to mention an earlier time when I left some money with him and later forgot about it.

I only commented, "If I am that type of person, then I don't have to serve God."

Words will fail if I try to describe how much hurt I felt by such an accusation. When Yishan came to meet me at SF International Airport, I expected him to comfort me.

My anxious expectation of his words and deed of comforting me was dampened when I saw him. He brought another man from the church and excitedly told me of the visitation he had conducted with some brothers and how many people had prayed to accept the Lord while I was in Taiwan. I swallowed hard my hurt and disappointment.

I *had to* unload my hurt and eventually did tell Yishan of the words of accusation I heard at the airport in Taiwan. He did not make any comment but went on to say, "This evening I won't be able to stay home with you. I have an appointment at 7:30 p.m. Thomas and I are going to visit a family."

He gave me the name of the family to be visited, but that name never registered with me. When I heard Yishan's words, my heart just sank, and I did not feel like uttering any more words.

The next morning when I woke up, Yishan was already downstairs, talking with someone on the phone. And for the next several days during the rest of the week, when I woke up in the morning, wishing to talk to Yishan, I was always disappointed. Every morning I woke up to an empty bed and a hurting heart, and someone else had already beaten me to the audience of Yishan's ears. (Years later Yishan told me it was the young man who went to the airport with him who had called every morning to talk to Yishan.)

The very next Sunday as usual, Yishan and I drove in separate cars to the new house church for worship service. (By that time we had left THC and started a new church of our own, SCC.) During that infant period of the new church, we were meeting at a member's home, and there was always a fellowship lunch after the worship and a prayer meeting following that. The lunch was mostly potluck-style. While most people brought food, the hostess and I each usually cooked a pot of rice and prepared more food than the rest. Usually, there were people who came without food. Yishan regularly left home earlier than I did, and he took the pot of rice with him.

That Sunday after I came back from Taiwan, we stayed for lunch and prayer meeting after the worship service just as usual. However, after the prayer meeting, Yishan continued to talk with some coworkers. I waited, hoping to come home together, be it in separate cars, so that we could spend some time together and have a good talk. However, Yishan said, "Why don't you go home first? I need to talk a little more with some coworkers. I'll come home in a while, and I'll bring the rice cooker home."

Obediently, I drove home alone. Although I was a bit disappointed, I did not give it too much thought. I just came back from Taiwan less than a week, I had jet lag, and I needed a nap. Surely, Yishan would be home when I woke up from my nap.

I must have been very tired because my nap lasted about three hours. By the time I woke up, it was completely dark inside and outside of the house. I looked at the clock radio, which said 6:00 p.m. I turned on the light, went downstairs, and was going to cook dinner, but there was no rice cooker. Then it hit me. *Yishan is still not home.* What had happened? Was he in a car accident? If he had delayed coming home, he usually would have called to inform me first.

Quickly, I went back upstairs to the bedroom, knelt down by the bed, and began to pray for Yishan. Well, at the moment when I was going to say, "Amen," I heard the downstairs entrance door opened. Yishan was home.

"How come you are home so late?" I asked.

"After you left, I finished talking to the coworkers and was going to come home, but Emma informed me of a certain couple that needed visitation. So we went to visit that couple and talked until just now." Yishan answered with great self-assurance.

"Couldn't you have called me and let me know you would be late coming home? You made me worry and wonder if you had been in an accident!"

I was fuming, but Yishan did not look a bit bothered and said, "At first, I thought it would be a short visit, and so I did not call you. As we talked, I just forgot about the time and did not realize it was so late."

Those words made me think that I was no longer important to Yishan and that he had just forgotten about me.

A few weeks later, Yishan was invited to preach at another church, and I would have to take his place speaking at our own worship service. That also meant I would have to ask a sister to teach the children's Sunday school class for me. By that time our worship service had been moved to an American church using a storefront in a shopping center, which was much roomier and more church-like. Our worship time was also moved to the afternoon since the host church was using that facility in the morning.

When I was home that afternoon, I realized that the sister who taught the children's Sunday school class for me had taken the Sunday school material home, and I had forgotten to ask it back from her. I told Yishan I was going to that sister's home to retrieve my Sunday school material since I would need it for next Sunday's class. However, Yishan said, "You need not go now. I'm going to her home this Thursday evening to visit her husband's nephew, who is staying with them. I'll then bring your Sunday school material back."

I figured I would still have Friday and Saturday to prepare my Sunday school lesson. So I said okay. I trusted Yishan's words.

On Thursday evening when Yishan came home from that visit, I did not see the Sunday school material he had promised to bring back. I asked him, "Where is my Sunday school material?"

"Oh, I forgot," he said, and he did not even say he was sorry. He was that type of man. In his whole life, I never heard him say sorry even once to me. Of course, he was never wrong and I was the one who was always at fault, for he said, "Why didn't you remind me when I left home?"

I exploded. I had suffered so much since I came back from attending Father's funeral in Taiwan. Not only had he failed to comfort me, but I had been feeling forgotten and forsaken as well. I had been convinced that I was no longer important to Yishan, and now I had my proof. In my whole life, I never shouted out so loud to a person as I did to Yishan that night. I just could not take it any longer.

The next morning when I got out of bed, I almost fell onto the floor. My legs were wobbly, and I could not stand. I almost had to crawl all the way downstairs. When I came upstairs later for my own prayer, I asked the Lord to forgive me and to teach me how to get back to health. I realized I had sinned. Our body is the temple of the Holy Spirit, and I did not do a good job of taking care of my own body. I had allowed anger to take control of me, and it had wrecked my health.

An unknown illness broke out on me. Although I had no more problem walking the rest of that day, I began to notice a strange symptom. My skin, especially the arms and legs and hands and even the soles of my feet, became very sensitive to the touch of cold. Whenever my skin came in contact with cold metal, I would feel as if it were burned. Even in hot summertime, I would have to wear long sleeves.

Still gradually, I began to notice that my head would sometimes shake uncontrollably, and later Yishan and someone else also noticed that. A few weeks after the outbreak of my strange illness, an even stranger phenomenon occurred. That day as I was sitting at my desk and reading the Bible, I began to feel drowsy, and I put my hands on the desk and laid my head on my hands for a short nap. When I woke up, instead of feeling numb and prickly in my hands as I used to do, I began to feel tiny pieces of ice traveling through the blood vessels of my hands. After that first occurrence, sometimes for no reason I would suddenly feel tiny ice passing through my arm or leg.

Yishan immediately took notice of my illness. Sometime later he commented—though only once—that I had gotten sick because I was *bad*. Even though that occasion of his saying this was not an unhappy one, it still would have made any woman's blood boil to hear her husband making such a remark, especially when he was the one who had triggered its onset in the first place. However, strangely enough, that comment did not irk me because I knew he liked to joke sometimes. That time I just chided him for having caused my illness.

I would not say that happiness vanished from my world. Nevertheless, it became an endangered species as far as my relationship with Yishan was concerned. It certainly became very fragile and had the potential of being crushed or smothered at any moment by any unkind word or action from any church member.

You see, Yishan and I were both hurt when we left THC and started our new church, but each of us had different ways of compensating for the hurt. At the beginning I confronted it headlong and was greatly hurt, but I was soon bathing in the comfort the Lord provided for us. The church we left behind was strangely burned by two inexplicable fires, almost four weeks apart, soon after we left. I was told that after the second fire, the fire chief gathered those present in church and told them, "Either it's arson by man, or it's an act of God."

From all the known circumstances concerning those two fires, I felt the Lord had vindicated us by revealing His holiness and righteousness.

The Lord gave us two more grandchildren in 1996, as I have mentioned in a previous chapter, so I was able to concentrate my mind and effort in helping my daughters as well as in enjoying my grandchildren.

Yishan reacted to hurt in a different way. He plunged himself headlong into endless church work—training, visitation, and duplicating tapes of his own teaching, to name just a few. By busying himself in these projects, he pretty much carried himself away from hurt and also away from dealing with any problems in our marriage relationship. For visitation he would always take somebody along. He no longer needed me for help. If it was a training session, it was even better because he had plenty of company. Most of them idolized him, and his ego was boosted all the more.

Thus, he was out of the house more and more, leaving me feeling lonely and rejected. A few times I pleaded with him to cut down on those activities or to come home early to have lunch with me. I told him I did not enjoy eating lunch by myself at home. He would either say, "Do you want me to ignore God's work?" Or he would give the excuse that everybody stayed for lunch after the fellowship meeting and it was not good for him as the pastor to leave the group alone.

It was a fellowship group *I* had originally started and led for more than a year. We *never* had lunch after the meeting. They came to our home for Bible study and fellowship, (Yishan went to pick up some of them, and others came by themselves.) And sometimes we had some refreshments at the end, and then they left. It was in 1996 when I was so busy with two new grandchildren that I handed the fellowship over for Yishan to lead. Soon after that, the group left my home and began to meet in a park and later moved to a woman's home. In the beginning I continued to join them a few times, but then I stopped attending the meeting because I felt I did not have enough time. It was then they began to have lunch together, and as a result, I was left out.

I began to have some recurring dreams that I knew were reflective of the fact that Yishan and I were drifting apart. In one of these recurring dreams, the two of us started out walking on a journey together, but Yishan walked so fast that he was soon out of sight. I trudged through water and rocks and had a hard time keeping up. I even boarded a bus trying to find Yishan. After a long time when I finally saw Yishan in the distance, I woke up. Each time when I woke up from the dream, I always felt sad and tired.

In another dream I saw myself and Yishan living in a circular house surrounded by glass windows. In the dream I was feeling very uncomfortable, and I thought, *How could we live in such a house? People can see us from all directions. How could we have privacy?* I had similar dreams like this quite a number of times. (My understanding of this dream is this: Although we never told people of our strained relationship, church people could observe, and they knew it.)

I also began to have difficulty falling asleep. Many times when I was finally drifting away, a terrible face would begin to appear. It was usually with an oval frame. It was like an oval picture hanging on a wall, and that face twisted its eyes and nose and wrinkled into different shapes, laughing at me. If I were an artist, I could make carvings of those twisted oval faces, and I knew I could become very rich by selling them.

When those faces appeared at the time when I was beginning to drift off, I was still somewhat conscious, and I would begin to say in my mind, "In the name of Jesus, I command Satan to leave." Sometimes that ugly (yet very artistic) face would vanish right away, but sometimes it would not leave until I had repeated the name of Jesus a few times.

I knew the real source of these disturbances to my relationship with Yishan. Satan was giving a legitimate excuse for Yishan to use— God's work. "Pastor Lin is so fervent and good at evangelism. He is so caring to the flock. His teaching is so good and edifying. He has led so many people to the Lord." Comments like these came from different people, and of course, they boosted Yishan's ego. It seemed that I was no longer needed in Yishan's work for the Lord.

The busier Yishan became, the less time he had left for me. That was why those twisted ugly faces were laughing at me. My husband and I were no longer working in one accord, and the wedged distance between us was getting bigger and bigger. Many church people constantly threw wedges between me and Yishan without realizing it, but a few of them seemed to do it deliberately.

In April 1997, Yishan went to Taiwan for a week and then to China to train church leaders for almost a month. I covered his work at our home church and organized prayer meetings to pray for him. At the end of one of those prayer meetings, a man verbally attacked me to my face, but a sister tried to speak up for me. The rest of the group was stunned. I felt rather like facing a mad dog, and when I found it was useless to reason with this man, I just kept my mouth shut. His wife could not bear to hear his torrents of senseless anger and hung her head down for quite a while. Then she left to wait for him in their car. When she passed by me, she spoke softly to me, "Mrs. Lin, I'm sorry." Later a brother also left and called at 11:30 p.m. after he was home to encourage me. When he saw that wife who was sitting in her car, she said to him, "Poor Mrs. Lin."

The next day an elderly woman who was present at the previous evening's prayer meeting and had watched the whole episode from beginning to the end asked me, "Mrs. Lin, did you have good sleep last night?"

And I was able to answer, "Praise the Lord! I felt great peace in my heart and was able to sleep well."

When Yishan came home in May, I told him of the unexpected, unfortunate episode, and he believed me. Then that mad dog called, and Yishan answered the phone. I did not know the intention of his call, but it seemed he tried to accuse me in front of Yishan. He began telling Yishan that he did not verbally abuse me. However, when Yishan told him his words seemed to contradict mine, he began to libel Yishan as "base" or "vile."

Satan tempted Jesus three times, and Yishan and I could not expect to be exempt.

A few weeks later, a seminary student whom I had befriended since I moved to California came to our home for a Wednesday night prayer meeting. She lived quite far away and usually came to church on Sunday only. That evening she talked to Yishan a long time, and when she left, I asked Yishan what she had told him. Yishan said that the mad dog had told her many complaints against me. I then asked Yishan, "If she heard of complaints against me, shouldn't she have come to me first and let me know? I have been befriending her and, of the whole church, I am the only one who has cared for her and tried to bridge the gap between her and the coworkers. Why did she come to you but not to me?"

Yishan answered, "Well, she says that I'm the pastor of the church, so she should let me know of grievances against you. But I think of how you have befriended her, and I believe she should have told you first instead of me."

Then later that evening when I was going to take a bath, our phone rang. Yishan answered and was on the phone a long time. I could tell who that caller was, but I went to take a bath. Once done, I immediately went to bed.

The next morning when Yishan and I went out for a walk I asked Yishan, "Did that mad dog call last night?"

"Yes."

"What did he say?"

"Well, he told me many complaints about you—"

"Did you believe all those accusations? Did you say anything in my defense?"

"Of course I did, but aren't you that type of person as he said?"

"*What?* You believe I'm that type of person? Okay. In that case, I don't have to come to SCC anymore. I'll go to an American church this Sunday!"

Although I did not shout at Yishan when he said those words, I wished I had slapped his face. I knew he had been brainwashed and could no longer tell right from wrong. As his wife, I had given him my all to help him in his ministry. I felt both Yishan as well as that mad dog had not only misunderstood me but had done me great injustice. Yishan had the title of the pastor and received the monthly salary, while I had no title and was paid only on a speaker basis. But I believed I had not done less for the church and probably had given more. Now that I had been maligned and libeled, and my own husband had believed other people rather than me. What did I have to work for as his wife? I was determined to leave the Chinese church once and for all.

Yishan was scared. He knew my words were not empty threats. He knew I meant it. Although he did not show any reaction to my face at that time, another man whom Yishan had confided in told me many months later, "Pastor Lin was worried when you told him you wanted to leave SCC. He told me to pray for you."

That following Sunday morning, I woke up around 10:00, and I prayed, "Lord, You know I'm going to an American church this morning. Please tell me which church to go to."

Well, I did not hear any audible voice, but I heard the answer in my head very clearly, "The English congregation did not offend you."

The Lord then went on to tell me that small flock of young people would suffer miserably if I left them without a shepherd.

My tears came out. I pleaded with the Lord, "Lord, if You want me to go to SCC, then You'll have to give me a message in record time because You know I have not prepared any sermon for this afternoon's English worship service."

If I were to go to the English worship service on time that afternoon, I would have to have a message ready in a little more than two hours. When we were in Schaumburg trying to sell our house, one Saturday I shut myself in the public library and wrote a sermon in four hours. That was my best record. But that Sunday in 1997, the Lord gave me a new record. The message was completed in a little more than two hours. The congregation was not aware of my struggles.

That incident, however, was not the only time the Lord intervened in our problems.

Earlier that year I went to Taiwan to visit my siblings during the lunar new year. While I was in Taipei, I tried to contact a woman in a church there because I had read a book published by that church. (Actually, it contained two books, but they were published as one.) Somebody had lent me that book, and I liked it so much that I decided to buy one for myself. It was not available in any bookstore here. When I went to Taiwan, I took the name and address of that church as well as the name of a woman listed as the publisher. However, I made repeated phone calls, and nobody answered the phone. I even tried to call at different times but was always met without success. I was very disappointed when I came back, but the trip to Taiwan and the additional trip two of my sisters took with me to Hong Kong for sightseeing and shopping were all very enjoyable. My eldest sister paid for my trip to Hong Kong as well as all the other expenses, including two suits and two pairs of new shoes I bought there.

About two or three months after I returned to the Bay Area, a package unexpectedly arrived, one addressed to "Rev. Yishan Lin." It was mailed from an address in Taipei. When I checked it out, it *was* the address of the church that had published the book I tried to get. Inside the mailer were two books. The original two books in one had been reprinted into two separate books.

I asked Yishan if he had ordered those two books. He said, "No. *You* are the one who wanted those two books. I'm not interested in them."

There was no enclosed letter, no explanation, nothing whatsoever inside the mailer, except those two books, the very books I had tried to get when I was in Taipei but without success, and yet those two books were mysteriously sent from that church and addressed to Yishan in his name, not in mine.

The main reason that prompted me to want those books was that the two women who wrote those books seemed to be very close to the Lord. The Lord communicated directly to them, guided them, and wonderfully used them in His ministry. *I wanted to be that kind of person.* I wanted to have those books so that I could read them again and again.

And yet when I was in Taipei, I was not successful in talking to anyone in that church. How did they have Yishan's name and address?

Yishan was not interested in those two books. Why were they sent to him and not addressed in my name?

Deep down inside, however, I knew it was the Lord who had told someone in that church to send those books as He had done a long time ago to the early believers in the book of Acts. The Lord had them send the books to Yishan and not to me because Yishan was the head of our family.

When I looked at that mail addressed in Yishan's name, I felt as if the Lord was telling me, "Yishan is your husband. Honor him."

At that moment I thought of Ephesians 5:22, Yishan's favorite verse, not mine. Normally, I had no problem with that verse. "Wives, submit to your husbands." It's a command from the Lord, and I did my best to obey it. It was only when Yishan was not doing his part of loving his wife that I found it difficult to submit to him.

I looked at the address and Yishan's name on that mail for a long time, and I knew it was time for me to change my attitude toward Yishan.

Yishan was the kind of man who wanted his wife to be gentle and submissive. When our relationship was smooth, I had no problem playing the submissive role. It was when I felt he did not love me or care for me that I found it difficult to respect him, even in public.

So that time the Lord intervened to slow down the deterioration of our relationship.

Yishan playing piano at home

Our God is omniscient and knows everything about us from beginning to the end. He really knows how to direct and guide our lives, but sometimes we are in the dark and may not understand why God does certain things.

Since Yishan basically remained the same and did not slow down his work or make any effort to win my respect, our relationship was sloping downward again before long. We took two trips together in 1997, one in June to Turkey and another in late July to Oregon and southern Washington with Angela's family. The trips were supposed to help improve our relationship, and they did accomplish the purpose in some measure. However, we bought a video camera earlier that year, and Yishan was so engrossed in using that new gadget that a lot of times I felt angry because he could not respond to me when I tried to talk to him.

Shortly after we came back from the family trip to Oregon toward the end of July, our relationship went down to the lowest point, at least from my end of the spectrum. I felt lonely all the time and found it hard to suppress a lot of anger toward Yishan.

On the surface I was enjoying my ministry, and in fact, I did. But inside I was hurting greatly. The worse was that some coworkers were adding fuel to the flame or rather pouring salt over the wound. Almost at every church board meeting I attended, I would hear some criticism aimed at me. Yishan never did anything or said anything to help me. The wedge between me and Yishan went only deeper. In two of those coworker meetings, separated by many months, I cooked dinner for those who came to my home to attend the meetings, and *yet* a few of them were daring enough to raise criticism against me. I could not see any reason behind all that criticism except that Satan, the accuser, had tried to create a mountain out of a molehill. After that second meeting at my home, I stopped inviting those people to my home for meetings. I no longer considered them worthy of my hospitality. I could feel nothing but outrage.

Why would people do such senseless things to me? It was only after Yishan went home to be with the Lord that I was able to find out why. My repeated action in helping a certain underdog in the church whom they did not deem worthy had turned them to be angry with me. In other words, jealousy had raised its ugly head in the church! Quite unfortunately.

I often cried to the Lord. He was the only one I could turn to. I said to the Lord, "Lord, I do not believe that You have called Yishan into the ministry to destroy our marriage. Yet You see how our marriage is being destroyed. Could You please touch Yishan's heart and turn it around? Could You tell him to slow down his work?"

Yet I was puzzled. The Lord seemed to turn a deaf ear to my prayer. I reasoned either the Lord was not hearing my prayer, or Yishan's heart was too hard for God to move. My anguish was almost unbearable, and yet I knew the Lord was trying to comfort me. I was just too puzzled to understand why the Lord did nothing to change Yishan.

It was not until Yishan went home to be with the Lord that I really understood why. The Lord *knew then* that Yishan had only a few more years left on this earth, and so He seemed to *spoil* Yishan and let him run ahead in the work he delighted in doing. That was why the Lord did not seem to slow Yishan down but instead kept telling me to be patient and to bear with Yishan, and when I was really hurt, He would do something extraordinary to comfort me.

One Tuesday in late October, I felt especially low. I had repeatedly asked Yishan to come home to have lunch with me instead of staying after the fellowship meeting, and he had totally ignored my pleading. That day I was home alone while he was at the fellowship. I cried to the Lord, and as usual, I heard nothing in return.

About 11:00 a.m., however, I felt I could not suppress my feelings anymore. I picked up the phone and called the place of the fellowship meeting. When the hostess answered the phone, I said, "Sister Holly, could you please help me?"

At that point I broke down sobbing, and I told her how I had suffered. I asked if she was kind enough to help, could she send Yishan home for lunch instead of keeping him there?

"No problem," she said with sympathy and understanding.

Sure enough, Yishan came home not too long after that, but one look at his face would tell you how much anger he had toward me.

What I have not mentioned is that during those months of emotional turmoil, I also suffered in the physical realm. I lost my singing voice in May, and on October 26, I began to develop ringing in my ears (tinnitus), which had since gotten increasingly louder and louder every time I suffered insomnia. It was only by God's grace that I did not break down and become insane.

One day in September or October, I found a piece of paper in my drawer with four Chinese words, "Look up to Jesus." It was a piece of paper I had written long time before that, and I had almost forgotten about it. At that moment the Lord seemed to remind me once again to look up to Him. So I confessed my sin to the Lord. I had allowed other people and the circumstances to attract my attention and forgotten to look up to Him.

Yet my situation did not improve until the first full week of November. That Monday morning I felt the greatest despair when I prayed about myself and about the sermon for the coming Sunday I would have to preach at the English worship service. After I finished praying, I saw lying on the floor an envelope in which I had put my notes. When I took out those notes I had written long ago and began to read them, I saw one that had the title "The Resurrection Miracle," which especially attracted me, and I decided to use it for that Sunday's sermon.

The Scripture passage for that sermon was Mark 16:1–6, and it talked about the big blocking stone the women faced when they were going to the tomb to anoint Jesus. In the sermon I mentioned, not only the devil is our greatest enemy, our own busyness, laziness, self-excuse, pride, stubbornness, and other people's criticism could all become our blocking stones. And yet "looking up, they saw the stone had been rolled away" (Mark 16:4).

That was exactly what happened to me. When I did look up to Jesus, I experienced the resurrection miracle.

That first Monday afternoon in November 1997, I knew I could not continue to allow all this bitterness to possess me. I cried out to the Lord, "Lord, remove all my bitterness from me."

Two days later, Thursday evening was the first time in a long while that Yishan was home and completely free. We watched a video together, a video I had ordered and just arrived that Monday, a video about a missionary pilot who experienced a miraculous escape from his kidnappers. When I watched that video, without my own realizing it, the Lord seemed to also let me experience a miraculous release from my emotional turmoil. By Friday morning I found that all my bitterness was completely gone, and I had perfect peace.

Still more unexpected was a card I received the very next day on November 8. The card was sent from a Chinese woman in Lancaster, Pennsylvania, and inside was enclosed a check for $200. It was a woman I had never met, but someone had given her my name and phone number. From time to time, she called me to talk about her problems, and I had counseled on her and prayed for her. I did not cash that check right away. I wanted to find out first why she had sent me that card and the check. That card had the words "Look to the Lord" on the front and inside was written Psalm 37:3–4. (Obviously, the Lord was emphasizing His comforting message to me.)

My first reaction upon receiving that card was to ask for the Lord's forgiveness, "Lord, forgive me. Indeed, I had forgotten to look up to You all these past months so that I had so much pain."

I was not able to talk to that woman until November 24 when she called to talk about some more problems she was facing. When I asked her the reason for sending me that card and the check, she said the Lord had told her to do that back *in late July*, but she did not do it right away. Then on October 25, the Lord urged her the second time to buy the card and not to delay it any longer. She had to go to two Christian bookstores, and even at the second store, she was not able to find an appropriate card. She was about to give up and go home when the Lord told her to look at the top shelf. She said she was too short and had to tiptoe, and then she saw that card. Her husband was a Caucasian, but she could not read English. When she took the card home to her husband, he said the message on the card was good, and he also wrote the check and the words "Psalm 37:3–4" on the card. That envelope was postmarked November 5 or 6.

The timing showed that the Lord *did* care for me and answered my prayers in such a marvelous way. Although she did not know it and did not buy the card in late July, it was actually the time when my relationship with Yishan began to slip again. Then in late October when I thought I could not bear it any longer and made that desperate phone call to make Yishan come home for lunch after the fellowship meeting, the Lord really remembered me and intervened again. I'm so thankful that dear sister in the Lord (one I still have not met) had to go through so much trouble in obeying the Lord's command to bring that encouragement to me.

That, however, was not the end of my trouble with Yishan. Two years later our marriage hit the bottom again, but I have to talk about that in the next chapter. Looking back now, I realize the Lord had upheld our marriage so that it became like an iceberg. Although people in the church kept chipping at the ice, nobody was able enough to break it apart. I marvel that, by God's grace, our marriage was never shipwrecked in spite of so many hidden rocks.

Chapter 23

Roller-Coaster Rides

$\mathcal{I}$ have mentioned that in spite of the many hidden rocks in our marriage, my marriage with Yishan was never shipwrecked. Why? I think one of the reasons is because of Yishan's three major illnesses. When Yishan was in good health, he was like a horse without reins, charging ahead in church work with all his might, and no one could slow him down. It was really by God's mercy that Yishan had those three major illnesses, for they forced Yishan to slow down, allowing him not only to spend more time with me but also making him depend more on me, thus preserving our marriage.

On November 1, 1997, Yishan and I were taking a walk together when he experienced a heart attack, but neither of us knew it. At first, nothing happened when we walked on a downhill street. After we turned uphill, Yishan began to feel chest pains and numbness in his right arm. We both stopped walking.

Neither of us knew anything about heart attacks at that time. When I asked him where he felt pain, he pointed to the middle of his chest where he used to feel heartburn before the Lord healed him of his stomach problem (see chapter 18). So I asked him, "Do you think it's heartburn or a heart attack?"

And he answered, "I don't know."

I don't remember if he mentioned the numbness in his right arm or not. Even if he did, neither of us was knowledgeable enough to pay much attention to it. It was much later in hindsight that he mentioned the difference between heartburn and heart attack was that he experienced numbness in his right arm during the latter.

At that point, I remember, I continued to ask him, "Do you think I should call an ambulance?"

And he said, "No, it's not that serious."

I then asked again, "Should we head home?" Again, he answered in the negative. So we resumed our walk, and he felt no more pain for the rest of the uphill climb or the rest of the walk that day.

That afternoon he drove forty-five minutes to another town to visit a church attendant who was still not a believer. In that visit he was able to lead that person in praying to receive Jesus as Lord and Savior. He made the journey and came home without any difficulty.

However, for the next two days when he went out to do his daily jogging, he felt chest pains again. Since I did not accompany him on those two occasions, I did not know the details. Yet I was concerned and urged him to see a doctor. At first he took no action. Then he began to ask a brother in the church who had been hospitalized for heart problems only about a month before. He said what Yishan had experienced was angina. "A precursor of heart attacks," said that brother.

It was after Yishan heard those words from that brother that he began seriously thinking of going to a doctor. I gave him the name and phone number of a family physician. By the time he went to see that physician, it was already February of 1998. When he saw that doctor, the latter did an EKG on Yishan and said his heart was abnormal and referred him to a cardiologist.

When that cardiologist saw Yishan, he told Yishan he had already had a minor heart attack, but the cardiologist said he would put Yishan on a regiment of exercises and medication to repair the damage of the heart muscles.

Around that time we were doing some house-hunting again. Since our new church was meeting on Sunday afternoons and using the facility of an American church, the two of us had only our study at home to use as a shared office. I found it difficult to study the Bible or to prepare a sermon when Yishan was talking on the phone, and he had a lot of phone calls when he was home. And since Corrie had started college the fall of 1996, we decided we did not need to stay in the M District anymore, and we would be able to find a house with more rooms for separate studies for each of us when we moved.

At that time Leslie was also expecting a baby girl with a due date coming up in April, and I had promised to go to Boston to help her after she gave birth.

In March, Yishan and I signed papers to purchase a new home in U City. Although it was a contingency contract, the builder's agent urged us to get our house sold as soon as possible. The housing market in the Bay Area was booming that year, and we were able to get a buyer within less than a month.

It was a horrendous month for both me and Yishan. We had to put a lot of books into boxes and move them downstairs to the garage. I also had to do a lot of cleaning. I had been a lot more careful in keeping our F City home in shape this time, but a lot of cleaning still needed to be done. Plus a lot more work was necessary for selling a house.

Leslie gave birth to Marisa pretty much close to the due date, and I was in Cambridge for two weeks to assist her. A lot of faxes were sent between F City and Cambridge during those two weeks—papers for me to sign or questions I sent out. Since Yishan could not quite make decisions without me, faxes were the best solutions during my absence from home.

When I returned to F City in late April, I found Yishan to be with more frequent chest pains. Since we had a lot of books and those boxes of books we moved to the garage were heavy, we had unknowingly and unfortunately put more strain on Yishan's heart.

I knew the cardiologist had informed Yishan that he would need to go to the hospital for an angiogram, and I decided to go with Yishan when he went for an appointment in the cardiologist's office on Thursday, May 7. I told the cardiologist of our upcoming move on May 14 and asked him if Yishan's surgery could be performed after that.

Since Yishan was really not that heavy as compared to most

overweight people who had heart problems, the cardiologist assured me not to worry and said that the angiogram would not have to be performed until after we had moved.

Unexpectedly, the next evening when Yishan was leading the Friday night Bible study at a member's home, he experienced more chest pains. Still the next morning, Saturday, when we were on the freeway (I was driving), Yishan suddenly said, "I think you need to take me to the hospital right now."

We got to the emergency unit about twenty minutes later. After a few minutes of waiting, he was admitted into an emergency room. By that time he was very pale, and his hands were icy cold. Plus his pulse only at sixty-two.

Yishan was kept at the hospital over the weekend, and his cardiologist performed an angiogram the following Monday evening. Since I could not go to the hospital until much later that evening, I asked Angela to accompany her dad before and after the surgery.

When I got to the hospital, I was told that the angiogram had just been completed and that the cardiologist was still there. When I saw him, he was still in his surgical gown, and he showed me two monitor screens on which the pictures of Yishan's major and minor arteries were displayed.

"I wonder," said the cardiologist when he began to explain those arteries to me, "that he only had a minor, not a major [heart attack]. You see, one of his major arteries was blocked 100 percent, a second one 75 percent. Only one artery is good, and still a secondary artery was blocked 80 percent. I wonder that he only had a minor, not a major." (Please note the doctor twice said. "I wonder.".)

"Well," I commented, "he is a pastor, and I think God has sent an angel to watch over His servant."

"Surely, I believe *somebody* was watching over him," the cardiologist answered.

Yishan was kept in the hospital for a total of five days. Because of the seriousness of his condition as seen from the angiogram, the cardiologist inserted a balloon to open up the blockage.

That Sunday right after Yishan's admission into the hospital was

Mother's Day. I had to take Yishan's place preaching a Mother's Day sermon, but I had no time to prepare the sermon at all. By God's grace, I was able to dig up one I had preached back in Schaumburg and accomplished the job quite well.

However, Tuesday was closing day at the title company, and Thursday's moving was coming up. And half of our house stuff was still not packed. I was able to sleep only three or four hours each night. Still, the thing I dreaded most was that Yishan would not be discharged by the moving day, and I would have to sleep in the new house all by myself.

Here I can only say that God's grace is always sufficient. At about 9:00 a.m. on Thursday, Yishan called me from the hospital saying that the cardiologist had seen him and said that he could go home that morning. I then called Angela, asking her to bring Boppy home, and Yishan was home around 10:00 a.m. Although he had to sit there most of the time while the rest of us were busy with moving, he *was* home, and I did not have to sleep in an almost empty new house by myself. That night when Yishan and I lay together on the mattress on the upstairs bedroom floor with the box spring standing against the window for cover (no window coverings yet for a new home), I still remember I felt so thankful that Yishan and I could start all over again.

From my previous chapter, you probably can see that my relationship with Yishan was not that smooth during those years. However, Yishan's heart attack and subsequent hospitalization served as a timely rain that quenched the parched ground, and for a short period, our relationship improved. We were brought closer when we were able to spend more time together in walking and talking, but unfortunately, not for long. Only two or three weeks later on the eve of my birthday, Yishan was asked to take a brother to the airport, and he did not come home until way past midnight. That night, again, I was kept up waiting for Yishan and worried about his well-being. I understood that he would come home in a short while, and yet I waited for hours before he finally did.

By that time I had moved from anxiety into anger, and I had

locked the bedroom door. When Yishan came home and found the bedroom door locked, he forced the entry and broke the lock of the new bedroom, which made me even angrier. *What a birthday present he had given me.* (It was not until now I realized that his breaking the new lock must have added a lot of strain to his heart.)

The very next day, my birthday, I was supposed to accompany Yishan and a few church members to drive down to Santa Cruz to view a conference facility for our upcoming summer retreat, but I ended up staying home by myself since I was so dissatisfied with Yishan's performance the previous night. Later that morning when a former church member called from Taiwan to wish me happy birthday, I tearfully told this dear sister what had happened the night before. (May the Lord bless this dear sister. Her second daughter and I share the same birthday, and for many years she called me every year to wish me happy birthday.)

(It was only a few months ago I learned from a brother, another former church member, that he had offered the other brother a ride to the airport for that night, but the latter had declined his offer and asked Pastor Yishan Lin instead. Yishan had actually told that brother he would drive him to the airport *only* when no other ride was offered him. Obviously, that brother had preferred Yishan to other members of the church as a chauffeur. The worst part about this story was the timing. It was only a little more than two weeks after Yishan's angiogram surgery, and yet that brother was not even thinking about the good of Yishan's health. This was another example showing how a church member had served to bring ruin to our marriage. Well, by now I realize that he was a very immature man.)

Our marriage was so strained that a little more than three months after we moved to the new home, Yishan's artery was blocked again, and he woke me up at 4:20 a.m., complaining of chest pains and asking me to take him to the hospital. The doctor had to reopen the blocked artery, and this time he inserted a stent to keep the artery from collapsing again.

This time, thanks to the tiny nitroglycerin tablet Yishan placed under his tongue right after he felt chest pain, a second heart attack was averted, and thus, Yishan sustained no more heart muscle damage. Later on he was told by the cardiologist that his heart muscle damage had been fully repaired.

Celebrating thirty-second anniversary in Hawaii

Once Yishan was fully recovered, he again galloped ahead at full force into weekly Bible training work for church members. A group of twenty or thirty-some people basked in his teaching, and he really enjoyed his ministry. When he came home he would often animatedly tell me how that evening of training went along while I just listened in silence. The short period of closeness I enjoyed with

Yishan was once more gone from us. During those evenings of his absence from home, I often had the feeling of being a living widow rather than being a beloved pastor's wife. As far as our marriage was concerned, I felt pretty much like a dying patient trying to hang on for dear life.

I felt so desperate about our marriage that I began a full-day fasting every Tuesday. Yishan knew of my fasting, but he did not know why. I never told him the true reason, and he seemed in no hurry to find it out.

An incident that occurred during this period will serve to illustrate how strained our marital relation was. It occurred on September 2, 1999.

That evening, a young couple that was about to be married came to our house for premarital counseling. My study was right next to the dining room where Yishan conducted the counseling session. Usually, I tried to go to one of the upstairs bedrooms and shut the door so that I could do my own things in quiet. However, there was no escape; Yishan's voice was so loud that I could not avoid hearing him anywhere in the house. I remember that evening I went to the small bedroom in the farthest corner upstairs and shut the door, but it really did not help much. Yishan's voice was still loud and clear, and I could hear every word he said.

After the session had ended and that young couple left, I could not suppress my feeling of what I heard that evening. When Yishan came upstairs, I said in what must be a belligerent tone to him, "Wow, you're very good in your counseling to tell that couple the husband has the responsibility of communicating with his wife. But have you yourself been practicing what you've taught?"

Yishan's response totally surprised me. "Well, it's only for other people to hear."

At that moment I could not help chiding him, "Then you are a hypocrite!"

(It's necessary for me to interject a few words here for Yishan's sake. I do not really think he was a hypocrite when he said, "It's only for other people to hear." For all his life, Yishan was never a person of quick response, at least not in words. That evening I had unintentionally backed him into a corner when I asked him if he was practicing what he had taught. In order to defend himself, he had failed to find better words and said those instead.)

That evening Yishan said no more, but what *I* really wanted was to have a good dialogue with him. Yet I did not want to talk to him face-to-face because I was afraid one of us would get angry in the middle of the talk, and negative consequences could result. Moreover, as a matter of fact, Yishan and I had not spoken to each other that much anymore, and I really doubted if we could carry on a good dialogue at all.

So I picked up a pen and wrote the following on the back side of a church program sheet. I wrote it in Chinese, and here is the translation.

> You said that women speak 25,000 words each day and men speak 12,500. Do you know how many words your wife speaks now? Do you care why your wife does not speak in friendly tones to you now?
>
> I only realize now it's truly pitiful to be a pastor's wife. Her income is in people's control, and her husband's time and energy are occupied by his work and other people's need, while nobody knows or cares about her needs. Even her own husband does not care; who else will?
>
> You're doing a very capable pastoral job, and so I do not mean much to your now. You have brothers and sisters to accompany you for visitation or evangelism, and I'm no longer needed. I can see clearly now I'm more a hindrance to you. I'm sorry, but I realize this only tonight.
>
> Whether you like what I write here or not, I have to let you know it, so that you may not say I have not told you so.

Back when we were living in Schaumburg, on a few occasions when I wrote letters to Yishan, pouring out my complaint or pointing out his mistakes, he would hug me and give me a kiss, a sign for truce or apology. Even though he never said, "I'm sorry," it was enough to satisfy me.

His reaction this time? Surely, he must be very angry because I found my letter in the trash bin under his desk the next morning. *It just broke my heart.* For years he treasured the letters of correspondence we exchanged before and after we were married, and *he had kept them in a bag for more than thirty years.* It was only in 1998 when we were getting ready to move to U City that he held that bag and asked me, "Should we still keep these letters?"

By that time our relationship was more or less strained, and I wondered if we would ever read or need those letters again. So I said, "Throw them away." And then he did. (Of course now I regret that I had allowed him to throw away those letters. For after he went home to be with the Lord, I looked all over the house in a frenzy for any letters he wrote to me, but of course, there was none except one he wrote from Taiwan while attending his father's funeral. I had kept that letter in my drawer, and that was why it had escaped being thrown away. And then when I began to write this book, I really wished I had all those letters to refresh a lot of memories.)

Needless to say, I was furious when I found that letter in the trash, and we exchanged some unkind words. I could not suppress my anger and disappointment, and picking up that letter out of the trash, I said, "In this case, what's the need of continuing in our marriage?"

Very quickly, Yishan retorted, "Okay, let's get a divorce."

"If we get divorced," I countered back, "then you'll have to get out of the ministry."

"No more ministry. That's fine with me."

Neither of us said anything more, but I knew he was not going to back down.

I was really hurt, and I kept crying out to the Lord, "Lord, have You called Yishan into the ministry to destroy our marriage?"

I knew it was not God's intention to destroy our marriage, but I just could not see any way out. I felt that my whole-day fasting every Tuesday was even more urgent.

One evening after dinner as Yishan was going to leave the house for another training session for church members, I suddenly thought, *Why should only the church members occupy Yishan's time and I can't enjoy him?* At that moment when he was about to open the door, I said, "Wait a moment."

Yishan halted, turned, faced me, and said in an angry tone, "What do you want?" I ran up to him and held him tightly and kissed him a long time.

Although Yishan was caught by surprise, I knew he enjoyed the kiss. I asked him if it was good, and he said so and rather victoriously left the house.

Our marriage was saved once more, and I wish I could say, "And we lived happily ever after." No, our marriage was for the most part like a roller-coaster ride at that time, going up and down, up and down. Whenever it seemed to go down to the lowest ebb, the Lord would allow something to happen to bring it up. And this letter I sent out for Christmas of 2000 sums up best what had happened.

> This Christmas I was unable to send out cards and letters in time for the holiday season. Having come back from a mission trip to Taiwan 11/24–12/7, I was still sorting things out on 12/17 when Yishan surprised me with another major illness and I had to call 911 and had him rushed to the hospital. It was massive bleeding of the stomach. The morning of Sunday 12/17, he informed me of having had diarrhea of loose, black-colored stools four times throughout the night and two more times in the morning. He was very pale and his hands were icy cold. Around 11:15 AM he asked me to take over the sermon preaching for that afternoon. Then at 11:55 I heard him throwing up in the kitchen. When I went over to look, he was

standing by the sink, torrents of pinkish red stuff gushing out of his mouth.

He stayed in the ICU five days and received transfusion of a total of ten units of blood. His doctor found a 0.5 cm hole in the lower part of his stomach and sealed it off by laser. He was discharged on Friday, Dec. 22. Many brothers and sisters of different churches had been praying for him and the Lord certainly had heard those prayers.

Needless to say, I was very busy, taking care of Yishan at home, plus doing his church work and answering countless phone calls. As a result of all these, maybe adding my own carelessness, I was also hit with another kind of illness, sneezing, coughing and fever and aching bones. Fortunately, mine was not really severe and I am very thankful. I am thankful that the Lord had spared Yishan for the second time. In fact, his hospitalization in 1998 (due to heart condition), dangerous as it was, seemed not as traumatic as this time.

It was really the Lord who had sustained me and Yishan throughout this ordeal. I am grateful as usual for the salvation and the hope we have in our Lord Jesus Christ. This Christmas has been extra meaningful to me after all."

At this point, I can only thank the Lord that our *roller-coaster ride* did not end at the lowest point but rather on a high note. God is to be glorified always for His work of grace and wonder.

Chapter 24

Marriage Saved

*I*t was during Yishan's five-day hospital stay when the doctor found his white blood cell count higher than normal and suspected of his having leukemia.

Subsequent tests at Stanford Hospital confirmed that Yishan had chronic mylogenic leukemia (CML). However, the doctor said to Yishan, "Right now you have three options. First, no need to do anything right away since your white blood cell count is still not that high, but you need to come in for blood tests every other week. Second, you can take a new pill called hydroxyurea, which acts like chemotherapy, but it can cause gout, so you'll also need to take another medication to counter its side effect. Third, I can send you to a leukemia treatment center in Portland, Oregon, to receive interferon chemotherapy. Interferon can damage the liver, but the damage can be reverted once the treatment stops. At this point we don't need to consider bone marrow treatment. It is too drastic. Right now I recommend the first and the second options, and we'll consider the third only later. CML develops slowly, and you're sixty-three. You should be able to go on seven or eight more years without problems."

Why did the doctor sound so positive?

It was possibly because she thought Yishan was strong and still quite healthy. When she did the bone marrow tap on Yishan, she had a hard time drilling the needle into Yishan's spinal cord, and when she finally finished drawing out the bloody marrow, she said

315

to Yishan, "Congratulations! You are the second patient with the strongest bones I have ever had. The other one is an athlete. Your bones are so hard!"

We told her Yishan did a lot of jogging every day and that was probably why he had strong bones.

Sometime after we moved to the new home in U City, I began sleeping alone in the guest room since Yishan's loud snoring often prevented me from falling asleep. So when I woke up the next morning after that visit to the Stanford doctor, I still felt tired (since I did not sleep well during that previous night), and as I continued to lie in the guest room's bed, I prayed, "Lord, the doctor wants Yishan to take that chemo pill. Should he take it right away or not? Lord, please speak to Yishan. Do not speak to me."

As I lay in bed with my eyes closed, I suddenly saw in the darkness a wall made of concrete blocks, and the large three-dimensional letters of these three words stood in blocks in front of that wall, "Hang in there."

I took those three words in front of the wall as an answer from the Lord to my prayer, and I thought He was speaking to me, "Hang in there. Do not worry." And because of this, I did not worry about Yishan's leukemia, not until much later.

(I never paid attention to the meaning of the wall behind those three words, not until much later. Of course, a wall usually means a blockade or a road meeting a dead end. It was not until after Yishan went home to be with the Lord that I understood God was actually indicating to me by the presence of that wall that Yishan's leukemia would not be cured. However, in the beginning I only paid attention to the three words, "Hang in there," and therefore, I was very hopeful and not worried.)

When words went out that Yishan had leukemia, everybody was concerned, and many began to pray for Yishan. Some even called long distance or overseas to ask their Christian friends to pray for Pastor Lin.

One day a woman asked me at church, "Mrs. Lin, Pastor Lin has leukemia. Don't you worry for him?"

And I immediately answered, "No, I don't worry. The Lord has told me to hang in there. I believe the Lord will take care of Pastor Lin. That's why I don't worry. I feel peace at heart."

What actually happened was that Yishan's vomiting blood and his five-day hospital stay had served to improve our relationship. The Lord intervened once more in our marriage, and instead of worrying about Yishan's leukemia, I had full confidence in the Lord that He would take care of Yishan, and therefore, I genuinely felt peace in my heart. I was very thankful that Yishan and I were united once again in our daily prayers for his health.

The whole church seemed to be unified all of a sudden. Everybody's goal was to get Pastor Lin back in health. Some coworkers even began to talk about paying for the expensive new drug that people believed was very effective.

Around that time news media began to publicize about a new miracle drug called Gleevac and talk about how CML patients were able to return to work after only a few weeks or a few months of treatment. However, because of its high cost (two to three thousand dollars a month), our medical insurance was not going to pay for it, we were told.

To Yishan and me, our focus continued to be on the Lord. *Pray, pray, and pray.*

Yishan's white blood cell count began to climb up very high in the month of May from 45,000 to 250,000. Not only that, he also began to develop a low fever which seemed never to go away, and he lost his appetite and began to feel tired. However, our church's short-term mission trip to Hungary was approaching. It was on May 26, and both Yishan and I had planned to go with three other church members. Actually, Yishan had gone to Hungary by himself in October of the previous year (2000). He had been there two weeks doing intensive teaching and training.

I was beginning to worry for Yishan because of his low fever and high white cell count, not because I was losing faith in the Lord but because Yishan insisted on going to Hungary. So I said to him, "What if you suddenly become critically ill in Hungary? How are we going to find the right help in a foreign country? Since you have been to Hungary before, why don't you stay home this time and let me lead the short-term mission team?"

"I want to go," said Yishan. "I'll be fine once I'm there."

Then two nights before we were to leave, Yishan received a phone call from Hungary asking him to preach a series of messages on four week nights plus two Sunday sermons. I heard Yishan answering, "I'm having low fever and feeling tired now. I'll speak on the first Sunday only and let Mrs. Lin preach the other messages."

Woe to me, I had to get ready quickly.

Thanks to God that I had accumulated some creation magazines and biblical archaeology books plus a number of other materials. After a short prayer, I knew what four messages to give—creation v. evolution, Noah's flood, archaeological evidences for the Bible, and prophecy.

I had been told that the Chinese church in Budapest consisted mainly of Chinese people who had gone to Eastern Europe as merchants and that all their meetings were conducted in the evening. When Yishan was there in October 2000, sometimes he had to speak well into late evenings or until midnight. Since these people had received Marxist indoctrination in China, no matter what level of their education, I reasoned that strong evidences for God's creation and the validity of the Bible would be beneficial for their faith in Jesus Christ.

That short-term mission trip turned out to be a success, praise be to God. The first night after Yishan spoke, ten people made decisions to trust Jesus, and another seven dedicated their lives to serve the Lord. I learned later that these people were greatly touched by Yishan, fearing they might not have another chance to hear him preach.

The first night after I spoke, a man in his late fifties or early sixties came up and tried to argue with me. I simply told him, "This is only my first message. I still have three messages to deliver. Wait until you hear all my messages. If you still have questions at that time, then we can have a discussion."

Before the end of my series of messages on Saturday evening, that man was changed. He became very humble. He invited Yishan and me with other guests to a nice Chinese restaurant *for lunch that Friday*. Although it was lunch, you might just call it a banquet. A much younger man who was probably in his mid to late thirties invited us to his home in the afternoon of the second Sunday. Only when we were there did I realize it was actually a party given in our honor. In our conversation that young man told me, "Last Wednesday night after I heard your first message, my wife and I came home, and I cried because you mentioned abortion in your message. Her first pregnancy was terminated in abortion, and we cried for that first child of ours."

That abortion, I was told, took place when they were still in China, and both of them were not yet believers. (I had not included abortion in my original note. However, in the message I did mention how God had created us, and therefore, abortion was really murder. It must have been the Holy Spirit who led me to add that.) I then went on to comfort that couple since they had done it in ignorance, and I told them the Lord would forgive them and that they'd get to meet that unborn child in heaven.

Praise the Lord, for He really blessed that mission trip and used us to change lives.

Yishan's low fever continued another day after we arrived in Budapest, and surprisingly, after that, his temperature became normal and remained so during the rest of our stay in Hungary. His first blood test after we came home also showed his white blood count to be normal, exactly as he had said before we left home.

In a way my prediction for him before we left for Hungary was also fulfilled. Since his appetite was very poor and because he could take only one or two bites from each dish at mealtime, I commented to him, "You know, you should have a banquet with many dishes in front of you. By taking small bites out of each dish, you can then gain weight."

During those ten days in Hungary, we were treated to several banquets at the Chinese restaurants. Those Chinese restaurants differed from the ones in the San Francisco Bay Area in one way. The former served many side dishes first before the main courses were served. So while we were there, each day Yishan was able to eat a lot more, and when we came back to Union City, he found that he had gained two pounds. I guess this was another reward from the Lord for his faith, but unfortunately, only for that time. A week after we came home, his low fever returned, and his white blood cells became erratic and began to go up and down again.

Shortly before we went to Hungary, it was reported in the news that FDA had taken an exception and approved Gleevac ahead of schedule for public release. People at church began to ask, "Why doesn't Pastor Lin use Gleevac?" We had to explain that his doctor had not prescribed it simply because she knew our insurance would not pay for it.

During the following two months, June and July, Yishan and I continued to ask the Lord to heal him, and it never crossed our minds to ask for that new drug, probably because we thought the insurance would not pay. And we considered we'd be greedy in asking for it. However, one Wednesday morning in August, I prayed, "Lord, if You see fit, could You please move Dr. M's heart to prescribe Gleevac for Yishan?"

Later that day around midafternoon, the phone rang. It was a nurse from Dr. M's office. She told Yishan, "Dr. M wants you to come to her office tomorrow to discuss the use of Gleevac."

The next day at her office, Dr. M said, "Although Gleevac costs about $2,000 a month, I'm going to prescribe it for you. The pharmaceutical company that manufactures it has an assistance program. I'm going to try to apply for it for you."

The cost turned out to be near $3,000 per month without the assistance. Yishan *did* get some assistance, but I never got to find out how much. Our own out-of-pocket expense for Gleevac totaled $799. (Yishan took it only a few months.) And I was certain our insurance paid a lot more for Yishan. Initially, it seemed to be a miracle drug indeed. Within two weeks after Yishan took it, he seemed to be completely normal and healthy. Yet a month later, his blood cell counts went out of control again, and he was back to fatigue and poor appetite. I realized the new drug was not a miracle drug after all.

I turned sixty that year. Yishan conspired with Angela to give me a surprise party at church. According to the Taiwanese custom, the son is supposed to celebrate his parent's sixtieth birthday. Since I only have daughters, Angela was obedient to this custom in celebrating first Yishan's sixtieth birthday and then mine. I was totally in the dark, and only later did I learn of Yishan's part in that scheme. It touched me so that I knew Yishan *did* care for me.

Unfortunately, our good days did not last long. At the end of August, someone came from Hungry to live with us, and he almost caused our marriage to totally fall apart.

I'll call this guy Dathan. He was one of the seven men and women who dedicated their lives to serve the Lord. Because he had responded to the altar call given by Yishan during that first Sunday night in Hungary, Yishan felt personally obligated to help this man, who was in his late thirties.

When we were in Hungary, Dathan told Yishan and me that he wanted to receive seminary training in the United States and that he had saved up enough money for the first year. "I visited a relative in the LA area a year ago," he said. "I have enough money saved up so that I'll be able to support myself for the first year."

Dathan knew Yishan was teaching at a seminary in Berkeley. He was interested in applying for that seminary, and Yishan promised to help. "When you come to the Bay Area," said Yishan, "you can stay with us at the beginning, and we'll help you find an apartment."

The missionary who was shepherding that Chinese church in Budapest highly recommended Dathan to us, and I had good impression of him. I thought what Yishan had said was reasonable, and therefore, I made no comment.

It was several months later through painful personal contacts that I learned Dathan was actually a proud and boastful man. Both Yishan and I had been conned, but Yishan continued to be misled by different ideas and did not wake up until much later.

Dathan left Hungary at the end of August, but by the time we met him at San Francisco International Airport, it was already September. We had to go to the airport twice that day since he failed to come at the said arrival time because of some passport problem. I did not know the difficulty we had that day would be really symbolic of what was going to come for our marriage.

When finally we brought Dathan home in the early morning hours of September 1, he told Yishan and me he had with him only $1,000, half of which had been given to him as a gift from the missionary who had pastored the Chinese church in Hungary. He said he had lost most of his savings because of the lost values of his stock investment.

At that point neither Yishan nor I questioned Dathan's honesty, and we were only full of compassion for him. The amount of money he had brought would be used up in a month in the Bay Area, we figured, since monthly room rental itself was around $500 at that time.

Yishan and I were willing to help Dathan receive seminary training. So we decided to let him stay with us and offer free room and board, at least until he could receive enough financial support from other sources.

When Dathan's pastor in Hungary heard of our decision to help out, he was greatly touched, and at the same time, he was concerned it could be adding too much burden to us. So he suggested to Yishan that Dathan be given some work to do at our home.

By that time, about a week or ten days after Dathan's arrival, I was beginning to feel a little different toward Dathan, possibly because his real character was beginning to show up in the light of daily contact. So when Yishan relayed to me those words from Dathan's pastor in Hungary, I was very hesitant. Honestly, I did not know what work I could trust him to do.

Dathan told me he was good at cooking and he also knew gardening. Those were the two areas where he could help me if he really wanted to help. So I let him cook some vegetables one evening, but I carefully instructed him on the one thing he needed to monitor here. Since Yishan's heart attack, I had tried to avoid putting too much vegetable oil in a hot wok, starting with only about one teaspoonful and adding a little more only after it was done.

Well, when Dathan finished cooking, he called me to the kitchen and said proudly to me, "See, it's done. Quick, isn't it?"

I took a quick look at the vegetables in the dish and asked dubiously, "Did you really do according to my instruction?"

"Sure," he said, "if you don't believe me, ask Pastor Lin. He is here."

I did ask Yishan, and his words seemed to back up Dathan at that time, but two days later when things were different, Yishan said he was not paying attention at that time. At that meal when I was eating the vegetables Dathan had cooked, I just did not feel right.

Two days later Dathan was cooking the same vegetables again, and I happened to be standing there. I watched him put one, two, and then three spoonfuls of oil into the hot wok before he put in the vegetables. (I had told him to put in only one teaspoonful.) I was silent at the beginning, but then I could not keep silent anymore. I asked Dathan, "The other night did you put in the same amount of oil at the beginning when you cooked those vegetables?"

"Yes, I did."

"Then why did you tell me you did according to my instructions?" I was very much annoyed at Dathan's dishonesty, and I told him, "Do you think that I, after being married and having been cooking for more than three decades, could not tell the difference of vegetable cooked with less oil and more added later from the ones cooked with a lot of oil at the beginning? Why did you try to fool me?"

"Oh, please do not say so."

From then on, I did not trust him to cook anymore, but Yishan still wanted me to give him some work. I felt forced to give Dathan some gardening work. I told him to dig up a peony I had planted too deep in the soil in the spring of 1999. Although that peony had been growing quite well, I thought it had not bloomed because I had planted it deeper than usual. I had one planted deeper in Schaumburg, Illinois, and it began to bloom in the third year and always did well all those years I lived there. I did not realize California weather was not the same as the conditions in Schaumburg, and my miscalculation had kept this peony from blooming even though it was thriving.

I had planned to dig up this peony and replant it, and I thought my chance for replanting had come with Dathan. Well, minutes later Dathan showed me a big hole in the ground with a peony rhizome lying at the bottom (the size of the rhizome had at least tripled), but the plant was missing.

"Where is the plant?" I asked Dathan.

"Dead. I threw it away."

"*What?* You threw it away? That plant was not dead. It was alive."

"Dead. Its leaves were withered."

"That plant was not dead," I tried to explain. "It's fall, so the leaves are beginning to turn dry. In the spring the plant will come alive."

I tried to comfort myself, "Well, at least I can replant the rhizome, and the peony will grow back next spring."

I walked away and did not say any more words. I was upset and did not feel like dealing with Dathan anymore, not realizing Dathan was actually ignorant in gardening. I was thinking of replanting that rhizome later, but to my consternation, when I returned later to the backyard, I found that not only Dathan had dug up that rhizome and thrown it away, but he had emptied all my flowerpots and stacked them up. Those were the pots I had planted freesias and hyacinths. They bloomed in the spring. The leaves died later, and in the fall nothing seemed to be there. I had told Dathan those were not empty pots, but obviously, he had his own ideas of gardening. (A few days later, I found some freesia bulbs on the ground in the backyard. Dathan had thrown them with the dirt on the ground. It was really the first time I met a person who was so ignorant of gardening and yet told me he knew how.)

Before the end of that month, I wanted Dathan to move out, but Yishan would not allow that. He insisted on letting Dathan stay until he could persuade the church to give financial support to Dathan.

Dathan became an eyesore to me in the house, but then I found out *I* had become an eyesore to Yishan. Our relationship was at its lowest during those months in all our thirty-six years of marriage.

Our church used to celebrate Thanksgiving with a potluck dinner plus sharing time for members to tell everyone about things they were thankful for that year. That Thanksgiving, because we were kicking off a fundraising drive for church building on December 1, it was decided that there would be no special church meeting, but each fellowship group would hold its own Thanksgiving meeting and dinner. It was announced in the Chinese bulletin, and of course, I was in the English service, and I did not know it. I did not know this decision until almost one or two weeks before Thanksgiving since I did not attend that church board meeting where the decision was made, and Yishan did not tell me until much later. (Usually, if I did not attend a church board meeting, Yishan would brief me on the meeting content and decision, but he never told me anything about that meeting. It showed how distant we had become!)

The church had six fellowship groups at that time, and Yishan and I usually went to different groups. When Yishan told me his group was going to have a catered dinner at a high-scale senior residence on Thanksgiving night, I did not like the idea. At the suggestion of a member who was working at that residence, he had been holding a few meetings there, hoping to be able to attract some of those residents. I had attended one or two of those meetings, and the results had not seemed desirable to me. So when he told me the idea of asking the chef of that residence to cook that group's Thanksgiving dinner, I just could not say amen. (As it turned out, he came home quite early that evening, saying the dinner was not good. From the scanty information he gave me, I could tell that meeting was not very exciting. As far as my memory goes, I think that was the last time he held a meeting at that residence.)

The group that I joined was going to have a potluck dinner on the Friday night after Thanksgiving. Since Yishan and I had been going to a lot of meetings in separate cars (Dathan had become his chauffeur) and I really longed to be together with him, especially during this time of year, I said to him on that Wednesday, "Would you like to join our group's potluck dinner this Friday?"

To my great surprise, he answered me very angrily, "Why is it always that I have to join you and you'll never join me?"

I tried to calm him down by saying, "If you don't want to come, that's fine. There's no need to be angry."

His words and action hurt me a great deal, especially because he did that right in front of Dathan. Although we talked in the Taiwanese language, which Dathan did not understand, his attitude had betrayed his lack of respect for me.

Actually, I had been suffering physically that whole week. It began on the previous Friday when I went for a yearly Pap smear. During the exam the doctor caused some bleeding, which later developed into a urinary tract infection. It was painful enough for me to move around. Little did I know that greater suffering would come just a few days later, and it would almost immobilized me and force me to crawl on the carpet around the house and use a wheelchair when I went out.

I'm not trying to exaggerate what I had to endure, although during the following months, I would go through the greatest suffering of my life. At the peak of my physical ordeal, I would feel as if a big cleaver was cutting the joint between my thigh and the body when I was *lying still* in bed, and there was the greater pain when I had to get up or tried to move.

Physical sufferings were always easier for me to endure. It was psychological hurt that really brought me pain. To me, what went on between me and Yishan during this period, especially because of the added strain of Dathan's presence in our home, amounted pretty much to mental torture. His lack of compassion and aloofness to me during this time of my great physical ordeal just added more agony to my whole being. I *was* mindful of his own lack of health, and so it was tragic that the two of us could not be really united in our prayer efforts. I knew the enemy must be having a good time, laughing at both of us, but I really felt helpless and wished that I had a magic wand to wave and make all this pain go away.

So two days after that flare-up from Yishan, around 11:30 a.m. on the Friday after Thanksgiving, Yishan came to the master bedroom, where I was lying awake in bed, and he said, "Dathan is going to cook noodles for lunch. Would you like him to cook some for you as well?"

"I did not have enough sleep over the night, and I'm trying to take a nap. Why don't you tell him to make noodles just for the two of you? I'll make my own later when I wake up from the nap."

I woke up at 12:20 p.m. and went down to the kitchen. Yishan and Dathan just finished saying grace and began eating, the two of them talking and laughing. I went to the stove, ready to cook noodles. However, I noticed some soiled spots that were not cleaned up, and feeling greatly annoyed, I said, "How come the dirty spots on the stove were not wiped clean?"

Immediately, Dathan said, "Surely, I did not cause them."

Dathan grew up during the long period of the cultural revolution in China, and I had noticed a lot of the young Chinese who grew up during that time had learned to be apt to defend themselves and were usually very eloquent. Obviously, Dathan was one of those. Of course, people had a right to defend themselves, but since Dathan came to live with us, I had learned enough to realize that no matter how wrong he was, he would go all the length to argue in order to shed all his own guilt.

His defensive attitude and his argument really hit my nerve, and I said, "Two nights ago I just cleaned up this stove, and I have not come to use it since then. If you did not soil the stove, then who has done it? Was it Pastor Lin who did it then?"

So I had to clean that stove before I began to cook. And then I noticed all of the dirty stuff scattered over the floor. It was so dirty that I could not find a clean spot to stand on. In fact, I had noticed the unclean floor days before, but because of my own physical pain, I had not been able to clean it. At that moment I was greatly agitated that neither Yishan nor Dathan had paid attention to the dirty floor or put in any effort to clean it. So I took a rag, and with great pain and effort, I bent down and wiped the floor clean. As I did that, I felt more and more anger inside. The two men sat by the table and talked and laughed, and neither of them offered to help me or tried to ease my burden. I was so angry that I could not help but burst out and say, "I can see that the two of you are more like a couple, and I'm but a housemaid!"

Yishan was enraged by my words and shouted like a roaring lion to me, "What do you mean by that?"

Yishan had a habit of roaring to me in anger in order to frighten me, but I was not intimidated. I also knew he had mistaken my words to have a homosexual connotation. That was why he was so enraged, but of course, that was not my intention. So I tried to clarify, "Of course, with the two of you talking and laughing and coming in and going out together all the time while I was always left all alone, don't you think that outside people would take you to be husband and wife if he were a woman?"

I was silently praying all that time, asking the Lord to look at our situation and help me, for He alone knew all human hearts and must have seen my loneliness.

Praise the Lord, for He gave me the stamina to endure all that physical and psychological pain, and I was able to clean up the floor and to cook not just my own lunch but also the food for that evening's potluck dinner.

Our God is really an all-knowing God, and nothing is impossible with Him. Bad as my marital relationship with Yishan was, it seemed the Lord was ready to do something to improve it.

First, on the morning of that very Thanksgiving Day, I had a dream before I woke up. In the dream I saw myself standing by the window on the left side of a long living room in a large house. (I never lived in a large house like that) with a high ceiling. From where I stood, I could see a large side yard with wooden fence on the side of the street, and there was a gate at the middle of that fence. As I was watching, I saw Yishan enter the yard through the gate, close it, and then come into the house. After he closed the gate, however, I saw the wind blow the gate open, and I thought, "I'll go out to close the gate." Yet as I turned to go out, I saw by the other side of the yard two small animals a little larger than house cats, beige and brown with black spots, and I saw a third large animal that was the mother of the two smaller ones. The face of the large animal was so fierce-looking that I was afraid to go out, and I thought, *Oh no, it's a leopard.* (In Chinese; it could also be a cheetah.) And then I woke up.

Actually, I had an identical dream a few years earlier before that, and I felt great turmoil when I woke up from that first dream, but I did not understand the meaning of that dream at that time even after I prayed for understanding. However, on that Thanksgiving morning after I woke up from that second identical dream, words appeared in my head, "This home no longer has defense or security." (The words *defense* and *security* came in English, but the rest of the sentence came in Mandarin. The word *home* in Chinese can also mean family.)

So that Thanksgiving morning when I woke up from that dream with those words in my head, I knew the Lord was giving me a diagnosis of our marital illness, and He had known it all along. Although I felt sad, it gave me hope nonetheless, knowing the Lord would not leave it the way it was.

Our God surely is a helper in our time of need. Three days later on Sunday morning, I woke up with two things in my mind—a movie that I watched decades ago and scenes of me sitting in the sanctuary of THC, listening to Yishan's preaching. Immediately, I felt the Lord was telling me, "Yishan has terribly misunderstood you. Go and communicate with him in such and such a way."

The movie that I watched decades ago was *My Geisha* with Shirley McClain and Jack Lemmon in the leading roles as a married couple. Their marriage was heading toward the rock all because the wife was a successful actress while the husband's directing career was not as brilliant as hers. McClain knew her husband's inferiority complex had caused the danger in her marriage, and since she loved him, she decided to do something about it. In the end, their marriage was saved. In their next movie, she played the role of a geisha, but she remained anonymous and gave all the credit to her husband.

Needless to say, I was in great awe and thanked the Lord and prayed for myself first before I went to talk to Yishan. When I went to his study and said, "Do you have time for talk?" he answered quite reluctantly, "What do you have to say?"

"Do you know that I enjoyed listening to your preaching?" I

began, trying to catch his attention, for I knew *why* and *what* the Lord had taught me. I knew if I had not said that first, he would not have listened to me or wanted to talk to me.

"I don't believe it," said Yishan.

"Yes," I said, "you forgot when we first began our ministries at THC how I used to sit in the sanctuary at Sunday services, and every time you preached, I always enjoyed your sermons."

"If you did, then why have you been angry toward me and treated me so shamefully?"

I was thus able to remind him of his own neglect of his wife at the beginning of the new church, and we were able to clear away all the misunderstandings of those nearly seven years. I was also able to point out to him Dathan's contribution to our marital problem.

Although Dathan would not move out until New Year's Day on 2002, my relationship with Yishan did begin to improve from that day on. Praise the Lord for His mercy and timely help!

Why did Yishan so biasedly favor Dathan and even blindly put our marriage at risk? Partially, I think, because we had no sons. Sometime after Dathan came to stay with us, one day Yishan told me that a deacon had commented to him that by having Dathan stay with us and help around the house, it was like Yishan had gained a son.

To me, those were poisoning words, but to Yishan, it was music to his ears. As a pastor, he was always kind to everyone in the church, his wife being the only exception. That deacon's words seemed to have helped Yishan to become blind to Dathan's faults at the beginning. In the end, however, the Lord allowed me to see that He vindicated me.

One Sunday afternoon in April 2002, long after the service was over and everyone else had left church except the two of us *and* another man, the latter suddenly asked Yishan a question when Yishan was about to lock the church door. In the church this man was quite well known for being *blunt*, and once he lost his temper with Yishan and shouted at him.

That afternoon, that brother asked Yishan, "Pastor, is there anyone else in the church besides me who dares to rebuke you?"

Yishan smiled and answered, "Yes, there is one, but I won't tell you who."

Praise the Lord that I *was* by Yishan's side to hear *this* question and answer. If Dathan were still staying with us, he would be driving Yishan home, and then I would not be there.

On the way home, I asked Yishan, "Who is that man in your answer to that brother's question?"

"Dathan," said Yishan. And upon further prodding from me, Yishan told me what had happened. It was just another example of how that man had no respect for me or Yishan. "I'm totally disappointed with him," said Yishan, and he gave me more examples of what Dathan had done.

(Dathan took classes at the seminary for about three years while staying on with SCC and then went back to China. By that time Yishan was home with the Lord and no longer here. Sometime later I heard some stories about Dathan that proved he was worse than what I had thought, one of those stories being that he caused some scandal in Southern California. That man was pretty much a charlatan who used us not just to gain entry into the United States but to obtain legal status as well.)

I believe the Lord had vindicated me as another means to bridge the gap between me and Yishan. In the end, He was the one who saved our marriage. Hallelujah! I'll always praise Him!

Chapter 25

Wounded Warrior

*I*n late January 2002, doctors at Stanford Hospital found that Yishan's leukemia had turned from chronic into the acute type and practically pronounced his death sentence. They said, "You only have a few months to live."

A week later we found that "a few months" was really euphemism the doctors used to cushion Yishan's shock. On a second visit a week later, they told him, "You actually only have a few weeks left." Later on we realized the doctors had not expected Yishan to live beyond early March.

"A few months" or "a few weeks" were not that much different. God turned it into four and a half months, to be exact.

I still remember that day in the doctor's office when Dr. M asked a male colleague to tell us the bad news because she herself was in a meeting. Dr. R began by asking a question, "Do you have a will?"

Since Yishan usually preferred having me answer questions for him when the conversation was conducted in English, I rather habitually answered, "We have wanted to have one set up but have not got around to doing it yet."

"You'd better do it soon," said Dr. R, "because 80 percent of your bone marrow has cancerous cells and you only have a few months to live."

Those words hit me like a lightning bolt. I did not know what Yishan's reaction was, for I dared not look at him, but I was afraid he might collapse. (I had heard a brother in church tell how his mother who was a medical doctor in China became paralyzed the day after hearing of the cancer pronouncement on her and died a month later.) So I prayed silently, "Lord, please give Yishan strength so that he may continue to trust in You."

I never looked at Yishan but continued praying silently for him. He told me later that he smiled at Dr. R, but neither of us spoke. Dr. R asked, "Well, what do you think?"

I answered Dr. R, "We are Christians. To us death had been dealt with by Jesus Christ two thousand years ago. Apostle Paul said in the Book of Philippians—"

I never got a chance to quote Philippians 1:23 because at that moment the door opened and Dr. M walked into the office. Dr. R said to her, "Mrs. Lin was quoting Apostle Paul."

However, even Dr. R was not able to finish his sentence. It seemed Dr. M was not listening but asked us instead, "Has Dr. R told you the news?"

I answered, "Yes, he did. I'd like to ask a question. Is Yishan's case really hopeless?"

"Once leukemia jumped Gleevac, there is no cure," she answered.

At that moment I expected her to continue saying, "Sorry, we doctors cannot help you anymore," and I was actually thinking, *Praise the Lord. Man's end is the beginning for God.*

Yet Dr. M continued to say, "We'll try to give you some low-dose chemotherapy, but it is not aggressive treatment. Aggressive treatment is useless. We only hope to slow down the progress of the cancer."

Neither Yishan nor I had any more to say, and after thanking her, we both got up. So did the two doctors. I thought Dr. M was going to shake hands with Yishan, but unexpectedly, she hugged him and planted a kiss on his face and said, "I know you are a man of faith, and the development of your leukemia has been different from all other patients."

Dr. M, a Lutheran, usually addressed Yishan as "Rev. Lin" and seldom called him "Yishan." When she hugged Yishan, I felt as if she were saying good-bye to him for the last time.

Medical doctors could no longer help Yishan; only God could. Truly, God did, for by March, doctors were surprised that Yishan's leukemia was under control, and he told Dr. M, "Many people have been praying for me." Dr. M confessed to Yishan that it could not have been the medication she had given to him. "It's *not* supposed to work."

Around that same time, I myself was suffering severe pain from a ruptured spinal disc. For more than a month in February and early March, I was crawling on the carpet at home and using a wheelchair when going out. I was in such great pain that I often cried out to the Lord, "Please kill me to end my misery. I cannot live on anymore in this pain." Although Yishan and I did pray together for each other's healing, I really had no more time or energy left to worry about his condition.

By mid-March, my own condition was improving, and I began to walk with a cane and no longer needed the wheelchair. I also began a twelve-session physical therapy that usually began with electro massage. During the electro massage, I had to lie still, and I usually read a small Christian magazine while lying there. One day around mid-April during the electro massage, I happened to be reading an article written by a widow. The writer described what she did on her fifty-third wedding anniversary, and as I read the story, a thought suddenly came to mind, *Am I going to be a widow before long?*

Tears came to my eyes and I quickly said in my heart, "Oh Lord, not so soon. My heart is not ready."

About a week after that, when I saw Yishan in the morning of April 22, he happened to be in the hallway outside the upstairs bathroom. As soon as he saw me, he took me closer to a window and opened up his mouth and showed me his tongue. There was a yellowish green band about one centimeter wide from the tip of the tongue all the way to its root. I asked him what it was, and he said, "I don't know. I'll ask the doctor on my next visit."

When he came home from his next doctor's visit, he informed me the band in the middle of his tongue was a yeast infection. My heart sank when I heard that. It meant that his body had lost its defense power and no longer had immunity, and deep down I felt as if my whole being were cast over by a dark shadow.

Beginning with that morning when Yishan showed me his yeast-infected tongue, I always smelled a foul odor emitting from his mouth every time I stood next to him. Together Yishan and I had visited many terminal cancer patients or frail elderly people in the nursing home, and every time I entered a nursing home, I could smell that odor. So from that day on, I began to pray, "Lord, if You're not going to heal Yishan, could You let me know at least two months ahead?"

I did not realize *then* it was too late for me to offer that prayer because the Lord would take Yishan home in less than two months. In hindsight, however, I think the Lord *did* reveal it to me exactly two months ahead when that first thought of becoming a widow came on that mid-April day during the electro massage in the neurosurgeon's office.

It was not until a few days after Yishan's going home when I learned of the full scope of the Lord's revelation in this regard. He revealed it *two months earlier to two other women* as well just as He did with the prophet Elijah. When Elijah was going to be taken to heaven, the Lord revealed it to many people, including Elisha (2 Kings 2:1–7). On the third evening after Yishan left the earth, a young woman from church came to visit me and said, "Mrs. Lin, I'm sorry I have not told you this earlier before. Two months before Pastor Lin passed away, I had a dream. I dreamed that a group of young people from our church, including myself, were going to a retreat. As we were walking, I saw Rick [a young man from church who was also her colleague at work] on a new red motorcycle, and I invited him to go to the retreat with us but he declined and left. As we walked along farther up the road, I saw Pastor Lin sweeping the floor in front of a cottage with a broom in his hand, and I asked him, 'Pastor, Pastor, how come you are here all alone?' He took out of his pocket a small box and showed me a thermometer and two toothpicks and said,

'Now I'm solely living on the thermometer and the two toothpicks.'
And then I woke up.

"After I woke up, I told my husband of my dream, but neither of
us knew what the dream meant. That following Friday when I went to
work, I saw Rick arriving with a new red motorcycle exactly identical
to the one I saw in the dream. Both my husband and I marveled about
the motorcycle part of the dream, but we still wondered what the
other part about Pastor Lin meant. Now I know the two toothpicks
meant two months because it was exactly two months earlier when
I had the dream, and toothpicks are fragile, exactly the condition of
Pastor Lin's health for the last two months."

Then I added, explaining to that woman, "Pastor Lin practically
lived on a thermometer during his last two months because he had a
low fever and used that thermometer daily to take his temperature."

When I mentioned this story to Angela, she said, "Two months
before Boppy left, God told me to clear my calendar for the next two
months and not to make any appointments. At first, I wondered why,
but then I understood it was for Boppy."

When I heard what Angela said, my tears came out, but I really
marveled at the work of our wonderful God. It seemed He wanted to
show me He had taken Yishan home at an appointed time.

Back in late April and early May of 2002, I did not know God
was going to take Yishan home soon, but one April morning Yishan
brought one of his prescription bottles to me and asked me to open
it. To me this was *not* a good sign. As a pianist and one who used to
do push-ups, Yishan had very strong arms, even stronger than a lot
of other Oriental men who were much younger, and I also used to
call on him for help whenever I needed someone with a strong arm.
Now that *he* had to ask *me* to open up a medicine bottle, it just showed
how weak he had become.

Yet I seemed to be in a daze and did not realize the significance
of Yishan's real condition, possibly because I was fooled by the
toughness Yishan tried to present *and* also because I myself was not
completely well from the ruptured disc. As a result, I failed to pay
close attention to *his* condition. Churches still invited him to speak,

and he still drove around the Bay Area to fulfill engagements. He said he had no intention of slowing down, and I could only pray for him, asking the Lord to give him strength. He told me he felt the Lord still had a lot of work for him to finish.

Not only that, but he had probably played tough to the Stanford doctors as well. That late January afternoon when we were told he only had a few months left, Dr. M said to Yishan, "If you are tired, we can give you blood transfusions to make you feel better."

And I remember Yishan answered her by saying, "I'll tell you when I'm tired."

It was not until three weeks before Yishan collapsed that I learned why he never told the doctor he was tired, although it was almost a daily occurrence when I saw him dozing off. That day I drove him to Stanford Hospital to receive an intravenous injection of medicine. Yishan told me this biweekly injection usually took only a short time. That day, however, there seemed to be some confusion among the hospital staff, and we had to wait a long time for the nurse to come. When one finally did come to put the needle into Yishan's arm, she had a hard time finding the right vein and poked Yishan's arms several times without success. Eventually, another nurse was called to perform the job, and when she succeeded in getting the vein, Yishan began sitting there without being able to do anything except waiting for the medication drip to empty out. Then after sitting there for some time, he sighed and said, "Ai, if I take a transfusion, it will take me a whole day sitting in the hospital."

It was only *then* I realized he considered transfusion a waste of his time. To him, only God's work took the first priority, and therefore, spending a whole day in the hospital without being able to perform any work seemed a waste of time.

Since I kept asking the Lord to tell me at least two months ahead of time if He was not going to heal Yishan, the Lord did finally reveal it clearly to me for the first time on Friday, May 31. That morning, when I woke up shortly before 9:00 a.m., I heard some strange noise in the backyard outside the window. Immediately, I pulled up the shade and looked into the backyard in the direction of the noise and saw an odd scene.

In June 1998, shortly after we moved to U City, I had someone plant a sizeable persimmon tree in one corner of the backyard, and a large wooden stake had also been driven into the ground to support that persimmon tree, leaving about twelve feet on the ground. By May 2002, the tree had grown to be about fourteen feet, two feet taller than the stake originally planted there to support that tree.

That morning on May 31, when I looked in the direction of the tree, I saw five or six branches of the persimmon tree lying on the ground, each piece about four or five feet long, and the tallest branch was missing from the tree. However, that twelve-foot stake was still there. I also saw a possum climbing on that tall stake, trying to get to the top. Possums are nocturnal animals, and that possum was obviously tired after a night's work of chopping down branches. This one seemed to be trying to get to the top to sleep, not realizing there was *no* treetop for it to climb to.

At that very moment, when my eyes saw those branches on the ground and that possum on the tree, words came into my head, "This tree is Yishan. He's being chopped down."

Tears rushed to my eyes, and I felt great sorrow and said to the Lord, "Oh, Lord, not so soon. My heart is not ready yet."

Can you imagine how difficult it was for me to suppress the urge to hug him and to cry and say, "I don't want you to leave!" when Yishan came to the master bedroom a few minutes later to pray with me?

In the past whenever either one of us had a special encounter with the Lord, it was always a delight for us to share the experience with each other. Yet that morning when the Lord told me that Yishan was being chopped down, I could neither tell Yishan about it nor express my sorrow. I was afraid that by revealing my emotion, I would add undue burden to him and thus jeopardize his health.

Six days later on Thursday morning, right after I woke up, words came into my head again, "Oh, God is using our sleeping in separate bedrooms during the past several months to prepare myself for living alone in the future."

Again, tears welled up in my eyes, and I said to the Lord in my heart, "Oh, Lord, not so soon. My heart is not ready yet."

Every day during the following week, I felt strongly that Yishan was going to leave me, and yet I still did not know it was going to be his final week.

On Sunday night following that Thursday morning, I lay in bed a long time without being able to fall asleep. There was the heavy burden in my heart, knowing that time was running out for Yishan. As I stayed awake in bed with my eyes closed, I saw clearly in the darkness three blackbirds lining up horizontally, and the one on the left shot up almost vertically. More words came into my head, "This bird is Yishan. He's flying away." And once again, tears flooded my eyes, and I said to the Lord in my heart, "Oh, Lord, not so soon. My heart is still not ready."

That very weekend happened to be our church retreat, and the speaker was Elder Wu, who was very well known among Chinese and Taiwanese Christians. Despite his illness, Yishan not only attended the retreat but had also accepted an invitation to speak at another Chinese church for that Sunday morning and planned to conduct a worship service on that afternoon at our own church for those who did not attend the retreat. (He always came back to hold a Sunday worship service for those who could not or chose not to attend the retreat. This was just another example of how much he cared for the Lord's flock.) Since I had to speak at our own English worship service every week except that Sunday, Yishan told me to stay at the retreat to the end to fully enjoy it, and he would arrange a ride for me to come back.

I did not agree to his plan, however, for I did not want to leave him driving back all that distance by himself. (*I* was the one who drove us to the retreat.) In the end, when I insisted on coming back with him on Sunday morning, he then said, "In this case, why don't you take over our own worship service in the afternoon, and I'll drive to the other church to speak in the morning. In this way I don't have to hurry back to our own church." Although I insisted on accompanying him to that other Chinese church, his decision prevailed, and in a sense, it turned out to be better that way. That afternoon there was traffic congestion on San Mateo Bridge, and Yishan was not able to get back in time. I saw him walking into church only when I was about one-third into my sermon.

Our thirty-sixth wedding anniversary fell on that weekend. To me it was a very significant occasion, especially because the Lord had healed our marriage, and I really wanted to celebrate it to make up for the hurts of the past several years. However, we could not do it right away because of our presence at the retreat, and when I mentioned it to Yishan, he said, "We'll do it after we go back."

So late that Sunday afternoon after the church service was over, we went to a Chinese restaurant and ordered some of Yishan's favorite dishes. In the course of the dinner, however, Yishan said, "I have no appetite." Our celebration had become meaningless. I just felt sadness.

It was later *that very Sunday night* when the Lord announced to me Yishan was flying away. Then two days later, Tuesday evening, when I opened up an English hymnal to choose hymns for that coming Sunday's English worship service, my eyes were directed to the title on the top of one of the pages that said, "It Is Well with My Soul," and words came into my head, "The Lord is going to take Yishan, but it is well with my soul."

My first reaction was the same as before. There were tears in my eyes, and I said to the Lord, "Oh, Lord, not so soon. My heart is not ready." Yet in fact, my heart was filled with greater sorrow, and I could not control myself but burst out weeping. After a short while, I did control myself and muffled my sobs because I did not want Yishan to hear me. (Yishan was upstairs in his study.) However, I could not help crying out to the Lord in my heart, "Lord, are You really going to take Yishan? Aren't You hearing my prayers? Has my whole week's fasting for him been in vain?"

I think I was a coward in the respect of expressing my emotion in front of Yishan during his final days. I did not want to adversely affect him then, and I'm still not sure if it might have been better for both of us if I had had more courage. I came to nearly express it only once on the Monday evening of his final week. He was sitting by his desk, reading the Bible, and I sat on the carpet at his feet, resting my head on his lap and wrapping my two arms around his body with my two hands at his back. When I did that, he turned in his swivel chair and laid both his hands on my back. It was not exactly an embrace, and we remained in that position for quite a while without uttering a single word. Yet I believe he knew in those moments my love for him. Then later on when I raised my head and sat in an erect position, he looked into my eyes and said, "If God does not heal me, I do not want you to stay in SCC. You can choose going back to your sisters in Taiwan or resume publishing your *Fish and Loaves.*"

Now I know in those words Yishan was revealing his love and concern for me. He obviously knew all along the attitude of the church coworkers toward me, and he did not want me to be hurt anymore by staying on in SCC after he was gone. Yet at that moment his words really brought back a lot of unpleasant memory to me, and I had to risk any danger of displeasing him by saying, "You know that all these past years I stayed on in this church only for the sake of helping you. Don't you remember that time when I decided to leave SCC and go to an American church instead? If the Lord had not kept me in SCC, I would have left long ago."

It was sad to think that even toward the end of Yishan's life, the church we founded together still stood between the two of us, although only in a shadowy way. In a spiritual sense, the dream I had in the Grand Canyon Lodge back in 1976 (chapter 8) was ironically fulfilled in the end. In that dream I saw Yishan having an affair with another woman, which made me very sad, and I began to cry. Although there was never really another woman involved in our marriage, yet in the end, the church had become the other woman to come between me and Yishan.

Since Yishan went home to be with the Lord, God has done a great deal to comfort me. Better yet, it has been really all in His knowledge, and He actually had made it known to me at the very beginning of our ministry; however, I did not fully figured it out until recently. The other day when I was flipping through my journal to refresh my memory for writing this book, I saw an entry in which I recorded a dream I had on the morning of September 23, 1981, after the publication of the first issue of *Fish and Loaves* and more than a month before Yishan began preaching his first sermon at the Taiwanese church.

In that dream I saw our bed was placed in the center of a very large bedroom with wooden floor, and when Yishan and I removed the bed, the wooden floor beneath revealed a very large hole. At that moment, a pastor and his wife (the couple whom we consulted with in chapter 11) came into the room, saying he needed twenty D batteries. Then I woke up from that dream.

"I don't know what that big hole under the bed means," I wrote in my journal. "Does it mean Yishan and I will have a big hole in our marriage? But I think that pastor needing twenty D batteries probably means he needs great power, a lot of prayers on his behalf so that he may receive great power for ministry. May God forgive me for not praying daily for that pastor."

In hindsight now, it's easy to understand that dream, but back in 1981, when Yishan and I were so fervently serving the Lord together, it was more like a puzzle to me. Now I do remember at the beginning I was troubled by that dream for a while because of its possible implication, but gradually, I forgot about it, especially by the time my marriage was in big trouble, although I did turn to that journal and think about the possible meaning of that dream, comparing it to our troubled marital state. Yet even at that time I was in so much hurt that I was not able to clearly see God's hand in it and for it to bring me any consolation. Of course, *now* I'm so thankful it was not God's purpose to destroy our marriage when He called Yishan into the ministry. I was in great awe the other day when I *rediscovered* this entry in my journal. We really serve a great and awesome omniscient God!

Now let me get back to Yishan's final week. On Thursday morning right after I woke up, I suddenly felt panic as words came into my head, "Oh no, Yishan is leaving soon, but we have not made any funeral arrangement." Honestly speaking, if the Spirit of God had not spoken to me, I would never have thought of those words myself.

Needless to say, I immediately felt great sorrow, but I controlled myself, and after wiping away the tears, I called out to Yishan, who was in his study, "Yi, have you prayed this morning?"

He answered by saying that he had prayed by himself but that he could pray with me again.

As soon as he came into the master bedroom, however, he said, "Today I need to go to the hospital for transfusion."

"Then how about the second deacons' training session tonight?" I asked. Since he had mentioned transfusion would take a whole day, I wondered if he would have enough time for the training session that evening. So I continued to ask, "Would you like to cancel it?"

He seemed to be annoyed at my question and said, "I can't cancel it! It's not easy to find a time everybody can come together."

So when we knelt together, I felt obligated to pray for him, asking the Lord to strengthen him. When our prayers ended, he said, "I feel much better now. There's no need for transfusion. I don't have to go to the hospital."

Whenever I thought back about that day, I always regretted that I had mentioned the meeting to him and prayed for him so that he changed his mind about going for transfusion. If I had not mentioned the deacons' training session for that evening, and Yishan had gone to the hospital to receive transfusion, would things have been different for us? Certainly, it would have been better, but I really have no way of finding it out. Only God knows.

The next morning, Friday, Yishan was up before I did. When I woke up, I heard him stirring in the kitchen downstairs. "Have you had breakfast yet?" I asked.

"I do not have a good appetite this morning," he answered. "I only ate a bit of the vegetables Mrs. Chan cooked for us."

Then the phone rang. It was a call from the office of Yishan's family doctor telling me to go there to pick up a free sample of medicine. Dr. M had told them Yishan needed this medicine, but the insurance would not pay for it. I figured out I would not have time to go to the doctor's office, so I called Angela to run the errand for me, but I could not reach her and had to leave a message on her cellular phone.

Actually, I felt rather distressed since I did not sleep well over the night, and I was thinking of going back to bed to make up for some sleep. I had to be in Oakland to do translation work that afternoon, and I was supposed to leave by 1:20 p.m. If I did not have enough sleep, I might have difficulty remaining awake while driving.

By the time Angela called back and I asked her to pick up the free sample medicine for Yishan, it was impossible for me to go back to bed. When it was near noon, I heard Yishan using the bathroom upstairs. I asked him, "You did not eat much this morning. What would you like to have for lunch?"

And he answered, "No, I'm thirsty. I don't want to eat. I just want something to drink."

"What would you like to drink then?"

He did not answer my question.

"How about grass jelly drink?" I suggested.

"Oh good. Grass jelly drink."

By that time I was upstairs and saw him coming out of the bathroom, his pajama pants half pulled up, something he would usually never have done. Then he walked past me with unsteady steps. These two irregularities really worried me, and I was wondering if Yishan was apt to stay home by himself.

When I brought a can of grass jelly drink to Yishan, I found him asleep in the bed. I had the can opened up in case he was too weak to pull up the tab himself, and I had also inserted a straw for him. But then I found there was already an unopened can on the small table by his bed, another sign that he was not very alert. I thought he was asleep, and I bent down to kiss him on his cheek, but he opened his eyes and smiled at me. He said he was not asleep, just tired. I touched his forehead and found it slightly hot. So I inserted a thermometer into his mouth, and indeed, he had a little fever. It really worried me even more.

I then asked him, "Are you going to receive transfusion today or not?"

He answered as if he had just remembered it, "Oh yes, I do want to receive transfusion. Could you call up the nurse at Stanford for me?"

Yishan usually handled all the doctor's phone calls himself, so it took me a long time to find out the number and made the call to the nurse. I had to leave our number on the nurse's beeper since she was not available right away.

Although I was hesitant to leave Yishan alone at home, eventually I did for two reasons. First, this was the first day of a new session for the special class of students for whom I was going to do the translation work. It would be difficult for the school to make a last-minute arrangement if I suddenly called to tell them I could not come in. Second, I figured I would be leaving Yishan alone only for a short while because I was going to ask Angela to take her dad to Stanford Hospital and she would be coming to pick him up pretty soon.

While I was getting dressed, the phone rang. It was the nurse. I told her Yishan's request for a transfusion, and she promised to make the arrangement. Yet before I finished my talk with the nurse, there was a knock at our front door, and I had to ask the nurse to hold for me. It was Angela bringing the sample medicine. I asked if she could take her dad to Stanford later, and she said she could. So when I got back to the nurse, I gave her Angela's numbers so that she could call Angela when things were ready.

I made two fatal mistakes that day. First, I should have stayed home, but I did not. Second, I thought of asking Angela if she had a key to my house when she brought the medicine, but because of all the bustle and hustle that day, the question slipped to the back of my mind, so I never got to ask her that question when I talked to her at the front door.

By the time I left my house for Oakland, it was already more than twenty minutes later than I had intended, and I knew I would be late. It was more than ten minutes later after I had already gotten into the freeway for some distance when I suddenly remembered I had failed to ask Angela that question about the key. I also realized that Angela did not have a key to my house. I had given her a key before, but she had lost it. Afew times she had to borrow our key, but I had not given her another one since she returned it the last time. I thought of heading back home, but in the split second, I continued to drive since I was already too late for my assignment in Oakland. So at that moment the only thing I could do was praying while I was driving, asking the Lord to send His angel to watch over Yishan.

When I got to Oakland, I found the classroom empty. There were no students, and the professor did not come in until more than ten or fifteen minutes later. She told me the students were still in registration, and we had a little talk while waiting for students to come in.

The class began more than an hour late. However, somewhere in the middle of my translating what the professor said, an administrator came into the classroom and told me, "Mrs. Lin, your son-in-law is waiting for you on the phone."

I followed her into her office and picked up the phone. Albert was on the line. "Mom, Angela had been trying to reach you. She said you did not turn on your cellular phone. Please call her immediately."

Since I arrived in Oakland, I had turned on my cellular phone because I was expecting Angela might call me. Back then I had not had a long history of using the cellular phone. Once I touched the "silence" key on the cellular phone by mistake, and it took me a long while before I was able to turn it back to normal.

So when I returned to the classroom, I immediately took out my phone and checked on it. It *was on*, and it was *not* silenced. Angela asked me why I did not turn on my phone, and it was not until two days later when she realized she had actually punched Yishan's cellular number that afternoon instead of mine. No wonder I never heard the phone ring!

When I reached Angela on her phone, she said, "Mommy, I'm worried. I knocked on the door a long time, and nobody answered. I cannot get into your house, and I have called the police. He wants to talk to you."

When I talked to the police he told me he wanted to make a forced entry into the house, but he needed my permission. I asked him how he was going to do that, and he said, "By breaking a window or a door."

I thought of all my downstairs doors and windows. If any of it was broken, there was no way I could get it fixed right away. Then anybody could get into my house anytime. So I said no, but I told Angela I would go home right away.

(I have the habit of locking every window of my house, but Yishan never locked the window of his study. Angela told me later since I did not give permission for the police to break into my house, he then used the ladder from the ambulance to climb into the upstairs through an unlocked window in Yishan's study. The emergency workers then got in and found Yishan lying on the bathroom floor, and at first, they had a hard time taking his vital signs since his pulse and blood pressure were both so low.)

I told the professor I had to leave, and immediately, I headed for home. It was nearly 4:30 p.m., so it was rush hour. Usually, it took me an hour to drive home in rush-hour traffic. But that afternoon I prayed while driving, asking the Lord to guide me, and I arrived home in thirty minutes. It was a miracle to me. When I got near home I saw an ambulance parked across the street from my house, and an EMT got into the ambulance and drove it away.

I parked my car in the garage and rode with Angela to the hospital. In the car Angela told me she asked the EMTs to take Yishan to Stanford Hospital, but they said by law they had to take him to the nearest hospital, so we were going to Washington Hospital (in F City), not to Stanford Hospital (in Palo Alto across the Bay.)

I wished the ambulance had taken Yishan to Palo Alto instead of F City that day. At Stanford Hospital, they had blood ready for Yishan. Plus, I was later told by Dr. M at Stanford that Yishan would have been given a large private room (for terminal patient) and we could have had twenty to thirty visitors at one time in that room without any problem. *The story would have been quite different.*

When Angela and I arrived at Washington Hospital, we found Yishan lying on a gurney out in the hallway of the ER; he was still waiting for an empty room. He was awake, although his eyes were closed. When I called his name, he opened his eyes, and I asked, "Did you know that you had collapsed and passed out?"

"At first, I did not know it," he said. "Later when I came to, I heard the knocks on the door, but I could not get up."

I immediately prayed for him, and he said, "Amen," his voice still very clearly audible.

After some more waiting, a room was vacated, and Yishan was wheeled in. Then after they had hooked him to the vital signs machine with the IV dripping regularly, I saw the pulse reading only at fifty-seven, and I commented to Angela, "It's so low."

She told me, "It was even lower when they first found him on the bathroom floor."

While I was looking at the machine, it suddenly started to blink, and a few seconds later, it went blank. The ER personnel tried to get it to work, but it took a long time before it went back to show numbers on it.

By that time a nurse had come in and began to work on Yishan. While her hands were on Yishan's abdomen, I noticed wavelike movements on that part, and so I realized Yishan had accumulated water in his abdomen. At that moment I remembered a scene that occurred about two weeks earlier. That day Yishan was walking up the stairs, and I happened to be standing nearby. Noticing his protruding abdomen, I said to him, "Wait a second. You're losing weight, but how come your tummy is getting bigger?"

Both Yishan and I had visited many terminal cancer patients, and we had learned that water accumulation was one of their symptoms. Obviously, Yishan knew his own condition then, and he did not want me to find it out. So that day he did not answer my question but just continued to walk upstairs. It was my own fault that I failed to pursue him further that day to find it out.

Then an on-call doctor, Dr. H, came in answer to the ER's call for Yishan's family doctor. Seeing the nurse working on Yishan, Dr. H said to her, "Don't you know he's a ____ [I did not hear that word properly, but it was probably end-stage] patient?" I guessed the doctor was trying to tell the nurse there was no need to work so hard on him.

At that moment Yishan's eyeballs rolled upward, showing the whites of his eye, but the nurse continued to work on her charge as if she did not notice it. Dr. H immediately said to the nurse, "Did you see his eyes?" She suddenly stopped, probably realizing it was not good to mention that in front of me, not knowing that I had already taken everything in.

After Dr. H left the room, I told Angela, who was standing nearby, what I had observed and what that meant. I then said to her, "We'd better pray hard for Ahma [Taiwanese word for *grandma*, Yishan's mom] if God does not heal Boppy." Yishan was the only son in the family and the one his mother really loved. If he did not survive, I was afraid my mother-in-law would not be able to take the loss.

The two things I observed on Yishan began to make me very anxious as I remembered the words that came to me the morning before, "Yishan is leaving soon, but we have not made any funeral arrangement."

At that moment I prayed silently, "Lord, You know Yishan and I have not talked about funeral arrangement, and I really do not know who should preside over Yishan's funeral service if You're going to take him home. Please give me the courage to ask him before it is too late."

I really agonized and hesitated over this topic, and I kept praying inside. Once both Dr. H and the nurse left the room, I was able to gather up enough courage and asked, "Yi, if God does not heal you, who do you want to preside over the service?"

"Yeah, who should we ask?" Yishan seemed to be lost in answering my question. I took it to be he had lost the ability to think.

Although Yishan had been ordained only a short decade, he had conducted close to twenty funerals, and I myself had done two up to that time. Many times he had mentioned the importance of funeral messages since they were good opportunities for witnessing to non-Christians and for giving out the gospel. Yishan had also mentioned more than once how he thought my sermons were much better than many other pastors'.

Since Yishan was not able to come up with a good answer and I really thought what he would agree, I suggested, "Would you like me to do it?"

"Very good, very good." He seemed to be relieved and pleased at the same time. Still, I wanted to be sure and asked him half-teasingly, "Do you really have so much confidence in me?"

Once again, he solemnly said, "Of course I have confidence in you. Why shouldn't I have confidence?"

At that time I was very thankful that I got it settled, but much later I realized, I was too naive and had invited too heavy a burden upon myself. (This is also why, as I have mentioned earlier, I'm thankful that God led our marriage to end on a high note since I was able to gain back his full confidence at the end.)

Angela and I waited in that room almost exactly three hours when Yishan was finally given blood. It was tragic that the EMTs did not send Yishan to Stanford but to Washington Hospital that day. At Stanford, they had blood ready for Yishan but not at Washington. Frozen blood could not be thawed in a hurry.

By that time I was thinking of going home to take a bath and change my clothes. I had come to the hospital in a hurry and therefore did not have time to change into something casual and more comfortable.

Although Yishan's condition seemed to be grave, I really had no idea how much longer he was going to hold on, the main reason being that he was very alert and was able to talk with a very clear voice all that time. I was expecting it to be a long night of vigil, and therefore, I wanted to go home to take a bath first and change into something comfortable and then come back to the hospital right away. I also wanted Angela to go home to Albert and her two young children, and I was planning to drive back to the hospital by myself.

However, Angela kept saying she wanted to wait until they moved Yishan to a regular hospital room since she heard them mention moving him to the floor. So we waited there about another hour, and still, nothing was done.

By that time Angela told me she had called Albert. He had taken their two children to his parents in Los Altos on the other side of the Bay, and there was no need for her to rush back home. In the end, she consented to take me home and said she would bring me back to the hospital again later.

We left the hospital sometime after 9:30 p.m. I told Yishan I would come back to the hospital to be with him in a short while, and he said okay.

After I got home, the first thing I did was kneel down by my bed and pray. Once I began to pray, I was deeply in communincation with the Lord, and even before I said a word, I *knew* God was *not* going to heal Yishan. Then I began to cry. I then said to the Lord, "Even if You don't heal Yishan, I will still praise You and worship You, but Lord, I ask You to have mercy on my mother-in-law. You know how much she loves Yishan. If You don't heal her son, please help her and comfort her so that she'll be able to cope with the loss."

I did not dare to spend much time in prayer and immediately headed downstairs to my study to call my younger sister in Taiwan. I told her Yishan's grave news and asked her to call Yishan's sister for me. But our talk was interrupted by an incoming call, and I had to cut the conversation short.

It was Dr. H, the on-call doctor, who had called. "Your husband may not last through the night," she said.

I felt incredulous and asked, "How come? When I left him in the hospital, he was still very much alert."

"His condition is not good," said Dr. H. "You must come to the hospital right away."

"I had planned to go back," I told her.

I began to shake all over even before I hung up the phone. I called Angela immediately. She was taking a shower, and Albert answered the phone. I told him the words of Dr. H, and he said they would come to pick me up. I then went to the kitchen to put two half-full bottles of drinking water together into one bottle. However, my hands were so shaky that I spilled some water and just gave up. I was only able to change my clothes but did not have time for a bath.

My wait for Albert and Angela to come seemed to last forever.

We went back to the ER and learned that Yishan had been moved to the fourth floor. They would not allow us to go from the ER to Yishan's room, and we had to go to the front entrance. Since it was past 8:00 p.m., it meant that Angela and I had to wait for the two visitors to come down so that we could have the visitor passes to go up.

Earlier that afternoon when I learned from Angela that Yishan had passed out, I called the deacons' board chairman to inform him. Every Friday night Bible study group had heard the news. Many church members had come to the hospital instead of going home after the Bible study, and two women were with Yishan when we got to the hospital. We had to wait for those two women to come down before we could go up since they were holding the two visitor's passes.

By the time Angela and I saw Yishan in that fourth-floor room, he looked very different from when I had left him two hours earlier. When I called his name and he opened his eyes, I saw his eyes were clouded, far from the clear brightness earlier that evening. Then when he tried to answer my question (I don't remember what I asked him), his voice was not only much weaker. But he mumbled, and the words were garbled, so I could not figure them out. I had to repeatedly ask him the same question several times before he was able to say them clearly enough. From then on, I could talk with him without any problem.

It was *then* I realized that in my two-hour absence from him, his spirit had taken on the journey of departure, but my arrival and calling his name had "brought him back." (Later on I asked the church members who were there prior to my arrival to learn about his condition in my absence. One said she called "Pastor Lin," but Yishan did not open his eyes. And only when she said, "We need you to come back to teach us the Bible," that he smiled wryly. Obviously, even then he knew his own condition and where he was heading.)

With my arrival, his reaction seemed to be different, and it gave me hope to try my best to keep him there. I did not want him to leave me too soon, and he seemed to prefer lingering as well. When I prayed with him and entreated the Lord to heal Yishan *even then*—after all, our Lord was able to bring Lazareth back to life even after he had been dead for four days—I could tell Yishan was echoing my prayer with a hearty *amen*, even though it was weaker than earlier.

We encountered a problem with the church members who kept sneaking into the room. When Angela and I arrived, the nurse told us, "Two visitors only," and even Albert could not stay in the room and had to go down again to the first floor waiting area. He eventually left for home. The problem was originally caused by church members who visited Yishan before we arrived. Since they talked too loudly and the other patient in the same room complained to the nurse so that she had to enforce the strict two-visitors rule.

Around 12:00 a.m., about fifteen minutes after we saw Yishan in that room, Angela asked me if she should call Corrie to come down to the hospital, and I gave her a nod. It must be the lack of traffic on the road that gave them a smooth ride because they arrived around 1:00 a.m.

After Corrie and Steve came into the room, I told Yishan, "Corrie and Steve are here." He opened his eyes, looked at her, and said softly, "You've come too?" Then quickly, he closed his eyes again. I believe he knew why Corrie had come, but he did not show any sadness or unwillingness to die. His faith was totally in exhibit that night, and he demonstrated perfect peace, knowing where he was going. It was *I* who did not want him to leave, and I continued to keep him here by engaging him in conversation.

However, I was not able to do that too long, for shortly after Corrie and Steve arrived, the nurse came in and said again, "Two visitors only."

Steve left the room and I followed him into the hallway so that Corrie and Angela could stay with their Dad. I talked with Steve for only a short while, and then I began to make calls to funeral homes. I prayed, asking the Lord to guide me, and it seemed He did. I only had the numbers of two funeral homes, although there were more in this area. God seemed to weed out one and leave me only one choice, for only one of the two who answered my calls was able to contact a funeral director to call me back. And later on, I realized God did choose the best one. It is closer to where I live, and it is a much nicer place. I'm thankful that the Lord was guiding me in this respect, even when I did not have a chance to make previous contacts to make a choice.

It was probably around 2:10 a.m. or a little earlier when I finished contacting the funeral home. At that moment someone from church who had just sneaked up to the fourth floor informed me, "Mrs. Lin, there are many people from church who are gathering on the first floor. They all want to see Pastor Lin."

I told her it was impossible for them all to come up, and I felt very uneasy to have so many people staying in the hospital all night. So I asked her to send them home, but she was not sure how to do that.

In the end, I felt obligated to go down to the first floor to thank those people, to have a short prayer with them, and then to come back quickly. I told Angela my intention, and she objected, saying, "Mommy, don't." I knew her concern. She was afraid Yishan might expire while I was gone. But I felt I had no choice, and I went down to the first floor lobby.

Honestly speaking, I was overwhelmed to see possibly more than forty people there at such a late hour. They seemed to be gathered into two groups—a larger group nearer to the elevator and a smaller group farther away. Those who were nearest to the elevator immediately swarmed around me once I got out of the elevator, and they all asked me, "How's Pastor Lin?" One or two of them pointed out that small group to me, "Those are the newly elected deacons. They're praying."

Those deacons seemed to be ending their prayers, and soon more people came over to me. I quickly announced to the group Yishan's condition and asked them to pray with me. Then I said I would have to go back upstairs shortly. Three or four people prayed, and I ended by praying last. Once I said, "Amen," I immediately got up and walked toward the elevator. However, a few people detained me by asking more questions, and while I was still trying to get away, I saw the same woman who had informed me earlier of this gathering walking toward me and hurriedly saying, "Mrs. Lin, quick. Your daughter wants you to go upstairs right away. It seems Pastor Lin is expiring."

When I got back to the room, it was already too late. Yishan had expired. Angela told me that after I went downstairs, at first Yishan seemed to hold on and breathe smoothly. Then he began gasping for air, and Angela called the nurse who came quickly and put an oxygen mask over Yishan. After that, he was able to breathe smoothly again, but five minutes later he began to pant and gag again. All of a sudden, he just stopped breathing. It was then she sent that church member to tell me to come up.

All of a sudden, I felt empty inside. I felt as if everything was dark around me, although I knew the hospital room was brightly lit. Yet I also felt as if a staying hand were holding my shoulder and said, "It was *I* who took Yishan away. *Nobody* could have stopped Me from doing that." Even though I did not hear any voice at that time, the sense of those words was so clear to me that even to this day I still remember every word.

I would have blamed myself for not having stayed at Yishan's bedside when he left this earth. Later on I was told that some church members (especially a few deacons who turned very nasty against me) *did* blame me exactly for that, and I might have felt guilty. Yet because of those comforting words from the Lord, when I saw Yishan's cold and still form lying on the hospital bed, I could not cry or shed tears even at that moment, but I really regretted having been away from him, even for only those twenty or so minutes.

Yishan passed away at 2:30 a.m., California time, on June 15, 2002. In Cambridge, Massachusetts, where Leslie lived at that time, it was 5:30 a.m. Angela called Leslie thirty minutes later and woke her up. Upon hearing Angela's voice, Leslie said, "It's Boppy, right?"

"Yes, how do you know that?" asked Angela.

"I just had a dream," said Leslie. "I dreamed that Boppy was in the hospital and somebody told me Boppy had died." (It seemed to be God's way of letting Leslie take part in the bedside vigil since He knew Leslie could not be there in time.)

So what can I say? Our God indeed is sovereign and perfect in control. "There is a time to die" (Ecclesiastes 3:2). This was evidently so in Yishan's case.

Although Yishan was a baritone and never a tenor in his life, he seemed to have fit the definition of a tenor perfectly. If my memory has not failed me, I think it was Richard Tucker, the American tenor, who said, "A tenor is one who is shot [or wounded] at the end of the third act, but instead of falling down and die, he gets up and begins to sing." [Tucker was talking about the third act of an opera.]

When Yishan was wounded, he did not fall down. He picked up his speed and worked even harder. He was a warrior wounded by three major illnesses—heart attack, massive ulcerous bleeding, and leukemia. Anyone of those three illnesses might have been fatal right away to someone else, but by God's grace Yishan was allowed to live four and half more years after the first heart attack and continued to do his favorite work for the Lord. Then in God's time, the wounded warrior was taken home by the Lord. He *did* literally fall down and could rise no more.

Moses said, "The days of our years are threescore and ten; and if by reason of strength they be fourscore years" (Psalm 90: 10a). That was not so with Yishan. He was only sixty-four and a half when the Lord took him.

Chapter 26

He Leads On

The night Yishan left this earth was practically the longest night in my life. In a certain sense, it was also the beginning of a very long night for me.

After Yishan expired and the visit of church members to his room died down, Angela called Albert, woke him up from sleep, and asked him to come to the hospital. Sometime after Albert arrived, I asked all the four family members who were present to join hands with me, and together we worshipped the Lord.

We could not go home right away though and had to wait for the hospital staff to give us the proper papers before we could leave. When Albert and Angela finally took me home, it was already past 5:00 a.m., and in a short while it was daybreak.

I tried to get some sleep but could not. Having been up all night had raised my blood pressure, which had given me a headache and made sleep impossible. I got up and began to call friends near and far, telling them the news of Yishan's departure.

In fact, by the time Albert and Angela took me home and left, the thought that I was all alone and that I would never be able to see Yishan again (except when I go to heaven to be reunited with him) so overwhelmed me that I wept and wept. From then on when I was making a phone call or whenever I saw or heard of something that reminded me of Yishan, I would weep. Many times when I was driving on the freeway or on roads that Yishan and I had traveled together, it was easy to be reminded of Yishan, and tears would always come out. Those tears came easily without any warning.

Although I knew Yishan had gone to a better place and that I would see him again someday, the fact that I was separated from him and could not have his company for who knows how long really made me very sad. I could not control the sadness or the weeping. I still remember the first time I went out for a walk after Yishan was gone. We used to go out walking together. Yishan knew I did not like walking alone; so there was only once or twice I went out by myself. About a month after Yishan was gone and all my relatives had gone back to Taiwan, I went out for a walk (for health reason) alone. As I walked on the sidewalks of those familiar streets, I could not help looking at the flowers planted in people's front yard and felt as if those flowers were talking to me. "See, you are all alone now! You and your husband used to walk together, but now you are only one person." Although I continued to walk, tears just rushed out of my eyes like a broken dam. Not only that, at the same time I felt as if my whole body were thrown up into the air and my heart had been wrenched out of my chest.

I love hymns. Singing hymns or listening to hymns usually brings me great joy. However, the first several months after Yishan was gone, hymns often brought me tears. When I was listening to them, some of those hymns sounded just so sad that tears would stream down my face. Or if I heard hymns about heaven or if those hymns brought back memories of bygone days, tears would surely flow out freely.

The sadness and weeping were so debilitating and so painful to me that I asked the Lord to take my sadness away. Although I did not hear any audible voice from the Lord, I was quite certain He answered my request by saying, "I made human beings, and I made your emotions. It's a miracle I will not perform. You'll have to deal with it yourself."

I was desperate, and I acted as if I had almost lost my mind. I went upstairs and downstairs, going into every room, trying to find if I could see Yishan. I ended up going through our photo albums one by one to look for Yishan's pictures. There were actually not that many pictures of Yishan because he loved photography, and most of the pictures in the albums were those he had taken of others instead of himself. I remember I always had to insist on taking pictures for him. Otherwise he would have practically left very few pictures of his own.

Back in Schaumburg in the days of the Cedar church, a year or two after *Fish and Loaves* was published, Yishan began taping the messages we preached. He was so interested in running a tape ministry that he continued it at SCC, which we started after leaving THC.

It was good that he left boxes and boxes of message tapes in the closet of his study. I took those tapes out and began listening to them one by one so that I could hear his voice.

When I listened to those tapes, sometimes I felt like the balm of Gilead was healing my heart, but sometimes his words brought back the memory of unhappy scenes at church or people who had hurt me. In the latter case, I would weep and feel sad. A lot of times I would end up praying for healing. I knew the Lord who had seen everything knew how I had suffered and that He would help me. It was during one of those times when I began to write this book, starting sometime in August 2002. Writing this book has been therapeutic for me, for in writing these stories I was able to see God's greater picture for the first time and truly understand the Lord's purpose for my life, and it provided closure for my many sufferings. Praise the Lord!

The day after Yishan's death was Father's Day. Weeks before that, Yishan had arranged for a guest speaker to come for that Sunday. Thus, instead of going to church, I was able to go to the funeral home that afternoon to discuss on funeral arrangements. It was good the Lord had told Angela to clear her calendar so that she was able to accompany me that whole afternoon. Even though I had helped people make funeral arrangements twice before, I was amazed and sometimes felt a little dismayed to realize that I had to go into so many details in making decisions for Yishan's funeral service. We spent a total of five hours there. In the middle of it, I was so fatigued (for having lost so much sleep in two nights) that I actually had to put my head down on the table for a little nap.

In such a time as this I was sure the Lord was holding me up with His strong arm and giving me His wisdom. I'll just give one example here. One of those decisions was for me to pick the kind and the pattern of the urn for Yishan's ashes. (Many times when Yishan was conducting a funeral service, he had commented on burial being too costly. We had both expressed our preference for cremation, and that was the only easy part in that whole afternoon's decision-making process.)

When I was shown the different kinds and colors of urns and the different patterns of just one type of urn, I felt lost. Angela was there to help me, but a lot of times I was the one who had to make the decision. There were at least sixty patterns for the type of urn I had picked. The picture of each was so small that it made my head dizzy just to look at them.

I bowed my head and asked the Lord to help me. I then picked one that looked the most beautiful, but I was really not sure how the actual urn would look. However, the funeral counselor had to check if it was in stock, and a few minutes later, she asked me to take another pick since the one I had just picked was not in stock. She said I would have to wait for at least a month and half if I wanted something not in stock because they would have to order for it from China. In the end, I decided not to take another pick. I told the funeral counselor I would rather wait.

When finally I was told that the urn had arrived sometime in August, we then set a date for interment service. A total of more than twenty people came for that service. When I looked at that urn, my heart was full of praise and thanks for the Lord. On the urn there were colorful flowers and *butterflies*—the very symbol of resurrection. I knew it was worth the wait, and indeed, the Lord had helped me in taking the right pick.

Earlier that year in February, upon hearing Stanford doctors' death sentence on Yishan, our three daughters with their husbands and fiancé came home for a family meeting. In the middle of that discussion, Leslie asked me a question, "Should Corrie move up her wedding date?"

I asked Corrie if that was possible, and she answered, "It will be difficult." Her wedding plan was to include the help of a lot of her and Steve's friends. Moving up her wedding date would really be too complicated. Upon hearing her explanation, I then said, "Let's keep the same date. If God wants Boppy to attend Corrie's wedding, He'll keep Boppy here longer. If He wants to take Boppy home before that, then His will be done."

Yishan's funeral service was held on June 29, 2002, and a week later on July 6, Corrie's wedding took place. The funeral service was so arranged that two of my sisters and one brother as well as one of Yishan's sisters could attend *both* services.

Neither the funeral nor the wedding was easy for me. I continued to lose so much sleep, and yet there were so many things to take care of that I just could not find the quiet time to prepare the message for the memorial service. Especially during the service when so many people were wiping tears from their eyes, I found it extremely difficult to control my own tears. In the middle of delivering the message, I had to stop and wipe the tears that had begun to form in my eyes. Thanks to the Lord, I was able to complete delivering that message without any problem. After we came home from the service, Yishan's sister commented that I was very strong. How wrong she was to have that thought! I'm sure the Lord was carrying me in His arms during those days just as it was said in the famous article "Footprints in the Sand."

It was the same with Corrie's wedding. She had asked me to walk down the aisle with her, and when we were standing together, waiting for the music to begin, I suddenly had to dry my eyes. Quickly, I prayed to the Lord for help. I was able to hold strong when I was walking and standing there. Then when the pastor who officiated the wedding asked who was giving Corrie away to be married, and I had to answer, "On behalf of my late husband and myself, I do," I almost choked. Nevertheless, before the wedding was over, I had to wipe my eyes again and again. I tried to be joyful for Corrie's sake, but it was impossible to suppress my own sadness.

Almost from the beginning when I lost Yishan, I found I had also lost my appetite. I knew I had to eat, and I forced myself to have at least two meals a day. But it was a losing battle. Although it was *always very hard* for me to lose weight before that, in less than six months after Yishan's passing, I lost more than twenty pounds and weighed only 102 pounds, the very same weight I was when I came to the United States in September 1965. (That summer before coming to the United States, I was very busy and lost some weight.) One can say that this was *the only good thing* for me from losing Yishan.

Difficult as my situation was, it was almost impossible to imagine that some people at church would make it even more difficult for me. Unfortunately, that was exactly what happened. *If* I had not been a Christian for so many years and known the Lord in such intimate ways, I might have ended up losing my faith after being treated in this way by those people. (I have known people who stumbled or even lost faith just for experiencing adversity, not to mention being treated unkindly by Christians.) I don't want to go into details about this. Suffice it to say that it was *so* difficult for me that by the Labor Day weekend of that year (less than three months after Yishan's departure), I decided to leave the church, and I went to Taiwan on October 31. Somebody said that I was "kicked out" into the street. Quite true.

(I think I must mention something here lest I should be misunderstood to be a bitter person. It was an act of kindness some church families showed to me and Yishan a few months back when I was unable to walk and had to use a wheelchair for a whole month. During that month those church families signed up to bring me and Yishan meals each day for a whole month, each day brought by a different family. I would never forget that kindness shown to us during our very difficult times. There were truly more people who showed kindness to me than those who were unkind.)

I stayed up almost the whole night on Friday before that Labor Day, not because I wanted to but rather the burden in my heart kept me from falling asleep. I got up to pray around 3:00 a.m., and I felt the Lord saying to me, "I'll set you free." I took it to mean that I could leave that church. I then went downstairs to pick up hymns for that coming Sunday's worship service. When I opened the hymnal,

I immediately saw the titles—one on the left-hand page said, "Cast Thy Burden Upon the Lord," and on the right-hand side said, "Peace I Leave with You."

The Lord is so good. He made His will and guidance so clear to me. Praise Him!

Yes, I'm free, but being free also means I'd have no job and no income. Yet I had no fear, for the Lord is faithful.

The very next day, which was Sunday, I told the chairman of the deacons' board that I was going to stay at church only until the end of October. That evening a couple I had helped years before when I was at another church came unexpectedly to visit me. When they left, they gave me an envelope, and when I opened it, I found a $200 check inside. Again, I felt the Lord was saying, "Do not be afraid. I'll be responsible for your financial needs."

The Lord is faithful. It's been more than thirteen years since Yishan went home to be with the Lord, and He has not let me suffer any lack. During 2004, He gave me a job to work as translator/interpreter for an American church in Milpitas, north of San Jose. It was a job I did not want to take at the beginning, but the Lord used three people to speak the same message to me, "Mrs. Lin, you are most suitable for this job." Although I *tried* to avoid taking that job in the process of application and interviews, it still fell into my lap eventually. However, I praise the Lord for giving me that job. I worked on that job for a total of nine months, and in the end, I realized I *needed* that job not only for the income, but more importantly, the Lord used it to restore in me faith in the love and goodness of church people. How wise our Heavenly Father is in guiding His children!

Maybe I can mention here something else that happened that same Labor Day weekend of 2002. That Friday or Saturday somebody said to me over the phone, "Mrs. Lin, I think you are hogging all the church ministries to yourself." This unjustified accusation, of course, only added more burden to the already overloaded sadness of my heart. It seemed nobody knew it, but God did.

Three weeks later I received a phone call from a woman in Oakland, one that I had taught in a seminary a few months earlier, but she was not a member of our church. Nor was she aware of my great difficulties at church. When I answered the phone, she said, "Mrs. Lin, three weeks ago the Lord told me to give you a Scripture verse and to pray for you to bless you. I'm sorry I have not called you until now."

"That's okay," I said. "What verse?"

"Ezekiel 13:22," she said.

I opened my Chinese Bible to Ezekiel 13:22 and read it, and then I knew the Lord was giving me encouragement while at the same time rebuking my accuser as well as the others who were giving me a hard time. Here, let me translate the Chinese version of Ezekiel 13:22 into English, and then you'll understand. "I did not cause the righteous grief, but you have brought grief to the righteous with your lies. And you have strengthened the hands of the wicked so that he will not turn from wickedness to be saved."

When encountering important Bible verses, I usually compared different versions since the difference in translation could render the meaning of that passage clearer and easier to understand. So after reading the Chinese Bible, I did compare it to other versions—KJV, NASB, NIV, TLB, GNB, RSV, and AMP.

The meaning of all the different English versions of Ezekiel 13:22 is pretty much the same to me, but the translation of those versions differ from the Chinese version, primarily in the order of the clauses as well as their different positions in the sentences. And it seems to me, at that time when I read that Chinese version, it really spoke directly to my heart and brought me no small consolation.

Remember my prayer for Yishan's mother? The night of June 14 when Yishan was in the hospital and I came home briefly to bathe but prayed instead, I asked the Lord to help my mother-in-law and comfort her if He was not going to heal her son so that she would be able to cope with the loss. The Lord *answered that prayer* in a most marvelous way.

My two sisters went to visit Yishan's mother in Hsinchu City before they came to the United States to attend Yishan's funeral. My eldest sister, who was the only Christian among my three sisters, told me the following story, which I was later able to confirm with Yishan's mother, and thus, I got a better understanding of exactly what happened to her.

After I called Yishan's second sister and told her of Yishan's departure, neither she nor her family members dared to inform their ninety-two-year-old mother of the sad news. They were afraid she would not be able to cope with it. Yet Yishan's mother saw everything—the phone call and how everybody hushed. She figured out it concerned Yishan, and she felt as if some large rock were lodged in her chest. She did not talk and could not eat for a whole day. She just sat there watching TV, and her daughter was really scared.

Then the next day while she sat there in front of the TV, she saw many ants on the left side of the long coffee table in front of her. Upon my further inquiry when I saw her in November, she explained those ants were light blue-gray in color and larger than their actual size in life, all of them crowded together in a boxlike rectangular frame that was also colored in light blue-gray. When I heard her explanation, I knew she had seen a vision, but at the time of its happening, neither she nor her second daughter understood it to be a vision. They both thought she had seen real ants. Yishan's sister did not see those ants. She only heard about them from her mother.

My mother-in-law said, "I had never seen so many ants at one time, and I felt prickly. So I got up and went to the kitchen to get a rag to wipe the ants, but when I returned to the table, the ants were no longer there."

"Still the next day," Yishan's mother continued, "when I was sitting here, I saw two lone ants, same color and size as the ones I saw in the previous day, moving in front of me on this table, one following the other, and then they were gone. After I saw those ants, the large rock was dislodged from my chest, and I did not feel sad anymore. Nor did the thought of loss ever bother me again."

How I want to praise our great God for showing such wonderful mercy on my aged mother-in-law! But why did the Lord use ants in those two visions?

There is a Chinese saying, "Human lives are like ants," meaning life is short and fragile. Indeed, in the sight of our great Creator, human beings are pretty much as fragile and insignificant as tiny ants. Yet God so loved us that He sent His Son, Jesus, to die on the cross in order to redeem us!

The first vision with many ants crowded together in one boxed frame represented many people attending Yishan's funeral in the church. I had at first estimated three hundred people at the most. However, as I continued to receive phone calls from people who planned to attend the funeral, I had to revise my estimation to 450, and we had to move to a larger church. In the end, some people had to go to an overflow meeting hall to watch closed-circuit TV of the service, and still others had to stand outside. I was told a total of six hundred came to the memorial service that day.

My mother-in-law's second vision involving only two ants was actually the Lord's revelation of a touching personal event—the reunion of Yishan with his saved father in heaven. Praise the Lord for comforting my mother-in-law in such a wonderful way!

Well, the Lord let me deal with my own grief for a *long* time. Of course, we know God has different plans for different individuals, and He usually does not necessarily deal with each one of us in the same way.

For the first month, I had one question in mind, but I never dared to ask God because I was afraid it might be an act of disbelief. I knew God never made mistakes, but I just could not understand why He chose not to heal Yishan. The question I really wanted to ask was, "Lord, You have the power to heal, and You need many workers for Your vineyard. Why didn't You heal Yishan so that he could continue to work for You?"

Of course, God is omniscient, and none of our thoughts can escape His notice. On a Wednesday night a few weeks later after I came home from the prayer meeting, I lay awake on the carpeted floor from midnight to 3:00 a.m. (I had to sleep on a hard surface instead of a mattress since my back pain from the degenerated disc was not completely healed.) By 3:00 a.m., I was quite tired and groggy, but all of a sudden, I felt clearly like a man was walking toward me and saying, "His work on earth is done."

Those words given in English (not Mandarin) were definitely clear in my mind. I'm sure it was the Lord's answer to my unuttered question.

One question was out of the way, but my heart still could not be consoled. "Rachel weeping ... and would not be comforted" (Matthew 2:18). It was *not* because I stubbornly refused to be comforted, although I *did* feel the Lord speaking to me and comforting me again and again, using the Bible or devotional articles, or through different speakers on the radio I listened to. I was not turning a deaf ear to the Lord's voice, but each time my uplifted spirit would just quickly sink again.

After spending four weeks in Taiwan, I came back on Thanksgiving evening. On the next morning when I saw the pile of fallen leaves in my backyard, I shed a lot of tears. Later that afternoon when I drove to the post office to pick up the vacation mail and saw on both sides of the street the red and yellow leaves on the trees and the fallen leaves on the ground, I was practically in tears all the way there. Autumn used to be my favorite season, but that first changing season of my widowhood served as a poignant reminder of the changing season in my own life and brought a lot of tears to my eyes.

That first Christmas Eve, I attended a service at Angela's church. Since I took a bath before I left home, after I came home, I immediately changed into pajamas and went to bed. Yet inevitably, I thought, *Oh no, nobody is going to say, "Merry Christmas," to me tomorrow morning.* However, I quickly stopped myself from further thoughts and was able to fall asleep right away.

On Christmas morning I woke up around 8:50 a.m., but I continued to lie in bed since I still felt tired. Suddenly, the phone next to my bed rang, and I picked it up and said, "Hello." Then I realized the phone was *dead* since I had unplugged it more than twenty-four hours ago and had not plugged it back in. I had also noticed the ring tone to be much softer than usual (that phone was unusually loud and noisy), and the ringing had actually come out not directly from the phone. No, it seemed to come out of the air at least a few inches on top of that phone. At that moment I knew God had allowed Yishan to come back to say, "Merry Christmas."

Having been married to Yishan for thirty-six years, it was very difficult if not impossible to remove Yishan from my thoughts, and I continued to grieve for him for three more years. (I grieved for a total of three and half years.) Leslie's family came to California for Christmas 2005, and they left on the evening of January 6, 2006. After they left, I busied myself in cleaning up the bathroom. Then when I sat down in front of the mirror, I felt lonely and sad again.

I had the habit of turning on the radio to listen to hymns or classical music (on different stations) when I sat in front of the bathroom mirror. When I first plugged the radio in, a man was talking, and I did not pay attention to what he said. However, when I began to feel sad, all of a sudden, I *heard* the voice on the radio saying, "Grieve no more. Rejoice! Does the Bible say, 'Rejoice in the Lord,' or 'Grieve in the Lord?'"

Wow! The Lord got my attention, and I heard Him speaking to me through that person. From that moment on, even though my grief did not go away immediately, those words began to work their effect on me. Every time I began to feel sad, those words would immediately come back to remind me that God wanted me to rejoice, not to grieve, and thus I was able to put a break on the sadness.

Today I seldom miss Yishan, fourteen years after his departure. And even once in a while when I miss Yishan again, I kneel and pray, and the Lord always helps me and gives me peace again. Occasionally, I still talk to friends about him, but there is *no more* grief. Of this I am sure. I can praise and thank the Lord because He has restored His fullness of joy in me. God has shown me His perfect grace by giving me ten grandchildren and a lot of joy as well. What more can I ask?

For a long time after I lost Yishan, I thought I would never have this joy again, *not without* Yishan. Yet the Lord has proven to me *again* nothing is impossible with Him (Matthew 19:26; Mark 10:27) and that *He* is the one who gives us the true joy. In January to February 2004, He led me on a short-term mission trip to a college campus in

New Mexico. (If Yishan were still here, I would not have made that trip, or if I did—or if *we* did—the result would be totally different.)

Sometime before that trip, a former seminary student of mine contacted me. She told me she had been working as a missionary with the Chinese students Bible study group on that New Mexico campus for more than a year. There was one person who deciside to accept Jesus, but *none* was willing to receive baptism. I asked her if all those students were from China, and she said yes. Those students were either working on master's degrees or PhDs, or they already had PhD and were working on postdoctoral studies. I then asked her to arrange four meetings for me so that I could bring the four messages I spoke in Hungary. She arranged for me to speak on two consecutive weekends—Saturday evenings and Sunday mornings.

While I was there, besides speaking on the weekends, I also accompanied my former student on some visitation errands during the weekdays, doing evangelism as well as caring for some families with special needs. Toward the end of that trip, I realized I was so full of joy that I had forgotten to feel sad.

After I came back, a few students were baptized on the following Easter Sunday and still a few more on that year's Christmas Sunday.

I knew the barrier to those students' faith was evolution, and the Lord used me to bring the breakthrough. That gave me a lot of joy. Praise the Lord!

On the Memorial Day of 2003, almost a year after Yishan's departure, I went out for a walk as usual. Around that time I heard on TV the news of a thirty-nine-year-old missing woman in Walnut Creek (almost an hour's drive from my place). She went out after lunch for a walk on a trail near her workplace and never returned, and many days later her body was found by the side of that trail. She had been assaulted and killed. So naturally, I was very careful when I went out for walks since I had no one to accompany me.

That Memorial Day I walked for about fifty minutes, and I was ready to come home. As I was going to cross the street to walk past the small park not too far from my home, I saw a cab parked in front of the park with its driver sitting inside, and these words (in Mandarin) came into my head, "This man is going to follow me."

Immediately, I knew God was warning me, but I continued on my course, crossed the street, and walked on the sidewalk outside the park. As I walked, I noticed that driver, a man from India, was watching me, and he began to move that cab. However, when he came to the intersection, he turned his cab around and began to drive in the same direction as I was walking. After the cab drove past me, I walked across the street and continued on the other side.

By that time, the cab was near the north end of the street, and it should have turned right to continue. However, that driver must have been afraid of losing sight of me since his cab was faster and he was ahead of me. He turned around and drove past me again in the opposite direction.

It was obvious by now this driver was trying to find out where I lived. On my previous walks, I had seen his cab parked on the street, and he probably had noticed I was alone.

If I continued to walk on that street, I would have to make two right turns around this block, and eventually, I would have to cross the street again (the same street I crossed when God warned me) before I could reach home.

Before I came near home, I stopped. If that driver was going to follow me, his cab would be coming on the street in front of my house, and indeed, I saw the cab passing me and going eastward. After passing me, he came back again, driving westward, and stopped in the middle of the block.

By this time I was tired and wanted to go home, but I couldn't. I decided to walk around this block one more time. However, I stopped to pray before I turned right and walked westward. I prayed, "Lord, take him away." I also decided to take a good look at his cab number (not the license plate number, which was too long), and if he continued to follow, I would knock on one of the neighbors' door and call the police to report the name of his cab company and the cab number. His cab number was 118.

That driver continued to watch me. Then when I walked past

him, he pulled his cab away. I continued to walk around the block and again came to the same place where I had to cross the street to reach home or to turn right to continue the walk. I stopped to look right and left and made sure the cab was not in sight. Then I crossed the street and came home. When I asked the Lord to take him away, I had a strong sense that the Lord said to that man, "Leave her alone, or I'll kill you." Of course, I had no way of ascertaining this, but the Lord *did* answer my prayer exactly as I had requested.

From that day on, I never ventured out to take another walk by myself, not until I moved away.

A week before this happened, I had begun to think about getting a treadmill. On rainy days or when it is too hot, I could stay home and exercise indoors.

After that Memorial Day, I began to look for ads in the newspaper, and I saw a Sears ad for a treadmill on sale at $1,299.95, one at $699.95, and another at $299.95. I thought I could afford the cheapest one and decided to get it.

Well, my birthday was coming up, and that Friday evening at the Bible study that I was leading my group members gave me two envelopes. One had five twenty-dollar bills inside, and the other a $200 check, a total of $300. I only had to pay $15 for the sales tax. I felt the Lord was saying, "See? I told you I'd provide for your financial need."

When I began using the treadmill, I could walk only as fast as 2.9 miles per hour. If I tried to run at 3.5 miles per hour, I would be panting like crazy and would have to quickly scale down back to 2.9 miles per hour. Praise the Lord for providing this equipment to make me stronger and healthier. Later on I could start at 3.5 miles per hour and quickly move to 4.0 and maintain between 4.2 and 4.6 for a much longer time. Then the Lord allowed me to see some very good results.

On January 29, 2006, I fell backward on a parking lot. As I got out of the car and turned to close the door, I felt a cord tripping my high heels. The feeling was unmistakable, although I knew there was no cord on the parking lot pavement. As I fell, I was afraid of a possible concussion like what happened to me back in 1973 (chapter 10). So as I fell, I tried to brace my neck in order to avoid danger to the back of my head, although I knew this was actually dangerous because I might suffer neck injury instead. Yet in that split second, I had no other choice.

Well, my right elbow and left hip simultaneously hit the pavement very hard, and I felt pain in both places; however, I was able to avoid being hit in the back of my head. I was stunned, but I was able to get up quickly. My neck was fine. I was able to walk as fast as usual as if nothing had happened. Only later in that evening I felt pain in my right elbow. That was all, no bleeding or bruises at all. I know of two or three people who fell at my age *on carpet* and suffered fractures in the hip or kneecap. I'm very thankful I was totally fine, thanks to the fact that the Lord gave me the treadmill to work on and to improve my health, especially my bones, so that I was able to get away without any fractures to any of my bones.

As for the invisible cord, obviously, Satan had tried to harm me, but God allowed it to happen to prove to me that my bones were strong enough to withstand the attack. More importantly, I was able to see the grace of God in my life one more time.

Then on August 26 of that same year, I was awarded an honorary doctor's degree by Andrew University of Berkeley, California. This whole thing was really out of the blue. Only a little earlier in late July or early August, I learned of this good news, but I had no idea what kind of degree I would be receiving. On the day of the commencement, I saw my name printed on the program with the degree of doctor of humanities. Again, this had to be the Lord's doing. He knew I had given up my graduate teaching assistantship and advanced degrees in order to help Yishan, and He has rewarded me what I thought to have been lost to me. He is really the God who gives liberally.

I taught *creationism* one semester and *Genesis* another semester at Andrew University during Yishan's final year on this earth. (At that time he was its honorary president.) A couple weeks after receiving the honorary degree, I was asked to teach *creationism* again. I'm so happy the Lord is continuing to use me, even without Yishan on my side, especially for this opportunity to train His workers for the vineyard. It is quite rewarding to see the result of my teaching. At the beginning of the semester, you could see the skepticism in my students about the six literal days of creation because of the wide spread influence of evolution. Yet after many weeks of presenting evidence about the *absurdity of evolution and millions of years* and evidences for the global flood as given in the Bible, about the middle of the semester, I could see the change of attitude in the students. I'm only thankful that the Lord has allowed me to gather all this information to share with the students so that they can believe in the total credibility of the Bible. *If* I had majored in music instead of English when I went to college, I probably would not have this ability today. Praise our wonderful God in the way He has been leading my life. He has made my life meaningful!

The Lord also gave me the joy of leading a young woman to accept Jesus Christ during my grieving period. It was either during my first trip back to Taiwan in 2002 or the second one in 2003. I can't remember correctly now. She was one of the students I came in contact with when I was doing the translation work for the Christian college in Oakland. While I was working there, I tried to witness for the Lord whenever I had a chance. This student also took a few personal study courses from me that were authorized by that college for making up credits. I gave her Christian books to read for those courses and designed the assignments whenever I could to help her (as well as other students who also took those courses) in paying attention to questions related to the gospel message.

She was one of the students I often prayed for during those years. From the assignments she handed in, I felt she was very responsive to the gospel. So I called her during my trip to Taiwan, and she came to see me. At the end of that visit, I asked her if she was willing to accept Jesus Christ as her Lord and Savior, and she consented. I then led her in praying to accept Jesus, and at the end of her prayer, I found she was very moved and was in tears. It was one bright spot during my otherwise bleak period of mourning for Yishan.

Here I would like to mention something else before I go on to talk about my next story. However, first I need to backtrack to our final year at THC. Sometime in late summer of that year (1994), a Caucasian man (I'll call him John) who went to the English service of that church came to see Yishan. Actually, both he and his wife went to Yishan's office, and Yishan came to my office to ask me to help them. John had married a much younger Chinese woman. She was at least in her sixth or seventh month of pregnancy, but she wanted to terminate it by abortion.

Quite unfortunately, this is a prevalent story. A young Chinese woman who came to the United States was willing to marry a much older American man in order to obtain a legal status to stay in this country. And once she got her wish, she would ask for a divorce and sometimes, as probably in this case, would also want an abortion.

I did not have a chance to ask John if she wanted a divorce, but at that time what I cared most was what John had told me. He loved her, and he did not want the abortion. He was in tears when he told me this.

I happened to have some pictures in my office, and when Yishan asked me to help, I took those pictures with me. Those were printed pictures for a *Sanctity of Human Life Sunday* I had kept with me since our days with the Cedar church back in Schaumburg. Those pictures, which were actually photos, showed babies in their mother's wombs in different poses, one even sucking his thumb, showing these babies to be *human beings*.

Since John's wife was not that proficient in English, I talked to her primarily in Mandarin, and later I translated to John what I had said to her. I gave her Psalm 139:13–16, and I said, "God made human life, and abortion is murder."

Even before I finished talking, she was in tears. But then she went on to say she had many problems, and she was afraid she would not be able to take care of all the child's needs. I then told her about our days when Yishan was a graduate student and I was a poor student wife and how God took care of us. I also told her of how once many years ago my marriage with Yishan was in trouble and I was contemplating jumping into Lake Michigan and how God helped me out. I knew John was a true believer, but I was not sure about her spiritual condition. So I spent some time emphasizing faith in Jesus Christ, and I encouraged her to put her trust in the Lord Jesus, who would help them.

That was the only time I talked to John and his Chinese wife, and I really did not know what came out of that conversation. By the end of that year, Yishan and I left THC, and we never saw them again.

Well, not exactly. Eight years later God allowed me to see John again in August of 2002, a little more than two months after Yishan went home to be with the Lord. I was then grieving for Yishan and also suffering from the mistreatment by some church deacons, but God comforted me in a big way.

That day in August 2002 as I was walking in an Oriental grocery store, pushing a shopping cart down some aisles, suddenly I saw a Caucasian man with a young Chinese girl. Immediately, I recognized both faces, even though it was the first time I saw that Chinese girl. The man was John, and the girl was obviously his daughter. She was, you might say, a carbon copy of her mother. She was tall for her age, about eight, but then her mother was tall, and so was John. She was slender and quite beautiful with an innocent child's face. And from the way she talked to John, you could tell they were intimate with each other just as father and daughter should be.

However, John did not recognize me. Since I did not feel in the mood to greet John to dig up the past, I just continued to watch them for a while, and then I left.

I believe it was the Lord who led me to see John and his daughter that day. I felt as if the Lord were saying to me, "See that girl? You saved her life." Although I was in mourning, I was overjoyed and very thankful that the Lord had given me the opportunity to talk to that Chinese woman eight years earlier so that she was willing to carry her pregnancy to full terms and give life to this beautiful girl. I also figured out that probably John's young wife had divorced him and that he had raised his daughter all by himself. I think that was why they showed such closeness.

I had forgotten another story until I was ready to get this book out to the agent. It happened after I left SCC and went to a Taiwanese church where both Yishan and I were asked to train Sunday school teachers before (see chapter 20). Many people knew me, and one of them, a brother around fifty (I'll call him Sam), told me one Sunday during lunch that he was going to visit an elderly brother (I'll call him Brother Chen) who had cancer and was living in a convalescent home in San Jose. "Brother Chen's faith is faltering now," Sam said.

Brother Chen was in his seventies, and the first day I went to that church, he went to the podium and gave a report of his short-term mission trip to Taiwan. I did not know him, but another Sunday he brought to church something and kept it in the freezer in the church kitchen and brought it out to me during lunchtime. It was a plastic box full of small fish eggs, usually used for sushi, expensive stuff. Such a loving brother was suffering, and I decided to visit him the next day.

I had to drive on the freeway for some distance and then on city streets for some blocks before I found it. When I got there, it was near lunchtime, but Brother Chen suggested we go outside to the courtyard to talk. (his wife was there but she was distracted.) It was a nice place.

Satan was obviously trying to interrupt us because there were many distractions, but I kept praying in my heart. Finally, Brother Chen was able to listen quietly, and I shared with him two important things.

The first was the story of a young woman around twenty-six who was seriously ill and died. She went to heaven and saw a beautiful city as described in Revelation 21. She came back to life twenty-nine minutes later a changed person. Not only was she physically healed, but her former materialistic way was completely gone. From then on she began to crave the Bible, and one day when she read Revelation 21, she was surprised to find it to describe the same thing she saw in heaven.

Then I told him in great details about the shroud of Turin, which had been proven to be the genuine burial cloth of Jesus when He was taken down from the cross. I first learned of this in 1974 and later bought books on this topic or checked them out from the public library of Schaumburg, and after moving to California, I learned more from the radio program I listened to and bought one video on this study.

Therefore, I told that elderly brother, "We believers of Jesus Christ are blessed, for we have the hope of eternal life."

Before I left, Brother Chen said to me, "Today my faith is greatly strengthened!" Praise the Lord!

Finally, I want to talk about my eldest sister. I lost her in December 2004, almost two and half years after Yishan's departure. It *would* have been very difficult for me to take *if* the Lord had not shown His will and help to me in more ways than one.

Earlier that year back in January 2004 when I first heard my eldest sister was going to be operated on for colon cancer, I pleaded with the Lord, "Lord, it's been only eighteen months since you took Yishan. Please do not take my sister now. I cannot take it. I still need her here on earth."

My sister had delayed in telling her husband about the tumor she had detected in one side of her body back in March 2002. She did not tell her husband until November 2003. However, even then, she still tried to avoid operation and delay it until January 2004. By that time it was already too late. Doctors found the cancer had spread, and they were not able to remove all the cancerous cells. Although they did remove a large mass, they had to rely on chemotherapy, and they pronounced that my sister had only three to six months to live.

When I heard that, I cried to the Lord, "Please give my sister more time, Lord. Please heal her."

I was told that my sister's naval was always reddish after the first operation, indicating infection since her cancerous cells were not totally removed. By July of that year, doctors had to operate on her a second time and removed another large mass. Still, my sister needed another round of chemotherapy, but she refused it this time. Doctors said she would then have only two to three months left without the chemotherapy.

When I heard that, tears kept flowing out, and I bargained with the Lord, "Lord, You have already had a lot of people with you there in heaven, and I'm sure You do not mind having one fewer person. You have already taken Yishan, and I still need my sister here on earth. Please do not take her."

In September of that year, my younger sister called me, "If you want to see Eldest Sister's face, you'd better come back." I took two weeks off from my translation work at Christ Community Church of Milpitas and went to Taiwan. I found my eldest sister in a condition similar to Yishan's in his final two months, and I was worried. After I came back, I continued to pray for her and kept bargaining with the Lord.

By the middle of that October, my younger sister told me that the doctors were wondering why my eldest sister was still around. "Is she getting better or worse?" I asked.

"No, she is not getting better or worse," she replied. "She is just the same." I knew it was *because* the Lord had heard my prayer and had left my sister the way she was.

Toward the end of October, I heard that my sister was having pain and doctors were going to give her morphine. Still, I was not ready, and I kept asking the Lord to keep my sister here.

Then around December 3, about a week before Yishan's birthday, which was December 10, I received a phone call from my younger sister. "I just came back from visiting Eldest Sister at the hospice," she said. "She is having such pain that she needs morphine now. However, the amount of morphine is very hard to control. If enough is not given, she is still in pain, and if she is given too much, then she'll be sleeping all the time. This is really not the best way out."

When I heard that, I felt very guilty. I knew the Lord had kept my sister here for *my* sake, but now that she was having such pain, I could not be selfish anymore. In tears I said to the Lord, "Lord, You know how much I really want my sister to be here, but I'm not sure what I should ask now. Now that she is having such great pain, Lord, I release her to You. You know what is best for her."

As soon as I released my sister to the Lord, these words came into my head, "Will it be on Yishan's birthday?"

Yishan's birthday, as I have mentioned, was December 10. On that evening I cooked a few of Yishan's favorite dishes and had Angela's family come over to remember his birthday with me. We even sang "Happy Birthday, Ahgong" before we ate. (*Ahgong* is *grandpa* in Taiwanese.) After the dinner Angela's family had to leave right away since they had a Bible study at home that evening. (Angela usually stayed to help with washing dishes.) Around 7:20 p.m. when I was washing dishes, the phone rang. It was my second sister, "Hwa [my younger sister] just called from the hospice. She said Eldest Sister had passed away at 11:04 a.m."

So my eldest sister went home to be with the Lord on December 11, 2004, in Taiwan, but it was still December 10 here in the States, Yishan's birthday, exactly as the Lord had hinted to me.

The Lord is sovereign, but He is merciful. He had mercy on me and gave me almost a full year's time to prepare myself to accept the loss of my eldest sister, the only Christian among my sisters.

If I continue to tell how the Lord has been guiding me and taking care of me, I think I can write another book maybe titled *Life without Yishan*. In fact, during this period, sometime in April of 2005, the Lord once again gave me a major delivery from harm, one no less scary or dramatic than my earlier encounter with the car thief (chapter 17). In fact, to think about it, I realize it involved my safety or my very life even more so, but the story is be too long to tell here.

So I think this is the proper place to end my story, and I just want to say the Lord is indeed *the God of orphans and widows* exactly as He has promised in the Bible. I know He'll never abandon me, and if we are willing to trust Him, *He'll lead us on* until the day we see Him face-to-face.

Shanghai International Airport

Chapter 27

A Bonus Chapter

*T*his chapter was not included in my original manuscript, which was first completed in December 2008, and it has since gone through many revisions. With all the revisions, the contents have stayed pretty much the same, except a few places I added this year because of a reminder from the Lord. A few times I wondered if I should be adding more chapters since the Lord has continued to work in my life. In the end, however, I decided not to add any more since this book was long enough to me.

It is really the Lord's idea for me to write this book. English is not my native language and writing in English really presents some challenges to me, although I was trained in it. The Lord gave me the title and a brief outline of chapters in the beginning. And as I prayed throughout the process of writing, something long forgotten would come into mind, and I would add another chapter. When finally I finished the original manuscript, I thought that was it.

Well, at the beginning June of 2014, my world seemed to have collapsed all of a sudden. My sleeping pills quit working, and I went through what I call *the mad, mad world of sleeplessness*. The most amount of sleep I could get each day was only three or four hours, which was far from what I needed, even for one who is in her seventies. A lot of the times I was not even getting three hours of sleep. Maybe two hours or a little more than an hour. (I would like to know if there is a medical doctor who could figure out what would be my chances of surviving this ordeal under normal circumstances with my age and the little amount of sleep I had during these nearly two months.) From the beginning I knew I could not have survived it long unless the Lord did something supernatural to help me.

As it turned out, supernatural things the Lord did, by way of two provisions He put in my hand in 2013 when I came back from my first medical trip to Taiwan. (I'll explain more later.)

Still, I had no idea what the Lord was going to do with my book.

Then one day during that sleepless period, I felt the Lord wanted me to add another chapter to this book.

I'm sure you can see why I call this chapter "A Bonus Chapter," but why should I include it here?

You'll understand it once you finish reading the rest of this chapter. At this point, it is probably best for me to go back a little so that you can understand the whole thing. I have mentioned in an earlier chapter some of the difficulties I went through in moving from U City to my current place in June 2011. It took me more than eleven months to get my house sold and move. It was a very difficult move for me, much more difficult than that time when Yishan and I moved from Schaumburg, Illinois, to the San Francisco Bay Area in August 1989 (see chapter 15). After all, in 1989, I was twenty-two years younger, and I still had Yishan on my side. In June 2011, when I moved to the current place, I was living alone, and although Angela and Corrie with their husbands did come to help me a lot, most of the time I had to do everything by myself. Plus it was another economic downtime and very difficult to get the house sold. So no matter from which angle you look at it, it was really much harder for a much older me to move, even though it was only a two-hour drive away. As a result of this last move (I knew it could be my last move on this earth), I became more and more sleep-deprived after I moved into the current home, which is almost a thousand square feet less than my previous one. And you will understand why I gave up organizing after unpacking and found it impossible to fit everything into this small place. This house became a wreck, and I still had to try to live in it and still try to thank the Lord in all circumstances.

I have kept reminding myself that with my age and all that the Lord has given me, I should always be thankful no matter what. Yet I realize I'm an ordinary human being, still living in my fleshly shell. Despite the fact that God has been working so many wonderful things in my life, a lot of times it is still very easy for me to be disturbed by difficulties, and it seems that difficulties have followed me all the days of my life. When I decided to move to the current city, I knew it was God's will for me. Yet after I moved here and began to experience again one difficulty after another, I began to wonder why God wanted me to move here. Quite a few times I asked, "Lord, have You moved me to this place so that You can shorten my life and that I'll go to see You sooner?" I was not trying to complain. I just could not understand why in following God's will, I still had to encounter all the difficulties that seemed to never go away.

During this same time, I had also another question in my mind. It had been so many years since the last issue of *Fish and Loaves* was published, and although the Lord has never told me to quit during this time, I'm beginning to see that I'll never reach my goal of resuming the publication. "If it is already so difficult for me just to get my everyday things done, how would I ever be able to have the extra time to do the publication work for the Lord?" I could not help but question myself.

Unexpectedly, I became very ill soon after the turn of the new year in 2013, about a year and a half years after moving here. I had to go to the ER one night after waking up Corrie's husband, Steve, in the middle of the night and asking him to take me there. I received a CT scan that night, and sometime later an ultrasound and still much later an MRI. After all these I felt the Lord was saying to me, "I'm going to take you home. How about that?"

"Well," I told the Lord, "You know that I'm not afraid of death. Ever since I studied the book of Philippians in Schaumburg more than thirty years ago and read what Paul said, 'It is far better for me to be with the Lord,' I have been waiting for You to take me home." When the Lord took Yishan home in 2002, I actually questioned Him, "Lord, have You taken the wrong person home? It is I who has been longing to go to heaven, and I have never wanted to live a long life. It was Yishan who had wanted to live a long life, and why did You take him home instead of me?" I know we should never question God, and yet it was so difficult for me at that time I just could not help asking the Lord that question. Of course, the Lord later told me that Yishan's work on earth was done and that I had to accept all that was God's good will and question it no more.

When my younger sister who lives in Taiwan heard of my illnesses (pains in many parts of my body, including toothache, prickly pains on the skins of my four limbs, difficulty in swallowing, difficulty in walking, etc.) and all the diagnoses given by various doctors (cyst on my pancreas, hepatitis B, besides possible fibromyalgia, which I learned about from a website link Angela sent me), my sister became very angry and said to me, "So you will sit there for six months and wait for that cyst to develop into cancer! Why don't you come back to Taiwan to seek medical help? There are many good doctors here in Taiwan now."

In the beginning I was very hesitant to go to Taiwan. I prayed, but the Lord did not give me the answer right away. Then some friends drove from F City to visit me in April, one of them a TCM (traditional Chinese medicine) doctor. She said after hearing my description of my symptoms without even feeling my pulse, "I think you should visit a TCM doctor and get some acupuncture treatments."

I ended up making two medical trips to Taiwan in 2013, one for six weeks from May to June and the second trip from the last day of October to late November. On the last night of my first trip while I was packing for my return flight, two women came to see me. One was a friend. The other was a total stranger who had heard so much about me from my friend that she was very interested and wanted to meet me. They gave me two bottles (one from each of them) of natural supplements that they claimed could help repair the damages done to my body by a medication I had taken for four years to treat my very minor osteoporosis problem. (Treating a minor problem brought many more serious problems to me! A gift from my former doctor, but in the end, I found it to be a gift from the Lord.)

Around September 20, 2013, I began to take that supplement, and a month later I found it to be working and helping me! When I went to Taiwan and met those two women again during my second trip, the younger woman was surprised and said to my friend, "Look! She's taking that supplement, only one dosage a day, and how come it's helping her?" I had been told that taking one dosage a day was only for those who want to maintain their health. In my case I should have taken more than a dosage a day.

My friend answered her, "Have you not heard her say that she prayed to the Lord to help her so that she could see the result even though she was only taking one dosage a day?"

I continued to take one dosage a day until February 2014. I felt then that I needed to increase the dosage so that my other damages could be healed as well.

I started to take sleeping pills back in 2004 or 2005. At that time, obviously because of my hysterectomy in 1989 and also because of my advancing age, my body was not able to produce enough hormone(s) needed to help me sleep. Up to June 2011 when I moved here, I was able to fall asleep after taking only one pill. After moving here, however, probably because of the stress of the many demands I had to face alone, I had to increase the dosage of sleeping pills every few months until December 2013 when I had to increase my dosage from one and a half to one and three quarter tablets.

On December 10, which was Yishan's birthday, I drove back to F City to lay fresh flowers at Yishan's nitch, and when the current pastor of SCC heard that, he invited me to lead the fellowship group that I used to lead until I moved away. It was the first time I led that group in more than two years. I met the pastor and his wife that day for the first time, but other than being together for the meeting and asking him to pray at the conclusion of the meeting, we did not engage in any conversation to get to know each other. He gave me the impression that he was a spiritual man. I was simply too busy talking to all the members who were so glad to see me again that I did not have time to talk to the pastor or his wife. (I guess I was overjoyed in seeing that group again that I did not really behave properly.)

Soon after coming back from that trip to F City, I began to have serious trouble with sleep again, and that was when I began to take the maximum two tablets of sleeping pills for each night.

My first four months of 2014 following that were packed with activities. I felt a need to receive acupuncture treatments again and also to replenish my supply of Chinese medicine prescribed by the TCM doctor, so I purchased an airline ticket. It was always a hassle for me to purchase an airline ticket online. Then Leslie came with her six-month-old baby, Xavier, and I needed her help in getting new software installed on the new laptop, which she had ordered for me and had arrived just in time. (In 2013, a few days after my arrival in Taipei, my three-year-old laptop broke down, and I had to spend close to $300 to get it fixed. I was afraid of losing important documents on my computer, and that was why I wanted a new laptop.) I left for Taiwan on March 26, 2014 and came back on April 16. It was near tax time, and I had to get it done before leaving for Taiwan. Plus I had to pack for my trip. Adding all these together, it was simply too overwhelming for me. No wonder I lost a lot of sleep, and that final week leading up to (and including) the night on the flight, I had a total of eighteen hours of sleep only. Just think—eighteen hours of sleep for a whole week! Would you be able to take it? During the three weeks in Taiwan, my sister took total care of me without my having to cook or wash dishes. Well, I made up a lot of sleep, and for several days I almost slept day and night, except for some necessary activities. Toward the second half of my stay, I was getting back to normal and slept not as much.

After returning home, because I had to do everything on my own and could never get things done in time, I soon slipped back to the habit of going to bed at two or three, but I still had difficulties falling asleep despite my taking the maximum dosage of sleeping pills already. I was heading for a disaster without realizing it.

The week before Mother's Day, I was surprised by a phone call and then a visit from the current pastor of SCC. He invited me back to preach at that church, and I did on May 18. On May 20, I led the fellowship group's Bible study again and then came back in the afternoon by Amtrak train. On the train the Lord unexpectedly gave me an opportunity to pray for a young woman who was very sick and groaning and turning. Obviously, the Lord heard my prayer and relieved some of her pain, and she was able to fall asleep. After waking up, she was able to eat a little food. I did not have enough time to pray more for her, and in fact, I was almost unable to get off the train in time when it arrived at my destination.

After coming home, as I thought more of what happened on the train, I was very thankful for our Lord Jesus Christ, who paid the ransom price for all of us on the cross so that we could become children of God and receive the privilege to come to His throne of grace to ask for anything. What a privilege it was for me to be God's channel of grace in seeing that woman get better right in front of my eyes after my simple prayer for her! She was obviously a nonbeliever. She did not even say, "Amen," when I finished praying for her in the name of our Lord, and yet that day she got introduced to the power of our Lord.

That day when I returned from F City, I was praising God on the train for seeing that He had smoothed the rough places of my life in the past few years (Isaiah 40:4). I have always believed God will honor His own word if we truly believe in Him, and this time He certainly did it again as He had done so many times in my past.

It seemed that while I was savoring the sweetness the Lord had given me, all of a sudden a most unbearable bitterness befell upon me, and I was almost suffocated by it. However, the Lord prevailed once again, upholding me with His righteous right hand. How would I be able to survive this two-month-long ordeal of sleeplessness with at most only three hours a day? Hypertension brought along by lost sleep is one of the most dreaded things that can happen to one, I've noticed in recent years in the news about the medical field, and personally, I had my own share of it in the past. I knew I might have lost my life under normal conditions.

However, as it turned out, as so many times in my life already, the Lord was in control, and although it is probably the lowest valley I had ever gone through in my life, much worse than the time following my loss of Yishan, the Lord was with me, talking to me almost daily. So far I had not been swamped over by the overwhelming floodwaters. How did He do it? First by that supplement I began to take in September of 2013, and then by something He taught me. The year before in June, right after I came back from Taiwan, I asked God, "Now that I can receive no more acupuncture treatments, Lord, what should I do?"

He told me, "Hit your head with your ten fingernails." And I found it to be very effective in relieving headaches caused by hypertension because of sleep loss.

As I have mentioned, by February of 2014, I began taking two dosages of that supplement each day instead of the one dosage daily in the beginning. Then one day around April or May (now I do not remember which date), I began to take three dosages each day, thinking I needed more of it.

A few days after taking the increased dosages, I noticed some more improvements to my body. I was fully aware of what the Lord was doing to repair the damages that had been caused by that medication I had taken for four years. Of course, I was thanking the Lord every day. Then a few days later, something totally unexpected happened, and I became scared and said, "Lord, halt it. Please tell that supplement to repair only the parts of my body that need to be repaired and not to go beyond. I don't want this new stuff." I knew my body was producing estrogen again, which my body had stopped producing for some years.

The Lord said to me, "You need that."

"I need that?" I was puzzled.

"Yes, you need it so that it will be easier for you to fall asleep again."

Indeed, *He is Lord and the Creator of our bodies.* Of course, He knows better what to do than anyone of us could ever imagine.

He then told me why all these years He had kept me from going back to the publication of *Fish and Loaves*. He clearly said, although not audibly, "I deliberately kept you from doing it because I'm not ready to use you again until I'm through with purifying you. That's why I'm dealing with this in you now. Your body has become pretty much a dead body that would have been put away in a few years, and physically, you were no longer fit to be used by Me. I'm leading you through the death and resurrection process so that you'll receive a new and more dynamic body to work for me again."

I must admit, as I have mentioned earlier in this chapter, before this whole thing occurred I had been living the last several years with dazed feelings, wondering how I would ever be used by the Lord again. Wow, instantly, not only did I feel great awe for the Lord, but I also became very excited knowing that the Lord was going to use me again.

At this point, someone might want to suggest that since this stuff is so good, I should recommend it to a lot of people so that they can receive the benefit as well. Not at all. I want to respond to that suggestion. I believe, as I have mentioned earlier, that the Lord has done supernatural things to help me, and it is not the stuff itself alone that has done the work. Just on the contrary. I think this stuff is actually quite dangerous since you just have no idea what kind of repair it is going to perform to your body, and it can easily get out of control. And that is exactly what it did to my body in the end. While it helped my body to produce some hormones again, it over-repaired my damaged esophagus, and I began to cough, knowing something had grown in my throat. At first, I thought it was my thyroid, but blood test showed it was not the thyroid. Then I realized that supplement had over-repaired my esophagus. That was why I stopped taking it. So clearly, it is the Lord who healed me, guiding that stuff to help me produce the needed hormones. If the Lord had not taken control in this situation, who knows what the whole result would have been?

Since this ordeal began, the Lord has been talking to me almost daily, and it seems clear that He is guiding me in the things He wanted me to do. He either let me talk to someone over the phone to help her or to bring someone to my home for me to minister to. For instance, one Sunday, since I was not able to sleep much during the previous night and thus was unable to attend church that morning, a woman noticed my absence and called me later and then came to visit me. While she was in my house, I happened to feel the need to go out to the backyard, and she began to follow me. While she was enjoying my small garden, the flowers and the pole beans and other plants I had planted, I told her about a small white butterfly I saw earlier that very spring. It was resting on one of my roses and was alarmed by my hand and flew away. However, before it opened up its wings and flew away, I had been able to catch a glimpse of something special on one corner of its folded wings—a small beautiful red line (about one centimeter long). It was so distinct as if it were drawing my attention to its Creator and saying to me, "This red line is my Creator's signature!"

As I talked more about God and His creation, that woman said to me, "Didn't God use evolution in the creation of everything?"

"Of course not!" I answered, and then I realized she had been deeply influenced by the theory of evolution (in some seminaries it is taught as theistic evolution), and I began to tell her how wrong the theory was and that the Bible was totally believable in its creation account and the story of Noah's flood.

Finally, she said, "Now I see."

Praise the Lord! Although I was not able to go to church, He brought someone to my home for me to minister to anyway.

What had happened earlier when I saw that beautiful red line on the underside of the small white butterfly's wing was that I felt great amazement as I thought more about that chance discovery. Of course, nothing happens by chance in God's economy. Normally, very few people (maybe nobody at all) would have noticed it if the butterfly was flying. The first thing is that it is so small and that it flies so quickly out of sight that no person would have noticed that small red line. Then the only chance for anybody to notice that red line is when the butterfly folds up its wings and one can see its underside. That was when I happened to get close to my rose flower and noticed it. I can only say it was a God-given opportunity for me to notice that very special marking on that butterfly. Of course, as I found out later, that small white butterfly is actually a pest that lay eggs on vegetable leaves or even tomatoes, and then the eggs turn into caterpillars, which cause a lot of damage to vegetables. Understandably, this white butterfly is not among butterflies collected for specimen, and so I'm quite sure no one has ever thought of catching them for specimen. So that chance discovery was really the Lord's gift to me.

So I would like to ask this question: What's the possibility of the theory of evolution working in this respect? Would evolution have produced this small butterfly with that special, short, but very distinct and beautiful red line on one corner of its wing? (Maybe I should say *wings* as a lot of created things are symmetrical in their patterns. However, since I did not get to see the other wing, I cannot assume that both wings are this way.)

That butterfly returned to my backyard garden many more times the whole summer, but I was never able to get another chance to get close to observe its wing again. I guess the Lord was saying, "Once is enough." I think I should be satisfied for the privilege to make that discovery.

It was during that time the Lord showed me several places in my book that I would need to add some more stories. One of those places was in the chapter on spiritual warfare (chapter 19), and there I added the story about the brother who was demon-possessed. When Yishan and I exercised the power of our Lord Jesus Christ to pray for him, he could not stand it and fell down on his couch.

There is something interesting about that chapter. One day my daughter Corrie came to my house to help me with the computer. However, to mention this story, I need to add a note that during those difficult days of very little sleep, I often experienced satanic attacks while working on the computer or when I was sleeping in the middle of the night or when I was about to fall asleep. Those experiences were quite frequent, and it is impossible for me to mention them all. Here I'll just mention one.

My mind got very easily confused as a result of losing so much sleep (it still is true even today). One night when I was about to fall asleep I was becoming groggy, and all of a sudden, I smelled something very awful, something like what you would smell when you go to an outhouse. At first I thought that a truck with septic tanks had passed my street and the smell had come into my house through the window. When I got up to close the window, I found that the window was actually closed. Still, it was not until the next day that I realized no truck of that type could have passed my street since we have sewers and there are no septic tanks in our area! Plus, of course, no truck driver would be working in the dead of the night!

During that time whenever I was working on my computer, I often encountered disturbances I knew were not natural. Although my computer skills and knowledge were limited, I knew those disturbances were by no means natural results of computer abnormality. So I often sent e-mails to my daughters, asking them to pray for me. However, none of my daughters ever responded to those e-mails, and I knew they must be thinking, *Oh, Mommy was having sleep trouble, and it's natural for her to think she was attacked by Satan. Some of her trouble with computer must have been caused by her lack of knowledge of the computer.*

Well, our God knows better. One day when Corrie was helping with me on the computer, something weird happened when she was working on the very chapter on spiritual warfare. Part of the text began to multiply itself again and again, and all of a sudden, that whole chapter just disappeared from the computer screen.

It caught Corrie by surprise, and she was stunned. Then she said, "Wow, I've never seen anything like this."

I just said, "Now that you've seen it with your own eyes, you know I've not been talking about imagined things." A little later she sent an e-mail to her two sisters, telling them about what her own eyes had seen.

All is not lost. Since Corrie had good computer skills and knowledge (she works as a website designer for a large computer company), very quickly she was able to use one of the previous versions of the book that I had sent to myself (from one computer to another) or to my daughters and pretty much recovered the whole chapter. Of course, I *did* have to spend some more time editing that chapter so that it was fully recovered. All that Satan accomplished was wasting some of my time.

Isn't this interesting? Satan tried to remove the very chapter he hates most! He sabotaged my book but failed, and instead he helped my three daughters see a broader scope of the spiritual warfare. Praise the Lord! He is always victorious.

Now I do remember there is another story that should have been added to that same chapter. Actually, more than a year ago when I was helping Leslie after the birth of her fifth baby, when one evening she was helping me editing this book on that chapter, she suggested I should add this story. At that time I thought the chapter was long enough, and I did not take her suggestion. Now I know this is another important story to add just as important as the one I added earlier in June.

This story took place a little more than a month *before* Yishan and I started our own SCC in F City. One late evening our phone rang, and Yishan answered it. While he was talking, I listened. From Yishan's end of the conversation, I figured out what was going on.

"Pastor, I'm sick," that brother (I'll call him Brother S) told Yishan. Yishan asked back, "You're sick?"

Earlier that evening we picked up Brother S and had dinner at another brother's home. (I'll call this one Brother M.) Later we took Brother S home before coming home ourselves. How had he suddenly become sick?

"Yes, yesterday my brother and I went to the Buddhist temple in San Jose, and I forgot to pray before I went." This Brother S had only been converted to the Lord and had been baptized for only a little more than a month. He had been a very devout Buddhist before his conversion and had been involved in a lot of Buddhist activities. His father's ashes were kept in a Buddhist temple in San Jose, and his brothers, one older and the other younger, were still Buddhists.

At that point I began to suspect there was something unusual in the spiritual realm, and I began to pray for Brother S and for Yishan and me. By the time Yishan hung up the phone, I was ready to go. Yishan told him that we were going over to his apartment to pray for him. Before we left our home, Yishan also called Brother M, informing him of the situation and asking him to pray for us all.

While Yishan was driving, I prayed out loud all the way until we arrived there. This way it was actually Yishan and I praying together, and he kept saying, "Amen."

It was an eight-unit apartment building with the stairway in the center between two units of apartments on each side of each floor. There was another stairway on the other end of the building. Yishan walked a lot faster ahead of me, and he just reached the top floor when he finished saying, "He had told me he would leave the door unlocked." With that, he began to push the door open while I was still one step lower on the stairway.

What happened next was so fast and so unexpected that I was almost unprepared to handle it.

Later Yishan told me that when he opened the door just a crack, he saw Brother S standing in the middle of his living room, and as soon as he saw Yishan, he ran out toward Yishan. Yishan grabbed Brother S's both hands, and the two began to struggle. The latter was almost twenty years younger and very strong, and Yishan almost had a hard time controlling him. Fortunately, Yishan was also quite strong, and he soon had the upper hand.

Since Yishan and I both had not expected all this, in the beginning we stammered but quickly said pretty much in unison, "In the name of Jesus, I command you to come out of him!"

Also very quickly, the two of them reversed their positions of standing ending with Yishan's back to the door and Brother S in Yishan's grip. The latter soon lost consciousness and fell backward to the floor. (Yishan was holding his hands. Otherwise, he would have fallen straight down backward, possibly ending with very bad consequences.) For a few minutes, he stayed there, stiff, motionless, and unconscious while the two of us continued praying, "In the name of Jesus, I command the demon to come out of him!"

A few minutes later, Brother S came to consciousness. Yishan raised him up, and he asked, "How come I'm lying here?"

At that moment I thought all was well. Then I noticed lying on the floor by the wall, there was a large cleaver, and I picked it up. Where had this cleaver come from?

As all of us walked into the apartment, Brother S's two brothers were inside, one right behind a kitchen counter, and when he saw the cleaver in my hand, he took it from me, opened a drawer, took out a small cardboard box, put the cleaver inside, and closed that drawer.

I then asked him, "Is this your cleaver?" He nodded his head.

Since those two brothers were not Christians, we did not ask them to join us in prayers, but Yishan and I soon began to pray for Brother S for complete release from demon-possession.

We then began to talk. I asked Brother S, "So you went to the Buddhist temple yesterday with your brother without praying?"

His older brother responded, "We did not go to the temple yesterday!"

Well, this was interesting to me. The older brother said they did not go to the temple yesterday, but Brother S said so to Yishan over the phone. If he had not said *that*, it would not have alerted me to the possibility of the presence of demons! Isn't our God always in control of every situation?

I forgot to mention that while Yishan and I were praying for Brother S outside by the door, Brother M came upstairs with another brother (Brother C) he had invited to come to pray with us. And then another man, one who obviously was one of the residents of those apartments, also came up and asked us what was going on.

I answered him by saying that this brother was demon-possessed and that we were praying for him.

"Demon or not," said that man, "next time call the cops first." He had seen the cleaver in my hand.

It was then we all went into the apartment.

Then Brother M said, "Brother C and I actually had arrived here earlier than you two did. When we came up the stairs and opened the door, we saw Brother S standing in the living room, and as soon as he saw us, he shot to the door toward us. We became scared and backed out and tried to hold the door closed. It was easier to open from the inside, and it took both of us to hold the door tight. Then we heard someone inside trying to pry the door open since we heard some metal sound. When it was quiet inside, we then both left and quickly ran to the other side of the street to wait for you. It was when we heard Pastor Lin shouting that we came over." Yishan's prayer was extra loud that evening. He was practically shouting.

So it seemed that Brother S had the cleaver in his hand when he ran toward Yishan. But then how did that cleaver land on the floor outside of the door? Well, Brother M said when he and Brother C came over the street, he heard like some kind of metal dropping on the floor.

How was all this possible? None of us knew how to explain it. Yet it was true that the cleaver came out of its resting place and ended up on the floor outside. I believe that an angel came to help us that evening by removing it out of Brother S's hand before he was able to harm Yishan and then let it drop to the floor. Both Yishan and I were so concentrated in praying that neither of us had heard the sound when that cleaver landed on the floor not even two feet away from us!

It was a very dangerous situation, and yet the Lord had protected us both without ourselves realizing it until later. What a blessing the Lord had given us. Ignorant bliss.

Yishan and I really had enough encounters with the powers of darkness for us to always believe that the Bible is talking about real spirit beings when it comes to Satan and demons!

Now let me get back to June of 2014 when I was having the sleep problem and trying to edit this book when the Lord told me what to do. One day He said to me, "You have the best evidence for creation."

"Me?" I never thought of that. (Actually, I had forgotten about this.)

The Lord reminded me of what I saw in Taiwan during a trip I took to Taiwan in September 2004 when I went to see my eldest sister who had colon cancer and three months later went home to be with the Lord.

On the second weekend of that trip, a friend invited me to go home with her to visit her parents who lived in central Taiwan. This friend, a former member of SCC, was working and living in Taipei, but she went back to see her parents every other weekend. Since her parents were aged and she wanted them to hear the gospel (they were Buddhists), she asked me to talk to her parents about Jesus. The next day after I was there, she took me to see Sun Moon Lake, a very famous tourist attraction that was about a twenty- or thirty-minute ride from her home. She hired a taxi to take us there.

I had been to that place thrice before. When we got there, I was disappointed that it did not look as nice as before. There was a big earthquake in Taiwan on the night of September 21, 1999. (It was actually on the morning of September 22, but people usually call it the 9/21 earthquake). The landscape of that area was somewhat altered as a result. I told my friend of my disappointment and suggested that we go back. When our driver heard that, he said, "I'll take you to see the epicenter of the 9/21 quake."

It was really providential that we were taken to the epicenter of that big quake. I was totally amazed and very delighted. When I saw that very spot experts believed to be the epicenter and the landscape of that whole surrounding area, I told my friend, "These are the best evidences for creation!"

Adjacent to that epicenter was a house, and a man was selling souvenirs of the earthquake. Quite unexpectedly and also to my delight, I saw two books filled with pictures taken throughout Taiwan after that earthquake, but most were taken near that area or in surrounding towns. I immediately bought both books, and the man gave me a photo with someone's signature as a bonus for buying those books.

Why was I so delighted in seeing that area and buying those two books, especially that photo? It was a picture of the very house in front of us, and the signature was that of the owner of that house. The house was damaged, but it had not collapsed, even though it was so close to the epicenter. But the strange thing about that house was that it became a place where gravity became very strange and everyone who entered had to stand with his or her body slanting backward. But the thing that most interested me is that a mountain appeared in the back of the house during that big quake. So the caption on the photo says, "Before the quake, no mountain; after the quake, a mountain [appeared]." (The peak of the mountain was just a little taller than the house originally, and therefore, it was not a mountain. But that mountain area was raised much higher than the house after the quake.)

How do you explain the appearance of that mountain? Through millions of years as evolutionists usually say? No, it came up overnight! It was not the only phenomenon from that quake. On my way back to Taipei, riding in the bus, I also saw not too far from the highway some low mountains that came up during that earthquake. (That area was of the same level as the highway before the quake.) And those land formations resembled a lot of badlands in the United States, which evolutionists claim to be results of millions of years. There is also another similar area in southern Taiwan near another highway that I saw on an earlier trip. It was dubbed "moonscape," but it was just another badlands formation. From the highway I could see that area was newly formed since they still did not have much vegetation. That area also appeared during that same quake. Those evidences show that evolutionists and those who believe God used evolution in creation (theistic evolution) are totally wrong as well!

I'm very thankful to the Lord for giving me that opportunity to observe with my own eyes those special evidences for God's creation. Although you won't be able to see clearly the badlands formation of those mountains if you go to Taiwan now because of the subtropical weather there and quick growth of plants and trees that have mostly covered up those areas, some of those evidences are nevertheless preserved forever in the two books I bought. Those are parts of what I presented to my students in the creationism class, and that was why my students were totally convinced. Praise the Lord!

This harrowing ordeal was finally over, but then I heard of something that almost knocked me over so that I would not be able to get up. It was a Tuesday evening in early July when I had dinner at Albert and Angela's house. After dinner, Albert told me, "We're going to move to Southern California."

I was not exactly surprised when I heard those words since Leslie had told me earlier after Angela visited her in May that she and Albert could move to Southern California. However, after I came home, for almost two hours, I could not sit down but kept walking around in the house, so shocked that Angela was going to be so far away from me and that it would not be easy for me to visit her.

Of course, Leslie lives in the Boston area, even farther away from me. Yet Angela had never lived too far away from me her whole life up till then. When she went to the University of Illinois, we lived in Schaumburg, only a three-hour drive apart. Then when she moved to Roseville (before she moved to this town in 2008), north of Sacramento, I was living in U City, still a three-hour drive apart. Now that I'm older, I really need my daughters to be around, but she is moving so far away that I would not be able to get to her by driving! So in those two hours when I walked around in the house, I kept asking, "Lord, what should I do?"

Twice I knelt down to pray. The first time I did not get any answer. The second time after I prayed, I remembered what the Bible says, "Therefore shall a man leave his father and his mother" (Genesis 2:24). The Word of God again showed its comforting power on me, and I was not worried anymore.

During my sleep-deprivation period, I was so incapacitated that I was not able to drive anywhere, whether to go for a doctor's appointment or to go for shopping. I had to rely on my daughters for driving me to those places. It was then I remembered that during two periods in the past, the Lord had foretold me of this. The first time was during the first month after Corrie was born. As she was so difficult to take care of, I often complained to the Lord, "Why did You give me a child so difficult to take care of?" And each time the Lord would say, "You should know that in the future this is the only daughter you can count on."

Then after I moved to my current place, I was not able to see either of my daughters easily all because both were too busy. I would then ask the Lord, "Why did you tell me to move here? Especially Corrie, it seems she does not care for me at all." Then the Lord would say this to me, "In the end, this is the only daughter you can depend on."

Angela and Albert moved away after the first week of August, and the Lord's words were fulfilled!

I flew to Southern California to visit Angela and Albert for almost a week and a half and came back on October 29. The night before that as I had difficulty with online check-in, I kept praying, "Lord, please give me an aisle seat so that it will be easier for me if I need to get up."

As soon as I walked into the airplane cabin, my heart sank since all the aisle seats had been taken, and so were most of the window seats. I asked silently, "Lord, what should I do?" I realized I had no choice but to take a middle seat, and I just walked forward. Then when I walked to row ten, the man who sat in the aisle seat on my left side suddenly got up and sat down in the middle seat. I noticed the woman sitting in the window seat saying something to the man, but I did not hear clearly what she had said.

I almost kept walking without thinking. Suddenly, I realized I should stop and then asked the man, "Sir, is the seat taken?' He said no, and I asked again, "Could I sit here?" And he answered, "You surely can!"

When I sat down, I heard him mutter something, but I did not fully realize what had taken place until I was home later that evening.

Honestly, to this day I still do not know exactly what had happened. I only figured out that the Lord must have answered my prayer by telling the woman to ask her husband to sit in the aisle seat until she saw someone fit to sit there. Then she would tell him to vacate that seat for that person. Although I did not hear clearly what she said to her husband when I got there, she must have told her husband, "This is the person. Give up your seat for her." Or she could have said, "Now you can sit next to me." All that I know was what I heard when I sat down, and that man said, "Must be someone special."

This reminded me of something my friend in New Orleans area had told me. I met her during my second trip to Israel in 2004, and we became fast friends. A year later something took place that I will not elaborate on here, but this friend began to tell some of her church friends about how I was "kicked out" of my church. A woman from her church felt a burden for me and was thinking of putting my name in the prayer box of her church.

However, my friend told me that the Lord told that woman, "Do not put her name in the prayer box with common people. She is special. Put her name on your windowsill so that you'll pray for her every time you see her name when you wash dishes."

I really have no idea why I am so special. I only know that God loves all of us, and if the Lord had not saved me, I would not be in the world today. I really owe a big debt to the Lord, and I ought to love Him and serve Him all the days of my life.

As I look back at my own life, I'm amazed at what God has been doing with me. (Yes, with Yishan as well, but he is gone now.) Especially when I first began my Christian life, I really had no idea that it would be such a wonderful way to me. As I have mentioned, when the Lord gave me that teaching job at my alma mater and let me know that I was connected to the heavenly hotline, I now suddenly realize what He has promised in Jeremiah 33:3, which says, "Call unto me, and I will answer thee, and show thee great and might things, which thou knowest not," is exactly what He has been doing to me. I do not know why the Lord should have chosen such a weak and small person such as me, but perhaps it is because Jesus Himself has said, "I thank thee, O Father, Lord of heaven and earth, because thou hast hid these things from the wise and prudent, and hast revealed them unto babes" (Matthew 11:25).

I admit I'm pretty much a baby in the Lord's kingdom. From time to time when I thought the Lord had made me a smart person, then something would happen that would quickly let me realize that I was not that smart but only as weak and ignorant as a little baby. That's how the Lord has kept me humble and dependent on Him a lot of times and at the same time let me enjoy His presence and blessing on me. I can only say I really have nothing to boast of my own. All that I have has come from the Lord, and without Him, I simply have no story to tell.

With all that I have experienced, how truly God is to be trusted. I can also say with certainty what some Bible scholars claim about Mark 16:9–20 to be wrong. Based on some early manuscripts, they say that these verses do not belong there since they were not included in the original manuscript.

In that passage Jesus said to His disciples, among other things, "And these signs will accompany those who have believed: in My name they will cast out demons, they will speak with new tongues; they will pick up serpents, and if they drink any deadly poison, it shall not hurt them; they will lay hands on the sick, and they will recover."

Among the things Jesus promised here, picking up serpents and drinking poison are the only two things I have not experienced. But we know Apostle Paul picked up a viper and got bitten without falling dead, as described in the book of Acts. I've also read of some early missionaries, some during 1930s to the 1940s, who were poisoned or unknowingly ate poisonous food without falling dead. One of those was a Chinese missionary sent out to an island in Indonesia. He was accompanied by another Christian who knew the language of a tribe there, and those indigenous people prepared a banquet to treat them. The next day the missionary asked his companion what those tribal people were talking about next door in the middle of the night since they were able to hear it in the next room, which was only separated by a wall. His companion said, "They were saying, 'How come he [the missionary] did not fall dead since we put poison in his food?'" As a result of that, those tribal people were able to see that the Jesus the missionary preached was truly God and there were many of them coming to the Lord.

I had also heard from an elderly pastor telling the story of a Brother Chang during the great revival period in Shangtung, China. One day Brother Chang was walking through a forest where tigers sometimes appeared to hurt or eat people, and so hunters set up traps to catch the tiger. However, Brother Chang was not aware of that, and since he was hungry that day when he was passing through the forest, when he saw food there he just picked it up and ate it. Just then he heard someone shouting at some distance away, "Do not eat that food!" But it was too late. By that time Brother Chang heard it, the food had already gone down into his stomach. And yet as Brother Chang continued on his way, he did not fall dead just as Jesus promised to His believers. Obviously in both cases, our Lord Jesus honored His own words! So I know Mark 16:9–20 definitely belongs in the original Greek manuscript.

In one of the issues of the magazine I published, *Fish and Loaves*, there was an article I had written and titled "Director." There I mentioned that in our life the most important factor is God's unseen hand directing our lives just as the importance of a movie director. William Shakespeare, the famous British playwright, said in *Macbeth*, "Life is but a shadow, full of sound and fury, signifying nothing." I do not totally agree with this famous saying. Yes, it is true *only* when one does not include God in his life. I felt this way when I was a teenager, only because I did not know the Bible or the Lord who created us all.

Yet after I began to understand the Bible and experience the Lord's working in my life, I knew my life was worth living. One day after I had been baptized more than eleven years, I suddenly realize this: God has used my father to give me my Chinese name, and it is a very good name full of biblical meanings. The two words are Guei Mei. The first means "expensive, precious, or noble," and the second means "beautiful." Yet the second word is actually composed of two parts, "lamb" or "sheep" on the top, and "big, large" on the bottom. Together, these two parts of the word pretty much say, "Magnify the Lamb!"

Wow! Although my father was not a Christian when I was born, he gave me a name saying, "I am expensive because I was purchased with the price of Christ's own life. So I'm precious and noble in God's sight. And God wants me to magnify the Lamb with my life. That will be a truly beautiful life."

Was it an accident that my father gave me such a name? I used to complain that it was too common because when I tried to find my name on the list published in the newspaper of all the people who passed the entrance exam to colleges, I found a total of six identical names, including mine (same last name as well as the given name), not to mention those whose names did not make the list! And actually, many women have the same given name as mine but with different family names.

That was why I used to hate the name my father had given me.

I used to think it was so common and so unoriginal! Yet after that discovery, I began to cherish it very much, knowing it had actually been given by the loving God through my father.

Our life is very meaningful when we have God as our director. It is empty and meaningless only when one excludes God from his or her life.

God has made my life *very* meaningful. It was especially so when I think of what happened during June and July of this past year. He led me through the experience of death and resurrection, changing my old, dying body into one that was younger and more dynamic, and I can sleep again without any medication. I do not know how to explain this medically, but I know God's unseen hand had directed all these changes and made them possible. He is the one who has given me this bonus chapter to the book as well as a bonus chapter to my life! Moreover, I think it is a bonus chapter from the merciful God who wants us all to come to Him and acknowledge Him as the Creator and accept His Son to be our Lord and Savior. "The Lord … is long suffering to us-ward, not willing that any should perish, but that all should come to repentance" (1 Peter 3:10).

(This chapter was completed in December 2014 and revised several times until October 2016)

Epilogue

That Sunday afternoon on June 16, 2002, when Angela and I sat in a conference room in the funeral home talking with the funeral counselor, I picked up an urn with double compartments, one for Yishan and the other for myself, and the counselor said, "God forbid, but in the future should you decide to remarry, your daughter can then use it."

At that moment I wanted to say to her, "God forbid I should remarry," but I kept my mouth shut.

I know the Bible allows a woman to remarry after her husband's death (Romans 7:2–3), but to me remarriage is just unthinkable. More than once people had out of good intention suggested to me, "Mrs. Lin, you're still young. You should remarry."

My answer has always been the same. "Unless God will allow Pastor Lin to come back, it is impossible for me to remarry."

I knew I was *not* boasting when I said that. Yishan and I had been close to each other most of the time (he was my best friend and I was his confidant) until his ministry pulled us apart, *and* yet I had loved him with all my heart and had given him all my best. I'm sure he had taken my heart with him when he went home to be with the Lord. I believe he is now waiting for me to go there to be reunited with him. After all, we two have been fused into one. As the Bible says, "The two shall become one." So there is part of him that has been left in me as well.

Perhaps you're still not convinced why I should be so devoted to Yishan after all. Well, for *one fact*, if not for anything else. During

November 24 to December 7 of 2000, I took a mission trip to Taiwan (chapter 23), and when I came back, Yishan told me a younger woman in the church who had some mental problem had called him and said that she wanted to move into our house. Yishan said, "How could you ask to move in since Mrs. Lin is not home?"

Yet she said, "Pastor, it's okay because I'm sanctified."

The whole thing may sound very ludicrous, but I felt very gratified when I thought of so many husbands cheating on their wives. Especially when the wife was absent from home, wouldn't it be a very good opportunity for the husband to cheat if he wanted to? So I'm forever grateful for Yishan's faithfulness to his wife. To me, it also exemplified his God-fearing character.

There were at least two times when Yishan showed extraordinary kindness to me. I've really forgotten about this until very recently. I'm sure the Holy Spirit had brought this to my attention, and of course, this just was another example of our human depravity. Well, not that of Yishan, but of mine. A lot of us often forget what our Lord Jesus Christ has done for us on the cross (and many other things that we take for granted, such as giving us free air and rain water) and become ungrateful. What I'm going to say here is really about Yishan's noble side. (Sorry, Pastor Doug, you did not get to read this part and also a few other places when you wrote the introduction for my book.)

The first time it occurred around 1981–82 when Yishan and I were helping with the Taiwanese church (chapter 7). I have mentioned a Mrs. Wang, whom we prayed for, but the Lord took her in her sleep. Later I drove there (a long distance to me) to attend her funeral while Yishan was at work. As I look back now, I know I have been a very poor motorist my whole life when it comes to car care. Yishan took care of all the necessary repair/maintenance with our car(s), and I never had to worry about it. In this respect Yishan had indeed pampered me. (He had pampered me in another area—mowing the lawn. The only time I did it was a month or two before the Lord took him home, and he said to me, "You should learn this in case I'm not here." That time when I pushed the lawn mower, for the first time

I realized how difficult it was for me to do the mowing! Well, you see, Yishan was much stronger, and I was the weaker vessel (1 Peter 3:7). I'm really a dummy as far as car care is concerned (one of my weakest areas). I think I must not have been careful during parallel parking. (It is always very difficult for me.) I got too close to the curb and had unknowingly rubbed the back tire against the curb, which made the tire wall very thin and eventually punctured it, so all the air leaked out. The worse thing was that I was so blissfully unaware of the whole thing but continued to drive and thus kept driving with not just a flat tire but also had damaged the tread. I somehow had an awareness that something was wrong. Yet I continued to drive while another motorist tried to point that out to me, and finally, I stopped the car and went out to take a look.

Of course, I was horrified to discover what I had done to my car. I had to take out the jack from the trunk and try to change the tire. Useless. I was too weak to help myself, and I had to call Yishan at work.

Since I had the only family car, Yishan asked a colleague who lived around that area to give him a ride to where I was. I remember his colleague was smiling when I saw them. (Right now I can see his smiling face right in front of me.) Then when they got close to me, since that car window was down, I heard the colleague say, "Yes." Obviously, he saw my flat tire and made that remark. Yishan must have told him what I had done to our car. When Yishan saw everything, he did not utter a single word but just began to take down the damaged tire and put on the spare tire. This was more than thirty years ago, and so I do not remember every detail. But I think he did not seem to be upset a bit by my stupidity. I remember he only said, "Well, what was done is done. We just need to get a new tire."

I actually had had a foreboding feeling (pretty much like a little child who had done wrong waiting to be punished) and was expecting to hear an outburst of rage from Yishan, "How could you have been so stupid?" Absolutely nothing. I think after he changed the tire, he drove back to work as I sat in the passenger seat and later waited in his company until it was time to go home. During the ride back to his office, we actually had a pleasant exchange of words with me filling him in on the funeral and other tidbits of information.

The second time it happened when we were living in F City or U City more than a decade later. I'm sorry, but the memory loss I have been suffering just does not allow me to recall the exact circumstance. I only remember it was on a parking lot in F City. It was on a Sunday when I was invited to preach at a Taiwanese church in a Bay Area town farther away from F City. By the time I came back, I was hungry and had gone into a place to eat, and when I came out, I found I had left my car key in the ignition and locked myself out. Good that we had two cars by that time. I called Yishan, and when he arrived, he just unlocked the car door for me using his own key without any comments again. All that I remember again is that he did not seem to be upset. He just accepted his stupid and forgetful wife with grace.

In these two incidents, I was the depraved wife, and he was the gracious husband. (Now I think you can see why I felt such a great loss when the Lord took Yishan home. It was not just that he depended on me for help in his ministry. I also needed him in many areas of my life.)

Then I also remember when we were living in Schaumburg, Illinois, once I was cooking when I heard Yishan playing on the piano a piece usually called "Love's Dream" by Franz Liszt (Liebestraum No. 3 in A-flat major). Classical music lovers all know this music is very romantic, and it is one of my most favorite pieces. So while I was cooking and also unexpectedly was able to enjoy Yishan playing such a romantic piece, I was not only delighted but thought, *How many women can have this joy of hearing her husband playing such beautiful music while she is cooking?* I know many famous pianists who are men, but at that moment I only felt myself so blessed to have such a husband.

I must admit that sometimes when I thought of how Yishan had given his last ounce of strength to serve the Lord and thus shortened his life on earth, leaving me to struggle with so many difficulties, I had the tendency to sigh and feel sad. Of course, many times my eyes were flooded with tears. Yet I was also mindful of the sovereignty of God and realized that this must have been in His plan. Then my heart was quieted, and I would feel the comforting of the Holy Spirit.

Looking back at my own life and Yishan's, I must admit that he really loved the Lord, not less than I had, although he became a believer much later than I did, and that was why the Lord loved Yishan so much. During Yishan's final years, quite a few times I asked myself, "Do I love Yishan more than I love the Lord?" I guess the Lord has taken Yishan away so that I can devote my total love to serve Him.

I think one or two years before Angela and Leslie entered colleges, I suggested to Yishan that we have a family worship every Sunday night. For years Yishan was never really the type of family leader as I had heard from the many speakers on Moody Radio. At that time he did accept my suggestion and every Sunday night the whole family would sit together on the living room couch (a long two-piece sectional) and sang one or two hymns and read some Bible passage, and each one took turns praying. Even the youngest, Corrie, also prayed; we gave her simple things to pray for. I remember we prayed for Angela and Leslie to receive a lot of scholarships and for a good college for each of them. We also prayed that Angela and Leslie would have good roommates in colleges and also that they would be able to lead their roommates to the Lord. The reason we prayed for good roommates for them was because I recalled some years back my friend Yvonne who lived in So Cal told me her daughter had entered UC Berkeley and she had a roommate who was an alcoholic. All our prayers for the two future college students were answered except one. Angela's roommate attended the intervarsity fellowship on the first Friday night and did not attend again. Years later Angela told me it was because they made her pray during that first meeting. The first meeting in her life, and of course, she was scared off. Well, the first Christmas after Angela graduated from college, that young woman called Angela to inform her she was baptized. Praise the Lord! Angela's roommate was actually a very nice young woman, but during the four years of college, Angela was frustrated a few times with her and called me to pray for her. I never stopped praying for her until she was baptized. Whenever Yishan and I prayed together, we included her in our prayers as well. You can certainly see Yishan did become the spiritual leader of the family before we moved to California.

One morning in June 2014 when I was lying in bed, suffering what I call "the mad, mad world of sleeplessness," which went on for almost two months, something came into my mind all of a sudden. It was as if the Lord were reminding me of another reason why He loved Yishan so much. That was his humility. Only a little more than a month before that, I was surprised by a visit from the current pastor of the church I was forced to leave behind, and he invited me to preach at that church again. That invitation was carried out very shortly. Then while I was in F City I heard of something about a pastor whom I had known back in seminary days (chapter 16). This man came to the Bay Area around the same time we did. He had a doctorate from a well-known seminary. Yishan had a PhD, and still, he had to attend a seminary to earn another degree before he could serve as a pastor. So between these two men, you might say that *that* man had an edge in serving the Lord. He should be ahead of Yishan in his service for the Lord.

However, it did not turn out that way. From all that I know, this man moved from one ministry to another and ended up serving in a fairly small church.

Do I despise this man? No, not at all. It just occurs to me that the reason Yishan was so effectively used by the Lord was because of his humility, while in the other man, I always could detect some pride in the words or deeds. (I'm not judging him. On the contrary, I feel great respect for his knowledge and ability. With the degree he has, he is worthy of a lot of my admiration.)

"God resists the proud but gives grace unto the humble" (James 4:6), and that was the reason in the different ways things turned out for each man. (To me all these are facts, not because Yishan was my husband. God Himself saw all the facts and made that difference.)

My younger sister who is not a believer has said to me a number of times since Yishan went home to be with the Lord, "Third Sister, if you had not gone to the United States but had stayed in Taiwan and continued to teach at your alma mater, today you would have owned many buildings." (I was making a lot of money when I was a teacher at my alma mater, especially with my side jobs of tutoring.)

Based on this world's value system, Yishan and I are two fools who have been willing to suffer hardships for the Lord's sake. I'm sure God had known that from the beginning, and that was why He put me and Yishan together to serve Him. We have been *matched for eternity.*

CPSIA information can be obtained
at www.ICGtesting.com
Printed in the USA
LVOW03s1458250118
563994LV00002B/384/P